Lecture Notes in Computer Science   8317

Commenced Publication in 1973
Founding and Former Series Editors:
Gerhard Goos, Juris Hartmanis, and Jan van Leeuwen

For further volumes:
http://www.springer.com/series/7410

T0212832

Carles Padró (Ed.)

Information Theoretic Security

7th International Conference, ICITS 2013
Singapore, November 28–30, 2013
Proceedings

 Springer

Editor
Carles Padró
Nanyang Technological University
Singapore
Singapore

ISSN 0302-9743   ISSN 1611-3349 (electronic)
ISBN 978-3-319-04267-1   ISBN 978-3-319-04268-8 (eBook)
DOI 10.1007/978-3-319-04268-8
Springer Cham Heidelberg New York Dordrecht London

Library of Congress Control Number: 2013957942

CR Subject Classification (1998): K.6.5, E.3, E.4, K.4.4, F.2.1

LNCS Sublibrary: SL4 – Security and Cryptology

Printed on acid-free paper

Springer is part of Springer Science+Business Media (www.springer.com)

Preface

ICITS 2013, the 7th International Conference on Information Theoretic Security, was held in Singapore during November 28–30, 2013. The conference took place on the One-North Campus of the Nanyang Technological University. The general chairs of the conference were Frédérique Oggier and Miklos Santha.

Information theoretic cryptography analyzes the existence and efficiency of cryptographic schemes whose security is not based on computational hardness assumptions. This research topic is connected to several areas of mathematics such as probability and information theory, algebra and algebraic geometry, combinatorics, coding theory and quantum information processing, among others.

Two different kinds of submissions were solicited for ICITS 2013. Only original research work could be submitted to the *Conference Track*, while submissions to the *Workshop Track* could consist of research work that had been recently published or submitted to other venues. Every submission was considered only for one track, chosen by the authors. The two-track format was initiated in ICITS 2012, the previous edition of the conference, and it has proved to be very successful in bringing together researchers from information theory, cryptography, and quantum computing, communities with different publication traditions.

The Program Committee received a total of 49 submissions, of which 14 were accepted for the Conference Track and 10 for the Workshop Track. All submitted papers were revised by the Program Committee, with the help in some cases of external reviewers. These proceedings contain the accepted papers for the Conference Track. The accepted works for the Workshop Track were presented at the conference but do not appear in this volume. The list of the contributions in the Workshop Track is given before the Table of Contents.

In addition to the contributed presentations, the program was completed with three invited talks:

- "*Multi-Linear Secret Sharing Schemes*," by Amos Beimel, Ben-Gurion University, Israel
- "*Entropic Uncertainty Relations and Their Applications in Quantum Cryptography*" by Marco Tomamichel, Centre for Quantum Technologies (CQT), Singapore
- "*New Results on Percolation Through Topological Quantum Error Correcting Codes*," by Gilles Zémor, Université de Bordeaux, France

Many people have contributed to the success of ICITS 2013. First of all, I thank all authors of submitted papers for choosing ICITS 2013 to disseminate their work. Many thanks to the members of the Program Committee. It was a pleasure to collaborate with such a team of motivated, talented, and hardworking scientists to put together the program of the conference. Reviewing and selecting the papers was a difficult task that required a lot of their time and efforts. I also thank the external reviewers for assisting the Program Committee in the reviewing process. I thank Adam Smith for his very good advice and for sharing his experience as program chair of ICITS 2012. Special thanks to the general chairs, Frédérique Oggier and Miklos Santha, for their invaluable work in organizing the conference, and many thanks to all people who assisted them in that challenging task: Noelle Chen from MAS General Office, NTU, Helen Chen and Nicholas Tee from SPMS IT support, NTU, Nweni Myint Aung from CITS, NTU, and Evon Tan from CQT, NUS.

November 2013   Carles Padró

ICITS 2013

The 7th International Conference on Information Theoretic Security
Singapore, November 28–30, 2013

General Chairs

Frédérique Oggier   Nanyang Technological University, Singapore
Miklos Santha   CNRS, Paris, France; CQT, Singapore

Program Chair

Carles Padró   Nanyang Technological University, Singapore

Program Committee

Simon R. Blackburn   Royal Holloway University of London, UK
Matthieu Bloch   Georgia Tech, USA
Ignacio Cascudo   CWI Amsterdam, The Netherlands
László Csirmaz   CEU Budapest, Hungary
Stefan Dziembowski   University of Warsaw, Poland
Serge Fehr   CWI Amsterdam, The Netherlands
Juan Garay   AT&T Labs – Research, USA
Masahito Hayashi   Nagoya University, Japan
Javier Herranz   Universitat Politècnica de Catalunya, Spain
Iordanis Kerenidis   CNRS, Université Paris Diderot, France
Lifeng Lai   Worcester Polytechnic Institute, USA
Leonid Reyzin   Boston University, USA
Tamir Tassa   The Open University of Israel
Stephanie Wehner   CQT and NUS, Singapore
Chaoping Xing   Nanyang Technological University, Singapore

ICITS Steering Committee

Carlo Blundo   University of Salerno, Italy
Ronald Cramer   CWI and Leiden University, The Netherlands
Yvo Desmedt, Chair   University College London, UK
Hideki Imai   University of Tokyo, Japan
Kaoru Kurosawa   Ibaraki University, Japan
Ueli Maurer   ETH Zürich, Switzerland
C. Pandu Rangan   Indian Institute of Technology, Madras, India

Sponsors

Lee Foundation, Singapore
CryptoWorks21, Institute for Quantum Computing, University of Waterloo, Canada
Centre for Quantum Technologies, Singapore

Lee Foundation

Workshop Track Presentations

1. One-Sided Device Independence of BB84 Via Monogamy-of-Entanglement Game
   Marco Tomamichel, Serge Fehr, Jedrzej Kaniewski, Stephanie Wehner
2. Secret Key Agreement Over a Lossy Optical Channel with a Passive Quantum Eavesdropper: Capacity Bounds and New Explicit Protocols
   Saikat Guha, Masahiro Takeoka, Hari Krovi, Mark M. Wilde, Cosmo Lupo
3. Efficient One-Way Secret-Key Agreement and Private Channel Coding Via Polarization
   David Sutter, Joseph M. Renes and Renato Renner
4. Composable Security of Measuring—Alice Blind Quantum Computation
   Tomoyuki Morimae, Takeshi Koshiba
5. Quantum Enigma Machines and the Locking Capacity of a Quantum Channel
   Saikat Guha, Patrick Hayden, Hari Krovi, Seth Lloyd, Cosmo Lupo, Jeffrey H. Shapiro, Masahiro Takeoka, Mark M. Wilde
6. Oblivious Transfer, the CHSH Game, and Quantum Encodings
   André Chailloux, Iordanis Kerenidis, Jamie Sikora
7. Non-Asymptotic Analysis of Privacy Amplification for Markov Chains
   Masahito Hayashi, Shun Watanabe
8. A Secret Images Sharing Scheme Using the Two-Variable One-Way Functions Approach with Public Values' Hiding
   Todorka Alexandrova
9. Security Analysis for a Relativistic Bit Commitment Experiment
   Jedrzej Kaniewski, Marco Tomamichel, Stephanie Wehner
10. Reference Frame Agreement in Quantum Networks
    Tanvirul Islam, Loïck Magnin, Brandon Sorg, Stephanie Wehner

Contents

How to Construct Strongly Secure Network Coding Scheme

Kaoru Kurosawa$^{(\boxtimes)}$, Hiroyuki Ohta, and Kenji Kakuta

Ibaraki University, Hitachi, Japan
kurosawa@mx.ibaraki.ac.jp

Abstract. We say that a network coding scheme is *strongly* 1-secure if a source node s can multicast n field elements $\{m_1, \cdots, m_n\}$ to a set of sink nodes $\{t_1, \cdots, t_q\}$ in such a way that any single edge leaks no information on any $S \subset \{m_1, \cdots, m_n\}$ with $|S| = n - 1$, where $n = \min_{t_i} \text{max-flow}(s, t_i)$ is the maximum transmission capacity. We also say that a *strongly* h-secure network coding scheme is *strongly* $(h + 1)$-secure if any $h + 1$ edges leak no information on any $S \subset \{m_1, \cdots, m_n\}$ with $|S| = n - (h + 1)$.

In this paper, we show the first explicit algorithm which can construct *strongly* k-secure network coding schemes. In particular, it runs in polynomial time for fixed k.

Keywords: Network coding · Strongly secure · Construction

1 Introduction

Consider a directed acyclic network $G = (\mathcal{V}, \mathcal{E})$, where $\mathcal{V}$ is the set of nodes and $\mathcal{E}$ is the set of edges. G has a source node s and a set of sink nodes $\{t_1, \cdots, t_q\}$, and each edge can transmit a single element of a finite field F. Let

$$n = \min_{t_i} \text{max-flow}(s, t_i),$$

where $\text{max-flow}(s, t_i)$ denotes the maximum flow that s can send to t_i.

Ahlswede et al. [1] showed that the source node s can send n field elements $(m_1, \cdots, m_n)$ to all the sink nodes simultaneously (i.e., *multicast*) by using a network coding scheme. Li, Yeung and Cai [8] proved that linear coding is enough to achieve this, where each intermediate nodes generates outgoing field elements as linear combinations of their incoming field elements. (See Fig. 1.) A linear network coding scheme can be expressed by an $n \times |\mathcal{E}|$ matrix U. Jaggi et al. [6] showed a polynomial time algorithm which can construct a linear network coding matrix U from a given network G.

A linear network coding scheme is called k-secure if a source node s can multicast $\sigma < n$ field elements $(m_1, \cdots, m_\sigma)$ in such a way that any k edges leak no information on $(m_1, \cdots, m_\sigma)$. (See Fig. 3 of Appendix A, where $k = 1$.)

C. Padró (Ed.): ICITS 2013, LNCS 8317, pp. 1–17, 2014.
DOI: 10.1007/978-3-319-04268-8_1, © Springer International Publishing Switzerland 2014

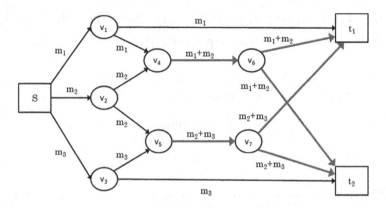

Fig. 1. Linear network coding scheme with $n = 3$

Cai and Yeung [4] proved that there exists a k-secure linear network coding scheme if and only if $\sigma \leq n - k$. In [3], the same authors gave an algebraic necessary and sufficient condition that a k-secure linear network coding matrix U must satisfy. Recently Tang et al. [14] showed a probabilistic algorithm for constructing k-secure linear network coding schemes.[1]

On the other hand, we say that a linear network coding scheme is *strongly* 1-secure if the source node can multicast n field elements $(m_1, \cdots, m_n)$ in such a way that any single edge leaks no information on any $S \subset \{m_1, \cdots, m_n\}$ with $|S| = n - 1$. We further say that a *strongly* h-secure network coding scheme is *strongly* $(h + 1)$-secure if any $h + 1$ edges leak no information on any $S \subset \{m_1, \cdots, m_n\}$ with $|S| = n - h - 1$. Harada and Yamamoto showed that there exists a strongly $(n - 1)$-secure linear network coding scheme if $|F|$ is suffi-ciently large [5, Theorem 3].[2] However, they did not give an explicit construction algorithm nor the concrete size of $|F|$.[3]

In this paper, we show an efficient construction algorithm of *strongly* k-secure network coding schemes. Let

$$L = |\mathcal{E}| + \sum_{i=1}^{k-1} \binom{n-1}{i} \binom{|\mathcal{E}|}{i+1}.$$

Then our algorithm runs in time $O(n^2 L)$ if $|F| > L$. This means that we solve the open problem of [5]. In particular, if k is fixed as a constant, then our algorithm runs in polynomial time in n and $|\mathcal{E}|$.

---

[1] See "Time Complexity" of [14, page 313].

[2] Our strongly $(n - 1)$-secure is their strongly 0-secure [5].

[3] They instead analyzed a case such that the source node multicasts $n' < n$ field elements [5, Sec. 6].

1.1   Related Works

Bhattad and Narayanan [2] constructed a linear network coding scheme such that a source node s can multicast n field elements $\{m_1, \cdots, m_n\}$ to the sink nodes in such a way that any $(n-1)$ edges leak no information on each m_i. Their security definition is different from strong $(n-1)$-security because it does not require strong k-security for $k < n-1$.

Silva and F.R. Kschischang [10] introduced the notion of universal k-secure coding schemes. A universal k-secure coding scheme is a transformation f : $\{m_1, \cdots, m_{n-k}\} \rightarrow \{x_1, \cdots, x_{n-k}\}$ which is independent of the underlying network. The source node just sends $\{x_1, \cdots, x_{n-k}\}$ to the sink nodes by using any linear network coding scheme. Then the resulting scheme is k-secure on $\{m_1, \cdots, m_{n-k}\}$.

Silva and F.R. Kschischang [11] generalized this notion to strong k-security. In their explicit construction, however, the source node can multicast only one or two messages, namely m_1 or (m_1, m_2).

Subsequently, Kurihara, Uematsu and Matsumoto [7] showed a universal strongly k-secure coding scheme such that the source node can multicast n messages to the sink nodes. Namely their coding scheme [7] is a transformation f : $\{m_1, \cdots, m_n\} \rightarrow \{x_1, \cdots, x_n\}$ such that the source node can send $\{x_1, \cdots, x_n\}$ to the sink nodes by using any linear network coding scheme over F so that the resulting scheme is strongly k-secure on $\{m_1, \cdots, m_n\}$.

The cost we must pay for these universal coding schemes is that each x_i is a vector over F of length T for some $T > 1$. Each m_i is also a vector over F of length T.[4] Hence the source node must run the underlying linear network coding scheme T times sequentially.

On the other hand, Shioji, Matsumoto and Uyematsu [13] showed some vulnerability of such universal coding schemes against stronger eavesdroppers.

2   Preliminaries

F denotes a finite field, and F_p denotes a finite field of order p. $w_H(\mathbf{x})$ denotes the Hamming weight of a vector $\mathbf{x}$. $\mathcal{I}_\ell$ denotes the $\ell \times \ell$ identity matrix. Let $X = (\mathbf{x}_i)$ denote a matrix such that the ith row is $\mathbf{x}_i$ for each i.

Let U be an $n \times |\mathcal{E}|$ matrix. Then

- For $A \subset \{1, \cdots, |\mathcal{E}|\}$, U_A denotes the submatirx of U such that the columns are restricted to A.
- $U_{A,h}$ denotes a matrix which consists of the last h rows of U_A.
- For $B \subset \{1, \cdots, n\}$, $U_{A,B}$ denotes the submatrix of U_A such that the rows are restricted to B.

---

[4] In the scheme of Kurihara et al. [7], $T \geq n' + n$ if the source nodes multicasts n' messages. So $T \geq 2n$ if the source nodes multicasts n messages.

Define

$$\text{Rank}_i(U) = \{A \subset \{1, \cdots, |\mathcal{E}|\} \mid |A| = rank(U_A) = i\} \tag{1}$$

It is clear that $\text{Rank}_i(T \cdot U) = \text{Rank}_i(U)$ if T is a nonsingular matrix. Therefore we write Rank_i instead of $\text{Rank}_i(U)$ henceforth when it is clear from the context. Note that $|\text{Rank}_i| \leq \binom{|\mathcal{E}|}{i}$.

For a vector $\mathbf{x} = (x_1, \cdots, x_N)$, let

$$support(\mathbf{x}) = \{i \mid x_i \neq 0\}.$$

2.1 Linear Network Coding

Let $n = \min_{t_i} \text{max-flow}(s, t_i)$, where $\text{max-flow}(s, t_i)$ denotes the maximum flow from the source node s to a sink node t_i. Then a linear network coding scheme can be expressed by

$$(m_1, \cdots, m_n) \times U = (d_1, \cdots, d_{|\mathcal{E}|}). \tag{2}$$

Here $(m_1, \cdots, m_n)$ is the message that the source node multicasts to the set of sink nodes, where $m_i \in \mathsf{F}$. U is an $n \times |\mathcal{E}|$ matrix over F which is called a linear network coding matrix. d_i is the field element which is sent through an edge e_i. For example,

$$U = \begin{pmatrix} 100110000101100 \\ 010001100111111 \\ 001000011010011 \end{pmatrix} \tag{3}$$

is the linear network coding matrix used in Fig. 1.

Jaggi et al. [6] showed a polynomial time algorithm which can construct a linear network coding matrix U from a given network G. Their algorithm works if $|\mathsf{F}| \geq q$, where q is the number of sink nodes.

2.2 k-Secure Linear Network Coding

Consider a linear network coding scheme such that

$$(m_1, \cdots, m_{n-k}, r_1, \cdots, r_k) \times V = (d_1, \cdots, d_{|\mathcal{E}|}), \tag{4}$$

where each r_i is randomly chosen from F. We say that such a linear network coding scheme is k-secure if any k edges leak no information on $(m_1, \cdots, m_{n-k})$.

Proposition 1. *[4, Theorem 2] Suppose that $|\mathsf{F}| > \binom{|\mathcal{E}|}{k}$. Then for any linear network coding matrix U, there exists an $n \times n$ nonsingular matrix T such that $V = T \times U$ is k-secure.*

Proposition 2. *[3, Lemma 3.1] The network coding matrix V of Eq. (4) is k-secure if and only if*

$$rank(V_A) = rank(V_{A,k})$$

for any $A \subseteq \{1, \cdots, |\mathcal{E}|\}$ such that $|A| \leq k$.

Corollary 1. *A network coding matrix V is 1-secure if and only if the last row of V consists of nonzero elements.*

2.3   Simple Proof of Proposition 2

In this subsection, we show a simpler proof of Proposition 2 than that of [3, Lemma 3.1]. Let $V = (\mathbf{v}_i)$, where $\mathbf{v}_i = (v_{i,1}, \cdots, v_{i,|\mathcal{E}|})$.

First consider a linear network coding scheme such that

$$(m_1, \cdots, m_{n-1}, r_1) \times V = \sum_{i=1}^{n-1} m_i \mathbf{v}_i + r_1 \mathbf{v}_n.$$

Corollary 1 states that it is 1-secure if and only if all the elements of $\mathbf{v}_n$ are nonzeros. This is because $r_1 \mathbf{v}_n$ works as the one-time pad to mask $(m_1, \cdots, m_{n-1})$ at each edge.

Next consider a 1-secure linear network coding scheme such that

$$(m_1, \cdots, m_{n-2}, r_1, r_2) \times V = \sum_{i=1}^{n-2} m_i \mathbf{v}_i + r_1 \mathbf{v}_{n-1} + r_2 \mathbf{v}_n.$$

Proposition 2 states that it is 2-secure if and only if $rank(V_{A,2}) = 2$ for any $A \subseteq \{1, \cdots, |\mathcal{E}|\}$ such that $|A| = rank(V_A) = 2$.

Without loss of generality, look at edges e_1 and e_2 and suppose that $rank(V_{\{1,2\}}) = 2$. Then from the above equation, we have

$$(d_1, d_2) = \left(\sum_{i=1}^{n-2} m_i v_{i,1}, \sum_{i=1}^{n-2} m_i v_{i,2} \right) + (r_1, r_2) \times V_{\{1,2\},2}$$

where

$$V_{\{1,2\},2} = \begin{pmatrix} v_{n-1,,1}, & v_{n-1,2} \\ v_{n,,1}, & v_{n,2} \end{pmatrix}.$$

Now $(r_1, r_2) \times V_{\{1,2\},2}$ is a random vector if and only if $rank(V_{\{1,2\},2}) = 2$. Therefore (d_1, d_2) leaks no information on $(m_1, \cdots, m_{n-2})$ if and only if $rank(V_{\{1,2\},2}) = 2$.

The proof for $k \geq 3$ is similar.

3   Strongly k-Secure Network Coding Scheme

3.1   Definition

Consider a linear network coding scheme of Eq. (2) such that each m_i is independently and uniformly distributed over F. Then strongly k-secure network coding schemes are defined as follows.

Definition 1.   1. Such a scheme is strongly 1-secure if any single edge leaks no information on any $S \subset \{m_1, \cdots, m_n\}$ such that $|S| = n - 1$.

2. A strongly h-secure network coding scheme is strongly $(h + 1)$-secure if any $h + 1$ edges leak no information on any $S \subset \{m_1, \cdots, m_n\}$ such that $|S| = n - h - 1$.

Harada and Yamamoto showed that there exists a strongly $(n - 1)$-secure linear network coding scheme if $|\mathsf{F}|$ is sufficiently large [5, Theorem 3]. However, they did not present an explicit construction algorithm. They did not give a concrete size of $|\mathsf{F}|$ either.

3.2 Necessary and Sufficient Condition

We can generalize Corollary 1 and Proposition 2 as follows.

Corollary 2. *In Eq. (2), the network coding matrix $U = (u_{i,j})$ is strongly 1-secure if and only if $u_{i,j} \neq 0$ for all (i, j).*

Proof. Equation (2) is written as

$$(m_1, \cdots, m_n) \times U = \sum_{i \neq j} m_i \mathbf{u}_i + m_j \mathbf{u}_j,$$

where $U = (\mathbf{u}_i)$. Corollary 2 states that any single edge leaks no information on $\{m_1, \cdots, m_n\} \setminus \{m_j\}$ if and only if all the elements of $\mathbf{u}_j$ are nonzeros. This is because $m_j \mathbf{u}_j$ works as the one-time pad to mask $\{m_1, \cdots, m_n\} \setminus \{m_j\}$. This argument holds for any m_j.   □

Proposition 3. *The network coding matrix U of Eq. (2) is strongly k-secure if and only if*

$$rank(U_A) = rank(U_{A,B})$$

for any $A \in \mathsf{Rank}_j$ and any $B \subset \{1, \cdots, n\}$ such that $|B| = j$ for $j = 1, \cdots, k$.

Proof. Suppose that U is strongly $(k-1)$-secure. We will show that any k edges leak no information on any $S \subset \{m_1, \cdots, m_n\}$ with $|S| = k$ if and only if $rank(U_{A,B}) = k$ for any $A \in \mathsf{Rank}_k$ and any $B \subset \{1, \cdots, n\}$ such that $|B| = k$.

Suppose that $S' = \{m_1, \cdots, m_n\} \setminus \{m_{i_1}, \cdots, m_{i_k}\}$. In this case, we consider that $(m_{i_1}, \cdots, m_{i_k})$ are random elements $(r_1, \cdots, r_k)$. Also let $B' = \{i_1, \cdots, i_k\}$. Then from Proposition 2 and the second example of Sec. 2.3, it is easy to see that any k edges leak no information on S' if and only if $rank(U_{A,B'}) = k$ for any $A \in \mathsf{Rank}_k$. This argument holds for any $\{i_1, \cdots, i_k\}$.   □

4   How to Construct Strongly 1-Secure Scheme

In this section, we show a deterministic polynomial time algorithm constructing strongly 1-secure linear network coding schemes.

Tang et al. [14] presented a *probabilistic* algorithm for constructing k-secure network coding schemes. We first show a deterministic polynomial time algorithm constructing 1-secure linear network coding schemes based on their algorithm. We next show a deterministic polynomial time algorithm constructing *strongly* 1-secure linear network coding schemes.

4.1 How to Increase Hamming Weight

For two given vectors $\mathbf{x} = (x_1, \cdots, x_N)$ and $\mathbf{y} = (y_1, \cdots, y_N)$ over F, we show how to find α which maximizes $w_H(\alpha \mathbf{x} + \mathbf{y})$ in time $O(N)$.[5] Define

$$\mathsf{zeros}(\mathbf{x}, \mathbf{y}) = \{-y_i/x_i \mid x_i \neq 0\}$$
$$= \{\alpha \mid \alpha x_i + y_i = 0 \text{ with } x_i \neq 0\}.$$

Lemma 1. *For any α such that $\alpha \in \mathsf{F} \setminus \mathsf{zeros}(\mathbf{x}, \mathbf{y})$, it holds that*

$$support(\alpha \mathbf{x} + \mathbf{y}) = support(\mathbf{x}) \cup support(\mathbf{y}).$$

Proof. Suppose that $\alpha \in \mathsf{F} \setminus \mathsf{zeros}(\mathbf{x}, \mathbf{y})$. Then $\alpha x_i + y_i = 0$ if and only if $x_i = y_i = 0$. This means that

$$support(\alpha \mathbf{x} + \mathbf{y}) = support(\mathbf{x}) \cup support(\mathbf{y}).$$

$\square$

Lemma 2. *If $|\mathsf{F}| > w_H(\mathbf{x})$, then we can find α such that $\alpha \in \mathsf{F} \setminus \mathsf{zeros}(\mathbf{x}, \mathbf{y})$ in time $O(N)$.*

Proof. Note that $|\mathsf{zeros}(\mathbf{x}, \mathbf{y})| \leq w_H(\mathbf{x}) < |\mathsf{F}|$. Therefore $\mathsf{F} \setminus \mathsf{zeros}(\mathbf{x}, \mathbf{y}) \neq \emptyset$. We can find α such that $\alpha \in \mathsf{F} \setminus \mathsf{zeros}(\mathbf{x}, \mathbf{y})$ by using the following algorithm in time $O(N)$. For simplicity, suppose that $\mathsf{F} = \mathsf{F}_p$ such that p is a prime.

(Algorithm HAMMING WEIGHT INCREASING**)**

Input: Two vectors $\mathbf{x} = (x_1, \cdots, x_N)$ and $\mathbf{y} = (y_1, \cdots, y_N)$ over F, where $|\mathsf{F}| > w_H(\mathbf{x})$.
Output: α such that $\alpha \in \mathsf{F} \setminus \mathsf{zeros}(\mathbf{x}, \mathbf{y})$.

1. Let $N_0 = w_H(\mathbf{x})$.
2. Let $a(0) = a(1) = \cdots = a(N_0) = 0$.
3. For $i = 1, \cdots, N$, do:
4.   If $x_i \neq 0$, then do:
5.   Compute $q_i = -y_i/x_i$. If $q_i \leq N_0$, then let $a(q_i) := 1$.
6. Output the least j such that $a(j) = 0$ as α.

$\square$

Consider $\mathbf{x} = (1, 1, 1, 0)$ and $\mathbf{y} = (0, 4, 2, 3)$ over F_5. Then $N_0 = w_H(\mathbf{x}) = 3$, and initially we have $a(0) = \cdots = a(3) = 0$. Next we compute $q_1 = 0$, $q_2 = -4 = 1$ and $q_3 = -2 = 3$. Hence we set $a(0) = a(1) = a(3) = 1$. Finally the least j such that $a(j) = 0$ is 2. Therefore we obtain $\alpha = 2$. In this case,

$$\alpha \mathbf{x} + \mathbf{y} = 2 \times (1, 1, 1, 0) + (0, 4, 2, 3) = (2, 1, 4, 3).$$

---

[5] Tang et al. [14] did not show such an algorithm.

4.2   How to Make a NonZero Row

Let $c \in \{1, \cdots, n\}$. For two $n \times \ell$ matrices $X = (\mathbf{x}_i)$ and $Y = (\mathbf{y}_i)$, we write

$$Y \cong_{\text{nonzero}(c)} X$$

if $\mathbf{y}_i = \mathbf{x}_i$ for all $i \neq c$, and $w_H(\mathbf{y}_c) = \ell$.

We show a polynomial time algorithm which outputs a nonsingular matrix T such that

$$T \cdot X \cong_{\text{nonzero}(c)} X$$

from any X which does not contain a column vector $(0, \cdots, 0)^T$ and any $c \in \{1, \cdots, n\}$ by using the HAMMING WEIGHT INCREASING algorithm.

(Algorithm NONZERO-ROW)

Input: A $n \times \ell$ matrix $X = (\mathbf{x}_i)$ over F which does not contain a column $(0, \cdots, 0)^T$, and $c \in \{1, \cdots, n\}$.

Output: A nonsingular matrix T such that $T \cdot X \cong_{\text{nonzero}(c)} X$.

1. Let $\mathbf{y} := \mathbf{x}_c$.
2. For $i = 1, \cdots, n$, do:
3.   If $i \neq c$, do:
4.   Choose α_i such that $\alpha_i \in \mathsf{F} \setminus \mathsf{zeros}(\mathbf{x}_i, \mathbf{y})$ by using the HAMMING WEIGHT INCREASING algorithm.
5.   Let $\mathbf{y} := \alpha_i \times \mathbf{x}_i + \mathbf{y}$.
6. Let $Q = (\mathbf{q}_i)$ be an $n \times n$ matrix such that

$$\mathbf{q}_i = \begin{cases} (\alpha_1, \cdots, \alpha_n) & \text{if } i = c \\ (0, \cdots, 0) & \text{if } i \neq c \end{cases}$$

  where $\alpha_c = 0$.
7. Output $T = \mathcal{I}_n + Q$.

Theorem 1. *The above algorithm outputs nonsingular matrix T such that $T \cdot X \cong_{\text{nonzero}(c)} X$ in time $O(n\ell)$ if $|\mathsf{F}| > \ell$.*

Proof. Let $\mathbf{z}_i$ denote the ith row of $T \cdot X$. Since $T = \mathcal{I}_n + Q$, we have

$$T \cdot X = (\mathcal{I}_n + Q) \cdot X = X + Q \cdot X.$$

Therefore

$$\mathbf{z}_i = \begin{cases} \mathbf{x}_i & \text{if } i \neq c \\ \mathbf{x}_c + \sum_{j=1}^{n} \alpha_j \mathbf{x}_j & \text{if } i = c \end{cases}$$

We next show that $w_H(\mathbf{z}_c) = \ell$. At line 4, if $|\mathsf{F}| > \ell$, we can find α_i such that $\alpha_i \in \mathsf{F} \setminus \mathsf{zeros}(\mathbf{x}_i, \mathbf{y})$ from Lemma 2. Then from Lemma 1, we can see that

$$w_H(\mathbf{z}_c) = |support(\mathbf{z}_c)| = |\cup_{i=1}^{n} support(\mathbf{x}_i)| = \ell$$

because X does not include $(0, \cdots, 0)^T$. Therefore $T \cdot X \cong_{\text{nonzero}(c)} X$.

Further by using the elementary row operation, it is easy to see that $\det(T) = \det(\mathcal{I}_n) = 1$. Hence T is nonsingular.

Finally, line 4 takes time $O(\ell)$ from Lemma 2. Line 5 also takes time $O(\ell)$. Hence the algorithm runs in time $O(n\ell)$. □

4.3   How to Construct 1-Secure Schemes

We can immediately obtain a deterministic polynomial time algorithm for constructing 1-secure linear network coding scheme from Sec. 4.2. Let U be a $n \times |\mathcal{E}|$ matrix of a linear network coding scheme. First compute $T = $ NONZERO-ROW (U, n). Next let $V = T \cdot U$. Then V is a 1-secure linear network coding matrix from Corollary 1 and Theorem 1. This algorithm runs in time $O(n|\mathcal{E}|)$ from Theorem 1.

An example of a 1-secure linear network coding scheme is shown in Appendix A. It is obtained by applying the above algorithm to Fig. 1 in such a way that $\alpha_1 = \alpha_2 = 1$.

4.4   How to Construct Strongly 1-Secure Schemes

We will now show a polynomial time algorithm which outputs a nonsingular matrix T such that $T \cdot U$ is strongly 1-secure from any linear network coding matrix U.

(**Algorithm** STRONGLY ONE-SECURE)

Input: An $n \times |\mathcal{E}|$ matrix U of a linear network coding scheme.
Output: A nonsingular matrix T such that $V = T \cdot U$ is strongly 1-secure.

1. Compute $T_0 := $ NONZERO-ROW(U, n).
2. Compute $U^* := T_0 \cdot U$.
   Let $U^* = (\mathbf{u}_i^*)$. Then $w_H(\mathbf{u}_n^*) = |\mathcal{E}|$.
3. For $i = 1, \cdots, n - 1$, choose β_i such that $\beta_i \in \mathsf{F} \setminus \mathsf{zeros}(\mathbf{u}_n^*, \mathbf{u}_i^*)$ by using the HAMMING WEIGHT INCREASING algorithm.
4. Output

$$
T = \begin{pmatrix} & & \beta_1 \\ & \mathcal{I}_{n-1} & \vdots \\ & & \beta_{n-1} \\ 0 & \cdots & 0 & 1 \end{pmatrix} \times T_0
$$

Theorem 2. *For any linear network coding matrix U, the above algorithm outputs T such that $V = T \times U$ is strongly 1-secure in time $O(n^2|\mathcal{E}|)$ if $|\mathsf{F}| > |\mathcal{E}|$.*

Proof. Let $V = (\mathbf{v}_i)$. Then $\mathbf{v}_n = \mathbf{u}_n^*$ and $\mathbf{v}_i = \mathbf{u}_i^* + \beta_i \mathbf{u}_n^*$ for $i = 1, \cdots, n - 1$. First from Theorem 1,

$$
w_H(\mathbf{v}_n) = w_H(\mathbf{u}_n^*) = |\mathcal{E}|.
$$

Next for $i = 1, \cdots, n - 1$, we have

$$
w_H(\mathbf{v}_i) = w_H(\mathbf{u}_i^* + \beta_i \mathbf{u}_n^*) = w_H(\mathbf{u}_n^*) = |\mathcal{E}|
$$

from Lemma 1. Hence all the elements of V are nonzero. This means that V is strongly 1-secure from Corollary 2.

Further T is nonsingular because T_0 is nonsingular from Theorem 1.

Finally from Lemma 2, we can run step 1 if $|\mathsf{F}| > |\mathcal{E}|$ in time $O(n|\mathcal{E}|)$. Therefore the algorithm runs in time $O(n^2|\mathcal{E}|)$.   □

An example of a strongly 1-secure linear network coding scheme is shown in Appendix A (Fig. 4). It is obtained by applying the above algorithm to Fig. 1 in such a way that $\alpha_1 = \alpha_2 = 1$ at step 1, and $\beta_1 = \beta_2 = 1$ at step 3.

5   How to Construct Strongly k-Secure Schemes

In this section, we show how to construct a strongly k-secure linear network coding scheme for $k \geq 2$.

5.1 D-Zero Projection of U

We first introduce a notion of D-zero projection of U, where U is an $n \times |\mathcal{E}|$ matrix of a linear network coding scheme and $D \subset \{1, \cdots, n\}$.

Definition 2. *We say that* $\mathbf{b}_A = (x_1, \cdots, x_n)^T$ *is a D-zero projection of U_A if* $\mathbf{b}_A = U_A \cdot (c_1, \cdots, c_{|D|+1})^T$ *for some* $(c_1, \cdots, c_{|D|+1}) \neq (0, \cdots, 0)$ *and* $x_i = 0$ *for all* $i \in D$, *where* $|A| = rank(U_A) = |D| + 1$.

Definition 3. *We say that an $n \times |\mathsf{Rank}_{|D|+1}|$ matrix W is a D-zero projection of U if each column $\mathbf{b}_A$ is indexed by $A \in \mathsf{Rank}_{|D|+1}$ and $\mathbf{b}_A$ a D-zero projection of U_A.*

It is an easy algebra to prove the following lemmas.

Lemma 3. *There exists a D-zero projection of U if*

$$rank(U_{A,D}) = |D|$$

for each $A \in \mathsf{Rank}_{|D|+1}$.

Lemma 4. *Let W be a D-zero projection of U. If the ith row of W consists of nonzero elements, then*

$$rank(U_{A,D\cup\{i\}}) = |D| + 1$$

for any $A \in \mathsf{Rank}_{|D|+1}$, where $i \notin D$.

An example is presented in Appendix B.

5.2   Construction of Strongly k-Secure Scheme

We now show an efficient algorithm which outputs a nonsingular matrix T such that $T \cdot U$ is strongly k-secure from any linear network coding matrix U for $k \geq 2$.

(Algorithm STRONGLY K-SECURE)

Input: A linear network coding matrix U.
Output: A nonsingular matrix T such that $V = T \cdot U$ is strongly k-secure.

1. Compute $T_0 :=$ NONZERO-ROW$(U, 1)$.
2. Compute $Y_0 := T_0 \times U$.
3. For $i = 1, \cdots, n - 1$, do:
4.   Let U^* be the first $|\mathcal{E}|$ columns of Y_{i-1}.
5.   For each $D \subset \{1, \cdots, i\}$ such that $i \in D$ and $|D| < k$, do:
6.   compute a D-zero projection W_D of U^* and let $X_i := (Y_{i-1}, W_D)$.
7.   Compute $T_i :=$ NONZERO-ROW$(X_i, i + 1)$.
8.   Compute $Y_i := T_i \times X_i$.
9. Output $T := T_{n-1} \times \cdots T_1 \times T_0$.

Theorem 3. *For any linear network coding matrix U, let*

$$L = |\mathcal{E}| + \sum_{i=1}^{k-1} \binom{n-1}{i} \binom{|\mathcal{E}|}{i+1}.$$

Then the above algorithm outputs T such that $T \cdot U$ is strongly k-secure in time $O(n^2 L)$ if $|\mathsf{F}| > L$.

The proof is given in Appendix C.

5.3   Example for $k = 2$

We show an example for $n = 3$ and $k = 2$. Let U be a $3 \times |\mathcal{E}|$ matrix of a linear network coding scheme. Our algorithm runs as follows.

1. Compute $T_0 :=$ NONZERO-ROW$(U, 1)$, and let $U^* := T_0 \times U$.
   This means that the first row of U^* consists of nonzero elements, and the other rows are the same as those of U.

$U^* = T \cdot U$
non-zero
***
***

2. Compute a $\{1\}$-zero projection $W_{\{1\}}$ of U^*.
   Here each column $\mathbf{b}_A$ of $W_{\{1\}}$ is indexed by $A = (i_1, i_2) \in \mathsf{Rank}_2$ and computed as
   $$\mathbf{b}_A = c_1 \mathbf{b}_{i_1} + c_2 \mathbf{b}_{i_2} = (0, x_2, x_3)^T$$
   for some $(c_1, c_2) \neq (0, 0)$, where $\mathbf{b}_i$ is the ith column of U^*.[6] Then $(U^*, W_{\{1\}})$ looks as follows.

U^*	$W_{\{1\}}$
non-zero	$0, \cdots, 0$
***	***
***	***

---

[6] Since the first row of U^* consists of nonzero elements, it holds that $rank(U^*_{A,\{1\}}) = 1$ for any $A \in \mathsf{Rank}_2$. Therefore there exists a $\{1\}$-zero projection of U^* from Lemma 3.

3. Compute $T_1 :=$ NONZERO-ROW$((U^*, W_{\{1\}}), 2)$.
   Compute $(U^*, W_{\{1\}}^*) := T_1 \times (U^*, W_{\{1\}})$.
   This means the 2nd row of $(U^*, W_{\{1\}}^*)$ consists of nonzero elements, and the other rows do not change. Hence $(U^*, W_{\{1\}}^*)$ looks as follows.

U^*	$W_{\{1\}}^*$
non-zero	$0, \cdots, 0$
non-zero	non-zero
***	***

4. Compute a $\{2\}$-zero projection $W_{\{2\}}$ of U^*.
   Here each column $\mathbf{b}_A$ of $W_{\{2\}}$ is indexed by $A = (i_1, i_2) \in$ Rank$_2$ and computed as
   $$\mathbf{b}_A = c_1 \mathbf{b}_{i_1} + c_2 \mathbf{b}_{i_2} = (x_1, 0, x_3)^T$$
   for some $(c_1, c_2) \neq (0, 0)$, where $\mathbf{b}_i$ is the ith column of U^*.[7] Then $(U^*, W_{\{1\}}^*, W_{\{2\}})$ looks as follows.

U^*	$W_{\{1\}}^*$	$W_{\{2\}}$
non-zero	$0, \cdots, 0$	***
non-zero	non-zero	$0, \cdots, 0$
***	***	***

5. Compute $T_2 :=$ NONZERO-ROW$((U^*, W_{\{1\}}^*, W_{\{2\}}), 3)$.
   Compute $X = (U^*, W_{\{1\}}^*, W_{\{2\}}^*) := T_2 \times (U^*, W_{\{1\}}^*, W_{\{2\}})$.
   Now the 3rd row of X consists of nonzero elements, and the other rows do not change. Hence X looks as follows.

U^*	$W_{\{1\}}^*$	$W_{\{2\}}^*$
non-zero	$0, \cdots, 0$	***
non-zero	non-zero	$0, \cdots, 0$
non-zero	non-zero	non-zero

Fig. 2. Example for $k = 2$

6. Outputs $T := T_2 \times T_1 \times T_0$.

In Fig. 2, $W_{\{1\}}^*$ is a $\{1\}$-zero projection of U^*, and $W_{\{2\}}^*$ is a $\{2\}$-zero projection of U^*. Since all the elements of U^* are nonzeros, it is clear that

$$rank(U_A^*) = rank(U_{A,\{1\}}^*) = rank(U_{A,\{2\}}^*) = rank(U_{A,\{3\}}^*) = 1$$

---

[7] Since the 2nd row of U^* consists of nonzero elements, it holds that $rank(U_{A,\{2\}}^*) = 1$ for any $A \in$ Rank$_2$. Therefore there exists a $\{2\}$-zero projection of U^* from Lemma 3.

for any $A \in \mathsf{Rank}_1$. Next from Lemma 4 and from Fig. 2, we have

$$rank(U_A^*) = rank(U_{A,\{1,2\}}^*) = rank(U_{A,\{1,3\}}^*) = rank(U_{A,\{2,3\}}^*) = 2$$

for any $A \in \mathsf{Rank}_2$. Therefore U^* is strongly 2-secure from Proposition 3.

The number of columns of $(U^*, W_{\{1\}}^*, W_{\{2\}})$ is at most $|\mathcal{E}| + 2 \cdot \binom{|\mathcal{E}|}{2}$. Therefore we can compute each T_i if $|\mathsf{F}| > |\mathcal{E}| + 2 \cdot \binom{|\mathcal{E}|}{2}$ from Theorem 1.

We show a strongly 2-secure linear network coding scheme in Appendix A (Fig. 5) which is obtained by applying our algorithm to Fig. 1.

A Example of Secure Linear Network Coding Schemes

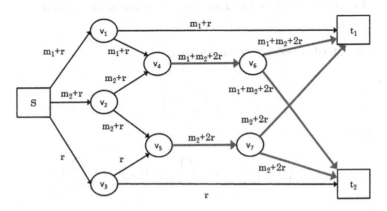

Fig. 3. 1-Secure linear network coding scheme (mod3)

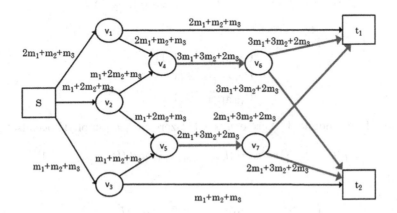

Fig. 4. Strongly 1-secure linear network coding scheme (mod5)

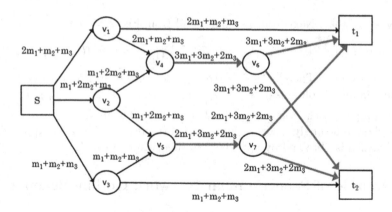

Fig. 5. Strongly 2-secure linear network coding scheme (mod11)

B Example of D-Zero Projection

Consider

$$U = \begin{pmatrix} 1 & 1 & 2 \\ 0 & 1 & 1 \end{pmatrix}$$

over F_5. Then

$$U_{\{1,2\}} = \begin{pmatrix} 1 & 1 \\ 0 & 1 \end{pmatrix}, U_{\{1,3\}} = \begin{pmatrix} 1 & 2 \\ 0 & 1 \end{pmatrix}, U_{\{2,3\}} = \begin{pmatrix} 1 & 2 \\ 1 & 1 \end{pmatrix}.$$

Therefore

$$\mathsf{Rank}_2 = \{\{1,2\}, \{1,3\}, \{2,3\}\}$$

because

$$rank(U_{\{1,2\}}) = rank(U_{\{1,3\}}) = rank(U_{\{2,3\}}) = 2.$$

Next

$$U_{\{1,2\},\{1\}} = (1,1)$$
$$U_{\{1,3\},\{1\}} = (1,2)$$
$$U_{\{2,3\},\{1\}} = (1,2)$$

Therefore from Lemma 3, there exists a $\{1\}$-zero projection of W because

$$rank(U_{\{1,2\},\{1\}}) = rank(U_{\{1,3\},\{1\}}) = rank(U_{\{2,3\},\{1\}}) = 1$$

Let

$$\mathbf{b}_{\{1,2\}} = -(1,0)^T + (1,1)^T = (0,1)^T$$
$$\mathbf{b}_{\{1,3\}} = -2 \cdot (1,0)^T + (2,1)^T = (0,1)^T$$
$$\mathbf{b}_{\{2,3\}} = -2 \cdot (1,1)^T + (2,1)^T = (0,-1)^T.$$

Then $\mathbf{b}_A$ is a $\{1\}$-zero projection of U_A for $A = \{1,2\}, \{1,3\}$ and $\{2,3\}$. Therefore W such that

$$W = (\mathbf{b}_{\{1,2\}}, \mathbf{b}_{\{1,3\}}, \mathbf{b}_{\{2,3\}}) = \begin{pmatrix} 0 & 0 & 0 \\ 1 & 1 & -1 \end{pmatrix}$$

is a $\{1\}$-zero projection of U. Finally the second row of W consists of nonzero elements. Therefore

$$rank(U_{\{1,2\},\{1,2\}}) = rank(U_{\{1,3\},\{1,2\}}) = rank(U_{\{2,3\},\{1,2\}}) = 2$$

from Lemma 4.

C Proof of Theorem 3

At line 5 and line 6, we can show that there exists such a D-zero projection W_D of U^* by induction on i based on Lemma 3. (See the footnotes of Sec. 5.3.) At line 8, the $(i+1)$th row of Y_i consists nonzero elements, and the other rows are the same as those of X_i. Therefore the final Y_{n-1} looks as follows, where $U^* = T \cdot U$. It is also easy to see that W_D^* is a D-zero projection of U^* for all $D \subset \{1, \cdots, n\}$ such that $|D| < k$ (Fig. 6).

U^*	$W_{\{1\}}^*$	$W_{\{2\}}^*$	$W_{\{1,2\}}^*$	$W_{\{3\}}^*$	$W_{\{1,3\}}^*$	$W_{\{2,3\}}^*$	—
non-zero	$0, \cdots, 0$	***	$0, \cdots, 0$	***	$0 \cdots 0$	***	—
non-zero	non-zero	$0, \cdots, 0$	$0, \cdots, 0$	***	***	$0 \cdots 0$	—
non-zero	non-zero	non-zero	non-zero	$0 \cdots 0$	$0 \cdots 0$	$0 \cdots 0$	—
non-zero	non-zero	non-zero	non-zero	non-zero	non-zero	non-zero	—
—	—	—	—	—	—	—	—
non-zero	non-zero	non-zero	non-zero	non-zero	non-zero	non-zero	non-zero

Fig. 6. The final Y_{n-1}

In the above figure, since all the elements of U^* are nonzeros, it is clear that

$$rank(U_A^*) = rank(U_{A,\{1\}}^*) = \cdots = rank(U_{A,\{n\}}^*) = 1$$

for any $A \in \mathsf{Rank}_1$. Next from Lemma 4 and from the above figure, we have

$$rank(U_A^*) = rank(U_{A,\{1,2\}}^*) = \cdots = rank(U_{A,\{n-1,n\}}^*) = 2$$

for any $A \in \mathsf{Rank}_2$. Similarly, we can see that

$$rank(U_A^*) = rank(U_{A,B}^*)$$

for any $A \in \mathsf{Rank}_j$ and any $B \subset \{1, \cdots, n\}$ such that $|B| = j$ for $j = 1, \cdots, k$. Therefore U^* is strongly k-secure from Proposition 3.

Lemma 5. *Let L_k be the number of columns of the final X. Then*

$$L_k \leq |\mathcal{E}| + \sum_{i=1}^{k-1} \binom{n-1}{i} \binom{|\mathcal{E}|}{i+1}.$$

Proof. Let $\#A$ denote the number of columns of a matrix A. Then

$$L_k = \#U + \sum_{h=1}^{k-1} \binom{n-1}{h} \sum_{|D|=h} \#W_D$$

If $|D| = h$, then we have

$$\#W_D = |\mathsf{Rank}_{h+1}| \leq \binom{|\mathcal{E}|}{h+1}$$

from Eq. (1), Therefore we have this lemma.   □

Therefore at line 7, we can compute each T_i if $|\mathsf{F}| \geq L \geq L_k$ in time $O(nL)$ from Theorem 1. To compute all T_i, it takes time $O(n^2 L)$.

At line 5, it takes $O(n|D|^2)$ time to compute each W_D. To compute all W_D, it takes time $O(\sum_{i=1}^{k} ni^2 \binom{n-1}{i})$ which is bounded by $O(n^2 L)$.

Finally the time complexity of line 2 and line 9 is bounded by $O(n^2 L)$. Therefore our algorithm runs in time $O(n^2 L)$.

References

1. Ahlswede, R., Cai, N., Li, S.-Y.R., Yeung, R.W.: Network information flow. IEEE Trans. Inf. Theory **46**(4), 1204–1216 (2000)
2. Bhattad, K., Narayanan, K.R.: Weakly secure network coding. In: Proceedings of NetCod 2005, April 2005
3. Cai, N., Yeung, R.W.: A security condition for multi-source linear network coding. In: Proceedings of the IEEE ISIT, pp. 561–565, 24–29 June 2007
4. Cai, N., Yeung, R.W.: Secure network coding on a wiretap network. IEEE Trans. Inf. Theory **57**(1), 424–435 (2011)
5. Harada, K., Yamamoto, H.: Strongly secure linear network coding. IEICE Trans. **91–A**(10), 2720–2728 (2008)
6. Jaggi, S., Sanders, P., Chou, P.A., Effros, M., Egner, S., Jain, K., Tolhuizen, L.M.G.M.: Polynomial time algorithms for multicast network code construction. IEEE Trans. Inf. Theory **51**(6), 1973–1982 (2005)
7. Kurihara, J., Uematsu, T., Matsumoto, R.: Explicit construction of universal strongly secure network coding via MRD codes. In: Proceedings of the IEEE ISIT 2012, Cambridge, MA, USA, pp. 1488–1492, July 2012
8. Li, S.-Y.R., Yeung, R.W., Cai, N.: Linear network coding. IEEE Trans. Inf. Theory **49**(2), 371–381 (2003)
9. Nishiara, M., Takizawa, K.: Strongly secure secret sharing scheme with ramp threshold based on Shamir's polynomial interpolation scheme. IEICE Trans. Fundam. (Jpn. Ed.) **J92–A**(12), 1009–1013 (2009)

10. Silva, D., Kschischang, F.R.: Security for wiretap networks via rankmetric codes. In: Proceedings of the IEEE International Symposium Information Theory, Toronto, Canada, pp. 176–180, 6–11 July 2008
11. Silva, D., Kschischang, F.R.: Universal weakly secure network coding. In: Proceedings of IEEE ITW 2009, pp. 281–285, June 2009
12. Silva, D., Kschischang, F.R.: Universal secure network coding via rank-metric codes. IEEE Trans. Inf. Theory **57**(2), 1124–1135 (2011)
13. Shioji, E., Matsumoto, R., Uyematsu, T.: Vulnerability of MRD-code-based universal secure network coding against stronger eavesdroppers. IEICE Trans. **93–A**(11), 2026–2033 (2010)
14. Tang, Z., Lim, H.W., Wang, H.: Revisiting a secret sharing approach to network codes. In: Takagi, T., Wang, G., Qin, Z., Jiang, S., Yu, Y. (eds.) ProvSec 2012. LNCS, vol. 7496, pp. 300–317. Springer, Heidelberg (2012)

Secure Two-Party Computation: A Visual Way

Paolo D'Arco and Roberto De Prisco[(⊠)]

Dipartimento di Informatica, University of Salerno,
Via Giovanni Paolo II, 132, 84084, Fisciano, SA, Italy
{paodar,robdep}@dia.unisa.it

Abstract. In this paper we propose a novel method for performing secure two-party computation. By merging together in a suitable way two beautiful ideas of the 80's and the 90's, Yao's garbled circuit construction and Naor and Shamir's visual cryptography, respectively, we enable Alice and Bob to securely evaluate a function $f(\cdot, \cdot)$ of their inputs, x and y, through a *pure physical* process. Indeed, once Alice has prepared a set of properly constructed transparencies, Bob computes the function value $f(x, y)$ by applying a sequence of simple steps which require the use of a pair of scissors, superposing transparencies, and the human visual system. A crypto-device for the function evaluation process is not needed any more.

Keywords: Yao's construction · Visual cryptography · Secure computation

1 Introduction

Yao's Construction. Latins said: *Verba volant, scripta manent.* Yao's construction disproves the saying. Indeed, [31,32], the papers which usually are cited when the construction is used or referred to, do not contain any description of it. It has never been written down by the author, but only provided to the community during an oral presentation (FOCS 1986). Fortunately, *verba* were captured by other researchers, who used the construction in subsequent papers, first of all [21]. Later on, it has been widely exploited in protocol design, but, apart some notable exceptions, it has more or less been considered as a powerful tool for establishing existential results. However, in the last years, since it has been shown that fine-tuned implementations, for reasonable input sizes, are becoming practical in many settings, new attention has been devoted to it. A version of the construction has been clearly described and proved secure according to precise definitions and assumptions in [28]. In a few other new recently introduced cryptographic primitives and protocols, e.g., *functional encryption* [7] or *non-interactive verifiable computing* [22], the construction plays a key role, and in [4] it has been even proposed to move from a view of Yao's construction as a cryptographic tool to a view of the construction as a *cryptographic goal*, which

C. Padró (Ed.): ICITS 2013, LNCS 8317, pp. 18–38, 2014.
DOI: 10.1007/978-3-319-04268-8_2, © Springer International Publishing Switzerland 2014

can be achieved with several security properties and privacy degrees[1]. From a certain point of view, Yao's idea is living nowadays a sort of *second life*.

Roughly speaking, Yao's construction, enables two parties, Alice and Bob, to privately evaluate a boolean function $f(\cdot, \cdot)$ on their inputs, x and y, in such a way that each party gets the result and, at the same time, *preserves* the privacy of its own input, apart from what can be inferred about it by the other party from its input and the function value $f(x, y)$. For example, if the function $f(\cdot, \cdot)$ is the xor function, given x xor y and one of the input, there is no way to preserve the other input.

In a nutshell, the construction works as follows: the boolean function $f(\cdot, \cdot)$ is represented through a boolean circuit $C(\cdot, \cdot)$ for which, for each x, y, it holds that $C(x, y) = f(x, y)$. Yao's idea is to use the circuit as a *conceptual guide* for the computation which, instead of a sequence of and, or and not operations on strings of bits x and y, becomes a *sequence of decryptions* on sequences of ciphertexts. More precisely, one of the party, say Alice, given $C(\cdot, \cdot)$, computes a new object $\tilde{C}$, which is usually referred to as the *garbled circuit* [2], where:

- to each wire w of $C(\cdot, \cdot)$, are associated in $\tilde{C}$ two random keys, k_w^0 and k_w^1, which (secretly, the correspondence is not public) represent 0 and 1, and,
- to each gate $G(\cdot, \cdot)$ of $C(\cdot, \cdot)$, corresponds in $\tilde{C}$ a gate table $\tilde{G}$ with four rows, each of which is a *double encryption*, obtained by using two different keys $k_{w_1}^a$ and $k_{w_2}^b$, for $a, b \in \{0, 1\}$, of a message which is itself a random key $k_{w_3}^c$, for $c \in \{0, 1\}$. In details, each double encryption $E_{ab} = E_{k_{w_2}^b}(E_{k_{w_1}^a}(k_{w_3}^c))$ uses *one of the four* possible pairs of keys $(k_{w_1}^a, k_{w_2}^b)$, associated to the input wires (w_1, w_2) of gate $G(\cdot, \cdot)$, and the message which is encrypted is the random key $k_{w_3}^c$, associated to the wire w_3 of output of the gate $G(\cdot, \cdot)$ *if and only if* $G(a, b) = c$. The four double encryptions E_{00}, E_{01}, E_{10} and E_{11} are stored in the gate table rows in *random* order.

Once $\tilde{C}$ has been computed, Alice sends to Bob all the gate tables $\tilde{G}$ associated to the circuit gates $G(\cdot, \cdot)$, and *reveals* the random keys k_w^0 and k_w^1, associated to all the *output* wires w, and their correspondences with the values 0 and 1. Moreover, for the input wires of the circuit, she sends to Bob the random keys $k_{w_1}^{x_1}, k_{w_2}^{x_2}, \ldots, k_{w_n}^{x_n}$ corresponding to the bit-values of her own input $x = x_1 x_2 \ldots x_n$. To perform the computation represented by $\tilde{C}$, then Bob needs only the keys associated to the input wires corresponding to *his own* input. This issue is solved by means of *executions* of 1-out-of-2 *oblivious transfer* protocols [18], through which Bob receives the random keys $k_{w_{n+1}}^{y_1}, k_{w_{n+2}}^{y_2}, \ldots, k_{w_{2n}}^{y_{2n}}$ corresponding to the bit-values of his own input $y = y_1 y_2 \ldots y_n$ and nothing else, while Alice from the transfer does not know which specific keys Bob has recovered.

Finally Bob, according to the topology of the original circuit $C(\cdot, \cdot)$, level after level, decrypts *one and only one* entry from each gate table $\tilde{G}$ in $\tilde{C}$, until he computes *one and only one* random key associated to each output wire. The binary string which corresponds to the sequence of computed random keys,

---

[1] The introduction of [4] offers a brief history of the construction and a nice accounting of the research efforts which followed.

associated to the output wires, is the value $C(x, y)$. Bob sends the result of the computation to Alice[2].

It is easy to check that the computation is correct and, intuitively, that the privacy of the inputs is preserved. The random keys held by Bob, the rows of each $\check{G}$, and the random keys obtained decrypting a row in each $\tilde{G}$, do not leak any information about the actual bits of Alice's input value.

Visual Cryptography. Visual cryptography is a special type of secret sharing in which the secret is an image and the shares are random-looking images printed on transparencies. It was introduced by Naor and Shamir [27] and, in a different form, by Kafri and Keren [24]. The captivating peculiarity of this type of secret sharing is that the reconstruction of the secret is performed without any computational machinery: it is enough to superpose the shares (transparencies) in order to reconstruct the secret. Roughly speaking, for black-and-white images, the bit value 0 is encoded as a transparent pixel, the bit value 1 is encoded as a black pixel, and the reconstruction operation is an **or** and is performed by the human visual system when the shares are superposed. Visual cryptography has been extensively studied (e.g. [1, 6, 11, 12, 14, 16, 17, 19, 23]); we refer the interested reader to [15] for a collection of surveys on several aspects of visual cryptography. For the goal of this paper we will be using a particular type of visual cryptography: probabilistic visual cryptography [13, 30].

Our Contribution. In this paper we merge together Yao's construction and properly defined visual cryptography schemes, in order to propose a method through which Alice and Bob can securely evaluate a function $f(\cdot, \cdot)$ of their inputs, x and y, through a *pure physical* process.

Our efforts were inspired and driven by the work of Kolesnikov [26], who showed that a different approach to the function evaluation process in Yao's construction can be pursued. Roughly speaking, instead of constructing the garbled circuit $\tilde{C}$ by using for each gate $G(\cdot, \cdot)$ a gate table $\tilde{G}$, containing a double encryption for each possible input pair of keys, Kolesnikov showed that it is possible to use *secret sharing schemes* designed to realize the functionalities implemented by the logical gates. Such schemes were referred to as *gate equivalent secret sharing schemes* (GESS, for short) [26]. Using a GESS, any time that two shares, say $sh^a_{w_1}$ and $sh^b_{w_2}$, associated to the input wires w_1 and w_2 of gate $G(\cdot, \cdot)$, are combined through the reconstruction function of the GESS, the secret s_{w_3}, associated to the output wire w_3 of gate $G(\cdot, \cdot)$ is recovered. It follows that an *explicit representation* $\tilde{G}$ of $G(\cdot, \cdot)$ is *not* needed any more, because all the information required to reconstruct the secret value associated to w_3, depending on the functionality of the target gate $G(\cdot, \cdot)$, is coded and, hence, *implicitly represented*, into the shares $sh^a_{w_1}$ and $sh^b_{w_2}$. Therefore, given the circuit $C(\cdot, \cdot)$, and by applying a bottom-up process, which starts from the circuit output wires and ends when the circuit input wires are reached, Alice can construct shares associated to the circuit input wires which encode *all the information* needed to evaluate $C(\cdot, \cdot)$ on every pair of inputs (x, y). Then, as in Yao's construction,

---

[2] A detailed description of Yao's protocol can be found in [28].

Alice sends directly to Bob the shares corresponding to the bit-values of her own input x, while Bob, by means of *executions* of 1-out-of-2 *oblivious transfer* protocols, receives the shares corresponding to the bit-values of his own input y. Finally, Bob applies iteratively the GESS reconstruction functions, until the secrets associated to the output wires, which correspond to the value $C(x, y)$, are obtained.

In this paper we provide a *generalization* of the above approach and a *visual implementation*.

Notice that, the technique used by Kolesnikov [26], does not immediately extend to visual secret sharing. In order to exploit visual secret sharing, some technical details and issues need to be addressed. The most important ones are two: (i) we need to define and construct a *visual counterpart* of a GESS scheme, and (ii) propose a physical method to perform the oblivious transfer. Both of them are goals of independent interests. We show that the GESS construction provided in [26] is a *special case* of a general construction which uses multi-secret sharing schemes, and that it can be instantiated by using a visual multi-secret sharing scheme. We also provide a construction. Regarding the oblivious transfer, even if physical metaphors have often been used for describing cryptographic primitives and protocols, only few papers have dealt with physical implementations. To our knowledge, the state of the art is summarized in [29], which is the first paper that rigorously addresses the issue of realizing cryptographic protocols by using tamper-evident seals (sealed envelopes and locked boxes). We could use an oblivious transfer protocol of [29], but since we discuss a simpler scenario, we propose an easier construction which uses *indistinguishable envelopes*. The main result we achieve can be (informally) stated as follows:

Theorem 1. *Every two-party computation representable by means of a boolean function $f(\cdot, \cdot)$ can be performed preserving the privacy of the inputs x and y through a pure physical visual evaluation process.*

2   Definitions and Tools

Let us start by setting up the notation and stating basic definitions. We follow essentially the treatment of [20, 28] (i.e., see Sect. 2 of [28] or Chap. 7 of [20]).

2.1   Notation

Efficient Algorithms. An efficient algorithm is a probabilistic algorithm running in $poly(k)$ time, where k is a security parameter. Efficient algorithms are referred to as *PPT algorithms*.

Negligible Functions. A function $f(\cdot)$ is negligible if it vanishes faster than the inverse of any fixed positive polynomial. That is, for any positive integer c, there exists an integer k_0 such that $f(k) \leq \frac{1}{k^c}$, for any $k \geq k_0$. We denote by $negl(k)$ a negligible function.

Algorithms and Random Variables. If $A(\cdot)$ is a probabilistic algorithm, then, for any x, the notation $A(x)$ refers to the random variable that assigns to the string σ the probability that A, on input x, outputs σ.

Distribution Ensembles. If S is an infinite set, and $X = \{X_s\}_{s \in S}$ and $Y = \{Y_s\}_{s \in S}$ are distribution ensembles[3], then we say the X and Y are *identically distributed*, $X \overset{p}{\equiv} Y$ for short, if, for every distinguisher D and for every $s \in S$, it holds that $Pr[D(X_s) = 1] - Pr[D(Y_s) = 1]$ is equal to 0. Similarly, if the Ds are PPT algorithms, and for all sufficiently large (in the length of the security parameter) $s \in S$ it holds that $|Pr[D(X_s) = 1] - Pr[D(Y_s) = 1]|$ is a negligible function $negl(s)$ in s, we say that X and Y are *computationally indistinguishable*, $X \overset{c}{\equiv} Y$ for short.

2.2   Secure Two-Party Computation

We consider two-party computation in presence of a *static semi-honest* adversary. The adversary controls one of the parties and, although it follows the protocol specification, it might try to learn extra information from the transcript of the messages received during the execution.

A two-party computation is a random process that maps pairs of inputs to pairs of outputs, one for each party. We refer to such a process as a *functionality* and denote it $f : \{0,1\}^* \times \{0,1\}^* \rightarrow \{0,1\}^* \times \{0,1\}^*$, where $f(x,y) = (f_1(x,y), f_2(x,y))$.

Let π be a two-party protocol for computing f. Intuitively, a protocol is secure if whatever a party can compute participating in the protocol can also be computed by himself by using *only* his own input and his own function value. More formally, for $i \in \{1,2\}$, denoting with the random variables $view_i^\pi(x,y)$, the view (i.e., input, random coins, messages received...) that party i has during the execution of $\pi(x,y)$, by $output_i^\pi(x,y)$ the output of party i, and by $output^\pi(x,y)$ the output of both parties, we state the following[4]:

Definition 1. *Let f be a functionality. A protocol π computes f in a perfectly (computationally) secure way, in presence of a static semi-honest adversary, if*

$$\{output^\pi(x,y)\}_{(x,y) \in \{0,1\}^*} = \{f(x,y)\}_{(x,y) \in \{0,1\}^*}$$

---

[3] A random variable is sufficient to represent the input, the output or any intermediate computation of a randomized entity in a *single* protocol execution. However, since it is of interest analyzing the behavior of protocol executions, according to input sizes depending on the security parameter k, *collections* of random variables are needed: an ensemble is exactly a family of random variables, where each of them, say X_s, is uniquely identified by an index s, related to the security parameter k.

[4] We deal in the following with a deterministic functionality. Hence, we state the simplified versions of the definitions in [20,28]. Moreover, we also state the definition for the unconditionally secure case. As we will show later, by using an unconditionally secure *physical* implementation of the oblivious transfer, known to be possible [29], the definition in the *physical* world is achieved by our protocol.

and there exists (PPT) algorithms Sim_1 and Sim_2 such that:

$$\{Sim_1(x, f_1(x, y))\}_{(x,y)\in\{0,1\}^*} \overset{p/c}{\equiv} \{view_1^\pi(x, y)\}_{(x,y)\in\{0,1\}^*},$$

$$\{Sim_2(y, f_2(x, y))\}_{(x,y)\in\{0,1\}^*} \overset{p/c}{\equiv} \{view_2^\pi(x, y)\}_{(x,y)\in\{0,1\}^*}.$$

3   Visual Gate Evaluation Secret Sharing

In this section, building on the definitions and the constructions provided in [26], we introduce the notion of *visual* gate evaluation secret sharing (VGESS, for short), and we show how to construct a VGESS scheme. We proceed as follows: (*i*) we recall some notions on secret and multi-secret sharing schemes and their visual version, (*ii*) we recall the definition of GESS schemes [26], (*iii*) we define a *general* construction for GESS schemes, GenGESS for short, in terms of multi-secret sharing schemes. The construction in [26] ends up to be a special instance of it. Finally, in order to take benefits from the general form, (*iv*) we define VGESS and, by using a visual multi-secret sharing scheme, (*v*) we realize an implementation.

3.1   Secret Sharing and Multi-Secret Sharing Schemes

Let us briefly introduce secret sharing and multi-secret sharing schemes[5].

Roughly speaking, a secret sharing scheme is a method through which a dealer shares a secret s among a set of parties, in such a way that, later on, some subsets of parties can reconstruct the secret, while others do not get any information about it. Similarly, a multi-secret sharing scheme enables the dealer to share more than one secret among the set of parties, in such a way that different subsets of parties reconstruct different secrets.

Let $\mathcal{P} = \{1, \ldots, n\}$ be a set of n parties. A collection of subsets $\mathcal{A} \subset 2^\mathcal{P}$ is monotone if $A \in \mathcal{A}$ and $A \subseteq B$ imply that $B \in \mathcal{A}$.

Definition 2. Access structure. *An access structure on the set of parties $\mathcal{P}$ is a pair $(\mathcal{A}, \mathcal{F})$ such that $\mathcal{A} \subset 2^\mathcal{P}$ is a monotone collection, $\mathcal{F} \subset 2^\mathcal{P}$, and $\mathcal{A} \cap \mathcal{F} = \emptyset$.*

$(\mathcal{A}, \mathcal{F})$ is a *specification* of the sets which reconstruct the secret and of the sets which do not get any information about it. Usually sets in $\mathcal{A}$ are called *authorized*, while sets in $\mathcal{F}$ are called *forbidden*. Sets in $2^\mathcal{P} \setminus (\mathcal{A} \cup \mathcal{F})$ are sets for which we *do not care*.

Let $S, SH_1, \ldots, SH_n$ be finite sets. The set S is usually referred to as the set of *secrets* and the sets $SH_1, \ldots, SH_n$ as the sets of *shares*. Moreover, denote

---

[5] We do not follow the traditional entropy-based characterization, e.g., [8,25], since in our analysis we are not going to use the entropy function. A comprehensive study of secret sharing schemes which does not use the language of information theory can be found in [5]. See also a recent survey [3].

with s and $sh_1, \ldots, sh_n$ elements belonging to S and $SH_1, \ldots, SH_n$, respectively, and for each $X = \{i_1, \ldots, i_m\} \subseteq \mathcal{P}$, with $SH_X = SH_{i_1} \times \ldots \times SH_{i_m}$ and with $sh_X = (sh_{i_1}, \ldots, sh_{i_m})$. Using the above notation, we state the following:

Definition 3. Secret sharing scheme (SSS for short). *Let S be a set of secrets, where $|S| \geq 2$. A secret sharing scheme $\Sigma = (Shr, Rec)$ with secret domain S realizing the access structure $(\mathcal{A}, \mathcal{F})$ is a pair of algorithms Shr and Rec where*

- *Shr is a probabilistic algorithm which takes as input a secret $s \in S$ and outputs a set of shares $sh_1, \ldots, sh_n$.*
- *Rec is a deterministic algorithm which takes as input a set of shares sh_X for $X \subseteq \mathcal{P}$, and outputs either $s \in S$ or $\perp$*

satisfying the following properties:

1. **Correctness.** *For each $A \in \mathcal{A}$, and for every secret $s \in S$, it holds that $Pr[Rec(Shr(s)_A) = s] = 1$*
2. **Privacy.** *For each $F \in \mathcal{F}$, and for every $s_1 \in S$ and $s_2 \in S$, it holds that $Pr[Shr(s_1)_F = sh_F] = Pr[Shr(s_2)_F = sh_F]$*

Property 1 guarantees that each authorized subset reconstructs the secret, while property 2 that each forbidden subset does not get any information from its subset of shares, since the subset is *compatible* with each possible secret with the same probability. Moreover, the definition does not assume *any* probability distribution on the set S, and can be weakened by not requiring perfect reconstruction or by requiring just statistical or computational privacy. Definition 3 can also be easily extended to *multi-secret* (*MSSS* for short), i.e., the case in which the dealer distributes more than one secret. Formally, it is necessary to consider, instead of a single set of secrets S and a single access structure $(\mathcal{A}, \mathcal{F})$, sets of secrets $S_1, \ldots, S_\ell$ and access structures $(\mathcal{A}_1, \mathcal{F}_1), \ldots, (\mathcal{A}_\ell, \mathcal{F}_\ell)$.

Remark. Notice that, in our construction we will consider a simple multi-secret sharing scheme, a 2-*MSSS*: the set of parties is $\mathcal{P} = \{1, 2, 3\}$, the sets of secrets are two and are equal, i.e., $S_1 = S_2 = S$, and the access structures are defined by $\mathcal{A}_1 = \{\{1, 2\}\}, \mathcal{F}_1 = \{\{1\}, \{2\}, \{3\}\}$ and $\mathcal{A}_2 = \{\{1, 3\}\}, \mathcal{F}_2 = \{\{1\}, \{2\}, \{3\}\}$.

3.2 Visual Cryptography

Visual cryptography schemes can be *deterministic* or *probabilistic*. The schemes introduced by Naor and Shamir are deterministic. The schemes introduced by Kafri and Keren are probabilistic. Deterministic schemes need to associate to each pixel of the secret image, a collection of $m \geq 2$ pixels in the shares. Parameter m is called the *pixel expansion* of the scheme. For probabilistic schemes it is possibile to have $m = 1$.

Given two images I_1 and I_2, with the same size, printed on transparencies, we denote with $\text{Sup}(I_1, I_2)$ the image that results from the superposition of the two images. Interpreting white as 0 and black as 1, for each pixel position (i, j), we have that $\text{Sup}(I_1, I_2) = I_1(i, j)$ or $I_2(i, j)$.

Let us start with the definition[6] of a probabilistic visual secret sharing scheme for a set $\mathcal{P} = \{1, 2\}$ of two parties, with access structure defined by $\mathcal{A} = \{\{1, 2\}\}$ and $\mathcal{F} = \{\{1\}, \{2\}\}$.

Definition 4. Probabilistic $(2, 2)$ -VCS. *Let S be a set of secret images, such that $|S| \geq 2$. A probabilistic $(2,2)$-VCS is a secret sharing scheme realizing the access structure defined by $\mathcal{A} = \{\{1, 2\}\}$ and $\mathcal{F} = \{\{1\}, \{2\}\}$ where Shr and Rec are such that*

– *Shr is a probabilistic algorithm which takes as input a secret $I \in S$ and outputs a pair of visual shares (sh_1, sh_2)*
– *Rec is the deterministic algorithm $\text{Sup}(\cdot, \cdot)$ which superposes sh_1 to sh_2*

satisfying the following properties:

– **Correctness**: *For each pixel position (i, j), if $I(i, j) = \bullet$ then $\text{Sup}(sh_1, sh_2)$ $(i, j) = \bullet$, and if $I(i, j) = \circ$ then $pr[\text{Sup}(sh_1, sh_2) \, (i, j) = \circ] > 0$.*
– **Privacy**: *For each pixel position (i, j), regardless of the values of $I(i, j)$, $pr[sh_1(i, j) = \circ] = pr[sh_2(i, j) = \circ]$, and, consequently, $pr[sh_1(i, j) = \bullet] = pr[sh_2(i, j) = \bullet]$.*

Notice that, in the above definition we require that black pixels are reconstructed perfectly.

In general, VCSs can be implemented by means of *distribution matrices*. Precisely, let n and m be two integers, where n represents the number of parties and m is the pixel expansion. A scheme is usually defined by two collections $\mathcal{C}_\circ$ and $\mathcal{C}_\bullet$ of $n \times m$ matrices with elements in $\{\circ, \bullet\}$. The *Shr* algorithm, for each secret pixel, chooses a distribution matrix M at random from $\mathcal{C}_\circ$, if the secret pixel is white, or from $\mathcal{C}_\bullet$, if the secret pixel is black, and uses row i of M to construct the pixel on the ith share. For example, the following collections of distribution matrices can be used to realize a probabilistic $(2, 2)$-VCS:

$$\mathcal{C}_\circ = \left\{ \begin{bmatrix} \circ \\ \circ \end{bmatrix}, \begin{bmatrix} \bullet \\ \bullet \end{bmatrix} \right\} \qquad \mathcal{C}_\bullet = \left\{ \begin{bmatrix} \circ \\ \bullet \end{bmatrix}, \begin{bmatrix} \bullet \\ \circ \end{bmatrix} \right\}$$

More precisely, assuming that the set S of secret images contains all black-and-white square images I of $n \times n$ pixels, and that $R = \{0, 1\}$, denoting the distribution matrices in $\mathcal{C}_\circ$ as $\mathcal{C}_{\circ,0}, \mathcal{C}_{\circ,1}$, and in $\mathcal{C}_\bullet$ as $\mathcal{C}_{\bullet,0}, \mathcal{C}_{\bullet,1}$, a probabilistic $(2, 2)$-VCS, can be realized as follows:

---

[6] In this abstract, to simplify the presentation of our approach, instead of providing general definitions, we concentrate on specific definitions of VCS for the tools we need in our construction.

Probabilistic $(2,2)$-VCS
$Shr(I)$

For every $i, j = 1, \ldots, n$,
     Choose uniformly at random $r_{i,j} \in R = \{0,1\}$
     Use $\mathcal{C}_{I(i,j),r_{i,j}}$ as distribution matrix for $sh_1(i,j)$ and $sh_2(i,j)$.
 Output (sh_1, sh_2)

$Rec(sh_1, sh_2)$ Return $I = \mathrm{Sup}(sh_1, sh_2)$.

An example of application of the scheme is given in Fig. 1.

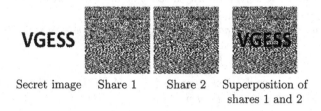

Secret image   Share 1   Share 2   Superposition of
shares 1 and 2

Fig. 1. Example of shares and superposition for a probabilistic $(2, 2)$-scheme.

The Probabilistic (2,2)-VCS satisfies Definition 4. More precisely:

Theorem 2. *The* Probabilistic $(2, 2)$ -VCS *construction realizes a probabilistic* $(2,2)$-*VCS.*

All proofs of our statements will appear in the full version of this paper.

We also remark that the Probabilistic (2,2) -VCS scheme is the same as the random grid scheme of Kafri and Keren [24].

Let us now define a 2-MVCS i.e., a visual multi-secret sharing scheme for a set $\mathcal{P} = \{1, 2, 3\}$ of three parties, with access structures defined by $\mathcal{A}_1 = \{\{1, 2\}\}, \mathcal{F}_1 = \{\{1\}, \{2\}, \{3\}\}$ and $\mathcal{A}_2 = \{\{1, 3\}\}, \mathcal{F}_2 = \{\{1\}, \{2\}, \{3\}\}$. The scheme will be used to share 2 secret images I_0 and I_1 which will be reconstructed, respectively, by $\mathcal{A}_1$ and $\mathcal{A}_2$.

Definition 5. Probabilistic 2-MVCS. *Let S be a set of secret images, such that $|S| \geq 2$. A probabilistic 2-MVCS is a multi-secret sharing scheme with domains $S_1 = S_2 = S$ realizing the access structure defined by $\mathcal{A}_1 = \{\{1, 2\}\}$, $\mathcal{F}_1 = \{\{1\}, \{2\}, \{3\}\}$ and $\mathcal{A}_2 = \{\{1, 3\}\}, \mathcal{F}_2 = \{\{1\}, \{2\}, \{3\}\}$, where Shr and Rec are such that*

- *Shr is a probabilistic algorithm which takes as input two secret images $I_0 \in S$ and $I_1 \in S$ and outputs three visual shares (sh_1, sh_2, sh_3).*
- *Rec is the deterministic algorithm $\mathrm{Sup}(\cdot, \cdot)$ which superposes a pair of shares.*

satisfying the following properties:

- **Correctness**: *For $h = 0, 1$, for each pixel position (i, j), if $I_h(i, j) = \bullet$, then $\mathrm{Sup}(sh_1, sh_{2+h})(i, j) = \bullet$, and if $I_h(i, j) = \circ$, then $pr[\mathrm{Sup}(sh_1, sh_{2+h})(i, j) = \circ] > 0$.*
- **Privacy**: *For each pixel position (i, j), $pr[sh_1(i, j) = \circ] = pr[sh_2(i, j) = \circ] = pr[sh_3(i, j) = \circ]$, and, consequently, $pr[sh_1(i, j) = \bullet] = pr[sh_2(i, j) = \bullet] = pr[sh_3(i, j) = \bullet]$.*

Notice that the definition does not state any requirement for the superposition of sh_2 and sh_3, that is we neither require a reconstruction nor an assurance of no information leakage for the combination of the two shares: we simply don't care as in our application they will never appear at the same time.

By using in a suitable way the collections of distribution matrices $\mathcal{C}_\circ, \mathcal{C}_\bullet$ of the Probabilistic (2,2)-VCS, a Probabilistic 2-MVCS can be realized as follows:

Probabilistic 2-MVCS

$Shr(I_0, I_1)$
For every $i, j = 1, \ldots, n$,
    Choose uniformly at random $r_{i,j} \in R = \{0, 1\}$
    Use $\mathcal{C}_{I_0(i,j), r_{i,j}}$ as distribution matrix for $sh_1(i, j)$ and $sh_2(i, j)$
    If $I_1(i, j) = \bullet$ then
        if $sh_1(i, j) = \circ$ then $sh_3(i, j) = \bullet$
        if $sh_1(i, j) = \bullet$ then $sh_3(i, j) = \circ$
    If $I_1(i, j) = \circ$ then
        if $sh_1(i, j) = \bullet$ then $sh_3(i, j) = \bullet$
        if $sh_1(i, j) = \circ$ then $sh_3(i, j) = \circ$
Output (sh_1, sh_2, sh_3)

$Rec(sh_i, sh_j)$
Return $I = \mathrm{Sup}(sh_i, sh_j)$.

It is possible to show that the Probabilistic 2-MVCS satisfies Definition 5. More precisely:

Theorem 3. *The* Probabilistic 2-MVCS *construction realizes a probabilistic 2-MVCS.*

3.3   GESS: Definition

At this point, we recall the definition of a GESS scheme given in [26]. Let us define a *selector* v as a pair of bits, that is $v \in V^2 = \{0, 1\} \times \{0, 1\}$. A *selection function Sel* takes as input a pair of pairs and a selector, and selects one element from each of the two pairs, according to the selector, i.e., $Sel : (((a_0, a_1), (b_0, b_1)), (v_1, v_2)) \to (a_{v_1}, b_{v_2})$.

Given a gate G and a selector $v = (v_1, v_2)$, we denote with $G(v)$ the output of gate G on input (v_1, v_2).

Definition 6. *A gate evaluation secret sharing scheme for gate G is a pair of algorithms (Shr,Rec) such that*

– *Shr is a probabilistic algorithm which takes as input two secrets $s_0 \in S$ and $s_1 \in S$ and outputs a tuple (t_1, t_2) where each t_i, for $i = 1, 2$, consists of two shares, i.e., $t_1 = (sh_{1,0}, sh_{1,1})$ and $t_2 = (sh_{2,0}, sh_{2,1})$*
– *Rec is a deterministic algorithm which takes as input two shares and outputs $s \in S$ or $\perp$*

satisfying the following conditions:

– **Correctness**: *For each $s_0 \in S$ and $s_1 \in S$, and for any selector $v \in V^2$, it holds that $Rec(Sel(Shr(s_0, s_1), v)) = s_{G(v)}$.*
– **Privacy**: *There exists a PPT algorithm Sim such that, for each $s_0 \in S$ and $s_1 \in S$, and for any selector $v \in V^2$, it holds that $Sim(s_{G(v)}) \stackrel{p}{\equiv} Sel(Shr(s_0, s_1), v)$.*

3.4   A General Construction for *GESS*

A *GESS* for a gate G (*GESS$_G$*, for short) can be implemented by using a 2-*MSSS* $\Sigma = (Shr_\Sigma, Rec_\Sigma)$. More precisely, we use two instances of Σ for a set of parties $\mathcal{P} = \{1, 2, 3\}$, denoted with the letters A and B to simplify the presentation[7]. Instance $A = (Shr_A, Rec_A)$ and instance $B = (Shr_B, Rec_B)$, with $Shr_A = Shr_B = Shr_\Sigma$ and $Rec_A = Rec_B = Rec_\Sigma$, have secret domains $S_1 = S_2 = \{s_0, s_1\}$, and both of them realize the pair of access structures defined by $\mathcal{A}_1 = \{\{1, 2\}\}, \mathcal{F}_1 = \{\{1\}, \{2\}, \{3\}\}$ and $\mathcal{A}_2 = \{\{1, 3\}\}, \mathcal{F}_2 = \{\{1\}, \{2\}, \{3\}\}$.

The construction is given in Table 1. In step 1, the two instances of Σ provide shares which reconstruct $s_{G(0,0)}$ and $s_{G(0,1)}$ (instance A) and $s_{G(1,0)}$ and $s_{G(1,1)}$ (instance B). Then, in step 2 the shares of A and B are viewed as sub-shares, and are rearranged and concatenated in order to construct shares which reproduce the functionality implemented by G. The random permutation bit b is used to hide the correspondence first-part/second-part of the share associated to the right wire and the secret which is reconstructed. Finally, in step 3, the shares for the wires of G are given in output.

Notice that the construction generalizes the construction given in [26]. Indeed, Kolesnikov's construction is a special case, where, assuming that the secrets s_0, s_1 are n-bit strings and R_0 and R_1 are also n-bit strings, chosen uniformly at random, the shares produced by the two instances of the 2-*MSSS* are $sh_1^A = R_0, sh_2^A = s_{G(0,0)} \oplus R_0, sh_3^A = s_{G(0,1)} \oplus R_0$, and $sh_1^B = R_1, sh_2^B = s_{G(1,0)} \oplus R_1, sh_3^B = s_{G(1,1)} \oplus R_1$, where R_0 and R_1 is the fresh randomness used by A and B, respectively, and the $Rec(\cdot, \cdot)$ function is the $\oplus$ (**xor**) function.

We show now that the general construction for GESS$_G$ satisfies Definition 6. More precisely:

Theorem 4. *The* GenGESS *construction realizes a GESS$_G$.*

---

[7] We stress that the scheme is the same, and it is used twice with independent and fresh randomness.

Table 1. General construction for a GESS scheme with a multi-secret sharing scheme.

GenGESS

$Shr(s_0, s_1)$

1. Run $Shr_A(s_0, s_1)$ and $Shr_B(s_0, s_1)$. Let the shares and the possible reconstructed secrets be denoted as follows:

MSSS scheme	$Shr_\Sigma(s_0, s_1)$	$Rec_\Sigma(sh_1^X, sh_2^X)$	$Rec_\Sigma(sh_1^X, sh_3^X)$
A	sh_1^A, sh_2^A, sh_3^A	$s_{G(0,0)}$	$s_{G(0,1)}$
B	sh_1^B, sh_2^B, sh_3^B	$s_{G(1,0)}$	$s_{G(1,1)}$

2. Choose uniformly at random a *permutation bit* $b \in \{0, 1\}$ and, denoting with $||$ the *concatenation* operator, constructs shares $sh_{1,0}$ and $sh_{1,1}$ for the left wire of G, and $sh_{2,0}$ and $sh_{2,1}$ for the right wire, as follows:

left wire	right wire (if $b = 0$)	right wire (if $b = 1$)
$sh_{1,0} = b||sh_1^A$	$sh_{2,0} = sh_2^A||sh_2^B$	$sh_{2,0} = sh_2^B||sh_2^A$
$sh_{1,1} = \bar{b}||sh_1^B$	$sh_{2,1} = sh_3^A||sh_3^B$	$sh_{2,1} = sh_3^B||sh_3^A$

3. Output $((sh_{1,0}, sh_{1,1}), (sh_{2,0}, sh_{2,1}))$

$Rec(c||sh_\alpha, sh_\beta||sh_\gamma)$

- If $c = 0$ then output $Rec_\Sigma(sh_\alpha, sh_\beta)$; else output $Rec_\Sigma(sh_\alpha, sh_\gamma)$.

3.5   Visual GESS

Visual gate evaluation secret sharing schemes (VGESS, for short) are a visual realization of a GESS scheme. More precisely, we state the following:

Definition 7. *A visual gate evaluation secret sharing scheme for gate G ($VGESS_G$, for short) is a pair of algorithms (Shr,Rec) such that*

- *Shr is a probabilistic algorithm which takes in input two secret images $I_0 \in S$ and $I_1 \in S$ and outputs a tuple (t_1, t_2) where each t_i, for $i = 1, 2$, consists of two visual shares, i.e., $t_1 = (sh_{1,0}, sh_{1,1})$ and $t_2 = (sh_{2,0}, sh_{2,1})$*
- *Rec is the deterministic algorithm $\mathrm{Sup}(\cdot, \cdot)$ which superposes a pair of shares.*

satisfying the following conditions:

- **Correctness**: *For each $I_0 \in S$ and $I_1 \in S$, and for any selector $v \in V^2$, it holds that, for each pixel position (i, j), if $I_{G(v)}(i, j) = \bullet$, then $\mathrm{Sup}(Sel((Shr(I_0, I_1), v))(i, j) = \bullet$, and if $I_{G(v)}(i, j) = \circ$, then $pr[\mathrm{Sup}(Sel((Shr(I_0, I_1), v))(i, j) = \circ] > 0$.*
- **Privacy**: *There exists a PPT algorithm Sim such that, for each $I_0 \in S$ and $I_1 \in S$, and for any selector $v \in V^2$, it holds that $Sim(s_{G(v)}) \stackrel{p}{\equiv} Sel(Shr(s_0, s_1), v)$.*

It is possible to check that the general construction for GESS$_G$, based on a multi-secret sharing scheme, realizes a VGESS$_G$ if the multi-secret sharing scheme therein used is substituted with a visual multi-secret sharing scheme. Indeed, the following result holds:

Corollary 1. *The* GenGESS *construction for a gate G realizes a VGESS$_G$ if the 2-MSSS is instanced with the* Probabilistic 2-MVCS.

4   A Visual Two-Party Protocol

In this section we describe our visual two-party protocol. We start by showing how to realize a physical oblivious transfer and then we provide a full specification of the protocol.

4.1   Physical Oblivious Transfer

The 1-out-of-2 oblivious transfer (1-out-of-2-OT, for short) functionality [18] is an extensively studied cryptographic primitive, which plays a key-role in secure computation. Several implementations under general assumptions (e.g., enhanced trapdoor permutations) and specific assumptions (e.g., factoring, discrete-log assumption) are available, secure w.r.t. semi-honest and malicious adversaries, respectively. It is well known that the oblivious transfer is sufficient for secure multi-party function evaluation. Actually, the protocol we are going to propose is an *unconditionally secure reduction* of secure two-party function evaluation to 1-out-of-2-OT.

Let Alice's secrets be n-bit strings z_0 and z_1, let σ be Bob's bit-choice, and let $\perp$ denote no output. The 1-out-of-2-OT functionality is specified by $((z_0, z_1, \sigma) \to (\perp, z_\sigma))$. The construction we propose is partially inspired to the approach pursued in [10], when the voter comes out from the booth.

A Physical 1-out-of-2 OT Protocol. Let us assume that the two secrets z_0 and z_1 are represented in form of transparencies, and Alice has two *indistinguishable envelopes* which *perfectly hide* the transparency inside. Alice and Bob proceed as follows:

1. Alice puts the two secrets in the two envelopes, one in the first and one in the second, and closes both of them. She also adds to each envelope a paper post-it with number 0 and number 1, depending on the secret which is inside. Then, she hands the two envelopes to Bob.
2. Bob turns his shoulders to Alice[8], checks that the envelopes are identical, takes the envelopes with the post-it corresponding to the secret he is interested in, removes the post-it from both envelopes, turns again in front of Alice, and

---

[8] If Alice thinks that Bob has had a career as illusionist, in order to be sure that Bob does not substitute the envelope that will be destroyed with an identical but fake one, might requests that Bob shows up in swimsuit.

Table 2. V2PC protocol

V2PC Protocol
Shares construction phase (performed by Alice)

1. Let I_0 and I_1 be two images that encode the values 0 and 1. Associate them to the output wire of the output gates.
2. For each gate G_h whose output wire ω_k has been associated to images s_0 and s_1
  (a) Let ω_i and ω_j be the input wires, and let VGESS_{G_h} be a visual GESS realizing gate G_h
  (b) Run $Shr(s_0, s_1)$, where s_0 encodes 0 and s_1 encodes 1, to obtain the shares $sh_{1,0}^{G_h}, sh_{1,1}^{G_h}$, and $sh_{2,0}^{G_h}, sh_{2,1}^{G_h}$. Let $sh_{1,0}^{G_h}, sh_{1,1}^{G_h}$ be the images s_0 and s_1 associated to 0 and 1 for the wire ω_i, and let $sh_{2,0}^{G_h}, sh_{2,1}^{G_h}$ be the images s_0 and s_1 associated to 0 and 1 for the wire ω_j.
3. Output the shares associated to wires $\omega_1, \ldots, \omega_n$ (Alice's input) and to $\omega_{n+1}, \ldots, \omega_{2n}$ (Bob's input).

Computation phase (performed by Alice and Bob)
1. Alice hands to Bob the shares $sh_{1,x_1}^{G_1}, sh_{1,x_2}^{G_2}, \ldots, sh_{1,x_n}^{G_n}$, corresponding to her input $x = x_1, \ldots, x_n$, associated to wires $\omega_1, \ldots, \omega_n$. 2. For every $j = 1, \ldots, n$, Alice and Bob execute the 1-out-of-2 OT protocol described before in which Alice's inputs are the shares $sh_{2,0}^{G_j}, sh_{2,1}^{G_j}$, associated to wire ω_{n+j}, while Bob's input is the bit y_j of his own input $y = y_1, \ldots, y_n$. 3. Bob, for $h = 1, \ldots, \ell$, applies the Rec algorithm of the VGESS_{G_h}, and computes the circuit output value $C(x, y) = f(x, y)$. 4. Finally Bob shows the result to Alice.

inserts under Alice surveillance the remaining envelope in a paper-shredder which reduces the envelop and its content in dust[9].

Theorem 5. *Assuming that indistinguishable envelopes which perfectly hide the transparency inside can be used, then the* Physical 1-out-of-2 OT *protocol realizes a physical perfectly secure 1-out-of-2-OT.*

4.2 Our Visual Two-Party Protocol

The protocol is the same reduction of secure function evaluation to 1-out-of-2 OT given via Construction 1 in [26], but with VGESSs instead of GESSs.

V2PC Protocol. Let $f : \{0,1\}^n \times \{0,1\}^n \to \{0,1\}^m$ be the target functionality and let $C(\cdot, \cdot)$ be a boolean circuit that computes $f(\cdot, \cdot)$, i.e., $C(\cdot, \cdot)$ is such that, for all inputs $x, y \in \{0,1\}^n$, it outputs $C(x, y) = f(x, y)$. Let us also assume

---

[9] An alternative could be that the envelope is burned in front of Alice. The key-property that need to be satisfied is that the physical process should be irreversible, the secret cannot be even partially recovered.

that the circuit is composed of q *wires*, labeled uniquely with $\omega_1, \ldots, \omega_q$, $2n$ of which are *input wires*, say $\omega_1, \ldots, \omega_{2n}$, and m of which are *output wires*, and ℓ *gates*, represented for $h = 1, \ldots, \ell$ by functions $G_h : \{0,1\} \times \{0,1\} \rightarrow \{0,1\}$. No circuit-output wire is also a gate-input wire. Along the same line of the original Yao's protocol, the description can be split in two phases: (i) shares construction phase, and (ii) interactive computation phase, described in Table 2.

At this point, we have all the elements needed to state and prove the following result:

Theorem 6. *Let $f : \{0,1\}^n \times \{0,1\}^n \rightarrow \{0,1\}^m$ be a boolean function, and let $C(\cdot, \cdot)$ be a boolean circuit that computes $f(\cdot, \cdot)$, i.e., $C(\cdot, \cdot)$ is such that, for all inputs $x, y \in \{0,1\}^n$, it holds that $C(x, y) = f(x, y)$. Then, assuming* indistinguishable envelopes *can be used, the* V2PC protocol *computes f in a perfectly secure way, in presence of a static semi-honest adversary.*

4.3 Efficiency and Implementation Details

Two observations need to be done in order to use the V2PC Protocol.

First of all, notice that in the V2PC Protocol the size of the shares associated to the right wire input gate, doubles at each level of the circuit. However, as shown in [26], it is the best that can be done in a perfectly secure reduction of secure function evaluation to OT which uses GESS schemes. It follows that the construction can be used in real-world applications only for small-depth circuits. Notice that the choice of using probabilistic visual cryptography schemes has been done to avoid further increase in the size of the shares. Indeed, the use of deterministic visual cryptography would have lead to an exponential extra factor in the increase of the size.

Then, notice that the correctness property of the VGESS definition 7 requires that the black area of the secret image will be reconstructed (deterministically) with black pixels, while the white area will be reconstructed, with some probability, with at least one white pixel. The rationale behind the definition is that in the reconstruction phase we will have to be able to visually distinguish the final output value of the function. The *quality* of the reconstructed image heavily depends on the depth of the circuit. Indeed, the more levels are in the circuit, the more image superpositions have to be performed. For each intermediate image reconstruction, the number of black pixels in the output can only increase. Thus, the size of the image that we use to encode the values of the output (0 and 1), must be sufficiently large in order to guarantee that the reconstruction of the output will have, with some probability, at least one white pixel in the white area of the original secret image. More specifically, denoting with d the depth of the circuit, we have that the probability that a specific pixel in the reconstructed white area is white is equal to $(\frac{1}{2})^d$. Assume that our secret image is defined by a matrix of $t \times t$ pixels and that our representation encodes the bit values, 0 and 1, as depicted in Fig. 2. The secret white area consists of $t^2/2$ pixels. Hence, the condition that we seek is that $\frac{1}{2^d} >> \frac{1}{t^2/2}$, which implies $t >> \sqrt{2^{d+1}}$. In the example which follows, where $d = 2$, we have chosen $t = 8$.

5   A Simple Example

In this section we provide a simple example of application of the proposed method. The secret function is

$$f((x_1, x_2), (y_1, y_2)) = (x_1 \text{ and } y_1) \text{ or } (x_2 \text{ and } y_2)$$

where (x_1, x_2) is the private input of Alice and (y_1, y_2) is the private input of Bob, with x_1, x_2, y_1 and y_2 being bits.

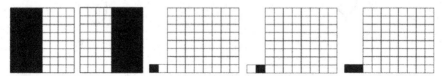

Image(0)$\equiv$ 0 Image(1)$\equiv$ 1 Permutation bit 0 Permutation bit 0 Permutation bit 1

Fig. 2. Bit representations: bit value, Image(0) and Image(1), and permutation bit, prepended to a blank image.

Binary values are represented as two images consisting of 8×8 pixels, more specifically we will use Image(0) and Image(1) shown in Fig. 2 to encode 0 and 1.

In the share construction phase of the V2PC protocol, Alice has to construct a VGESS for each gate. Alice starts from gate G_3. Gate G_3 gives the output value of f, which can be either 0 or 1. Alice constructs the VGESS$_{G_3}$ which uses the two *2-MVCS* A and B. The shares of scheme A reconstruct the secrets $s_{G_3(0,0)}, s_{G_3(0,1)}$, and those of scheme B reconstruct $s_{G_3(1,0)}, s_{G_3(1,1)}$. Since G_3 is an **or** gate we have that scheme A reconstructs $Image(0), Image(1)$, and scheme B $Image(1), Image(1)$.

To finish up the construction of the shares for VGESS$_{G_3}$ Alice has to choose, at random, the permutation bit b. In the example we are constructing we assume that the share of scheme A are placed on the left, so that $b = 0$ for Sh_1^A and clearly $\bar{b} = 1$ for Sh_1^B. The random bit will be visually represented as a 2-pixel image which encodes 0 as one black pixel and one white pixel and 1 as two black pixels[10].

The 2-pixel image will be prepended to the share image (and will become part of the share). Figure 2 shows the permutation bit prepended to a blank share.

Figure 3 (left) shows the shares for G_3, including the permutation bit.

Now Alice can go on and consider gate G_1. The output of G_1 can be either $0||Sh_1^A$ or $1||Sh_1^B$, where the first element is the permutation bit. Hence the

---

[10] Notice that, for the permutation bit, we are using a deterministic (2, 2)-VCS with pixel expansion $m = 2$. We have used this solution for the permutation bit because, first of all it is possible to use a scheme with pixel expansion since each permutation bit propagates only from one level of the circuit to the subsequent one, and secondly because a scheme with pixel expansion allows a deterministic reconstruction.

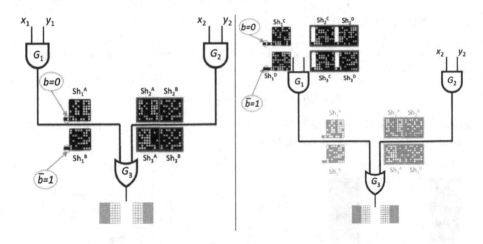

Fig. 3. Shares construction for gate G_3 (left) and gate G_1 (right).

secrets that we need to share are $\{0||Sh_1^A, 1||Sh_1^B\}$. Share Sh_1^A corresponds to the wire value 0, while share Sh_1^B to the wire value 1. Since G_1 is an **and** gate, Alice will need to use two *2-MVCS* schemes C and D such that scheme C reconstructs $s_{G_1(0,0)} = 0||Sh_1^A$ and $s_{G_1(0,1)} = 0||Sh_1^A$, and scheme B reconstructs $s_{G_1(1,0)} = 0||Sh_1^A$ and $s_{G_1(1,1)} = 1||Sh_1^B$.

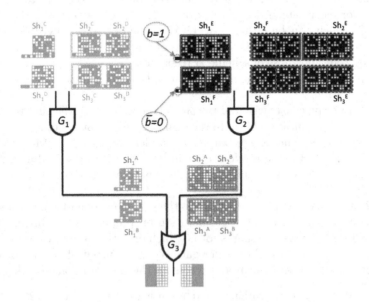

Fig. 4. Shares construction for gate G_2

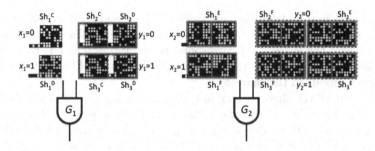

Fig. 5. Visual circuit for the computation of f

Also for gate G_1 Alice has to choose the permutation bit that will allow the correct reconstruction. Also in this case we decided to use $b = 0$. Figure 3 (right) shows the shares for G_1.

Finally Alice constructs the shares for G_2. The output wire of G_2 has to be able to reconstruct either $Sh_2^A || Sh_2^B$ (when the wire value is 0) or $Sh_3^A || Sh_3^B$ (when the wire value 1). Gate G_2 is an **and** gate, hence Alice will need to use two 2-$MVCS$ schemes E and F such that scheme E reconstructs $s_{G_2(0,0)} = Sh_2^A || Sh_2^B$ and $s_{G_2(0,1)} = Sh_2^A || Sh_2^B$, and scheme F reconstructs $s_{G_2(1,0)} = sh_2^A || Sh_2^B$ and $s_{G_2(1,1)} = Sh_3^A || Sh_3^B$.

Also for gate G_2 Alice has to choose a permutation bit that will allow the correct reconstruction. In this case we decided to use $b = 1$. Figure 4 shows the shares for G_2.

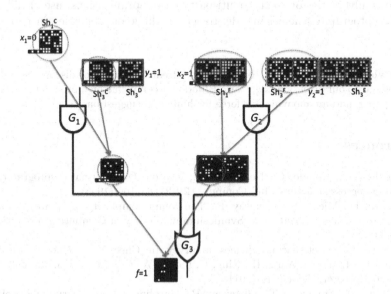

Fig. 6. An example of visual evaluation of the circuit for the computation of f for the input $((1, 0), (1, 1))$

Alice has now completed the construction phase and all the shares that she needs for the computation are the ones shown in Fig. 5. The figure shows for each input wire the shares that correspond to the values 0 and 1. For example for the left input wire of G_1 the value 0 corresponds to share Sh_1^C while the value 1 corresponds to the share Sh_1^D.

Notice that all the shares shown in the figure are known only to Alice so far. At this point Alice chooses the shares that represent the values of her input. As an example, assume that Alice's input values are $x_1 = 0$ and $x_2 = 1$. Alice can throw away Sh_1^D and Sh_1^E and keep Sh_1^C, that represents $x_1 = 0$, and Sh_1^F, that represents $x_2 = 1$. Alice passes both shares, Sh_1^C and Sh_1^F to Bob. Then Alice and Bob run two executions of the 1-out-of-2 physical OT protocol so that Alice will pass to Bob only the shares that correspond to Bob's input. As an example assume that Bob's input values are $y_1 = 1$ and $y_2 = 1$. After the execution of the two 1-out-of-2 OT protocols, Bob has all the shares that correspond to his input values and can perform the visual computation of $f((1,0),(1,1))$, as depicted in Fig. 6.

6   Conclusions

Chapter 7 of [15] describes several applications of visual cryptography. In this paper we have shown a new application: every two-party computation representable by means of a boolean function $f(\cdot, \cdot)$ can be performed preserving the privacy of the inputs x and y through a pure physical visual evaluation process.

Several extensions are possible: study non-trivial extensions to cope with malicious adversaries or to the multi-party case, optimizations, use of different visual cryptography schemes in order to achieve different properties, just to name a few.

Acknowledgment. We would like to thank Alfredo De Santis for discussions and for pointing out to our attention [29], Carlo Blundo for comments on a preliminary version of this paper, and an anonymous referee for hints and suggestions.

References

1. Ateniese, G., Blundo, C., De Santis, A., Stinson, D.R.: Visual cryptography for general access structures. Inf. Comput. **129**(2), 86–106 (1996)
2. Beaver, D., Micali, S., Rogaway, P.: The round complexity of secure protocols. In: Proceedings of 22nd ACM Symposium on Theory of Computing, pp. 503–513 (1990)
3. Beimel, A.: Secret-sharing schemes: a survey. In: Chee, Y.M., Guo, Z., Ling, S., Shao, F., Tang, Y., Wang, H., Xing, C. (eds.) IWCC 2011. LNCS, vol. 6639, pp. 11–46. Springer, Heidelberg (2011)
4. Bellare, M., Hoang, V.T., Rogaway, P.: Garbling schemes. Cryptology ePrint archive, report 2012/265 (2012)

5. Bellare, M., Rogaway, P.: Robust computational secret sharing and a unified account of classical secret-sharing goals. In: Proceedings of the 14th ACM Conference on Computer and Communications Security (ACM CCS), ACM (2007)
6. Blundo, C., D'Arco, P., De Santis, A., Stinson, D.R.: Contrast optimal threshold visual cryptography schemes. SIAM J. Discrete Math. **16**, 224–261 (2003)
7. Boneh, D., Sahai, A., Waters, B.: Functional encryption: definitions and challenges. In: Ishai, Y. (ed.) TCC 2011. LNCS, vol. 6597, pp. 253–273. Springer, Heidelberg (2011)
8. Capocelli, R.M., De Santis, A., Gargano, L., Vaccaro, U.: On the size of shares for secret sharing schemes. In: Feigenbaum, J. (ed.) CRYPTO 1991. LNCS, vol. 576, pp. 101–113. Springer, Heidelberg (1992)
9. Canetti, R.: Security and composition of multiparty cryptographic protocols. J. Cryptol. **13**, 143–202 (2000)
10. Chaum, D.: Secret-Ballot receipts and transparent integrity. http://www.vreceipt.com/article.pdf
11. Cimato, S., De Prisco, R., De Santis, A.: Colored visual cryptography without color darkening. In: Blundo, C., Cimato, S. (eds.) SCN 2004. LNCS, vol. 3352, pp. 235–248. Springer, Heidelberg (2005)
12. Cimato, S., De Prisco, R., De Santis, A.: Optimal colored threshold visual cryptography schemes. Des. Codes. Crypt. **35**, 311–335 (2005)
13. Cimato, S., De Prisco, R., De Santis, A.: Probabilistic visual cryptography schemes. Comput. J. **49**(1), 97–107 (2006)
14. Cimato, S., De Prisco, R., De Santis, A.: Colored visual cryptography without color darkening. Theor. Comput. Sci. **374**(1–3), 261–276 (2007)
15. Cimato, S., Yang, C.-N. (eds.): Visual Cryptography and Secret Image Sharing. CRC Press, Boca Raton (2012). ISBN: 978-1-4398-3721-4
16. De Prisco, R., De Santis, A.: Using colors to improve visual cryptography for black and white images. In: Fehr, S. (ed.) ICITS 2011. LNCS, vol. 6673, pp. 182–201. Springer, Heidelberg (2011)
17. De Prisco, R., De Santis, A.: Color visual cryptography schemes for black and white secret image. Theoretical Computer Science. http://dx.doi.org/10.1016/j.tcs.2013.09.005 (to appear)
18. Even, S., Goldreich, O., Lempel, A.: A randomized protocol for signing contracts. Commun. ACM. **28**(6), 637–647 (1985)
19. Eisen, P.A., Stinson, D.R.: Threshold visual cryptography schemes with specified whiteness levels of reconstructed pixels. Des. Codes. Crypt. **25**, 15–61 (2002)
20. Goldreich, O.: Foundation Cryptography, vol. II. MIT Press, Cambridge (2004)
21. Goldreich, O., Micali, S., Wigderson, A.: How to play any mental game. In: STOC, pp. 218–229 (1987)
22. Gennaro, R., Gentry, C., Parno, B.: Non-interactive verifiable computing: outsourcing computation to untrusted workers. In: Rabin, T. (ed.) CRYPTO 2010. LNCS, vol. 6223, pp. 465–482. Springer, Heidelberg (2010)
23. Hofmeister, T., Krause, M., Simon, H.U.: Contrast-optimal k out of n secret sharing schemes in visual cryptography. Theor. Comput. Sci. **240**, 471–485 (2000)
24. Kafri, O., Keren, E.: Encryption of pictures and shapes by random grids. Opt. Lett. **12**(6), 377–379 (1987)
25. Karnin, E., Greene, J., Hellman, M.: On secret sharing systems. IEEE Trans. Inf. Theor. **29**(1), 3551 (1983)
26. Kolesnikov, V.: Gate evaluation secret sharing and secure one-round two-party computation. In: Roy, B. (ed.) ASIACRYPT 2005. LNCS, vol. 3788, pp. 136–155. Springer, Heidelberg (2005)

27. Naor, M., Shamir, A.: Visual cryptography. In: De Santis, A. (ed.) EUROCRYPT 1994. LNCS, vol. 950, pp. 1–12. Springer, Heidelberg (1995)
28. Lindell, Y., Pinkas, B.: A proof of security of Yao's protocol for two-party computation. J. Cryptology **22**, 161–188 (2009)
29. Moran, T., Naor, M.: Basing cryptographic protocols on tamper-evident seals. Theor. Comput. Sci. **411**, 1283–1310 (2010)
30. Yang, C.-N.: New visual secret sharing schemes using probabilistic method. Pattern Recogn. Lett. **25**, 481–494 (2004)
31. Yao, A.C.: Protocols for secure computations. In: Proceedings of 23rd IEEE Symposium on Foundations of Computational Science, pp. 160–164 (1982)
32. Yao, A.C.: How to generate and exchange secrets (extended abstract). In: Proceedings of 27th IEEE Symposium on Foundations of Computational Science, pp. 162–167 (1986)

Measure-Independent Characterization of Contrast Optimal Visual Cryptography Schemes

Paolo D'Arco, Roberto De Prisco[✉], and Alfredo De Santis

Dipartimento di Informatica, Università di Salerno, via Giovanni Paolo II, 132,
84084 Fisciano, SA, Italy
{paodar,robdep,ads}@dia.unisa.it

Abstract. The *contrast* in visual cryptography has received a lot of attention. It has been studied using three different measures. In this paper we follow a *measure-independent* approach, which, by using the structural properties of the schemes, enables us to provide a characterization of optimal schemes that is independent of the specific measure used to assess the contrast. In particular we characterize and provide constructions of optimal schemes for the cases of $(2, n)$-threshold and (n, n)-threshold schemes. Then, we apply the measure-independent results to the three measures that have been used in the literature obtaining both new characterizations and constructions of optimal schemes and alternative proofs of known results.

Keywords: Secret sharing · Visual cryptography · Optimal contrast

1 Introduction

Secret Sharing. Secret sharing allows the sharing of a secret among a set of participants. Let $\mathcal{P} = \{1, 2, \ldots, n\}$ be a set of participants and let s be a secret. Participant i receives some information s_i, a *share*, computed from the secret s. Some subsets of participants, called *qualified*, by using collectively their shares, will be able to reconstruct the secret s. All other subsets of participants, called *forbidden*, will not have any information about the secret s. The reconstruction process involves mathematical operations on the shares which have to be performed using a computer.

Visual Cryptography. Visual cryptography is a form of secret sharing in which the secret is an image and the shares are also images printed on transparencies. The peculiarity of this form of secret sharing is that the reconstruction of the secret is obtained by superposing the shares (transparencies) belonging to the qualified set of participants that is reconstructing the secret. No machinery to perform mathematical operations is required. The reconstruction process is performed by the human visual system which basically computes an "or" of the superposed

C. Padró (Ed.): ICITS 2013, LNCS 8317, pp. 39–55, 2014.
DOI: 10.1007/978-3-319-04268-8_3, © Springer International Publishing Switzerland 2014

pixels. A *visual cryptography scheme* is a way to accomplish the visual secret sharing. We will restrict the attention to (k, n)-threshold visual cryptography schemes, for which the qualified subsets of participants are all the subsets with cardinality greater or equal to k.

Previous Results. Visual cryptography has been introduced by Naor and Shamir [28]. A similar and related idea had been proposed by Kafri and Keren [23]. The approach used by Kafri and Keren is called *random grid* visual cryptography because it uses random images as building blocks for the schemes. The approach used by Naor and Shamir is called *deterministic visual cryptography* because the reconstruction is guaranteed in a deterministic way. A *probabilistic* model has been introduced by Yang [34]: in the reconstructed image it is allowed that some pixels be erroneously reconstructed as long as the probability of such mistakes can be controlled. The three models (deterministic, probabilistic and random grid) are related to each other. The random grid model in fact corresponds to the probabilistic model. In [15] it has been proved that it is possible to trade the probability error of a probabilistic scheme with the pixel expansion.

Deterministic visual cryptography has been widely studied. Many papers have explored various aspects: minimal pixel expansion (e.g., [5,7,21], optimal contrast (e.g., [6,9,22,24]), general access structures (e.g., [2,27]), perfect reconstruction of black pixels (e.g., [7,8,31]), generalization to colored pixels (e.g. [1,13,14,16,18–20,25,32,37]), and other issues (e.g. [4,35,36]). Recently also the random grid model has received considerable attention (e.g., [10–12,29,30,33]).

We remark that the above citations are not comprehensive. We refer the interested reader to [17] for more pointers to the literature.

Our Contribution. In this paper we focus the attention on the contrast measure used for the deterministic model. Almost all the papers that have studied the contrast have used the measure proposed by Naor and Shamir [28]; we will denote with γ_{NS} such a measure. Verheul and van Tilborg [32] have proposed an alternative measure; we will denote it with γ_{VV}. Eisen and Stinson [21] provided yet another measure with a discussion that emphasizes why their measure is better than the other two; we will denote with γ_{ES} the measure introduced in [21]. However, with the exception of [21,32], all the papers that study contrast optimal schemes consider γ_{NS}.

In this paper we study contrast-optimal visual cryptography schemes using an approach that does not depend on the particular measure that one uses to assess the contrast. More specifically we characterize the contrast for a *family* of contrast measures, which we call *linear contrast measures*. The measures γ_{NS} and γ_{ES} are members of such a family. This allows us to apply the results to both measures. In the case of γ_{NS}, since contrast optimal schemes are already known, we simply obtain alternative constructions and proofs of optimality. In the case of γ_{ES} we provide novel results since no optimal schemes with respect to this measure are known. The measure γ_{VV} does not belong to the family of linear contrast measures. However with some adjustments to the proof techniques, we show that the approach used to study linear contrast measures can be applied also to γ_{vv} for a particular class of schemes. Thus, for such a particular class of schemes, we provide contrast optimal schemes also with respect to γ_{vv}. The above results are proven for the cases of $(2, n)$-threshold and (n, n)-threshold schemes.

2   The Model

A secret image I has to be visually shared among a set $\mathcal{P} = \{1, 2, \ldots, n\}$ of n participants. A trusted party, called the *dealer*, in order to share I, creates n images printed on transparencies, called *shares*, and distributes them to the participants, giving one share to each participant. Some subsets of participants, called *qualified*, will be able to reconstruct the secret by simply superposing their shares. All other subsets of participants, called *forbidden*, cannot infer any information about the secret image neither by superposing their shares nor by any other computation on the shares.

A *scheme* is a method for encoding the secret image I into the n shares. The encoding process associates, to each pixel of the secret image I, a collection of m subpixels[1] in each of the n shares.

A *distribution matrix* M is an $n \times m$ matrix that represents the encoding of a pixel by means of the n shares. More precisely, row i of M represents the collection of subpixels that is printed on share i, which is used to encode the secret pixel of I. We will use 0 to denote a white pixel and 1 to denote a black pixel. With this notation the superposition of pixels corresponds to the **or** operation. Since the symbols $\circ$ and $\bullet$ are self-explanatory, where convenient, we will also use $\circ$ and $\bullet$ to denote, respectively, white and black.

A scheme is specified by *two collections* $\mathcal{C}_\circ = \{M_\circ^1, M_\circ^2, \ldots, M_\circ^{r_0}\}$ and $\mathcal{C}_\bullet = \{M_\bullet^1, M_\bullet^2, \ldots, M_\bullet^{r_1}\}$ of distribution matrices. In order to share a secret pixel of I, the dealer will randomly choose a distribution matrix from $\mathcal{C}_\circ$ if the secret pixel is white, and from $\mathcal{C}_\bullet$ if the secret pixel is black. The sharing process is repeated for *every* pixel of the secret image.

An *access structure* $\mathcal{A} = (\mathcal{Q}, \mathcal{F})$ is a specification of the qualified subsets of participants $\mathcal{Q}$ and of the forbidden subsets of participants $\mathcal{F}$. Notice that if $Q \in \mathcal{Q}$ then any superset Q' of Q must belong to $\mathcal{Q}$. Another natural requirement is that any subset P of participants is either qualified or forbidden[2]. In most cases the access structure is a *threshold* access structure: $\mathcal{Q}$ consists of all the subsets of at least k participants, while $\mathcal{F}$ consists of all the subsets with at most $k - 1$ participants, with $2 \leq k \leq n$. In such a case we talk about (k, n)-*threshold* visual cryptography.

Since the shares are represented by rows of matrices, the following notation will be useful. Given a matrix M and a set of participants P, we will denote

---

[1] For deterministic visual cryptography it must be $m \geq 2$, i.e., the pixel *expansion* is unavoidable. The probabilistic and the random grid visual cryptography models allow $m = 1$.

[2] In a more general form, it is possible to consider access structures where there are some subsets that are neither qualified nor forbidden; in such a case we simply don't care about what those subsets of participants can do with the shares.

with $M[P]$ the submatrix of M consisting only of the rows corresponding to participants in P. Moreover we will denote with $\text{Sup}(M)$ the superposition of the shares represented by the rows of M. Notice that $\text{Sup}(M)$ is a binary vector (like a row of M) where the ith element is equal to the or of the ith column of M. Using this notation we have that $\text{Sup}(M[Q])$ is the pixel reconstructed by the participants of a qualified set Q. Given a vector v, we will denote with $w(v)$ the Hamming weight of v, that is the number of 1s (i.e., the number of black pixels) in v.

Definition 1. *A (k,n)-threshold scheme $\mathcal{S}$ consists of two collections $\mathcal{C}_\circ$ and $\mathcal{C}_\bullet$ of $n \times m$ distribution matrices such that there exists two integers ℓ and h, $0 \le \ell < h \le n$, for which the following conditions are satisfied.*

1. *(Reconstruction) For any qualified set Q, for any $M \in \mathcal{C}_\circ$, we have that $w(\text{Sup}(M[Q])) \le \ell$ and for any $M \in \mathcal{C}_\bullet$, we have that $w(\text{Sup}(M[Q])) \ge h$.*
2. *(Security) For any forbidden set F, it holds that the two collections $\mathcal{C}_\circ[F] = \{M[F] | M \in \mathcal{C}_\circ\}$ and $\mathcal{C}_\bullet[F] = \{M[F] | M \in \mathcal{C}_\bullet\}$ are indistinguishable in the sense that they contain the same matrices with the same frequencies.*

We will refer to ℓ and h as to the *contrast thresholds*.

Base matrices. In many schemes the collection $\mathcal{C}_\circ$ (resp. $\mathcal{C}_\bullet$) consists of all the matrices that can be obtained by permuting all the columns of a matrix $B_\circ$ (resp. $B_\bullet$). For such schemes, the matrices $B_\circ$ and $B_\bullet$ are called the *base matrices* of the scheme. When a scheme is described with base matrices the contrast and the security properties can be simplified to the following:

1. *(Reconstruction) For any qualified set Q, we have that $w(\text{Sup}(B_\circ[Q])) \le \ell$ and that $w(\text{Sup}(B_\bullet[Q])) \ge h$.*
2. *(Security) For any forbidden set F, the two matrices $B_\circ[F]$ and $B_\bullet[F]$ are the same up to a permutation of the columns.*

Canonical schemes. Often, the base matrices can be described in a very convenient way by means of *column multiplicities*. This is possible when a base matrix that contains a specific column, consisting of i black pixels and $n - i$ white pixels, with a multiplicity μ, contains *also all the other possible columns* that have exactly i black pixels and $n - i$ white pixels, each of them with the same multiplicity μ. When the above holds, we say that the scheme is in *canonical form* and we can describe the base matrices by listing the multiplicities μ_i of the columns that have exactly i black pixels. The white base matrix will be specified by $\mu_0^\circ, \mu_1^\circ, \ldots, \mu_n^\circ$. The black base matrix will be specified by $\mu_0^\bullet, \mu_1^\bullet, \ldots, \mu_n^\bullet$.

Example. As an example we consider a $(2,3)$-threshold scheme in canonical form given by $\mu_0^\circ = 2, \mu_1^\circ = 0, \mu_2^\circ = 0, \mu_3^\circ = 1$ and $\mu_0^\bullet = 0, \mu_1^\bullet = 1, \mu_2^\bullet = 0, \mu_3^\bullet = 0$. The base matrices and are:

$$B_\circ = \begin{bmatrix} \circ\circ\bullet \\ \circ\circ\bullet \\ \circ\circ\bullet \end{bmatrix} \qquad\qquad B_\bullet = \begin{bmatrix} \bullet\circ\circ \\ \circ\bullet\circ \\ \circ\circ\bullet \end{bmatrix}$$

An example of application of the above scheme is provided below. The size of the shares and of the reconstructed images is 3 times the size of the secret image since the pixel expansion is $m = 3$. The "+" sign denotes shares superposition.

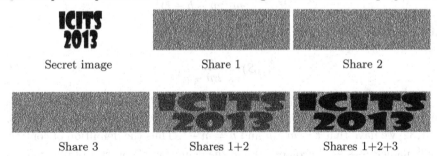

| Secret image | Share 1 | Share 2 |

| Share 3 | Shares 1+2 | Shares 1+2+3 |

3 Contrast: Properties and Notions

The contrast quantifies *how well* the secret image I can be seen by the human visual system in the reconstructed form, obtained by superposing a subset of shares. In the example provided above the contrast of shares 1+2+3 is clearly better than the contrast of shares 1+2. The overall quality of the reconstructed image depends on how much reconstructed black pixels differ from reconstructed white pixels. Such a difference depends on the threshold parameters ℓ and h and on the pixel expansion m. Hence, the contrast is a function $\gamma(\ell, h, m)$. Regardless of the specific definition used for γ, according also to the discussion in [21], there are some natural requirements for any *meaningful* definition of contrast:

Fact 1. *A meaningful measure of contrast requires that $\gamma(\ell, h, m)$ be: (i) a decreasing function of ℓ; (ii) an increasing function of h; (iii) a decreasing function of m.*

Indeed, if we decrease ℓ while keeping the same values of h and m, we are *improving* the quality of the reconstruction of *white* pixels, without changing anything else. Hence, the contrast should not decrease. Similarly, if we increase h while keeping the same values of ℓ and m, we are *improving* the quality of the reconstruction of *black* pixels, without changing anything else. Again, the contrast should not decrease. Finally, if we decrease m without changing the values of ℓ and h, we are *maintaining the same difference* in the reconstruction of white and black pixels but we are "reducing the scale" at which we use such a difference. Once again the contrast should not decrease.

Throughout the paper we will always consider meaningful definitions of contrast. So when we say "contrast" we implicitly mean "meaningful contrast".

Three measures of contrast have appeared in the literature: γ_{NS} (Naor and Shamir [28]), γ_{VV} (Verheul and van Tilborg [32]) and γ_{ES} (Eisen and Stinson [21]). The measure introduced by Naor and Shamir [28]) is defined by:

$$\gamma_{\text{NS}}(\mathcal{S}) = \frac{h - \ell}{m}. \tag{1}$$

Verheul and van Tilborg [32], on the other hand, defined:

$$\gamma_{\mathrm{VV}}(\mathcal{S}) = \frac{h - \ell}{m(2m - h - \ell)}, \qquad (2)$$

while, Eisen and Stinson [21], used:

$$\gamma_{\mathrm{ES}}(\mathcal{S}) = \frac{h - \ell}{2m - h}. \qquad (3)$$

Notice that the definition of the thresholds ℓ and h that we use in this paper is different from that used in $[21,32]^3$. If we denote with $\hat{\ell}$ and $\hat{h}$ the thresholds of [21,32] we have that $\hat{\ell} = m - h$ and $\hat{h} = m - \ell$. Thus the definition of contrast of [32], namely $\frac{\hat{h}-\hat{\ell}}{m(\hat{h}+\hat{\ell})}$, becomes (2) and the definition of contrast of [21], namely $\frac{\hat{h}-\hat{\ell}}{m+\hat{\ell}}$, becomes (3).

It is easy to check that $\gamma_{\mathrm{NS}}, \gamma_{\mathrm{ES}}$ and γ_{VV} are meaningful. However, in [21], the authors have pointed out some differences among them. They have emphasized, through some examples, that γ_{NS} associates *the same* value of the contrast to reconstructed images which have clearly a different visibility, and γ_{VV} associates the same value of the contrast to *all* images where black is perfectly reconstructed, *independently of* the quantity of blackness in the reconstruction of white pixels. According to these observation γ_{ES} is a better choice for measuring the contrast. We refer the reader to [21] for more details.

The following two facts are well known (see Lemmas 3.5 and 3.6 in [6]).

Fact 2. *Given a scheme $\mathcal{S}$ defined with collections of distribution matrices $\mathcal{C}_\circ$ and $\mathcal{C}_\bullet$, with contrast $\gamma_{\mathrm{NS}}(\mathcal{S})$, there exists a scheme $\mathcal{S}'$ defined with base matrices $B_\circ$ and $B_\bullet$ with contrast $\gamma_{\mathrm{NS}}(\mathcal{S}') = \gamma_{\mathrm{NS}}(\mathcal{S})$.*

Fact 3. *Given a scheme $\mathcal{S}$ defined with base matrices $B_\circ$ and $B_\bullet$ with contrast $\gamma_{\mathrm{NS}}(\mathcal{S})$, there exists a canonical scheme $\mathcal{S}'$ with contrast $\gamma_{\mathrm{NS}}(\mathcal{S}') = \gamma_{\mathrm{NS}}(\mathcal{S})$.*

When studying contrast optimal schemes, the above two facts are often used to restrict the attention, without loss of generality, to *canonical schemes*. Facts 2 and 3 have been proved considering the measure of contrast γ_{NS}. However, the proof can be generalized to include any measure of contrast γ that can be expressed in the form

$$\gamma = \frac{f(\ell, h, m)}{g(\ell, h, m)}, \qquad where\ f\ and\ g\ are\ linear\ functions\ of\ \ell, h, m. \qquad (4)$$

---

[3] The authors of [32] used two thresholds, $\hat{\ell}$ and $\hat{h}$, to measure the *level of whiteness* in the reconstruction of a white or a black pixel, while we use two thresholds, ℓ (low) and h (high), to measure the *level of blackness* in the reconstruction of a white or a black pixel. In [21] the thresholds measure the level of blackness too, but are expressed as $m - \hat{h}$ and $m - \hat{\ell}$. In the first paper on visual cryptography [28] explicit thresholds ℓ and h are not used, but the conditions are stated in terms of the level of blackness, too.

More precisely, let ℓ, h and m be integer values, such that $0 \leq \ell \leq h \leq m$ and let $f(\ell, h, m)$ and $g(\ell, h, m)$ be functions

$$f(\ell, h, m) = \begin{cases} 0 & \text{if } \ell = h \\ > 0 & \text{if } \ell < h \end{cases} \qquad g(\ell, h, m) = \begin{cases} 0 & \text{if } \ell = h \\ > 0 & \text{if } \ell < h \end{cases}$$

such that, for any integers a and b, it holds that

$$f(a(\ell_1 + \ell_2), a(h_1 + h_2), a(m_1 + m_2)) = af(\ell_1, h_1, m_1) + af(\ell_2, h_2, m_2)$$

and

$$g(b(\ell_1 + \ell_2), b(h_1 + h_2), b(m_1 + m_2)) = bg(\ell_1, h_1, m_1) + bg(\ell_2, h_2, m_2).$$

We will refer to definitions of contrast that satisfies (4) as *linear*.

The following two lemmas provide a generalization of Facts 2 and 3.

Lemma 1. *Given a scheme $\mathcal{S}$ defined with collections of distribution matrices $\mathcal{C}_\circ$ and $\mathcal{C}_\bullet$, with contrast thresholds ℓ and h, pixel expansion m, and a linear contrast $\gamma(\mathcal{S}) = f(\ell, h, m)/g(\ell, h, m)$, there exists a scheme $\mathcal{S}'$ defined with base matrices $B_\circ$ and $B_\bullet$ with contrast $\gamma(\mathcal{S}') = \gamma(\mathcal{S})$.*

(We defer all the proofs to the full version of the paper.)

Lemma 2. *Given a scheme $\mathcal{S}$ defined with base matrices $B_\circ$ and $B_\bullet$, with contrast thresholds ℓ and h, pixel expansion m and a linear contrast $\gamma(\mathcal{S}) = f(\ell, h, m)/g(\ell, h, m)$, there exists a canonical scheme $\mathcal{S}'$ with contrast $\gamma(\mathcal{S}') = \gamma(\mathcal{S})$.*

Since γ_{ES} is linear, Facts 2 and 3 are true *also* for γ_{ES}. Hence, for γ_{NS} and γ_{ES} (as well as any other linear contrast), we can focus our attention on canonical schemes. The definition of contrast γ_{VV} is not linear. Hence, we do not know whether in this case we can restrict the attention to canonical schemes. The transformations used in Lemmas 1 and 2, indeed, *reduce* the value of γ_{VV}.

Throughout the rest of the paper we will use γ without subscript when we want to deal with any linear measure of contrast, and we will use the subscript (i.e., $\gamma_{\text{NS}}, \gamma_{\text{ES}}$, and γ_{VV}) when we want to deal with a specific measure of contrast.

Lemma 3. *Let $\mathcal{S}$ be a (k, n)-threshold scheme defined with base matrices and let $\gamma(\mathcal{S})$ a linear contrast. Then, there exists a scheme $\mathcal{S}'$ with contrast $\gamma(\mathcal{S}') \geq \gamma(\mathcal{S})$ and satisfying the following property: $B_\circ$ and $B_\bullet$ do not contain identical columns.*

By Lemmas 1, 2 and 3, we know that when the contrast is linear, there exists a scheme with optimal contrast γ that is in canonical form and such that the two base matrices do not contain identical columns. Hence, from now on, without loss of generality, we restrict our attention to schemes having such two properties.

4   Previous Results

In this section we briefly survey the known results about γ_{NS}, γ_{ES} and γ_{VV}.

4.1   Results About γ_{NS}

The problem of finding contrast optimal schemes with respect to γ_{NS} has been well studied and many results are known. Both bounds and schemes achieving the bounds are known. For $k = 2$ we have the following bound, proved in [9] and in [22].

Theorem 4. *In any $(2, n)$-threshold scheme we have that $\gamma_{NS} \leq \frac{\lceil n/2 \rceil \lfloor n/2 \rfloor}{n(n-1)}$.*

Constructions of $(2, n)$-threshold schemes with optimal γ_{NS} are known: the pixel expansion is $m = \binom{n}{\lfloor n/2 \rfloor}$, the black base matrix consists of all binary vectors of weight $\lfloor n/2 \rfloor$, and the white base matrix consists of equal rows each with weight $\binom{n-1}{\lfloor n/2 \rfloor - 1}$.

For the case of $k = n$, the paper by Naor and Shamir [28] provides a strict bound on the contrast: $\gamma_{NS} \leq \frac{1}{2^{n-1}}$ (it is also proves that $m \geq 2^{n-1}$). A construction of (n, n)-threshold schemes with optimal γ_{NS} is also provided.

For general k, Krause and Simon [24] have proved that the optimal contrast γ_{NS} of (k, n)-threshold schemes is about $4^{-(k-1)}$:

Lemma 4. *For any (k, n)-threshold scheme we have that*

$$\gamma_{NS} \leq 4^{-(k-1)} \frac{n^k}{n(n-1)\cdots(n-(k-1))}.$$

Other bounds and constructions, optimal with respect to γ_{NS}, for $(3, n), (4, n)$, $(5, n)$ and $(n-1, n)$-threshold schemes can be found in [6].

4.2   Results About γ_{VV}

In [32] Verheul and Van Tilborg introduced γ_{VV} as a measure for the contrast. To our knowledge it is the only paper in which it has been used. The authors provided the following intuitive justification for the measure: "Consider the contrast of two adjacent buildings A and B in the night, formed by the number of illuminated windows. Then, the contrast formed by 100 illuminated windows in A and 99 in B, is much less[4] than 1 illuminated window in A and 0 in B".

Following such an intuition, they referred to schemes with perfect black reconstruction as to schemes with *maximal contrast*. Moreover, they proposed two constructions for (k, n) threshold schemes with perfect black reconstruction, based on the use of functionals defined over finite fields, described some structural properties of threshold schemes, and provided some lower bounds on the pixel expansion. The first one, which applies to general schemes, is:

---

[4] According to the measure γ_{NS} the contrast in both cases is the same.

Theorem 5. *For any (k,n) threshold scheme with contrast thresholds ℓ and h, and pixel expansion m, it holds that $m \geq (h - \ell)2^{k-1}$.*

The second lower bound on the pixel expansion refers to the class of *uniform* schemes [32]. No explicit analysis of the contrast is provided.

4.3   Results About γ_{ES}

The contrast measure γ_{ES} has been introduced in [21]. Although there are good reasons to consider this measure better than the others, as far as we know, no other paper has considered γ_{ES} as definition of contrast. In [21] γ_{ES} has been used as a motivation to study the pixel expansion subject to fixing the contrast threshold ℓ and h (or, more precisely[5], $\hat{\ell}$ and $\hat{h}$). Beside providing a linear program that allows to find, if it exists, a $(2,n)$-threshold scheme achieving minimum pixel expansion, Eisen and Stinson proved the following theorem.

Theorem 6. *The following are necessary conditions for the existence of a $(2,n)$-threshold scheme with pixel expansion m and contrast parameters $\hat{\ell}$ and $\hat{h}$*

$$m \geq \begin{cases} n\hat{h}, & \text{if } \hat{\ell} = 0 \\ \frac{n\hat{h}}{\hat{l}n + \hat{h} - \hat{l}}, & \text{if } \hat{h} \geq m/2 \\ \frac{4(\hat{h} - \hat{\ell})(n-1)}{n}, & \text{otherwise.} \end{cases} \tag{5}$$

The bounds on m provided in [21] are not given in a form that can be easily used to obtain bounds on γ_{ES}. Hence there are no explicit known bounds on γ_{ES}.

5   Optimal Contrast for $(2,n)$-Threshold Schemes

In this section we present a characterization of $(2,n)$-threshold schemes with optimal contrast γ. The characterization shows that, regardless of the particular measure γ, the contrast optimal scheme has a specific form: the black base matrix $B_\bullet$ consists of all and only the columns with a specific weight w, that is $\mu_w^\bullet = 1$, for some $w, 1 \leq w \leq n - 1$, and $\mu_i^\bullet = 0$, for $i \neq w$. The specific measure γ determines the value of w. The white base matrix $B_\circ$ contains only all-black and all-white columns and the multiplicities of these two type of columns is uniquely determined by w. The security property determines the corresponding white base matrix.

Lemma 5. *There exists a $(2,n)$-threshold scheme with optimal contrast γ for which the base matrix $B_\circ$ contains μ_0° —the column with all 0s— and μ_n° —the column with all 1s— while all other μ_i°, for $1 \leq i \leq n - 1$ are 0.*

---

[5] We state the following theorem using the original contrast thresholds $\hat{\ell} = m - h$, $\hat{h} = m - \ell$ as they appear in the original paper.

As a consequence of the previous lemma, in a contrast optimal $(2, n)$-threshold scheme, matrix $B_\circ$ contains only all-0 or all-1 columns, that is, we have that an optimal scheme has $\mu_1^\circ = \mu_2^\circ = \ldots = \mu_{n-1}^\circ = 0$ while μ_0° and μ_n° are greater than 0. Since $\mu_0^\circ > 0$ and $\mu_n^\circ > 0$, by Lemma 3 we have that $\mu_0^\bullet = 0$ and $\mu_n^\bullet = 0$.

Before proceeding to the next lemma, let us introduce some notation needed to prove the lemma. Given a black base matrix $B_\bullet$ in canonical form, we partition it into chunks, each one containing all the columns of a given weight. If $B_\bullet$ consists of $\mu_{i_1}, \ldots, \mu_{i_z}$, with $1 \leq i_1 < \ldots < i_z \leq n - 1$, then

$$B_\bullet = C_\bullet^{i_1} || C_\bullet^{i_2} || \ldots || C_\bullet^{i_z}$$

where $C_\bullet^{i_j}$ is the chunk containing all the columns with weight j. Each column appears with multiplicity μ_{i_j}. Restricting the attention to one specific chunk $C_\bullet^{i_j}$, we have that in $C_\bullet^{i_j}$ each row contains the same number a_{i_j} of 0s and the same number b_{i_j} of 1s. Notice that, by the security condition, $\sum_{j=1}^z a_{i_j}$ must be equal to μ_0°, that is, the number of all-0 columns in $B_\circ$, and that $\sum_{j=1}^z b_{i_j}$ must be equal to μ_n°, that is, the number of all-1 columns in $B_\circ$. Hence, we can partition also $B_\circ$ in chunks that corresponds to the chunks of $B_\bullet$. Chunk $C_\circ^{i_j}$ contains a_{i_j} all-0 columns and b_{i_j} all-1 columns, and we have that

$$B_\circ = C_\circ^{i_1} || C_\circ^{i_2} || \ldots || C_\circ^{i_z}.$$

An example will clarify the notation. Let $n = 5$ and assume that $B_\bullet$ has $\mu_1 = 2$, $\mu_3 = 1$ and $\mu_4 = 1$, that is the black base matrix contains 2 occurrences of every column with weight 1, one occurrence of every column of weight 3 and one occurrence of every column with weight 4. The chunks are:

$$B_\bullet = \begin{bmatrix}
C_\bullet^1 & C_\bullet^3 & C_\bullet^4 \\
1000010000 & 1111110000 & 11110 \\
0100001000 & 1110001110 & 11101 \\
0010000100 & 1001101101 & 11011 \\
0001000010 & 0101011011 & 10111 \\
0000100001 & 0010110111 & 01111
\end{bmatrix}$$

$$B_\circ = \begin{bmatrix}
C_\circ^1 & C_\circ^3 & C_\circ^4 \\
0000000011 & 0000111111 & 01111 \\
0000000011 & 0000111111 & 01111 \\
0000000011 & 0000111111 & 01111 \\
0000000011 & 0000111111 & 01111 \\
0000000011 & 0000111111 & 01111
\end{bmatrix}$$

Now let h_j be the number of 1s that we obtain by stacking two rows of chunk $C_\bullet^{i_j}$ and ℓ_j be the number of 1s that we obtain by stacking two rows of chunk $C_\circ^{i_j}$. Then we have that

$$h = h_1 + h_2 + \ldots + h_z$$

and

$$\ell = \ell_1 + \ell_2 + \ldots + \ell_z.$$

Moreover, if we let m_j be the number of columns in chunk $C_\bullet^{i_j}$ (or $C_\circ^{i_j}$ since they have the same size), we have

$$m = m_1 + m_2 + \ldots + m_z.$$

In the above example we have $h_1 = 4, h_2 = 9$ and $h_3 = 5, \ell_1 = 2, \ell_2 = 6$ and $\ell_3 = 4, m_1 = 10, m_2 = 10$ and $m_3 = 5$:

$$h = 4 + 9 + 5 = 18,$$
$$\ell = 2 + 6 + 4 = 12,$$
$$m = 10 + 10 + 5 = 25.$$

Lemma 6. *For any linear contrast γ, there exists a contrast optimal canonical $(2,n)$-threshold scheme whose multiplicities for $B_\bullet$ are $\mu_i^\bullet = 0$, for all but one i, with $1 \le i \le n - 1$.*

The next theorem follows from Lemma 6 strengthening the result, by stating that the multiplicity can be 1.

Theorem 7. *For any linear contrast γ, there exists a contrast optimal $(2,n)$-threshold scheme whose base matrix $B_\bullet$ is defined by $\mu_w^\bullet = 1$, for some w, with $1 \le w \le n - 1$, and $\mu_i^\bullet = 0$ for $i \neq w$, with $1 \le i \le n - 1$.*

Theorem 7 characterize explicitly the structure of the scheme that achieves maximal contrast for all linear measures of contrast. In particular for γ_{NS} and γ_{ES}.

The specific value of w that maximizes the contrast is (not surprisingly) different in each case.

First, we consider γ_{ES}. In the following we prove that in order to maximize γ_{ES} we have to choose either $w = \lfloor n(2 - \sqrt{2}) \rfloor$ or $w = \lceil n(2 - \sqrt{2}) \rceil$.

The case of γ_{NS} has been already studied and it is known that choosing $w = \lfloor n/2 \rfloor$ one gets optimal contrast. As a sanity check, exploiting the same proof technique used for γ_{ES}, we will prove that our analysis gives the same result, obtaining an alternative proof of the result.

Before proceeding with the calculation of the value of w that maximizes the contrast, we observe that, regardless of which contrast measure we are considering, for a contrast optimal scheme that satisfies Theorem 7 we have that

$$m = \binom{n}{w}, \qquad h = \binom{n}{w} - \binom{n-2}{w}, \qquad \text{and} \qquad \ell = \binom{n-1}{w-1}.$$

5.1   Value of w that Maximizes γ_{ES}

In order to compute the value of w which maximizes γ_{ES}, we proceed as follows. Notice that:

$$\gamma_{ES} = \frac{h - \ell}{2m - h} = \frac{\binom{n}{w} - \binom{n-2}{w} - \binom{n-1}{w-1}}{2\binom{n}{w} - \left(\binom{n}{w} - \binom{n-2}{w}\right)}.$$

Let us call the numerator N and the denominator D, that is

$$N = \binom{n}{w} - \binom{n-2}{w} - \binom{n-1}{w-1}$$

and

$$D = 2\binom{n}{w} - \left(\binom{n}{w} - \binom{n-2}{w}\right).$$

Using the well-known equalities

$$\binom{n}{w} = \frac{n}{w}\binom{n-1}{w-1} \quad \text{and} \quad \binom{n}{w} = \binom{n-1}{w} + \binom{n-1}{w-1}$$

from which we get

$$\binom{n-1}{w} = \binom{n}{w} - \binom{n-1}{w-1}$$

we can express N and D as follows:

$$
\begin{aligned}
N &= \binom{n}{w} - \binom{n-2}{w} - \binom{n-1}{w-1} \\
&= \frac{n}{w}\binom{n-1}{w-1} - \binom{n-2}{w} - \binom{n-1}{w-1} \\
&= \left(\frac{n}{w} - 1\right)\binom{n-1}{w-1} - \left[\binom{n-1}{w} - \binom{n-2}{w-1}\right] \\
&= \left(\frac{n}{w} - 1\right)\binom{n-1}{w-1} - \left[\frac{n-1}{w}\binom{n-2}{w-1} - \binom{n-2}{w-1}\right] \\
&= \left(\frac{n}{w} - 1\right)\binom{n-1}{w-1} - \left(\frac{n-1}{w} - 1\right)\binom{n-2}{w-1} \\
&= \left(\frac{n}{w} - 1\right)\frac{(n-1)!}{(w-1)!(n-1-(w-1))!} - \left(\frac{n-1}{w} - 1\right)\frac{(n-2)!}{(w-1)!(n-2-(w-1))!} \\
&= \frac{(n-2)!}{(w-1)!(n-w-1)!}\left(\frac{n-1}{w} - \frac{n-1-w}{w}\right) \\
&= \frac{(n-2)!}{(w-1)!(n-w-1)!} \tag{6}
\end{aligned}
$$

$$
\begin{aligned}
D &= \binom{n}{w} + \binom{n-2}{w} \\
&= \frac{n!}{w!(n-w)!} + \frac{(n-2)!}{w!(n-w-2)!}
\end{aligned}
$$

$$= \frac{(n-2)!}{w!(n-w-2)!} \left(\frac{n(n-1)}{(n-w)(n-w-1)} + 1 \right)$$

$$= \frac{(n-2)!}{w!(n-w-2)!} \left(\frac{n(n-1) + (n-w)(n-w-1)}{(n-w)(n-w-1)} \right)$$

$$= \frac{(n-2)!}{(w-1)!(n-w-1)!} \left(\frac{n(n-1) + (n-w)(n-w-1)}{w(n-w)} \right) \qquad (7)$$

From Equations (6) and (7) we have that

$$\gamma_{\mathrm{ES}} = \frac{N}{D} = \frac{w(n-w)}{n(n-1) + (n-w)(n-w-1)} = \frac{wn - w^2}{w^2(1-2n) + 2n(n-1)}.$$

We are interested in finding the maximum value of γ_{ES} and also the value of w that maximizes γ_{ES}. We start by computing the first derivative:

$$\frac{\partial}{\partial w} \gamma_{\mathrm{ES}}(n, w) = \frac{(n-1)(w^2 - 4wn + 2n^2)}{(w^2 + w(1-2n) + 2n(n-1))^2}.$$

Then we compute the roots of the first derivative, which are the roots of the equation $w^2 - 4wn + 2n^2 = 0$, which are $(2 - \sqrt{2})n$ and $(2 + \sqrt{2})n$. Since $(2 + \sqrt{2})n > n$ and $2 \le w \le n - 1$ the only point where $\frac{\partial}{\partial w} \gamma_{\mathrm{ES}}(n, w)$ is 0 is $w_0 = (2 - \sqrt{2})n$. Moreover for $w < w_0$, we have that $\frac{\partial}{\partial w} \gamma_{\mathrm{ES}}(n, w) > 0$ and for $w_0 < w \le n - 1$ we have that $\frac{\partial}{\partial w} \gamma_{\mathrm{ES}}(n, w) > 0$. Hence the function $\frac{\partial}{\partial w} \gamma_{\mathrm{ES}}(n, w)$ reaches its maximum in w_0.

Recalling that w must be an integer, we have that the maximum contrast γ_{ES} is reached either at $w_1 = \lfloor (2 - \sqrt{2})n \rfloor$ or at $w_2 = \lceil (2 - \sqrt{2})n \rceil$ and we have that

$$\max \gamma_{\mathrm{ES}} = \max \left\{ \frac{\lfloor (2 - \sqrt{2})n \rfloor n - \lfloor (2 - \sqrt{2})n \rfloor^2}{\lfloor (2 - \sqrt{2})n \rfloor^2 (1 - 2n) + 2n(n-1)}, \right.$$
$$\left. \frac{\lceil (2 - \sqrt{2})n \rceil n - \lceil (2 - \sqrt{2})n \rceil^2}{\lceil (2 - \sqrt{2})n \rceil^2 (1 - 2n) + 2n(n-1)} \right\}$$

5.2   Value of w that Maximizes γ_{NS}

Using the same approach we can easily derive the value ω which maximizes γ_{NS}. Indeed:

$$\gamma_{\mathrm{NS}} = \frac{h - \ell}{m} = \frac{\binom{n}{w} - \binom{n-2}{w} - \binom{n-1}{w-1}}{\binom{n}{w}}$$

$$= \frac{\frac{(n-2)!}{(w-1)!(n-w-1)!}}{\frac{n!}{w!(n-w)!}} = \frac{w(n-w)}{n(n-1)} = \frac{1}{n(n-1)}(wn - w^2)$$

The maximum of this function is reached in the same point where the function $wn - w^2$ reaches its maximum, which is $w = n/2$. Since w must be an integer, we need to consider as possible points of maximum $\lfloor n/2 \rfloor$ and $\lceil n/2 \rceil$. However, it is not difficult to see that the value of $wn - w^2$ is the same in both cases, so we can choose any of the two values, for example $w = \lfloor n/2 \rfloor$. Obviously we have that the maximum value is the same as the one of Theorem 4 (i.e., we just get an alternative proof of the same result):

$$\max \gamma_{\mathrm{NS}} = \frac{\lceil n/2 \rceil \lfloor n/2 \rfloor}{n(n-1)}.$$

5.3   Value of w that Maximizes γ_{VV} for Schemes in Canonical Form

The definition of contrast γ_{VV} is not linear. Hence, Lemmas 1, 2 and 3 do not work, and we do not know whether we can restrict our attention to the canonical form. Lemma 6 does not work, too.

However, for the class of canonical schemes we are able to prove that Lemma 5 holds also for γ_{VV} and by an analysis similar to that of γ_{NS} and γ_{ES} we can prove that the maximum contrast γ_{VV} is

$$\max \gamma_{\mathrm{VV}} = \frac{1}{n}.$$

Notice that the optimal construction in canonical form implied by our analysis coincides with the maximal contrast construction for $(2, n)$ threshold visual schemes described in [32]. However, we remark that our proof technique does not say anything about whether constructions not in canonical form can achieve a better value of γ_{VV}.

6   Contrast Optimal (n, n)-Threshold Schemes

We prove that the construction of [28] for (n, n)-threshold schemes is optimal with respect to *any* linear contrast γ. The construction of [28], in terms of base matrices, is defined as follows: the base matrix B_o consists of all the binary vectors with *even* weight, and the base matrix $B_\bullet$ consists of all the binary vectors with *odd* weight. The authors proved that such a construction gives contrast optimal, with respect to γ_{NS}, and minimum pixel expansion schemes. The second construction for (k, n)-threshold schemes given in [32], for $k = n$ is the same as the construction of [28]. In [9], it was shown the following result:

Theorem 8. *Let S_o and $S_\bullet$ be two $n \times m$ boolean matrices such that the same column does not appear in both. Then, S_o and $S_\bullet$ are base matrices of an (n, n)-threshold scheme with pixel expansion m and relative difference $\alpha(m) \leq \frac{\mu}{m}$ if and only if all the columns with even weight appear in S_o with multiplicity $\mu = \frac{m}{2^{n-1}}$ and all the columns with odd weight appear in $S_\bullet$ with the same multiplicity μ. Consequently, $\mu \geq \alpha(m) \times m$, $\alpha(m) \leq \frac{1}{2^{n-1}}$, and $m \geq 2^{n-1}$.*

Notice that, in the language of [9,28], the relative difference $\alpha(m)$ is γ_{NS}. The theorem states that the only way to construct contrast optimal (n,n)-threshold schemes with $\gamma_{NS} = \frac{1}{2^{n-1}}$ is by using $B_\circ$ and $B_\bullet$, as defined above (or base matrices obtained by concatenating several copies of $B_\circ$ and $B_\bullet$).

Going through the proof of Theorem 8 in [9], we notice that the steps are justified either by the *Reconstruction* property or by the *Security* property of Definition 1. Moreover, the additional assumption that $S_\circ$ and $S_\bullet$ do not contain identical columns, is not a limitation in studying contrast optimal schemes with respect to any linear contrast γ. Indeed, Lemma 3 confirms that, looking for contrast optimal constructions for the class of linear measures of contrast, we can restrict our attention to base matrices that do not contain identical columns. Hence, we can conclude that the results holds for any linear contrast γ.

Actually, we can say a bit more: there is a *unique way* to construct (n,n)-threshold schemes by means of base matrices, and the characterization of the matrices is *independent of* the contrast measure—either linear or not— that is used to quantify the contrast:

Theorem 9. *Two $n \times m$ boolean matrices, $S_\circ$ and $S_\bullet$, are the base matrices of an (n,n)-threshold scheme with contrast thresholds ℓ and h if and only if $S_\circ$ contains all the columns with even weight with multiplicity $h - \ell$ and $S_\bullet$ contains all the columns with odd weight with multiplicity $h - \ell$. Moreover, S_0 and S_1 might contain additional identical columns.*

Notice that the identical common columns, make the reconstructed image overall clearer or darker, depending on the number of black subpixels that the identical common columns introduce in each share. For γ_{NS}, γ_{ES} and γ_{VV}, the construction with no common columns is optimal with respect to the contrast and to the pixel expansion.

7   Conclusions and Future Work

In this paper we have provided a measure-independent approach to the study of the contrast for visual cryptography schemes. Our work was motivated by the fact that although the contrast measure γ_{ES} appears to be better than other definitions, most of the known results are for the definition γ_{NS}. Interesting directions for future work include the extension of the analysis to the case of (k,n)-threshold schemes for any k and the study of the relation of the results presented in this paper with other models (random grid and probabilistic). The results about γ_{VV} presented in this paper hold for the class of canonical schemes and we do not know whether considering other classes of schemes can lead schemes with better contrast. Studying this question is an open problem. Another open problem is to see whether the characterization given in Theorem 9, which holds for schemes given with base matrices, holds also for schemes described in terms of collections of matrices $\mathcal{C}_\circ$ and $\mathcal{C}_\bullet$.

References

1. Adhikari, A., Sikdar, S.: A new (2, n)-visual threshold scheme for color images. In: Johansson, T., Maitra, S. (eds.) INDOCRYPT 2003. LNCS, vol. 2904, pp. 148–161. Springer, Heidelberg (2003)
2. Ateniese, G., Blundo, C., De Santis, A., Stinson, D.R.: Visual cryptography for general access structures. Inf. Comput. **129**, 86–106 (1996)
3. Ateniese, G., Blundo, C., De Santis, A., Stinson, D.R.: Constructions and bounds for visual cryptography. In: Meyer auf der Heide, F., Monien, B. (eds.) ICALP 1996. LNCS, vol. 1099, pp. 416–428. Springer, Heidelberg (1996)
4. Ateniese, G., Blundo, C., De Santis, A., Stinson, D.R.: Extended schemes for visual cryptography. Theor. Comput. Sci. **250**, 143–161 (2001)
5. Blundo, C., Cimato, S., De Santis, A.: Visual cryptography schemes with optimal pixel expansion. Theor. Comput. Sci. **369**, 169–182 (2006)
6. Blundo, C., D'Arco, P., De Santis, A., Stinson, D.R.: Contrast optimal threshold visual cryptography schemes. SIAM J. Discrete Math. **16**, 224–261 (2003)
7. Blundo, C., De Bonis, A., De Santis, A.: Improved schemes for visual cryptography. Des. Codes. Crypt. **24**, 255–278 (2001)
8. Blundo, C., De Santis, A.: Visual cryptography schemes with perfect reconstruction of black pixels. J. Comput. Graph. **22**, 449–455 (1998)
9. Blundo, C., De Santis, A., Stinson, D.R.: On the contrast in visual cryptography schemes. J. Cryptol. **12**, 261–289 (1999)
10. Chen, S.-K., Lin, S.-J.: Optimal (2, n) and (2, ∞) visual secret sharing by generalized random grids. J. Vis. Commun. Image Represent. **23**, 677–684 (2012)
11. Chen, T.-H., Tsao, K.-H.: Visual secret sharing revisited. Pattern Recogn. **42**, 2203–2217 (2009)
12. Chen, T.-H., Tsao, K.-H.: Threshold visual secret sharing by random grids. J. Syst. Softw. **84**, 1197–1208 (2011)
13. Cimato, S., De Prisco, R., De Santis, A.: Colored visual cryptography without color darkening. In: Blundo, C., Cimato, S. (eds.) SCN 2004. LNCS, vol. 3352, pp. 235–248. Springer, Heidelberg (2005)
14. Cimato, S., De Prisco, R., De Santis, A.: Optimal colored threshold visual cryptography schemes. Des. Codes. Crypt. **35**, 311–335 (2005)
15. Cimato, S., De Prisco, R., De Santis, A.: Probabilistic visual cryptography schemes. Comput. J. **49**(1), 97–107 (2006)
16. Cimato, S., De Prisco, R., De Santis, A.: Colored visual cryptography without color darkening. Theor. Comput. Sci. **374**(1–3), 261–276 (2007)
17. Cimato, S., Yang, C.-N. (eds.): Visual Cryptography and Secret Image Sharing. CRC Press, USA (2012). ISBN 978-1-4398-3721-4
18. De Prisco, R., De Santis, A.: Using colors to improve visual cryptography for black and white images. In: Fehr, S. (ed.) ICITS 2011. LNCS, vol. 6673, pp. 182–201. Springer, Heidelberg (2011)
19. De Prisco, R., De Santis, A., Color visual cryptography schemes for black and white secret images. Theor. Comput. Sci. http://dx.doi.org/10.1016/j.tcs.2013.09.005, to appear
20. Hou, Y.-C.: Visual cryptography for color images. Pattern Recogn. **36**, 1619–1629 (2003)
21. Eisen, P.A., Stinson, D.R.: Threshold visual cryptography schemes with specified whiteness levels of reconstructed pixels. Des. Codes. Crypt. **25**, 15–61 (2002)

22. Hofmeister, T., Krause, M., Simon, H.U.: Contrast-optimal k out of n secret sharing schemes in visual cryptography. Theor. Comput. Sci. **240**, 471–485 (2000)
23. Kafri, O., Keren, E.: Encryption of pictures and shapes by random grids. Opt. Lett. **12**(6), 377–379 (1987)
24. Krause, M., Simon, H.U.: Determining the optimal contrast for secret sharing schemes in visual cryptography. Comb. Probab. Comput. **12**, 285–299 (2003)
25. Koga, H.: Proposal of a lattice-based visual secret sharing scheme for color and gray-scale images. IEICE Trans. Fundam. Electron. Commun. Comput. Sci. **81–A(6)**, 1262–1269 (1988)
26. Kuhlmann, C., Simon, H.U.: Construction of visual secret sharing schemes with almost optimal contrast. In: Proceedings of the 11th ACM-SIAM Symposium on Discrete Algorithms, San Francisco, pp. 262–272, 9–11 January 2000
27. Lu, S., Manchala, D., Ostrovsky, R.: Visual cryptography on graphs. J. Comb. Optim. **21**, 47–66 (2011)
28. Naor, M., Shamir, A.: Visual cryptography. In: De Santis, A. (ed.) EUROCRYPT 1994. LNCS, vol. 950, pp. 1–12. Springer, Heidelberg (1995)
29. Shyu, S.-J.: Image encryption by random grids. Pattern Recogn. **40**, 1014–1031 (2007)
30. Shyu, S.-J.: Image encryption by multiple random grids. Pattern Recogn. **42**, 1582–1596 (2009)
31. Simon, H.U.: Perfect reconstruction of black pixels revisited. In: Liśkiewicz, M., Reischuk, R. (eds.) FCT 2005. LNCS, vol. 3623, pp. 221–232. Springer, Heidelberg (2005)
32. Verheul, E.R., van Tilborg, H.C.A.: Constructions and properties of k out of n visual secret. sharing schemes. Des. Codes. Crypt. **11**, 179–196 (1997)
33. Wang, R.-Z., Lan, Y.-C., Lee, Y.-K., Huang Shyu, S.J., Chia, T.L.: Incrementing visual cryptography using random grids. Opt. Commun. **283**, 4242–4249 (2010)
34. Yang, C.-N.: New visual secret sharing schemes using probabilistic method. Pattern Recogn. Lett. **25**, 481–494 (2004)
35. Yang, C.-N., Chen, T.-S.: Size-adjustable visual secret sharing schemes. IEICE Trans. Fundam. Electron. Commun. Comput. Sci. **88–A**(9), 2471–2474 (2005)
36. Yang, C.-N., Chen, T.-S.: Aspect ratio invariant visual secret sharing schemes with minimum pixel expansion. Pattern Recogn. Lett. **26**, 193–206 (2005)
37. Yang, C.N., Laih, C.-S.: New colored visual secret sharing schemes. Des. codes. crypt. **20**, 325–335 (2000)

On (k, n) Visual Cryptography Scheme with t Essential Parties

Teng Guo[1,2](✉), Feng Liu[1], ChuanKun Wu[1], YaWei Ren[1,2,3], and Wen Wang[1,2]

[1] State Key Laboratory of Information Security,
Institute of Information Engineering, Chinese Academy of Sciences,
Beijing 100093, China
{guoteng,liufeng,ckwu,renyawei,wangwen}@iie.ac.cn
[2] University of Chinese Academy of Sciences, Beijing 100190, China
[3] School of Information Management,
Beijing Information Science and Technology University, Beijing 100192, China

Abstract. In visual cryptography schemes (VCS), we often denote the set of all parties by $P = \{1, 2, \cdots, n\}$. Arumugam et al. proposed a (k, n)-VCS with one essential party recently, in which only subset S of parties satisfying $S \subseteq P$ and $|S| \geq k$ and $1 \in S$ can recover the secret. In this paper, we extend Arumugam et al.'s idea and propose a (k, n)-VCS with t essential parties, say (k, n, t)-VCS for brevity, in which only subset S of parties satisfying $S \subseteq P$ and $|S| \geq k$ and $\{1, 2, \ldots, t\} \in S$ can recover the secret. Furthermore, some bounds for the *optimal pixel expansion* and *optimal relative contrast* of (k, n, t)-VCS are derived.

Keywords: Visual cryptography · Essential parties · Pixel expansion · Relative contrast

1 Introduction

A (k, n) visual cryptographic scheme (VCS) is a special type of secret sharing method introduced by Naor and Shamir [1], which encodes a binary secret image S into n share images in such a way that the physical stacking of any more than or equal to k share images will reveal S, while any fewer than k share images provide no information about S. Any VCS with n parties contains the following two stages:

Encoding Stage: Firstly, a binary secret image S is encoded into n share images by some VCS. Secondly, the n share images are printed on n transparencies. Finally, the ith transparency is distributed to party i for $1 \leq i \leq n$.

Decoding Stage: Some subset of parties superimpose their transparencies carefully. If this subset is qualified, the secret image S can be perceived from the stacking result.

In general, a secret pixel has to be encoded into a block of m pixels on each share image, where m is called *pixel expansion* and is expected to be as small

C. Padró (Ed.): ICITS 2013, LNCS 8317, pp. 56–68, 2014.
DOI: 10.1007/978-3-319-04268-8_4, © Springer International Publishing Switzerland 2014

as possible. In a qualified decoded image, the blocks decoded from a black pixel have more black pixels than blocks decoded from a white pixel, which ensures the emergence of the secret. The *relative contrast* measures the above difference and is expected to be as large as possible. In general, *optimal pixel expansion* and *optimal relative contrast* cannot be achieved by the same VCS [20].

Naor and Shamir [1] gave two methods to construct (k, n)-VCS, and their construction of (k, k)-VCS is optimal in the sense that the *pixel expansion* reaches minimum and *relative contrast* reaches maximum simultaneously. Droste [2] devised a clever algorithm to find solutions of (k, n)-VCS, and his scheme performs especially well for small k and n. Verheul et al. [3] studied the construction and properties of (k, n)-VCS by coding theory and linear algebra. Eisen et al. [4] studied (k, n)-VCS with specified gray levels of decoded blocks, and established the connections between $(2, n)$-VCS and some block designs, such as BIBD and PBD. Hofmeister et al. [5] characterized the exact *optimal relative contrast* of (k, n)-VCS by linear programming.

Ateniese et al. [6] firstly realized general access structure VCS, in which subsets of parties are divided into qualified sets and forbidden sets. Tzeng et al. [7] gave a new model of VCS, where for certain qualified sets, a white pixel is reconstructed as black while a black pixel is reconstructed as white and we perceive a complement of the secret image. Blundo et al. [8] proved a lower bound on the *optimal pixel expansion* of VCSs satisfying the model of Tzeng et al. [7], and for $(2, n)$-VCS, they provided schemes achieving the bound. Liu et al. [9] and Wang et al. [10] proposed shift tolerant VCSs such that the shares are not required to be aligned exactly in the decoding stage. Horng et al. [11] and Hu et al. [12] and Chen et al. [13] tried to propose cheating prevention VCSs such that fake shares can be detected in the decoding stage. Wang et al. [14] and Yang et al. [15] and Shyu et al. [16] constructed region incrementing VCSs, in which the secret information can be revealed gradually region by region. Guo et al. [17,18] realized VCSs directly by an algorithm.

Arumugam et al. [19] initiated the study of (k, n)-VCS with one essential party, in which party 1 is specified as essential and only subset S of parties satisfying $|S| \geq k$ and $1 \in S$ can recover the secret. (k, n)-VCS with one essential party is suitable for situations where one party is the leader and the secret image should not be retrieved in his absence. However, in a large company, there is usually a board of directors who are all essential for big decision makings. In such a case, the secret image should not be retrieved in the absence of any director. In this paper, we extend Arumugam et al.'s idea to (k, n)-VCS with t essential parties, which is denoted as (k, n, t)-VCS for brevity. The successful decoding of a (k, n, t)-VCS not only requires that the number of parties at the scene is no less than k, but also requires that the t essential parties are all at the scene. The proposed (k, n, t)-VCS is especially suitable for group decision makings with multiple essential parties. From another viewpoint, Arumugam et al.'s scheme can be seen as a $(k, n, 1)$-VCS under the proposed model. Furthermore, we give a construction of (k, n, t)-VCS from a given $(k-t, n-t)$-VCS and an optimal (t, t)-VCS. Some bounds for the *optimal relative contrast* and *optimal pixel expansion* of (k, n, t)-VCS are derived from the known parameters of $(k - t, n - t)$-VCS and (t, t)-VCS. Finally, we compare the exact formulae for *relative contrast* and *pixel expansion* of the two (k, n, t)-VCSs obtained by the accumulative array method [6] and the proposed method, and prove that the proposed method gives better results.

This paper is organized as follows. In Sect. 2, we give some preliminaries of VCS. In Sect. 3, we present the proposed (k, n, t)-VCS and its analysis. The paper is concluded in Sect. 4.

2   Preliminaries

2.1   Basic Definitions

We first give some knowledge of access structure. Denote all parties as $P = \{1, 2, \cdots, n\}$ and the power set of P as 2^P. $\Gamma = (Q, F)$ is called an access structure if $Q \subseteq 2^P$ and $F \subseteq 2^P$ and $Q \cap F = \emptyset$. The elements of Q are called qualified sets and the elements of F are called forbidden sets. If for any element of Q, all of its supersets are also in Q, then Q is said to be monotone increasing. If for any element of F, all of its subsets are also in F, then F is said to be monotone decreasing. $\Gamma = (Q, F)$ is said to be a strong access structure if Q is monotone increasing and F is monotone decreasing and $Q \cup F = 2^P$. $Q_0 = \{A \in Q : A' \notin Q \text{ for all } A' \subsetneq A\}$ represents the set of all minimal qualified subsets of P. $F_M = \{A \in F : A' \in \Gamma_{Qual}, \text{ for any } a \in P \setminus A, A' = A \cup \{a\}\}$ represents the set of all maximal forbidden subsets of P. In (k, n, t)-VCS, the set of all qualified sets is $Q = \{A \subseteq P : |A| \geq k \text{ and } \{1, 2, \ldots, t\} \subseteq A\}$ and the set of all forbidden sets is $F = \{A \subseteq P : |A| < k \text{ or } \{1, 2, \ldots, t\} \nsubseteq A\}$, where parties $\{1, 2, \ldots, t\}$ are specified to be essential.

Next we set up our notations. Let S be an $n \times m$ Boolean matrix and X be a subset of $P = \{1, 2, \cdots, n\}$ and Z be a subset of $M = \{1, 2, \cdots, m\}$ and $|X|$ be the cardinality of X. $S[X][Z]$ represents the $|X| \times |Z|$ matrix S constrained to rows in X and columns in Z. $S[X]$ represents the $|X| \times m$ matrix S constrained to rows in X. The OR result of rows of $S[X]$ is denoted by S_X and its Hamming weight is denoted by $w(S_X)$.

The formal definition of general access structure VCS is given as follows:

Definition 1 (VCS [6]). *Let $\Gamma = (Q, F)$ be an access structure on a set P of n parties. The two $n \times m$ Boolean matrices (S^0, S^1) constitute a solution of (Γ, m)-VCS if they satisfy the following conditions:*

1. *(Contrast) There exists a positive real number α and a set of thresholds $\{t_X | X \in Q\}$ such that for any party set $X \in Q$, we have $w(S_X^0) \leq t_X - \alpha m$ and $w(S_X^1) \geq t_X$.*
2. *(Security) For any party set $Y \in F$, $S^0[Y]$ and $S^1[Y]$ are equal up to a column permutation.*

Remark: The number α is called the *relative contrast* and m is called the *pixel expansion* and αm is called the *contrast*.

2.2   Previous Results

2.2.1   Some Bounds of VCS

Theorem 1 ([6]). *Let $\Gamma = (Q, F)$ be a strong access structure and F_M be the set of all maximal forbidden sets of Γ. Then there exists a Γ-VCS with pixel expansion $m = 2^{|F_M|-1}$ and relative contrast $\alpha = 2^{-|F_M|+1}$.*

Theorem 2 ([20]). *Let S^0 and S^1 be the two basis matrices of a Γ-VCS with pixel expansion m and relative contrast α. If S^0 and S^1 have d common columns, then by deleting the d common columns, we obtain a new Γ-VCS with pixel expansion $m - d$ and relative contrast $\frac{\alpha m}{m-d}$.*

Theorem 3 ([21]). *There exists a (k, n)-VCS with pixel expansion*

$$
m = \begin{cases} \binom{n}{k} 2^{k-2} & \text{if } \binom{n}{k} \text{ is even,} \\ \left(\binom{n}{k} + 1\right) 2^{k-2} & \text{if } \binom{n}{k} \text{ is odd.} \end{cases}
$$

and relative contrast $\alpha = \frac{1}{m}$.

2.2.2   The Cumulative Array Method

Ateniese et al. gave a construction of strong general access structure VCS by cumulative array method [6]. Let $F_M = \{B_1, B_2, \dots, B_t\}$ be the set of all maximal forbidden sets of a Γ-VCS with n parties. The cumulative array $CA = (c_{ij})$ of F_M is the n by t matrix defined by

$$
c_{ij} = \begin{cases} 0 & \text{if } i \in B_j, \\ 1 & \text{otherwise.} \end{cases}
$$

Let M^0 and M^1 be basis matrices for a (t, t)-VCS. Let X_i be the set of integers j such that $c_{ij} = 1$. The following two basis matrices S^0 and S^1 constitute a solution of Γ-VCS.

$$
S^0 = \begin{bmatrix} M^0_{X_1} \\ M^0_{X_2} \\ \vdots \\ M^0_{X_n} \end{bmatrix} \quad \text{and} \quad S^1 = \begin{bmatrix} M^1_{X_1} \\ M^1_{X_2} \\ \vdots \\ M^1_{X_n} \end{bmatrix}
$$

where $M^0_{X_i}$ (resp. $M^1_{X_i}$) is the OR result of rows X_i of M^0 (resp. M^1).

For (k, n, t)-VCS, the set of maximal forbidden sets $F_M = \{X \subseteq P : \{1, 2, 3, \cdots, t\} \subseteq X$ and $|X| = k - 1$ or $X = P/i$ where $i \in \{1, 2, 3, \cdots, t\}\}$. It is easy to see that $|F_M| = \binom{n-t}{k-t-1} + t$. Since the optimal (t, t)-VCS [1] has pixel expansion 2^{t-1} and relative contrast 2^{-t+1}, the (k, n, t)-VCS constructed by cumulative array method has pixel expansion $m = 2^{\binom{n-t}{k-t-1}+t-1}$ and relative contrast $\alpha = 2^{-\binom{n-t}{k-t-1}-t+1}$.

3   Our Work

In this whole section, Γ and Γ^* are defined as follows. $\Gamma = (Q, F)$ is an access structure on $P_t = \{t+1, t+2, \ldots, n\}$ and $\Gamma^* = (Q^*, F^*)$ is an access structure on $P = \{1, 2, \ldots, n\}$, where $Q^* = \{Z \cup \{1, 2, 3, \cdots, t\} : Z \in Q\}$ and $F^* = \{Z \cup T : Z \subseteq P_t \wedge T \subsetneq \{1, 2, 3, \cdots, t\}\} \cup \{X \cup \{1, 2, 3, \cdots, t\} : X \in F\}$. In such a case, parties $\{1, 2, 3, \cdots, t\}$ are specified to be essential, since the absence of any of them will make the secret image be unavailable, no matter how many parties are at the scene.

3.1   Construction of VCS with t Essential Parties

Let M^0 and M^1 be the basis matrices for the optimal (t, t)-VCS [1], where M^0 consists of all possible column vectors with even Hamming weight exactly once and M^1 consists of all possible column vectors with odd Hamming weight exactly once. Let $\hat{S}^0$ and $\hat{S}^1$ be the basis matrices for a Γ-VCS with pixel expansion m, where $\hat{S}^0$ is the white basis matrix and $\hat{S}^1$ is the black basis matrix.

Let $X = \{1, 2, \cdots, t\}$, then $M^0[X][i]$ represents the ith column of M^0, where $1 \le i \le 2^{t-1}$. Let $mM^0[X][i] = \underbrace{M^0[X][i] \circ M^0[X][i] \circ \cdots \circ M^0[X][i]}_{m}$ denote the concatenation of m copies of column vector $M^0[X][i]$. The basis matrices S^0 and S^1 for the constructed Γ^*-VCS are defined as follows:

$$S^0 = \begin{bmatrix} mM^0[X][1] \ldots mM^0[X][2^{t-1}] & mM^1[X][1] \ldots mM^1[X][2^{t-1}] \\ \hat{S}^0 \quad \ldots \quad \hat{S}^0 & \hat{S}^1 \quad \ldots \quad \hat{S}^1 \end{bmatrix}$$
$$S^1 = \begin{bmatrix} mM^0[X][1] \ldots mM^0[X][2^{t-1}] & mM^1[X][1] \ldots mM^1[X][2^{t-1}] \\ \hat{S}^1 \quad \ldots \quad \hat{S}^1 & \hat{S}^0 \quad \ldots \quad \hat{S}^0 \end{bmatrix} \quad (1)$$

Remark: Arumugam et al.'s scheme [19] works the same way as the proposed scheme with a special "(1, 1)-VCS" having basis matrices $M^0 = [0]$ and $M^1 = [1]$.

In the following, we will construct a (4,5,2)-VCS with essential parties $\{1, 2\}$ from a (2,3)-VCS and the optimal (2,2)-VCS.

Example 1. We are given a (2,3)-VCS with basis matrices $\hat{S}^0$ and $\hat{S}^1$, and the optimal (2,2)-VCS with basis matrices M^0 and M^1. We use the above construction in Eq. (1) to build a (4,5,2)-VCS, whose basis matrices are denoted as S^0 and S^1.

$$\hat{S}^0 = \begin{bmatrix} 0 & 0 & 1 \\ 0 & 0 & 1 \\ 0 & 0 & 1 \end{bmatrix} \text{ and } \hat{S}^1 = \begin{bmatrix} 1 & 0 & 0 \\ 0 & 1 & 0 \\ 0 & 0 & 1 \end{bmatrix} \quad (2)$$

$$M^0 = \begin{bmatrix} 0 & 1 \\ 0 & 1 \end{bmatrix} \text{ and } M^1 = \begin{bmatrix} 0 & 1 \\ 1 & 0 \end{bmatrix} \quad (3)$$

From Eqs. (1) and (3), we have the following:

$$S^0 = \begin{bmatrix} 0\,0\,0\,1\,1\,1\,0\,0\,0\,1\,1\,1 \\ 0\,0\,0\,1\,1\,1\,1\,1\,1\,0\,0\,0 \\ \hat{S}^0 \mid \hat{S}^0 \mid \hat{S}^1 \mid \hat{S}^1 \end{bmatrix}$$

$$S^1 = \begin{bmatrix} 0\,0\,0\,1\,1\,1\,0\,0\,0\,1\,1\,1 \\ 0\,0\,0\,1\,1\,1\,1\,1\,1\,0\,0\,0 \\ \hat{S}^1 \mid \hat{S}^1 \mid \hat{S}^0 \mid \hat{S}^0 \end{bmatrix}$$

Combining the above with Eq. (2), the basis matrices S^0 and S^1 for the (4,5,2)-VCS are explicitly given as follows:

$$S^0 = \begin{bmatrix} 0\,0\,0\,1\,1\,1\,0\,0\,0\,1\,1\,1 \\ 0\,0\,0\,1\,1\,1\,1\,1\,1\,0\,0\,0 \\ 0\,0\,1\,0\,0\,1\,1\,0\,0\,1\,0\,0 \\ 0\,0\,1\,0\,0\,1\,0\,1\,0\,0\,1\,0 \\ 0\,0\,1\,0\,0\,1\,0\,0\,1\,0\,0\,1 \end{bmatrix}$$

$$S^1 = \begin{bmatrix} 0\,0\,0\,1\,1\,1\,0\,0\,0\,1\,1\,1 \\ 0\,0\,0\,1\,1\,1\,1\,1\,1\,0\,0\,0 \\ 1\,0\,0\,1\,0\,0\,0\,0\,1\,0\,0\,1 \\ 0\,1\,0\,0\,1\,0\,0\,0\,1\,0\,0\,1 \\ 0\,0\,1\,0\,0\,1\,0\,0\,1\,0\,0\,1 \end{bmatrix}$$

The set of all qualified sets is $Q = \{\{1,2,3,4\}, \{1,2,3,5\}, \{1,2,4,5\}, \{1,2,3,4,5\}\}$. The set of all maximal forbidden sets is $F_M = \{\{1,3,4,5\}, \{2,3,4,5\}, \{1,2,3\}, \{1,2,4\}, \{1,2,5\}\}$. It is easy to verify that $w(S_X^1) \geq 11$ and $w(S_X^0) = 10$ for all $X \in Q$, and $S^0[X]$ and $S^1[X]$ are equal up to a column permutation for all $X \in F_M$. Hence S^0 and S^1 indeed constitute a (4,5,2)-VCS, where the pixel expansion is $m = 12$ and the relative contrast is $\alpha = \frac{1}{12}$. From Sect. 2.2.2, we know that the (4,5,2)-VCS constructed by cumulative array method has pixel expansion $2^{|F_M|-1} = 16$ and relative contrast $2^{-|F_M|+1} = \frac{1}{16}$. Hence our method outperforms the cumulative array method in both parameters with respect to (4,5,2) access structure.

Figures 1, 2, 3 and 4 in Appendix are the experimental results for the above (4,5,2)-VCS, where Fig. 1 shows the binary secret image with letters "LOIS" on it, and Fig. 2 shows the five share images, and Fig. 3 shows all qualified decoded images, and Fig. 4 shows all maximal forbidden decoded images. If $X = \{1,2,3,4,5\}$, $w(S_X^0) = 12$ and $w(S_X^1) = 10$ and $w(S_X^1) - w(S_X^0) = 2$, and if $X \in Q/\{1,2,3,4,5\}$, $w(S_X^1) = 11$ and $w(S_X^0) = 10$ and $w(S_X^1) - w(S_X^0) = 1$. Hence in Fig. 3, the 4th image is clearer than other three images.

LOIS

Fig. 1. A binary secret image of size 200×100

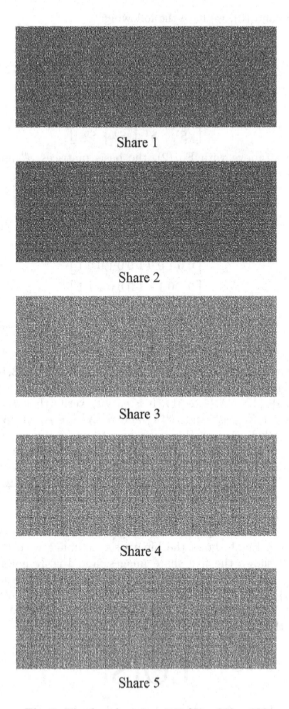

Fig. 2. The five share images of size 800×300

Stacking result of Shares 1234

Stacking result of Shares 1235

Stacking result of Shares 1245

Stacking result of Shares 12345

Fig. 3. All qualified decoded images of size 800×300

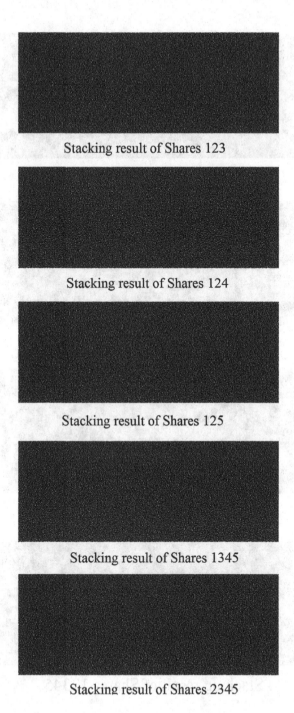

Fig. 4. All maximal forbidden decoded images of size 800×300

3.2   Analysis of the Proposed VCS with t Essential Parties

Theorem 4. *Given a Γ-VCS with pixel expansion m and relative contrast α and basis matrices $\hat{S}^0$ and $\hat{S}^1$, and the optimal (t, t)-VCS [1] with basis matrices M^0 and M^1, the two basis matrices S^0 and S^1 defined by Eq. 1 constitute a solution of Γ^*-VCS with pixel expansion $2^t m$ and relative contrast $\frac{\alpha}{2^t}$.*

Proof: First we prove the security property of the constructed Γ^*-VCS. For any forbidden set $X \in F^*$, either *case 1: $X \in \{Z \cup B : Z \subseteq P_t \wedge B \subsetneq \{1, 2, 3, \cdots, t\}\}$* or *case 2: $X \in \{A \cup \{1, 2, 3, \cdots, t\} : A \in F\}$* holds.

Case 1: Since $T = \{1, 2, 3, \cdots, t\} \not\subseteq X$, from the security property of the optimal (t, t)-VCS, we know that there exists a permutation σ on $\{1, 2, \ldots, 2^{t-1}\}$ such that $M^1[B][j] = M^0[B][\sigma(j)]$ holds for any $j \in \{1, 2, \ldots, 2^{t-1}\}$, where $B = X \cap T$. Apply permutation σ to S^0 and S^1 in the following way, where S_σ^0 represents the permuted S^0 and S_σ^1 represents the permuted S^1.

$$S_\sigma^0 = \begin{bmatrix} mM^0[T][\sigma(1)] \ldots mM^0[T][\sigma(2^{t-1})] \, mM^1[T][1] \ldots mM^1[T][2^{t-1}] \\ \hat{S}^0 \qquad \cdots \qquad \hat{S}^0 \qquad \hat{S}^1 \qquad \cdots \qquad \hat{S}^1 \end{bmatrix}$$

$$S_\sigma^1 = \begin{bmatrix} mM^0[T][\sigma(1)] \ldots mM^0[T][\sigma(2^{t-1})] \, mM^1[T][1] \ldots mM^1[T][2^{t-1}] \\ \hat{S}^1 \qquad \cdots \qquad \hat{S}^1 \qquad \hat{S}^0 \qquad \cdots \qquad \hat{S}^0 \end{bmatrix}$$

In such a case, the left half part of $S_\sigma^0[B]$ (resp.$S_\sigma^1[B]$) is the same as the right half part of $S_\sigma^0[B]$ (resp.$S_\sigma^1[B]$). Therefore, $S_\sigma^0[X]$ and $S_\sigma^1[X]$ are equal up a column permutation, which leads to the satisfaction of the security property in this case.

Case 2: Since $A = X/\{1, 2, 3, \cdots, t\} \in F$, from the security property of the given (Γ, m)-VCS, we know that there exists a permutation σ on $\{1, 2, \ldots, m\}$ such that $\hat{S}^1[A][j] = \hat{S}^0[A][\sigma(j)]$. Apply permutation σ on the first m columns of S^0, and then the second m columns of S^0, $\cdots$, until the 2^{t-1}th m columns of S^0. Apply permutation σ on the $(2^{t-1}+1)$th m columns of S^1, and then the $(2^{t-1}+2)$th m columns of S^1, $\cdots$, until the 2^tth m columns of S^1. Since the above permutations to S^0 and S^1 do not change their first t rows, the permuted S^0 and the permuted S^1 are the same constrained to rows X, which leads to the satisfaction of the security property in this case.

Since the pixel expansion of the optimal (t, t)-VCS is 2^{t-1}, the pixel expansion of the constructed Γ^*-VCS is $m \times 2^{t-1} \times 2 = 2^t m$.

Now, we turn to prove the contrast property of the constructed Γ^*-VCS. For any qualified set $X \in Q^*$, $X = \{1, 2, 3, \cdots, t\} \cup H$, where $H = X/\{1, 2, 3, \cdots, t\} \in Q$. From the contrast property of the given Γ-VCS, we know that $w(\hat{S}_H^1) - w(\hat{S}_H^0) \geq \alpha m$.

$$w(S_X^1) - w(S_X^0) = w(\hat{S}_H^1) + (2^t - 1)m - (w(\hat{S}_H^0) + (2^t - 1)m)$$
$$= w(\hat{S}_H^1) - w(\hat{S}_H^0) \geq \alpha m$$
$$= (\frac{\alpha}{2^t})2^t m$$

Hence the relative contrast of the constructed Γ^*-VCS is $\frac{\alpha}{2^t}$. $\square$

Remark: Theorem 2.3 in [19] can be derived from Theorem 4 by setting $t = 1$. Corollaries 1 and 2 follow immediately from Theorem 4.

Corollary 1. *Let k, n and t be positive integers satisfying $t < k$ and $2 \leq k - t \leq n - t$. Given a $(k - t, n - t)$-VCS with pixel expansion m and relative contrast α, there exists a (k, n, t)-VCS with pixel expansion $2^t m$ and relative contrast $\frac{\alpha}{2^t}$.*

Corollary 2. *Let k, n and t be positive integers satisfying $t < k$ and $2 \leq k - t \leq n - t$. Let m and α be the optimal pixel expansion and optimal relative contrast of $(k - t, n - t)$-VCS. Let m^* and α^* be the optimal pixel expansion and optimal relative contrast of (k, n, t)-VCS. Then $m^* \leq 2^t m$ and $\alpha^* \geq \frac{\alpha}{2^t}$ hold.*

Recall the definition of Γ and Γ^* given in the beginning of Sect. 3. In the following, we give an upper bound on the *optimal relative contrast* α^* and a lower bound on the *optimal pixel expansion* m^* of the constructed Γ^*-VCS.

Theorem 5. *Let m and α be the optimal pixel expansion and optimal relative contrast of Γ-VCS. Let m^* and α^* be the optimal pixel expansion and optimal relative contrast of Γ^*-VCS. Then $m^* > m$ and $\alpha^* < \alpha$ always hold.*

Proof: Let S^0 and S^1 be the basis matrices of a Γ^*-VCS, with optimal pixel expansion m^*. Let $\hat{S}^0$ and $\hat{S}^1$ denote the $n - t$ by m^* matrix obtained from S^0 and S^1, where

$$
\hat{S}^0 = \begin{bmatrix} S^0_{\{\{t+1\}\cup T\}} \\ S^0_{\{\{t+2\}\cup T\}} \\ \vdots \\ S^0_{\{\{t+n-t\}\cup T\}} \end{bmatrix} \quad \text{and} \quad \hat{S}^1 = \begin{bmatrix} S^1_{\{\{t+1\}\cup T\}} \\ S^1_{\{\{t+2\}\cup T\}} \\ \vdots \\ S^1_{\{\{t+n-t\}\cup T\}} \end{bmatrix}
$$

where $T = \{1, 2, 3, \cdots, t\}$ and $S^0_{\{\{t+1\}\cup T\}}$ represents the *OR* result of rows $\{\{t+1\} \cup T\}$ of S^0.

We claim that $S^0[T]$ and $S^1[T]$ are equal up to some column permutation, otherwise the secret can be reconstructed by only considering the shares hold by all essential parties. Therefore, row vector S^0_T and S^1_T contain the same number of 1s, say d. In such a case, $\hat{S}^0$ and $\hat{S}^1$ both contain at least d all 1 columns. By deleting d all 1 columns from each of $\hat{S}^0$ and $\hat{S}^1$, we obtain two basis matrices for Γ-VCS with pixel expansion $m = m^* - d$, referring to Theorem 2, which is always smaller than m^*.

Now, let S^0 and S^1 be the basis matrices of a Γ^*-VCS, with optimal relative contrast α^* and pixel expansion m^o. Consider basis matrices $\bar{S}^0$ and $\bar{S}^1$ constructed similarly as above. For any $X \in Q$, we have $H = X \cup \{1, 2, 3, \cdots, t\} \in Q^*$, and thus

$$w(S_X^{\bar{1}}) - w(S_X^{\bar{0}}) = w(S_H^1) - w(S_H^0)$$
$$\geq \alpha^* m^o$$

The constructed Γ-VCS has relative contrast $\alpha = \frac{\alpha^* m^o}{m^o - d}$, which is always larger than α^*. $\qquad\square$

Remark: The proof of Theorem 2.7 in [19] assumes the existence of a Γ^*-VCS with *optimal pixel expansion* m^* and *optimal relative contrast* α^*. However, in general, the above two optimal parameters cannot be achieved simultaneously by the same VCS [20]. The above flaws can be easily made up by assuming the existence of a Γ^*-VCS with *optimal pixel expansion* m^* and the existence of another Γ^*-VCS with *optimal relative contrast* α^*, and then proving the two conclusions separately.

To conclude this section, we compare the basic parameters of two (k, n, t)-VCSs constructed by the proposed scheme and cumulative array method [6].

- From Sect. 2.2.2, we know that the (k, n, t)-VCS constructed by cumulative array method has pixel expansion $m = 2^{\binom{n-t}{k-t-1}+t-1}$ and relative contrast $\alpha = 2^{-\binom{n-t}{k-t-1}-t+1}$.
- From Theorem 3, we know that there exists a $(k-t, n-t)$-VCS with pixel expansion $m \leq (\binom{n-t}{k-t} + 1)2^{k-t-2}$ and relative contrast $\alpha \geq \frac{2^{-k+t+2}}{\binom{n-t}{k-t}+1}$. Combining this fact with Theorem 4, we know that the (k, n, t)-VCS constructed by the proposed scheme has pixel expansion $\leq (\binom{n-t}{k-t} + 1)2^{k-2}$ and relative contrast $\geq \frac{2^{-k+2}}{\binom{n-t}{k-t}+1}$.

For $n \geq 5$ and $2 \leq k - t < n - t$, the exponential part $\binom{n-t}{k-t-1} + t - 1$ is asymptotically much larger than the exponential part $k - 2$. Hence the proposed scheme is asymptotically much better than cumulative array method for (k, n, t) access structure.

4 Conclusion

In this paper, we propose a (k, n)-VCS with t essential parties, which includes Arumugam et al.'s scheme [19] as a special case with $t = 1$. Similar to [19], we then explore some bounds on the *optimal pixel expansion* and *optimal relative contrast* of the proposed (k, n, t)-VCS. At last, we show that for (k, n, t) access structure, the proposed scheme surpasses cumulative array method significantly in both parameters.

Acknowledgments. This work was supported by 863 Program grant No. Y370071102, the "Strategic Priority Research Program" of the Chinese Academy of Sciences grant No. XDA06010701, the IIE's Projects grant No. Y3Z001B102 and NSFC grant No. 61303256.

References

1. Naor, M., Shamir, A.: Visual cryptography. In: De Santis, A. (ed.) EUROCRYPT 1994. LNCS, vol. 950, pp. 1–12. Springer, Heidelberg (1995)
2. Droste, S.: New results on visual cryptography. In: Koblitz, N. (ed.) CRYPTO 1996. LNCS, vol. 1109, pp. 401–415. Springer, Heidelberg (1996)
3. Verheul, E., Tilborg, H.V.: Constructions and properties of k out of n visual secret sharing schemes. Des. Codes Crypt. 11(2), 179–196 (1997)
4. Eisen, P.A., Stinson, D.R.: Threshold visual cryptography schemes with specified whiteness levels of reconstructed pixels. Des. Codes Crypt. 25, 15–61 (2002)
5. Hofmeister, T., Krause, M., Simon, H.U.: Contrast-optimal k out of n secret sharing schemes in visual cryptography. Theoret. Comput. Sci. 240(2), 471–485 (2000)
6. Ateniese, G., Blundo, C., De Santis, A., Stinson, D.R.: Visual cryptography for general access structures. Inf. Comput. 129, 86–106 (1996)
7. Tzeng, W.G., Hu, C.M.: A new approach for visual cryptography. Des. Codes Crypt. 27, 207–227 (2002)
8. Blundo, C., Cimato, S., De Santis, A.: Visual cryptography schemes with optimal pixel expansion. Theoret. Comput. Sci. 369, 169–182 (2006)
9. Liu, F., Wu, C.K., Lin, X.J.: The alignment problem of visual cryptography schemes. Des. Codes Crypt. 50, 215–227 (2009)
10. Wang, D.S., Dong, L., Li, X.B.: Towards shift tolerant visual secret sharing schemes. IEEE Trans. Inf. Forensics Secur. 6(2), 323–337 (2011)
11. Horng, G.B., Chen, T.H., Tsai, D.S.: Cheating in visual cryptography. Des. Codes Crypt. 38, 219–236 (2006)
12. Hu, C.M., Tzeng, W.G.: Cheating prevention in visual cryptography. IEEE Trans. Image Process. 16(1), 36–45 (2007)
13. Chen, Y.C., Horng, G., Tsai, D.S.: Comment on "cheating prevention in visual cryptography". IEEE Trans. Image Process. 21(7), 3319–3323 (2012)
14. Wang, R.Z.: Region incrementing visual cryptography. IEEE Signal Process. Lett. 16(8), 659–662 (2009)
15. Yang, C.N., Shih, H.W., Wu, C.C., Harn, L.: k out of n region incrementing scheme in visual cryptography. IEEE Trans. Circuits Syst. Video Technol. 22(6), 779–810 (2012)
16. Shyu, S.J.: Efficient construction for region incrementing visual cryptography. IEEE Trans. Circuits Syst. Video Technol. 22(5), 769–777 (2012)
17. Guo, T., Liu, F., Wu, C.K.: Threshold visual secret sharing by random grids with improved contrast. J. Syst. Softw. 86, 2094–2109 (2013)
18. Guo, T., Liu, F., Wu, C.K.: k out of k extended visual cryptography scheme by random grids. Sig. Process 94, 90–101 (2014)
19. Arumugam, S., Lakshmanan, R., Nagar, A.K.: On (k, n)*-visual cryptography scheme. Des. Codes Crypt. (2012). doi:10.1007/s10623-012-9722-2
20. Blundo, C., De Santis, A., Stinson, D.R.: On the contrast in visual cryptography schemes. J. Crypt. 12(4), 261–289 (1999)
21. Adhikari, A., Dutta, T.K., Roy, B.: A new black and white visual cryptographic scheme for general access structures. In: Canteaut, A., Viswanathan, K. (eds.) INDOCRYPT 2004. LNCS, vol. 3348, pp. 399–413. Springer, Heidelberg (2004)

New Lower Bounds for Privacy
in Communication Protocols

Iordanis Kerenidis[1,2], Mathieu Laurière[3(✉)], and David Xiao[1]

[1] CNRS, LIAFA, Université Paris 7, Paris, France
{jkeren,dxiao}@liafa.univ-paris-diderot.fr
[2] CQT, NUS Singapore, Singapore, Singapore
[3] LIAFA, Université Paris 7, Paris, France
lauriere@liafa.univ-paris-diderot.fr

Abstract. Communication complexity is a central model of computation introduced by Yao [22], where two players, Alice and Bob, receive inputs x and y respectively and want to compute $f(x, y)$ for some fixed function f with the least amount of communication. Recently people have revisited the question of the privacy of such protocols: is it possible for Alice and Bob to compute $f(x, y)$ without revealing too much information about their inputs? There are two types of privacy for communication protocols that have been proposed: first, an information theoretic definition ([9,15]), which for Boolean functions is equivalent to the notion of information cost introduced by [12] and that has since found many important applications; second, a combinatorial definition introduced by [13] and further developed by [1].

We provide new results for both notions of privacy, as well as the relation between them. Our new lower bound techniques both for the combinatorial and the information-theoretic definitions enable us to give tight bounds for the privacy of several functions, including Equality, Disjointness, Inner Product, Greater Than. In the process we also prove tight bounds (up to 1 or 2 additive bits) for the external information complexity of these functions.

We also extend the definitions of privacy to bounded-error randomized protocols and provide a relation between the two notions and the communication complexity. Again, we are able to prove tight bounds for the above-mentioned functions as well as the Vector in Subspace and Gap Hamming Distance problems.

Keywords: Communication complexity · Information complexity · Lower bound · Privacy

1 Introduction

Communication complexity is a central model of computation, first defined by Yao, [22], that has found applications in many areas of theoretical computer

C. Padró (Ed.): ICITS 2013, LNCS 8317, pp. 69–89, 2014.
DOI: 10.1007/978-3-319-04268-8_5, © Springer International Publishing Switzerland 2014

science. In the *2-party communication complexity setting*, we consider two players, Alice and Bob with unlimited computational power. Each of them receives an input, say $x \in \mathcal{X}$ for Alice and $y \in \mathcal{Y}$ for Bob, and their goal is to compute $f(x, y) \in \mathcal{Z}$ for some fixed function f with the minimum amount of communication.

Imagine now that Alice and Bob still want to collaboratively compute $f(x, y)$, while retaining privacy of their input. The loss of privacy measures how much information about (x, y) is leaked to an eavesdropper who has only access to the transcript (*external* privacy), or how much information about one party's input is leaked through the transcript to the other pary (*internal* privacy). A perfectly private protocol will reveal no information about x and y, other than what can be inferred from the value of $f(x, y)$.

For example, if Alice and Bob both want to output the minimum of $x, y \in \{0, 1\}^n$ and the identity of the person holding it, then the deterministic communication protocol with optimal communication is the trivial protocol of complexity $2n$. In fact one can show that any deterministic protocol that has optimal communication is not private at all against an eavesdropper since basically both players have to send the input to the other one. However a perfectly private deterministic protocol exists, alas with much worse communication complexity: the two parties initiate a counter $i = 0$ and in each round $i = 0$ to $2^n - 1$, Alice announces "Yes" if $x = i$, otherwise "No"; Bob announces "Yes" if $y = i$, otherwise "No". If neither party says "Yes" then they increment i, otherwise the protocol ends when someone says "Yes". It is clear that from the transcript, one only learns what can be inferred from the value of the function and nothing more.

In order to quantify privacy, Bar-Yehuda *et al.* [9] provided a definition of *internal privacy* of a function f according to an input distribution μ, a variation of which has been subsequently referred to as *internal information cost* ($\mathrm{IC}_\mu^{int}(f)$). At a high level, it measures the amount of information Alice learns about Bob's input from the transcript and vice versa. A second type of information cost, called *external information cost* ($\mathrm{IC}_\mu^{ext}(f)$) was defined in [12] and measures the amount of information that is learned by an external observer about Alice and Bob's inputs given the messages they exchanged during the protocol. The notion of internal and external information cost has recently found many important applications in communication complexity, including better communication lower bounds for important functions, direct sum theorems and new compression schemes [2, 3, 5–8, 12, 20].

Klauck [15] also defined an information theoretic notion of privacy, which we denote here by $\mathrm{PRIV}_\mu^{int}(f)$, which is closely related to the internal information cost (the only difference being that we subtract the information that the function reveals about the inputs, which the players are allowed to learn). In fact, the two notions are basically equivalent for boolean functions and all our results about PRIV can be translated to results about information cost. These definitions have the advantage of being easily related to other tools in information theory, but are not easily seen in a combinatorial way.

Feigenbaum *et al.* [13] gave a combinatorial definition of privacy for the uniform distribution over inputs that was extended by Ada *et al.* [1] to any distribution μ, called *average case objective privacy-approximation ratio*, that we will refer to simply as *external privacy-approximation ratio* (we only study this average-case notion, and not a related worst-case notion also defined in that work), and we denote this by $\mathrm{PAR}_\mu^{ext}(f, P)$. It is equal to the expected value over the inputs (x, y) drawn from some distribution μ of the following ratio: the number of inputs that are mapped to the same value by f (that are indistinguishable from (x, y) by looking only at the function's output) over the number of inputs giving rise to the same transcript as the one of (x, y) (that are indistinguishable of (x, y) by looking only at the protocol's transcript). They also defined *(average) subjective (or internal) privacy-approximation ratio* (here again we will omit "average") which we denote $\mathrm{PAR}_\mu^{int}(f, P)$, which captures how much more one player learns about the input of the other one by the transcript than by the value of the function, and equals the ratio of the number of Alice's possible inputs x that are indistinguishable by looking only at Bob's input y and the output of the function, over the number of x's that are instiguishable by looking at y and the full transcript plus the symmetric ratio for Bob. Last, they computed lower bounds for the privacy-approximation ratio of several functions, however restricting themselves to the case of uniformly distributed inputs.

More recently, Ada *et al.* in [1] have modified the definition of privacy-approximation ratio, which we denote as $\mathrm{PAR}_\mu^{ext}(f)$ and $\mathrm{PAR}_\mu^{int}(f)$, so that it measures the size of subsets of $\mathcal{X} \times \mathcal{Y}$ not just by counting the number of elements, but relative to the inputs' distribution μ. They showed that the logarithm of this new definition of internal PAR can be lower bounded by the zero-error internal information cost (which nevertheless can be arbitrarily smaller for certain functions with large output range). They also proved a tradeoff between privacy and communication complexity for a specific function (**Vickrey-auction**) and the uniform distribution of inputs. We note that in [13] and [1] only deterministic protocols were considered. Moreover, the relation between PRIV and PAR was not very well understood.

Our Results: We prove new relationships between PRIV, PAR and communication complexity, as well as providing new lower bound techniques for the two notions of privacy, PRIV and PAR, both external and internal, enabling us to give tight bounds for the privacy of various functions in the case of deterministic protocols. We also extend the definitions of PRIV and PAR to bounded-error randomized protocols, and derive linear lower bounds for various functions.

New lower bounds for external PAR *of deterministic protocols for boolean functions:* For boolean functions we give new lower bounds techniques, relating it to the rank of the function and the deterministic complexity.

Theorem 1. *For boolean f, for any distribution μ with full support,* $\mathrm{PAR}_\mu^{ext}(f) \geq \mathrm{rank}(\mathcal{M}_f) - 1$.

Theorem 2. *For boolean f, for any distribution μ with full support,* $\log \mathrm{PAR}_\mu^{ext}(f) \geq \sqrt{\mathbf{D}(f)}$.

Observe that this implies that $\log \mathrm{PAR}_\mu^{ext}(f)$ is in fact *polynomially* related to the deterministic communication complexity. Notably, it therefore holds that the *only* boolean functions with low privacy loss (as measured using PAR^{ext}) are functions that have low communication complexity (this is not the case with non-boolean functions as was already observed by [13]).

New lower bounds for external PAR *of deterministic protocols for non-boolean functions:* For simplicity we restrict ourselves to full support distibutions μ, but it is possible to extend the results to general distributions by considering summations over only the rectangles whose intersection with μ's support is not empty. First, we present a general lower bound technique for $\mathrm{PAR}_\mu^{ext}(f)$ via linear programming. We relate it to two other well known lower bound techniques for communication complexity (see [14]): the *rectangle* bound ($\mathrm{rec}(f)$) and the *partition* bound ($\mathrm{prt}(f)$). This linear program, whose optimal value is denoted by $\widetilde{\mathrm{PAR}}_\mu(f)$, can be written as a weighted sum of rectangle bounds $\mathrm{rec}^z(f)$, where the weight is equal to the weight of the inputs (x, y) according to μ that are mapped to z by f. It is, hence, easy to compute for many functions:

Theorem 3. *For all f, for any distribution μ with full support,* $\mathrm{PAR}_\mu^{ext}(f) \geq \widetilde{\mathrm{PAR}}_\mu(f)$.

Theorem 4. *For all f, for any distribution μ with full support,* $\widetilde{\mathrm{PAR}}_\mu(f) \geq \sum_{z \in \mathcal{Z}} \left| f^{-1}(z) \right|_\mu \cdot \mathrm{rec}^z(f)$.

Moreover, we bound external PAR as a weighted sum of the size of the z-fooling sets F_z of $\mathcal{M}_f$:

Theorem 5. *For all f, for any distribution μ with full support,* $\mathrm{PAR}_\mu^{ext}(f) \geq \sum_z \left| f^{-1}(z) \right|_\mu \cdot |F_z|$.

New lower bound techniques for external IC *and* PRIV: We prove a new lower bound on the external zero-error information cost which, using the equivalence between IC and PRIV given in Theorem 12, will in turn give new lower bounds on $\mathrm{PRIV}_\mu^{ext}(f)$.

Theorem 6. *Fix a function f. Suppose there exists $\delta > 0$ and a distribution μ over the inputs of f, such that for all monochromatic rectangles R of f, $\mu(R) \leq \delta$. Then it holds for every protocol P that computes f without error on any input that $\mathrm{IC}_\mu^{ext}(P) \geq \log(1/\delta)$.*

We remark that our theorem allows us to prove exact bounds for zero-error IC up to an *additive* constant term (with a small constant, between 1 and 2).

Theorem 7. *For each of $f = \mathrm{EQ}, \mathrm{GT}, \mathrm{DISJ}$, there exists μ such that $\mathrm{IC}_\mu^{ext}(f) \geq n$. Also, there exists μ such that $\mathrm{IC}_\mu^{ext}(\mathrm{IP}) \geq n - 1 - o(1)$.*

These are much sharper than typical lower bounds on IC, which work in the bounded-error case and incur multiplicative constants [6,7,10,16]. The only other such sharp lower bounds we are aware of are due to Braverman *et al.* [4] who study the AND and DISJ functions. However they prove sharp bounds for the internal IC of DISJ, not for the external IC as we study here.

Our bound proves an *optimal* lower bound on the zero-error information cost of certain functions (i.e. without any additive constant loss). For the one bit AND, we show that there exists μ with $IC_\mu^{ext}(AND) \geq \log_2 3$. This matches the bound of [4] (they also proved optimality via different techniques).

Privacy for bounded-error randomized protocols: We define for the first time PAR and PRIV for bounded-error protocols. Such protocols can be much more efficient than deterministic ones and it is important to see whether they remain private or not. These definitions capture again how much more information is leaked by the protocol than by the output of the function, where now we consider randomized protocols that compute the function with some bounded error. We show that for any protocol, PRIV is a lower bound on PAR, both for the external and internal notions.

Theorem 8. $\forall \mu, f, \epsilon,$ $PRIV_{\mu,\epsilon}^{ext}(f) \leq \log PAR_{\mu,\epsilon}^{ext}(f)$ and $PRIV_{\mu,\epsilon}^{int}(f) \leq 2 \log PAR_{\mu,\epsilon}^{int}(f) - 2$.

Internal PRIV is lower bounded by internal IC, which was shown in [16] to subsume almost all known lower bounds for communication complexity, i.e. smooth rectangle, γ_2-norm, discrepancy, etc. Hence,

Corollary 1 (Informal). *In the bounded error setting, for all boolean f whose internal information complexity equals communication complexity, all notions of privacy loss (PRIV, PAR, external, internal) are equivalent to each other and to the communication complexity.*

Interestingly, PAR sits between information and communication complexity, and it is an important open question whether these two notions are equal for all functions (and hence make PAR equal to them).

Applications: We exhibit the power of these new lower bound techniques for PAR and PRIV by proving optimal lower bounds on most of the examples of functions left open in [13] and more: Equality, Disjointness, Inner Product, Greater Than (Millionaire's problem).

Table 1. Lower bounds for specific functions, zero error.

Problem	PAR_μ^{ext}		$PRIV_\mu^{ext}$
	[13] (for uniform μ)	**Our contribution** (for μ with full support)	(for some μ)
Equality	-	2^n	$n-1$
Disjointness	$\left(\frac{3}{2}\right)^n$	$2^n - 1$	$n-1$
Inner Product	-	$2^n - 1$	$n-2-o(1)$
Greater Than	$2^n + \frac{1}{2^{n+1}} - \frac{1}{2}$	$2^n - 1$	$n-1$

Comparison between the two notions of privacy: For the case of bounded-error protocols, the two notions of privacy seem to be practically equal for most functions. However, for the zero-error case, they can diverge for certain functions. In

Table 2. Lower bounds for specific functions, with bounded error

	$\mathbf{PRIV}_{\mu,\epsilon}^{\text{int}}, \mathbf{PRIV}_{\mu,\epsilon}^{\text{ext}}$ (for some μ)	$\mathbf{PAR}_{\mu,\epsilon}^{\text{int}}, \mathbf{PAR}_{\mu,\epsilon}^{\text{ext}}$ (for some μ)
Equality	$\Theta(1)$	$\Theta(1)$
Disjointness	$\Theta(n)$	$2^{\Theta(n)}$
Inner Product	$\Theta(n)$	$2^{\Theta(n)}$
Greater Than	$\Theta(\log n)$	$2^{\Theta(\log n)}$

order to understand the differences between the notions, we study their robustness when we change slightly the input distribution and we show that the information theoretic notion of privacy is more robust to such changes. Moreover, we show that while PRIV is always less than the expected communication complexity of the protocol, the same is not true for PAR. We also discuss an error in the appendix of [13] where they claim that PRIV is not as robust as PAR.

2   Preliminaries

We consider three non empty sets $\mathcal{X}, \mathcal{Y}, \mathcal{Z}$ and a function $f : \mathcal{X} \times \mathcal{Y} \to \mathcal{Z}$. μ denotes a distribution over $\mathcal{X} \times \mathcal{Y}$, and for any set $E \subseteq \mathcal{X} \times \mathcal{Y}, |E|_\mu :=$ $\sum_{(x,y)\in E} \mu(x,y)$. $\mathcal{M}_f$ is the matrix of f: $\mathcal{M}_f[x,y] := f(x,y)$. A *rectangle* of $\mathcal{X} \times \mathcal{Y}$ is a product set $A \times B$ where $A \subseteq \mathcal{X}, B \subseteq \mathcal{Y}$.

We let P denote a two-party communication protocol. Protocols may use both public and private random coins. We let r denote the ensemble of all random coins (public and private) a protocol may use; we let R denote a random variable of all these coins, and R_{pub} denote just the public coins. Given a (possibly randomized) protocol P, for any input $(x,y) \in \mathcal{X} \times \mathcal{Y}$ and random coins r, $P(x,y,r)$ is the value output by Alice and Bob upon running the protocol, and $T_P(x,y,r)$ is the transcript, comprising all messages and public coins. We omit r in the previous if P is deterministic. Let $\mathbf{CC}(P)$ be the maximum number of bits communicated by P over all choices of inputs and random coins. Let $\mathbf{D}(f) = \min_P \mathbf{CC}(P)$ where P ranges over all *deterministic* protocols computing f. Let $\mathbf{R}^\epsilon(f) = \min_P \mathbf{CC}(P)$ where P ranges over all randomized protocols computing f with error at most ϵ on each input.

In the following paragraph we let P be a *deterministic* protocol that perfectly computes a function f. For any input $(x,y) \in \mathcal{X} \times \mathcal{Y}$, the monochromatic f-region of (x,y) is defined as $\mathrm{D}_{x,y}^f := f^{-1}(f(x,y))$, and is equal to the monochromatic P-region $\mathrm{D}_{x,y}^P$ of (x,y). The monochromatic P-rectangle of (x,y) is defined as $\mathrm{D}_{x,y}^{T_P} := T_P^{-1}(T_P(x,y))$ (the fact that this is a rectangle and not an arbitrary subset is a well-known consequence of P being a communication protocol). For any output $z \in \mathcal{Z}$, the monochromatic f-region of z is: $f^{-1}(z) := f^{-1}(\{z\})$, which is equal to the monochromatic P-region of z, $P^{-1}(z)$. Let $\mathcal{R}_z^P$ be the set of P-rectangles covering $P^{-1}(z)$, that is: $\mathcal{R}_z^P := \{\mathrm{D}_{x,y}^{T_P} | (x,y) : P(x,y) = z\}$. Let $\mathcal{R}^P = \cup_{z \in \mathcal{Z}} \mathcal{R}_z^P = \{\mathrm{D}_{x,y}^{T_P} | (x,y) \in \mathcal{X} \times \mathcal{Y}\}$ be the set of all P-rectangles. For each

$z \in \mathcal{Z}$, $\text{cut}_P(f^{-1}(z))$ is the number of P-rectangles in $f^{-1}(z)$; $\mathcal{R}(\mathcal{X} \times \mathcal{Y})$ is the set of all rectangles in $\mathcal{X} \times \mathcal{Y}$.

For three random variables A, B, C the conditional mutual information is defined as $\mathbf{I}(A; B|C) := \mathbf{H}(A|C) - \mathbf{H}(A|BC)$, where $\mathbf{H}$ denotes Shannon entropy: if X and Y are two random variables $\mathbf{H}(X) = \sum_x \mathbb{P}\{X = x\} \log(1/\mathbb{P}\{X = x\})$ and $\mathbf{H}(X|Y) = \mathbb{E}[-\log(\mathbb{P}(X|Y))]$. We recall some simple facts about information and entropy (more details about information theory can be found in the textbook of Cover and Thomas [11].) For any random variables X, Y, Z, W, the Chain Rule says that $\mathbf{H}(X, Y) = \mathbf{H}(X) + \mathbf{H}(Y|X)$ and $\mathbf{I}(X, Z; Y) = \mathbf{I}(X; Y) + \mathbf{I}(Z; Y|X)$. Another easy fact (see for example [1]) is that:

$$|\mathbf{I}(X; Y|W) - \mathbf{I}(X; Y|W, Z)| \leq \mathbf{H}(Z) \tag{1}$$

We let D_{KL} denote the KL-divergence, $\mathsf{D}_{\mathsf{KL}}(X \parallel Y) = \mathbb{E}_{x \sim X} \log \frac{\Pr[X=x]}{\Pr[Y=x]}$. It is easy to see that $I(X; Y) = \mathsf{D}_{\mathsf{KL}}(XY \parallel X'Y)$ where X' is an independent copy of X. We will also use the following data processing inequality for KL-divergence (we include a proof in the appendix for the sake of completeness):

Lemma 1. *For any X, Y and any deterministic function L, the following holds:*

$$\mathsf{D}_{\mathsf{KL}}(X \parallel Y) \geq \mathsf{D}_{\mathsf{KL}}(L(X) \parallel L(Y)) \tag{2}$$

2.1 Definitions of Privacy

In the following, (X, Y) denotes a pair of random variables, distributed according to μ, and P denotes a (possibly randomized) protocol.

Information Cost: We define the external and internal information cost, notions that have recently found many applications in communication complexity [2,6,7,12]. The external information cost measures the amount of information that is learned from someone who looks at the messages exchanged between Alice and Bob during the protocol about their inputs. The internal information cost measures the amount of information that Alice learns about Bob's input and vice versa.

Definition 1. *The external information cost of P is defined as $\mathrm{IC}_\mu^{ext}(P) := \mathbf{I}(X, Y; T_P(X, Y, R))$. The external information cost of f is $\mathrm{IC}_{\mu,\epsilon}^{ext}(f) := \inf_P \mathrm{IC}_\mu^{ext}(P)$ where the minimum is over all protocols P computing f with distributional error ϵ.*

Definition 2. *We define the internal information cost of P as $\mathrm{IC}_\mu^{int}(P) := \mathbf{I}(X; T_P(X, Y, R)|Y) + \mathbf{I}(Y; T_P(X, Y, R)|X)$. The internal information cost of f is $\mathrm{IC}_{\mu,\epsilon}^{int}(f) := \inf_P \mathrm{IC}_\mu^{int}(P)$ where the minimum is over all protocols P computing f with distributional error ϵ.*

Information-theoretic privacy: In [9], the definition of privacy ($\mathcal{I}_{c-i}^{det}$ in their notations) is basically the same as what we now call $\mathrm{IC}_\mu^{int}(P)$ (they used the max instead of the sum of the two terms). A related notion of privacy has been defined by Klauck in [15]. We give a distribution-dependent version of his definition. At a high level, it quantifies how much *more* an observer learns about the inputs from the transcript than from the value of the function. We also define an internal version of the definition. We assume that the output of a randomized protocol depends only on the transcript (i.e. $P(x, y, r)$ is a deterministic function of $T(x, y, r)$).

Definition 3. *The external privacy of P is defined as* $\mathrm{PRIV}_\mu^{ext}(f, P) := \mathbf{I}(X, Y; T_P(X, Y, R)) - \mathbf{I}(X, Y; f(X, Y))$. *For $\epsilon \geq 0$, the external ϵ-error privacy of f is defined as the following, where the infimum is taken over all protocols P computing f with distributional error at most ϵ:* $\mathrm{PRIV}_{\mu,\epsilon}^{ext}(f) := \inf_P \mathrm{PRIV}_\mu^{ext}(f, P)$. *We let* $\mathrm{PRIV}_\mu^{ext}(f) := \mathrm{PRIV}_{\mu,0}^{ext}(f)$.

Definition 4. *The internal privacy of P is defined as* $\mathrm{PRIV}_\mu^{int}(f, P) := \mathbf{I}(X; T_P(X, Y, R)|Y) - \mathbf{I}(X; f(X, Y)|Y) + \mathbf{I}(Y; T_P(X, Y, R)|X) - \mathbf{I}(Y; f(X, Y)|X)$. *For $\epsilon \geq 0$, the internal ϵ-error privacy of f is defined as the following, where the infimum is taken over all protocols P computing f with distributional error at most ϵ:* $\mathrm{PRIV}_{\mu,\epsilon}^{int}(f) := \inf_P \mathrm{PRIV}_\mu^{int}(f, P)$. *We let* $\mathrm{PRIV}_\mu^{int}(f) := \mathrm{PRIV}_{\mu,0}^{int}(f)$.

It is easy to see that our definition is equivalent to the one in [15] for deterministic or zero-error protocols.

Combinatorial privacy PAR: We present here the definition of PAR for *deterministic* protocols given by [1], which modified the original definition in [13] in order to measure the size of regions relative to the inputs' distribution.

Definition 5. *The external privacy-approximation ratio of a deterministic protocol P for f is defined as:* $\mathrm{PAR}_\mu^{ext}(f, P) := \mathbb{E}_{(x,y)\sim\mu}\left[\frac{\left|\mathrm{D}_{x,y}^f\right|_\mu}{\left|\mathrm{D}_{x,y}^{T_P}\right|_\mu}\right] = \mathbb{E}_{(x,y)\sim\mu}\left[\frac{\left|\mathrm{D}_{x,y}^P\right|_\mu}{\left|\mathrm{D}_{x,y}^{T_P}\right|_\mu}\right]$ *(where the equality holds because P has zero error). The external privacy-approximation ratio of a function f is defined as:* $\mathrm{PAR}_\mu^{ext}(f) := \inf_P \mathrm{PAR}_\mu^{ext}(f, P)$ *where the infimum is over all deterministic P computing f with zero error.*

Definition 6. *The internal privacy-approximation ratio of a deterministic protocol P for f is defined as:* $\mathrm{PAR}_\mu^{int}(f, P) := \mathbb{E}_{(x,y)\sim\mu}\left[\frac{\left|\mathrm{D}_{x,y}^f \cap \mathcal{X}\times\{y\}\right|_\mu}{\left|\mathrm{D}_{x,y}^{T_P} \cap \mathcal{X}\times\{y\}\right|_\mu}\right] + \mathbb{E}_{(x,y)\sim\mu}\left[\frac{\left|\mathrm{D}_{x,y}^f \cap \{x\}\times\mathcal{Y}\right|_\mu}{\left|\mathrm{D}_{x,y}^{T_P} \cap \{x\}\times\mathcal{Y}\right|_\mu}\right]$. *The internal privacy-approximation ratio of a function f is defined as:* $\mathrm{PAR}_\mu^{int}(f) := \inf_P \mathrm{PAR}_\mu^{int}(f, P)$ *where the infimum is over all deterministic P computing f with zero error.*

The external PAR equals a weighted sum of the number of rectangles tiling each f-monochromatic region.

Theorem 9 ([1]). *For any deterministic protocol P, we have:* $\mathrm{PAR}_\mu^{ext}(f, P) = \sum_{z \in \mathcal{Z}} \left| f^{-1}(z) \right|_\mu \cdot \mathrm{cut}_P(f^{-1}(z))$.

This result was stated in [1] but for completeness we present a proof in the appendix.

We now extend the definition to randomized protocols. In the following, the expectations are taken over inputs x, y and random coins r. A simple calculation shows that the following definition coincides with the definition of [1,13] in the case of deterministic zero-error protocols.

Definition 7. *We define:*

- *The external* PAR *of a randomized protocol P as:*

$$\mathrm{PAR}_\mu^{ext}(f, P) := \mathbb{E}_{x,y,r} \left[\frac{\mathbb{P}_{X,Y,R}((X,Y)=(x,y) \mid T_P(X,Y,R)=T_P(x,y,r))}{\mathbb{P}_{X,Y}((X,Y)=(x,y) \mid f(X,Y)=f(x,y))} \right].$$

For $\epsilon \geq 0$, the external ϵ-error PAR *of f is defined as the following, where the infimum is taken over all protocols P computing f with error at most ϵ:*
$\mathrm{PAR}_{\mu,\epsilon}^{ext}(f) := \inf_P \mathrm{PAR}_\mu^{ext}(f, P)$.

- *The internal* PAR *of a randomized protocol P as:*

$$\mathrm{PAR}_\mu^{int}(f, P) := \mathbb{E}_{x,y,r} \left[\frac{\mathbb{P}_{X,Y,R}(Y=y \mid T_P(X,Y,R)=T_P(x,y,r) \wedge X=x)}{\mathbb{P}_{X,Y}(Y=y \mid f(X,Y)=f(x,y) \wedge X=x)} \right]$$

$$+ \mathbb{E}_{x,y,r} \left[\frac{\mathbb{P}_{X,Y,R}(X=x \mid T_P(X,Y,R)=T_P(x,y,r) \wedge Y=y)}{\mathbb{P}_{X,Y}(X=x \mid f(X,Y)=f(x,y) \wedge Y=y)} \right].$$

For $\epsilon \geq 0$, the external ϵ-error PAR *of f is defined as the following, where the infimum is taken over all protocols P computing f with error at most ϵ:*
$\mathrm{PAR}_{\mu,\epsilon}^{int}(f) := \inf_P \mathrm{PAR}_\mu^{int}(f, P)$.

Remark 1. There is another way to generalize the definition of PAR for 0-error protocols. This alternative definition is deferred to the appendix.

3   Relations Between Privacy Notions and Communication

We prove a number of relations between the different notions of privacy, communication complexity and information cost both for deterministic and randomized protocols. We summarize them in Fig. 1. In the diagram, an arrow $A \leftarrow B$ indicates that $A \leq B$ (up to constants). The quantities indicate *worst-case* complexity except for Dist (see Theorem 13). Relations between:

- PAR and PRIV are given in Theorem 8 (which was proved in [1] only for the *deterministic 0-error internal* case);
- **D** (resp. $\mathbf{R}^\epsilon$) and PAR is given by Theorem 11;
- IC and PRIV are given in Theorem 12 (which was proved in [1] only for the *deterministic 0-error internal* case);
- The expected distributional complexity and IC (or PRIV) for every possible input distribution is given in Theorem 13;
- PRIV^{ext} and PRIV^{int} is given in Theorem 14;
- PAR^{ext} and PAR^{int} comes from Theorem 15 (for the deterministic case).

We start by proving that PRIV provides a lower bound for the log of PAR:

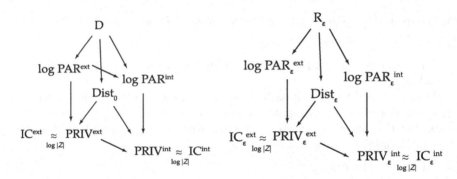

Fig. 1. Lower bounds diagrams for deterministic and bounded error cases

3.1 Relations Between the Different Notions of Privacy and Communication Complexity

We provide below the proof of Theorem 8. The other theorems are proven in the appendix.

Theorem 8 [restated]. For any input distribution μ and any (deterministic or randomized) protocol P, it holds that $\mathrm{PRIV}_\mu^{ext}(f, P) \leq \log\left(\mathrm{PAR}_\mu^{ext}(f, P)\right)$ and $\mathrm{PRIV}_\mu^{int}(f, P) \leq 2 \cdot \log\left(\mathrm{PAR}_\mu^{int}(f, P)\right) - 2$. As a consequence, $\forall \mu, f, \epsilon$ it holds that $\mathrm{PRIV}_{\mu,\epsilon}^{ext}(f) \leq \log\left(\mathrm{PAR}_{\mu,\epsilon}^{ext}(f)\right)$ and $\mathrm{PRIV}_{\mu,\epsilon}^{int}(f) \leq 2 \cdot \log\left(\mathrm{PAR}_{\mu,\epsilon}^{int}(f)\right) - 2$.

Proof. For external privacy, this is a consequence of Bayes rule, and for internal privacy, this is a consequence of Bayes rule and an argument about the worse of the two terms comprising internal PRIV and PAR. The details of this proof will appear in the full version of the article ([17]).

Remark 2. Note that when the protocol is externally (resp. internally) perfectly private, the inequality is tight since $\mathrm{PRIV}_\mu^{ext}(f, P) = 0$ and $\mathrm{PAR}_\mu^{ext}(f, P) = 1$ (resp. $\mathrm{PRIV}_\mu^{int}(f, P) = 0$ and $\mathrm{PAR}_\mu^{int}(f, P) = 2$).

3.2 Applications: Tight Bounds on PAR and PRIV for Specific Functions

For boolean functions, PRIV is essentially lower bounded by Information Cost, which subsumes almost all known lower bounds for communication complexity, i.e. smooth rectangle, γ_2-norm, discrepancy, etc [16]. Hence, Theorem 8 implies

Corollary 1 [restated]. For all f, μ, ϵ such that $\mathbf{R}^\epsilon(f) = O(\mathrm{IC}_{\mu,\epsilon}^{int}(f))$, it holds that $\log \mathrm{PAR}_{\mu,\epsilon}(f) = \mathrm{PRIV}_{\mu,\epsilon}(f) = \mathbf{R}^\epsilon(f)$ up to constant factors (for both internal and external notions).

Interestingly, the notion of PAR sits between information and communication complexity, and it is an important open question whether these two notions are equal (which would also make PAR equal to them). For the bounds in Table 2, the results follow immediately from known lower bounds on the IC of these functions: for EQ the lower bound is trivial, for DISJ one can look at IC directly [6,7], while for EQ, IP, GT one can look at their discrepancies [10]. Then, using Theorem 12 and 8 we obtain bounds on internal PAR. Note that the bounds also hold for external PRIV and PAR (since internal is always at most external, see Theorem 14). Moreover, we can also get similar lower bounds for the functions Vector in Subspace and Gap-Hamming distance by the results in [16].

4 New Lower Bound Techniques for PAR and PRIV of Deterministic Protocols

In Subsects. 4.1 and 4.2, we assume μ to be full-support for simplicity. By restricting the summations to the rectangles that intersect the support of μ, it is possible to get similar results for a general distribution.

4.1 External PAR of Boolean Functions

Let f be a *boolean* function, P a deterministic protocol for f and T its transcript. Let n_0 and n_1 be the number of P-rectangles with output 0 and 1 ($n_0 = |\mathcal{R}_0^P|, n_1 = |\mathcal{R}_1^P|$). We lower bound PAR by the communication matrix rank.

Theorem 1 [restated]. *For boolean f, for any distribution μ with full support,*

$$\mathrm{PAR}_\mu^{ext}(f) \geq \min\{\mathrm{rank}\,(\mathcal{M}_f)\,\mathrm{rank}\,(\mathcal{M}_{\mathrm{not}f})\} \geq \mathrm{rank}\,(\mathcal{M}_f) - 1.$$

The proof will appear in the full version of the article ([17]) and uses Theorem 9 in [1]. Moreover, we are going to use the following result of Yannakakis, which restated in our notation says that

Lemma 2 (Lemma 1 in [21]). *For boolean f and any deterministic protocol P, $\log \min(n_0, n_1) \geq \sqrt{\mathbf{D}(f)}$.*

In fact, Yannakakis proves only that $\log n_1 \geq \sqrt{\mathbf{D}(f)}$, but it is easy to verify that the proof is independent of the value of the monochromatic rectangles, so it similarly follows for the 0-rectangle case. Using in addition the fact that $\mathrm{PAR}_\mu^{ext}(f) \geq \min(n_0, n_1)$, we have

Theorem 2 [restated]. For boolean f, for any distribution μ with full support, $\log \mathrm{PAR}_\mu^{ext}(f) \geq \sqrt{\mathbf{D}(f)}$.

Note that Theorem 1 is not true in general for non-boolean functions (see Appendix).

4.2   External PAR for Non-boolean Functions

Definition 8. *Let* $\widetilde{\mathrm{PAR}}_\mu(f)$ *be the value of the following linear program:*

$$\min_{w_{z,R}} \sum_{z,R} w_{z,R} \cdot \left|f^{-1}(z)\right|_\mu \quad s.t. \quad \forall\,(x,y) \in f^{-1}(\mathcal{Z}): \sum_{R:R\ni(x,y)} w_{f(x,y),R} = 1 \quad (3)$$

$$\forall\,(x,y) \in f^{-1}(\mathcal{Z}): \sum_{R:R\ni(x,y)} \sum_z w_{z,R} = 1 \quad (4)$$

$$\forall\,z,\ \forall\,R: \quad w_{z,R} \geq 0. \quad (5)$$

where the z's and the R's are always taken respectively in $\mathcal{Z}$ and in $\mathcal{R}(\mathcal{X} \times \mathcal{Y})$.

Intuitively, from conditions (4) and (5), we can interpret $w_{z,R}$ as a probability distribution. In fact, $w_{z,R}$ is the probability to pick R and outputs z on (x,y). This is because condition (3) forces the probability of outputting $f(x,y)$ on (x,y) to be 1.

Theorem 3 [restated]. *For all f, for any distribution μ with full support,* $\mathrm{PAR}_\mu^{ext}(f) \geq \widetilde{\mathrm{PAR}}_\mu(f)$.

Proof. Let P be a deterministic protocol for f and T its transcript. We can show that $w_{z,R} := \mathbf{1}_{R \in \mathcal{R}_z^P}$ satisfies the conditions of Definition 8 and deduce the lower bound. The details of this proof will appear in the full version of the article ([17]).

Relation with rectangle linear program: We relate this linear program to the rectangle bound defined in [14]. For uniform output distribution, we can generalize this relation to the partition bound (see Appendix).

Definition 9. $\mathrm{rec}^z(f)$ *is the optimal value of the following linear program, where R is taken in $\mathcal{R}(\mathcal{X} \times \mathcal{Y})$:*

$$\min_{w_R} \sum_R w_R \quad s.t. \quad \forall(x,y) \in f^{-1}(z): \sum_{R:R\ni(x,y)} w_R = 1 \quad (6)$$

$$\forall(x,y) \in \mathcal{X} \times \mathcal{Y} \setminus f^{-1}(z): \sum_{R:R\ni(x,y)} w_R = 0 \quad (7)$$

$$\forall R: \quad w_R \geq 0. \quad (8)$$

Theorem 4 [restated]. *For all f, for any distribution μ with full support,* $\widetilde{\mathrm{PAR}}_\mu(f) \geq \sum_{z \in \mathcal{Z}} \left|f^{-1}(z)\right|_\mu \cdot \mathrm{rec}^z(f)$.

The proof will appear in the full version of the article ([17]).

Relation between PAR *and fooling sets:* Recall that a z-fooling set $(z \in \mathcal{Z})$ for $f : \mathcal{X} \times \mathcal{Y} \to \mathcal{Z}$ is a subset $F_z \subseteq f^{-1}(z)$ such that: $\forall\,(x,y) \in F_z$, $f(x,y) = z$ and $\forall\,(x_1,y_1),(x_2,y_2) \in F_z$, $(x_1,y_1) \neq (x_2,y_2)$ it holds that $f(x_1,y_2) \neq z$ or $f(x_2,y_1) \neq z$. By Theorem 9 in [1] and the following theorem we lower bound PAR by fooling sets.

Theorem 10 ([18]). *If F_z is a z-fooling set for f, then any covering of $f^{-1}(z)$ by monochromatic rectangles has at least $|F_z|$ rectangles.*

Theorem 5 [restated]. For all f and any set of z-fooling sets $\{F_z\}_{z \in \mathcal{Z}}$, for any distribution μ with full support, $\text{PAR}_\mu^{ext}(f) \geq \sum_{z \in \mathcal{Z}} \left| f^{-1}(z) \right|_\mu \cdot |F_z|$.

4.3   New Lower Bound Techniques for External IC

We show lower bounds on the external information complexity, which using Theorem 12 will in turn give new lower bounds on information-theoretic privacy. Our lower bounds hold for zero-error randomized protocols, which of course imply the same bounds for deterministic protocols.

Theorem 6 [restated]. Fix a function f. Suppose there exists $\delta > 0$ and a distribution μ over the inputs of f, such that for all monochromatic rectangles R of f, $\mu(R) \leq \delta$. Then it holds for every P that computes f without error on any input (i.e. even on pairs of inputs lying outside μ's support) that $\text{IC}_\mu^{ext}(P) \geq \log(1/\delta)$.

The proof will appear in the full version of the article ([17]).

Corollary 2. *For any function f with a fooling set S of size $|S| = k$, there exists a distribution μ such that for all protocols P that compute f with zero error over μ, it holds that $\text{IC}_\mu^{ext}(P) \geq \log k$.*

The proof of this corollary will appear in the full version of the article ([17]). Note that Theorem 6 can be used to prove an optimal lower bound on the zero-error information complexity of certain functions. For example, for one bit AND, the hard distribution μ is uniform over $(0, 1)$, $(1, 0)$, $(1, 1)$, and our theorem implies that $\text{IC}_\mu^{ext}(P) \geq \log_2 3$. This matches a recent exact bound (which is in particular an upper bound) by Braverman *et al.* [4].

4.4   Applications: Tight Bounds on External PAR and PRIV for Specific Functions

Our applications in Table 1 follow from the lower bounds techniques that we have seen and applying well known facts about the rank or the size of the fooling sets of the communication matrix of the functions in question.

The proofs will appear in the full version of the article ([17]).

5   Quality of the Two Definitions

5.1   Privacy for Deterministic Protocols

Deterministic protocols: for deterministic protocols, the two definitions of privacy, PRIV and PAR, can be arbitrarily different for the same distribution. In high level, PRIV captures the expected privacy loss of a protocol, while PAR captures a more "risk-averse" notion of privacy, where a protocol is penalized heavily for high-privacy-loss events, even if they occur with small probability.

In the appendix, we show that this difference makes PRIV a much more robust definition: an ϵ change in the input distribution causes at most an ϵn change in PRIV, so PRIV is "smooth". Furthermore, PRIV always remains less than the expected communication of the protocol, which we believe to be another natural property. We prove that this is not the case for PAR: sometimes an ϵ change in the input distribution can cause PAR to change exponentially, and PAR can grow arbitrarily larger than the expected communication. Finally we also point out an error in the appendix of [13] and show that for the example they gave, in fact PRIV is just as good as PAR at distinguishing two protocols in their example.

Bounded-error case: As we explained in Sect. 3.2, in the case of bounded-error randomized protocols, the two notions of privacy are in fact both equal to the communication complexity for all boolean functions for which we have a tight bound on their communication complexity. Moreover, for functions with large output, we still do not have any example where PRIV and PAR are different when we are allowed bounded error.

Acknowledgements. We would like to thank Salil Vadhan for useful comments regarding our definition for bounded error and for observing that the original proof of Theorem 6 could be greatly simplified. We would also like to thank Omri Weinstein and Lila Fontes for useful discussions.

This work was partially supported by the ANR Blanc project ANR-12-BS02-005 (RDAM) and ANR Jeune Chercheur project CRYQ, ANR Blanc project QRAC (ANR-08-EMER-012), and EU ANR Chist-ERA project DIQIP.

A   Appendix

A.1   Complements to Sect. 2

Omitted Proofs. The proofs of Lemma 1 and Theorem 9 will appear in the full version of the article [17].

Discussion About the Definition of PAR. In Sect. 2, definition 7, we have defined PAR for randomized bounded-error protocols relatively to the transcript and the output value of the function. This definition is consistent with the one for deterministic protocols. However it is also possible to extend the definition of PAR by taking the output of the protocol instead of the output of the function:

Definition 10. – *An   alternative   definition   for   the   exter-nal   PAR   of   a   randomized   protocol   P   is:* $\mathrm{PAR}_\mu^{ext,alt}(P) :=$ $\mathbb{E}_{x,y,r}\left[\frac{\mathbb{P}_{X,Y,R}((X,Y)=(x,y)\,|\,T_P(X,Y,R)=T_P(x,y,r))}{\mathbb{P}_{X,Y}((X,Y)=(x,y)\,|\,P(X,Y)=P(x,y))}\right]$. *For $\epsilon \geq 0$, the external ϵ-error PAR of f is defined as the following, where the infimum is taken over all protocols P computing f with error at most ϵ:* $\mathrm{PAR}_{\mu,\epsilon}^{ext,alt}(f) := \inf_P \mathrm{PAR}_\mu^{ext,alt}(P)$.

– *An alternative definition for the internal* PAR *of a randomized protocol P is:*

$$\text{PAR}_{\mu}^{int,alt}(P) := \mathbb{E}_{x,y,r}\left[\frac{\mathbb{P}_{X,Y,R}(Y=y \mid T_P(X,Y,R)=T_P(x,y,r)\wedge X=x)}{\mathbb{P}_{X,Y}(Y=y \mid P(X,Y)=P(x,y)\wedge X=x)}\right]$$
$$+ \mathbb{E}_{x,y,r}\left[\frac{\mathbb{P}_{X,Y,R}(X=x \mid T_P(X,Y,R)=T_P(x,y,r)\wedge Y=y)}{\mathbb{P}_{X,Y}(X=x \mid P(X,Y)=P(x,y)\wedge Y=y)}\right].$$

For $\epsilon \geq 0$, the external ϵ-error PAR *of f is defined as the following, where the infimum is taken over all protocols P computing f with error at most ϵ:*
$$\text{PAR}_{\mu,\epsilon}^{int,alt}(f) := \inf_P \text{PAR}_{\mu}^{int,alt}(P).$$

A.2   Omitted Roofs from Sect. 3

We have proven Theorem 8 in Sect. 3. We prove here the other theorems stated in this section.

Relations Between the Different Notions of Privacy and Communication Complexity. Firstly we show that for any protocol (deterministic or randomized), the external privacy-approximation ratio is at most exponential in the communication of the protocol.

Theorem 11. *For any protocol P,* $\text{PAR}_{\mu}^{ext}(f,P) \leq 2^{\mathbf{CC}(P)}$.

The proof will appear in the full version of the article [17].

The relation between internal IC and internal PRIV for deterministic protocols was explained in [1]. It is possible to improve the lower bound and to show the same relationship for external notions and any (deterministic or randomized) protocol.

Theorem 12. *For any protocol P and any distribution μ,*

$$\text{PRIV}_{\mu}^{int}(f,P) \leq \text{IC}_{\mu}^{int}(P) \leq \text{PRIV}_{\mu}^{int}(f,P) + 2\log(|\mathcal{Z}|)$$
$$\text{PRIV}_{\mu}^{ext}(f,P) \leq \text{IC}_{\mu}^{ext}(P) \leq \text{PRIV}_{\mu}^{ext}(f,P) + \log(|\mathcal{Z}|)$$

Proof. By definition of IC and PRIV we have, respectively for the external and the internal notions:

$$\text{IC}_{\mu}^{int}(P) - \text{PRIV}_{\mu}^{int}(f,P) = \mathbf{I}(X;f(X,Y)|Y) + \mathbf{I}(Y;f(X,Y)|X) \leq 2\log(|\mathcal{Z}|),$$
$$\text{IC}_{\mu}^{ext}(P) - \text{PRIV}_{\mu}^{ext}(f,P) = \mathbf{I}(X,Y;f(X,Y)) \leq \log(|\mathcal{Z}|).$$

For the lower bounds, note that mutual information is always positive.

Moreover, if $\text{Dist}_{\mu,\epsilon}$ for $\epsilon \geq 0$ represents the *expected* distributional complexity of a randomized ϵ-error protocol with respect to some input distribution μ, we have:

Theorem 13 ([11]). *For any randomized ϵ-error protocol and any input distribution,* $\text{Dist}_{\mu,\epsilon}(P) \geq \text{IC}_{\mu,\epsilon}^{ext}(P)$.

The proof of this well-known fact can be found in [11] for example.
Note that, since $\text{IC}_{\mu,\epsilon}^{ext}(P) \geq \text{IC}_{\mu,\epsilon}^{int}(P)$, we also have: $\text{Dist}_{\mu,\epsilon}(P) \geq \text{IC}_{\mu,\epsilon}^{int}(P)$.

Relation Between Internal and External Privacy. We first study the case of PRIV and then focus on PAR.

Theorem 14. $\text{PRIV}_\mu^{int}(f, P) \leq \text{PRIV}_\mu^{ext}(f, P) + \log(|\mathcal{Z}|)$.

Proof. Braverman [7] proved that: $\text{IC}_\mu^{int}(P) \leq \text{IC}_\mu^{ext}(P)$. Hence, with 12:

$$\text{PRIV}_\mu^{int}(f, P) \leq \text{IC}_\mu^{int}(P) \leq \text{IC}_\mu^{ext}(P) \leq \text{PRIV}_\mu^{ext}(f, P) + \log(|\mathcal{Z}|).$$

Moreover, we show that internal PAR is smaller than external one for deterministic protocols:

Theorem 15. *For any deterministic protocol P computing f:*

$$\text{PAR}_\mu^{int}(f, P) \leq 2 \cdot \text{PAR}_\mu^{ext}(f, P).$$

The proof will appear in the full version of the article [17].

However, Theorem 15 does not hold in general for ϵ-error randomized protocols. For instance, consider that Alice receives an s-bit string x, and Bob receives x plus an n-bit string y, such that x and y are independent, and they want to compute the function that reveals x: $f(x, y) = x$. The protocol they use, where only Bob sends messages, is the following: if $x = 0^s$ then Bob sends y, otherwise he sends a random n-bit string (independent of x and y). Then:

$$\text{PAR}_\mu^{int}(f, P) = \mathbb{E}_{x,y,t}\left[\frac{\mathbb{P}(XY = xy | T = t, X = x)}{\mathbb{P}(XY = xy | X = x)}\right] + 1$$

$$= \sum_{x,y,t} \mathbb{P}(X = x, Y = y, T = t)\frac{\mathbb{P}(Y = y | T = t, X = x)}{\mathbb{P}(Y = y | X = x)} + 1$$

$$= 2^n \sum_{x,y,t} \mathbb{P}(X = x, Y = y, T = t)\mathbb{P}(Y = y | X = x, T = t) + 1$$

$$= 2^n \left(\sum_{x \neq 0, y, t} \frac{1}{2^{2n+s}} \frac{1}{2^n} + \sum_{x = 0, y = t} \frac{1}{2^{n+s}} \cdot 1\right) + 1 = 2^{n-s} + o(1)$$

and:

$$\text{PAR}_\mu^{ext}(f, P) = \mathbb{E}_{x,y,t}\left[\frac{\mathbb{P}(X = x, XY = xy | T = t)}{\mathbb{P}(X = x, XY = xy | f(X, Y) = f(x, y))}\right]$$

$$= \sum_{x,y,t} \mathbb{P}(X = x, Y = y, T = t)\frac{\mathbb{P}(X = x, Y = y | T = t)}{\mathbb{P}(Y = y)}$$

$$\text{(since } f(x, y) = x\text{)}$$

$$= 2^n \sum_{x,y,t} \mathbb{P}(X = x, Y = y, T = t)\mathbb{P}(X = x, Y = y | T = t)$$

$$= 2^n \left(\sum_{x \neq 0, y, t} \frac{1}{2^{2n+s}} \frac{1}{2^{n+s}} + \sum_{x = 0, y = t} \frac{1}{2^{n+s}} \frac{1}{2^s}\right) = 2^n + o(1)$$

Hence, if x is of length $s = n/2$, then $\text{PAR}_\mu^{int}(f, P) = 2^{n/2} + o(1)$ is exponentially bigger than $\text{PAR}_\mu^{ext}(f, P) = o(1)$.

A.3   Omitted Proofs for Sect. 4

Relation with Partition Linear Program. It is also possible to lower bound $\text{PAR}_\mu^{ext}(f)$ by $\frac{1}{|\mathcal{Z}|} \cdot \text{prt}(f)$, where $\text{prt}(f)$ is defined in [14]. The details of this fact wille appear in the full version of the article [17].

Rank Argument Fails for Non-boolean Functions. For instance, consider the following function that take three values: let $\text{EQ}' : \{1, \ldots, m\}^2 \rightarrow \{0, 1, 2\}$ be the function defined by:

$$\text{EQ}'(x, y) = \begin{cases} 0 & \text{if } x \neq y \text{ and } x < m \text{ or } y < m \\ 1 & \text{if } x = y \text{ and } x < m \text{ or } y < m \\ 2 & \text{otherwise } (x = m \text{ or } y = m). \end{cases} \quad \text{whose matrix is:} \quad \begin{pmatrix} 1\,0 \cdots 0\,2 \\ 0\,1 \cdots 0\,2 \\ \vdots\ \vdots\ \ddots\ \vdots \\ 0\,0 \cdots 1\,2 \\ 2\,2 \cdots 2\,2 \end{pmatrix}.$$

Then, for any (zero-error) protocol P solving EQ', the number of 0-rectangles and the number of 1-rectangles are at least the minimum number of such rectangles for EQ_{m-1}:

$$\text{EQ}_{m-1} : \{1, \ldots, m-1\}^2 \rightarrow \{0, 1\}, \ (x, y) \mapsto 1 \text{ iff } x = y.$$

But the number of 2-rectangles can be only 2. Now, if we pick a distribution μ and δ satisfying $\left|\text{EQ}'^{-1}(0)\right|_\mu = \left|\text{EQ}'^{-1}(1)\right|_\mu = \delta/2 < 2^{-(2m-2)}$ and $\left|\text{EQ}'^{-1}(2)\right|_\mu = 1 - \delta$, then one can see that $\text{PAR}_\mu^{ext}(\text{EQ}') \leq 3$. Hence for this function EQ' and this distribution μ: $\text{PAR}_\mu^{ext}(\text{EQ}', P) \leq 3$ whereas : $\text{rank}\left(\mathcal{M}_{\text{EQ}'}\right) \geq \text{rank}\left(\mathcal{M}_{\text{EQ}_{n-1}}\right) = 2^{n-1}$.

Proofs of Applications. An advantage of our techniques is that they give bounds for *any* distribution of input μ, and not only for a uniform distribution as in [13]. Since any of these problems can be solved by sending Alice's entire input (n bits), the communication complexity is always upper-bounded by n, hence so PAR is always upper-bounded by 2^n. The lower bounds stated in Table 1 can be proved using Theorem 1.

Now we explain briefly how to obtain the results of Theorem 7 (see the full version of the article ([17]) for the details). For the lower bounds for EQ, DISJ, GT, we can apply Corollary 2 using an appropriate fooling set, followed by the relationship between IC and PRIV given in Theorem 12. For IP it is possible to use the well-known fact that all 0-monochromatic rectangles of the IP function contain at most 2^n elements.

A.4   Privacy for Deterministic Protocols

Robustness over the Input Distribution. We show that PAR is not robust over the input distribution μ. More precisely, we give an example of a function and of two distributions with exponentially small statistical distance, but whose privacy-approximation ratio is constant for one and exponential for the other.

Proposition 1. *There exists a function f and two input distributions μ_1, μ_2 satisfying $|\mu_1 - \mu_2| \leq 2^{-n/2}$ in statistical distance, and yet such that $\mathrm{PAR}_{\mu_1}^{ext}(f) = \Theta(1)$ and $\mathrm{PAR}_{\mu_2}^{ext}(f) = \Omega(2^{n/2})$.*

Proof. Let $m = 2^n$ and $f : \{0, \ldots, m\}^2 \to \{0, 1, 2\}$ be the function defined by:

$$f(x, y) = \begin{cases} 0 & \text{if } x \neq y \text{ and } x \neq m \text{ and } y \neq m \\ 1 & \text{if } x = y \text{ and } x \neq m \text{ and } y \neq m \\ 2 & \text{otherwise } (x = m \text{ or } y = m). \end{cases} \quad \text{whose matrix is:} \quad \begin{pmatrix} 1 & 0 & \cdots & 0 & 2 \\ 0 & 1 & \cdots & 0 & 2 \\ \vdots & \vdots & \ddots & \vdots & \vdots \\ 0 & 0 & \cdots & 1 & 2 \\ 2 & 2 & \cdots & 2 & 2 \end{pmatrix}.$$

Let μ_1 be the following distribution: with probability 2^{-n} pick a random element of $f^{-1}(0) \cup f^{-1}(1)$, and with probability $1 - 2^{-n}$ pick a random element of $f^{-1}(2)$.

Set $\epsilon = 2^{-n/2}$ and let μ_2 be the following distribution: with probability $2^{-n} + \epsilon$ pick a random element of $f^{-1}(0) \cup f^{-1}(1)$, and with probability $1 - 2^{-n} - \epsilon$ pick a random element of $f^{-1}(2)$.

Consider now the protocol P, where first Alice and Bob exchange a single bit to check whether $x = m$ or $y = m$ and if they are both different than m, Alice and Bob solve Equality (by having Alice send her entire input to Bob). Then we have:

$$\mathrm{PAR}_{\mu_1}^{ext}(f) \leq \mathrm{PAR}_{\mu_1}^{ext}(f, P) = \left|f^{-1}(0)\right|_{\mu_1} \cdot n_0 + \left|f^{-1}(1)\right|_{\mu_1} \cdot n_1 + \left|f^{-1}(2)\right|_{\mu_1} \cdot n_2$$
$$\leq \left(\left|f^{-1}(0)\right|_{\mu} + \left|f^{-1}(1)\right|_{\mu_1}\right) \cdot 2^n + \left|f^{-1}(2)\right|_{\mu_1} \cdot 3 = \Theta(1)$$

On the other hand, any protocol for this function must solve Equality so n_0 and n_1 must be at least 2^n, since they have to be larger than the rank of the matrix. Consider the optimal protocol P for f

$$\mathrm{PAR}_{\mu_2}^{ext}(f) = \mathrm{PAR}_{\mu_2}^{ext}(f, P) = \left|f^{-1}(0)\right|_{\mu_2} \cdot n_0 + \left|f^{-1}(1)\right|_{\mu_2} \cdot n_1 + \left|f^{-1}(2)\right|_{\mu_2} \cdot n_2$$
$$\geq \left(\left|f^{-1}(0)\right|_{\mu_2} + \left|f^{-1}(1)\right|_{\mu_2}\right) \cdot 2^n = \left(\frac{1}{2^n} + \epsilon\right) \cdot 2^n = \Omega(2^{n/2}).$$

One can finally verify that $|\mu_1 - \mu_2| = \epsilon = 2^{-n/2}$.

In fact, the right way to look at the robustness of PAR is to talk about $\log \mathrm{PAR}_{\mu}^{ext}(f)$. Even in this case, we see that an exponentially small change to the input distribution can change the $\log \mathrm{PAR}_{\mu}^{ext}(f)$ from constant to $\Omega(n)$.

On the other hand, we can prove that when the statistical distance of the input distributions is ϵ, then the PRIV changes by at most $O(\epsilon n)$. This implies that in our previous example, PRIV changes only by an exponentially small amount.

Theorem 16. *For any protocol P and any two input distributions μ, μ' with statistical distance $|\mu - \mu'| \leq \epsilon$, it holds that : $|\mathrm{PRIV}_{\mu}^{ext}(P) - \mathrm{PRIV}_{\mu'}^{ext}(P)| \leq O(\epsilon n)$ and $|\mathrm{PRIV}_{\mu}^{int}(P) - \mathrm{PRIV}_{\mu'}^{int}(P)| \leq O(\epsilon n)$.*

Proof. The proof is a consequence of the fact that two statistically close joint distributions must have similar mutual information. To prove this formally we use the following lemma:

Lemma 3 (Lemma 3.15 of [19]). *For any random variables $XY, X'Y'$ such that $|XY - X'Y'| \leq \epsilon$ and where X, X' take value in $\{0, 1\}^n$, it holds that*

$$|H(X \mid Y) - H(X' \mid Y')| \leq 4(H(\epsilon) + \epsilon n).$$

The details of this proof will appear in the full version of the article [17].

Relationship Between Communication and Privacy. A natural methodology for studying privacy is to measure the amount of information revealed by the transcript above and beyond what is supposed to be revealed. We believe that both PRIV and PAR were designed with this methodology in mind.

One intuitive bound that "natural" measures of information should satisfy is the following: a transcript of length c can reveal at most c bits of information. As a consequence, the privacy loss should also be bounded by the communication (appropriately normalized of course: for example in the case of PAR, one would compare $\log$ PAR to communication).

When taking an expectation over randomized protocols, as one does for instance when measuring the complexity of zero-error randomized protocols, one would therefore also expect that the privacy loss revealed should be bounded by the expected communication. While PRIV does indeed satisfy this property, we observe that PAR does not:

Remark 3. For the `Greater Than` function GT under the uniform input distribution $\mathcal{U}$, the following holds:

1. For all zero-error protocols P solving GT, $\mathrm{PAR}_{\mathcal{U}}^{ext}(P) \geq 2^n - 1$.
2. There exist a zero-error protocol for GT where the expected communication is constant.

The first point was proved in Theorem 1. The second point follows from the trivial protocol that exchanges their inputs bit-by-bit starting with the highest order bits until the players find a difference, at which point they terminate because they know which player has the greater value. Then clearly under uniform inputs, for each $i \geq 1$ the probability of terminating after $2i$ bits is $1 - 2^{-i}$, and so the expected communication is $2 \sum_{i=1}^{\infty} i \cdot 2^{-i} = 4$ regardless of the size of the inputs.

Thus, the above remark shows that PAR can tend to infinity even though the expected communication is constant, which violates the "natural" property that c bits of communication can reveal at most c bits of information.

On the other hand, one could argue that PAR captures a "risk-averse" notion of privacy, where one does not want the expected privacy loss but rather the privacy loss with higher weights assigned to high-privacy-loss events. In this case one may also want to look at worst-case choices of inputs and random coins; worst-case inputs were defined in [1,13], although they did not study worst-case random coins since they focused on deterministic protocols.

Error in Appendix of [13]. An example was given in the appendix of [13] that claimed to exhibit a function f and two protocols P, Q such that $\text{PAR}_{\mathcal{U}}^{ext}(P) = O(1)$ and $\text{PAR}_{\mathcal{U}}^{ext}(Q) = 2^{\Omega(n)}$, whereas it was claimed that $\text{PRIV}_{\mathcal{U}}^{ext}(P) = \text{PRIV}_{\mathcal{U}}^{ext}(Q) = \Theta(n)$. This was interpreted to mean that PRIV was not sufficiently precise enough to capture the difference between these two protocols.

However the second claim is incorrect as a calculation reveals that $\text{PRIV}_{\mathcal{U}}^{ext}(P) = O(1)$ and so PRIV does indeed distinguish between the two protocols. The flaw in their argument was in using the geometric interpretation of PRIV: the characterization of [9] that they use only applies to the *worst* distribution for a function (which for the function they give is *not* uniform), whereas they explicitly want to study the uniform distribution. For the worst distribution μ it is indeed the case that $\text{PRIV}_{\mu}^{ext}(P) = \Theta(n)$, but not for the uniform distribution. Therefore, for their example, PRIV is actually just as capable as PAR in distinguishing the two protocols P, Q.

References

1. Ada, A., Chattopadhyay, A., Cook, S., Fontes, L., Koucký, M., Pitassi, T.: The Hardness of Being Private. In: 27th Annual IEEE Conference on Computational Complexity, CCC'12, pp. 192–202 (2012)
2. Barak, B., Braverman, M., Chen, X., Rao, A.: How to compress interactive communication. In: Proceedings of the 42nd STOC, pp. 67–76 (2010)
3. Brody, J., Buhrman, H., Koucky, M., Loff, B., Speelman, F., Vereshchagin, N.: Towards a reverse Newman's theorem in interactive information complexity, CCC (2013)
4. Braverman, M., Garg, A., Pankratov, D., Weinstein, O.: From information to exact communication, In: STOC, pp. 151–160 (2013)
5. Braverman, M., Garg, A., Pankratov, D., Weinstein, O.: Information lower bounds via self-reducibility. In: Bulatov, A.A., Shur, A.M. (eds.) CSR 2013. LNCS, vol. 7913, pp. 183–194. Springer, Heidelberg (2013)
6. Bar-Yossef, Z., Jayram, T., Kumar, R., Sivakumar, D.: An information statistics approach to data stream and communication complexity. In: Proceedings of the 43rd Annual IEEE Symposium on Foundations of Computer Science, pp. 209–218 (2002)
7. Braverman, M.: Interactive information complexity. ECCC, report No. 123, STOC'12 (2011)
8. Braverman, M., Moitra, A.: An information complexity approach to extended formulations. In: STOC'13 (2013)
9. Bar-Yehuda, R., Chor, B., Kushilevitz, E., Orlitsky, A.: Privacy, additional information and communication. IEEE Trans. Inf. Theory **39**(6), 1930–1943 (1993)

10. Braverman, M., Weinstein, O.: A discrepancy lower bound for information complexity. In: Proceedings of the APPROX-RANDOM 2012, pp. 459–470 (2012)
11. Cover, T.M., Thomas, J.A.: Elements of Information Theory, 2nd, Hardcover, New York, pp. 776 2006 ISBN: 0-471-24195-4
12. Chakrabarti, A., Shi, Y., Wirth, A., Yao, A.: Informational complexity and the direct sum problem for simultaneous message complexity. In: 42nd IEEE FOCS, pp. 270–278 (2001)
13. Feigenbaum, J., Jaggard, A.D., Schapira, M.: Approximate privacy: foundations and quantification. In: Proceedings of the 11th Conference on Electronic Commerce (EC)., ACM Press, New York, pp. 167–178 (2010)
14. Jain, R., Klauck, H.: The partition bound for classical communication complexity and query complexity. In: 25th IEEE Conference on Computational Complexity (2010)
15. Klauck, H.: On quantum and approximate privacy. In: Proceedings STACS (2002)
16. Kerenidis, I., Laplante, S., Lerays, V., Roland, J., Xiao, D.: Lower bounds on information complexity via zero-communication protocols and applications. FOCS **2012**, 500–509 (2012)
17. Kerenidis, I., Laurière, M., Xiao, D.: New lower bounds for privacy in communication protocols, http://eccc.hpi-web.de/report/2013/015/ (full version, 2013)
18. Kushilevitz, E., Nisan, N.: Communication Complexity. Cambridge University Press, New York (1997)
19. Mahmoody, M., Xiao, D.: Languages with efficient zero Knowledge PCPs are in SZK. ECCC technical report TR2012-052 (2012)
20. Jain, R.: New strong direct product results in communication complexity. J. ACM (2013)
21. Yannakakis, M.: Expressing combinatorial optimization problems by linear programs. J. Comput. Syst. Sci. **43**, 441–466 (1991)
22. Yao, A.C-C.: Some complexity questions related to distributive computing. In: Proceedings of the 11th ACM Symposium on Theory of Computing (STOC), pp. 209–213 (1979)

On the Transmit Beamforming for MIMO Wiretap Channels: Large-System Analysis

Maksym A. Girnyk[✉], Frédéric Gabry, Mikko Vehkaperä,
Lars K. Rasmussen, and Mikael Skoglund

Communication Theory Laboratory, KTH Royal Institute of Technology,
Osquldas väg 10, 10044 Stockholm, Sweden
{mgyr,gabry,mikkov,lkra,skoglund}@kth.se
http://commth.ee.kth.se

Abstract. With the growth of wireless networks, security has become a fundamental issue in wireless communications due to the broadcast nature of these networks. In this work, we consider MIMO wiretap channels in a fast fading environment, for which the overall performance is characterized by the ergodic MIMO secrecy rate. Unfortunately, the direct solution to finding ergodic secrecy rates is prohibitive due to the expectations in the rates expressions in this setting. To overcome this difficulty, we invoke the large-system assumption, which allows a deterministic approximation to the ergodic mutual information. Leveraging results from random matrix theory, we are able to characterize the achievable ergodic secrecy rates. Based on this characterization, we address the problem of covariance optimization at the transmitter. Our numerical results demonstrate a good match between the large-system approximation and the actual simulated secrecy rates, as well as some interesting features of the precoder optimization.

Keywords: MIMO wiretap channel · Large-system approximation · Random matrix theory · Beamforming.

1 Introduction

Wireless networks have developed considerably over the last few decades. As a consequence of the broadcast nature of these networks, communications can potentially be attacked by malicious parties, and therefore, security has taken a fundamental role in today's communications. The notion of physical layer security (or information-theoretic security) was developed by Wyner in his fundamental work in [1]. The *wiretap channel*, which is the simplest model to study secrecy in communications, was introduced therein, consisting of a transmitter

The present research was supported by the Swedish Research Council (VR).

C. Padró (Ed.): ICITS 2013, LNCS 8317, pp. 90–102, 2014.
DOI: 10.1007/978-3-319-04268-8_6, © Springer International Publishing Switzerland 2014

and two communication channels: to a legitimate receiver and to an eavesdropper. The *secrecy capacity* of the wiretap channel is then defined as the maximum transmission rate from the transmitter to the receiver, provided that the eavesdropper does not get any information. Finding the aforementioned secrecy capacity is a difficult problem in general, due to its non-convex nature.

Notwithstanding, multiple-input multiple-output (MIMO) communications [2,3] have become an emerging topic during the last two decades due to their promising capacity gains. Similar to communication networks without secrecy constraints, the overall performance for channels with secrecy constraints is limited by the channels' conditions. In particular, the legitimate parties need to have some advantage over the eavesdropper in terms of channel quality to guarantee secure communications. Many techniques have been proposed to overcome this limitation; one example is the use of multi-antenna systems, as in [4–7], where the secrecy capacity of the MIMO wiretap channel with multiple eavesdroppers (MIMOME) was characterized. These results extend to the problem of secret-key agreement over wireless channels, as in [8] where key-distillation strategies over quasi-static fading channels were investigated, and [9] where the secret-key capacity of MIMO ergodic channels was considered. Finding the precoder matrix achieving the MIMO secrecy capacity has been attempted in [4,7], however the general form of the optimal covariance matrix remains unknown. Nevertheless, in certain regimes, the optimal signaling strategies have been derived. The high SNR case was investigated in [7], while the optimal transmitting scheme at low SNR was found in [10]. In [11], the authors characterized the secrecy capacity for some special cases of channel matrices with certain rank properties. The special case where the transmitter and legitimate receiver have two antennas, whereas the eavesdropper has a single antenna, has been addressed in [5]. More recently, the same problem has been investigated in a computationally efficient way in [12] by developing the *generalized singular value decomposition* (GSVD)-based beamforming at the transmitter, and deriving the optimal transmit covariance matrix. Optimal signalling in presence of an isotropic eavesdropper has been recently investigated in [13]. In particular the authors in [13] found a close-formed expression for the optimal covariance matrix in the isotropic case as well as lower and upper bounds on the secrecy capacity for the general case.

All the references above considered quasi-static scenario, where the changes in channel gains were slow enough, so that the transmitter could adapt its radiation pattern to each channel realization. If, on the contrary, wireless channels are subject to ergodic fading, a codeword spans many fading realizations and traditional notion of secrecy rate is no longer suitable. Hence, the concept of *ergodic secrecy rate*, proposed in [14,15], has to be used to characterize the performance of the wiretap channel. In [16–18] the problem of finding achievable ergodic secrecy rates was addressed for multiple-input single-output (MISO) channels. In the context of MIMO channels, in [19], following a previous work in [20], the authors characterize the secrecy capacity of an uncorrelated MIMOME channel with only statistical channel state information (CSI) at the transmitter and investigate the optimal input covariance matrix under a total power constraint.

Unfortunately, for general fast-fading MIMOME channels evaluation of ergodic secrecy rates is problematic due to the necessity of averaging over the channel realizations. Hence, asymptotic approaches based on methods from *random matrix theory* [21] have been proposed to circumvent these difficulties. Typically, such techniques assume that the number of antennas at the transmitter and the receiver tend to infinity at a constant rate. Then, an explicit expression – or a *deterministic equivalent* – of the ergodic mutual information (MI) is obtained. The expression is then shown to describe well the behavior of the systems with realistic (finite) numbers of antennas.

In this paper, we make a first step in studying the problem of the ergodic secrecy rate maximization under power constraint in MIMO wiretap channels. After computing the deterministic equivalents of the two MIMO channels, we address the problem of the transmit precoder optimization. We further show that despite being capacity achieving for a point-to-point MIMO channel, the water-filling strategy becomes a poor choice in the wiretap setting. For instance, under the assumption that the transmitter performs the GSVD-based beamforming, we derive the ergodic-secrecy-rate maximizing transmit covariance matrix, which outperforms the water-filling solution.

2   System Model

Consider a scenario, where Alice, equipped with an M-antenna transmitter, wants to communicate a message to Bob, who is equipped with an N_{M}-antenna receiver. The message has to be kept secret from unauthorized parties. Meanwhile, Eve tries to eavesdrop the message with the aid of an N_{E}-antenna receiver. The corresponding setup, depicted in Fig. 1, has the following channel model

$$y_{\mathrm{M}} = H_{\mathrm{M}}x + n_{\mathrm{M}}, \tag{1a}$$

$$y_{\mathrm{E}} = H_{\mathrm{E}}x + n_{\mathrm{E}}, \tag{1b}$$

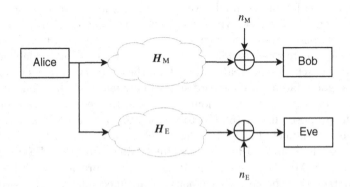

Fig. 1. The MIMO wiretap channel.

where $x \sim \mathcal{CN}(\mathbf{0}_M, \mathbf{I}_M)$, $n_{\mathrm{M}} \sim \mathcal{CN}(\mathbf{0}_{N_{\mathrm{M}}}, \mathbf{I}_{N_{\mathrm{M}}})$, $n_{\mathrm{E}} \sim \mathcal{CN}(\mathbf{0}_{N_{\mathrm{E}}}, \mathbf{I}_{N_{\mathrm{E}}})$, and the Kronecker model [22] is used, viz.,

$$\boldsymbol{H}_{\mathrm{M}} = \sqrt{\frac{\rho_{\mathrm{M}}}{M}} \boldsymbol{R}_{\mathrm{M}}^{1/2} \boldsymbol{W}_{\mathrm{M}} \boldsymbol{T}_{\mathrm{M}}^{1/2} \in \mathbb{C}^{N_{\mathrm{M}} \times M}, \tag{2a}$$

$$\boldsymbol{H}_{\mathrm{E}} = \sqrt{\frac{\rho_{\mathrm{E}}}{M}} \boldsymbol{R}_{\mathrm{E}}^{1/2} \boldsymbol{W}_{\mathrm{E}} \boldsymbol{T}_{\mathrm{E}}^{1/2} \in \mathbb{C}^{N_{\mathrm{E}} \times M}, \tag{2b}$$

where $\boldsymbol{T}_{\mathrm{M}}$ and $\boldsymbol{R}_{\mathrm{M}}$ are the transmit and receive correlation matrices of the channel between Alice and Bob, $\boldsymbol{T}_{\mathrm{E}}$ and $\boldsymbol{R}_{\mathrm{E}}$ are the transmit and receive correlation matrices of the channel between Alice and Eve, while $\boldsymbol{W}_{\mathrm{M}}$ and $\boldsymbol{W}_{\mathrm{E}}$ have i.i.d. $\mathcal{CN}(0,1)$ entries. The channel described by (1a) is referred to as the *main channel*, whereas the channel described by (1b) is called the *eavesdropper channel*.

For a given transmit covariance matrix, $\boldsymbol{P} \triangleq \mathsf{E}\{\boldsymbol{xx}^{\mathsf{H}}\}$, under the assumption that Alice uses Gaussian signals, the per-antenna achievable ergodic secrecy rate is expressed as

$$R_{\mathrm{s}} = \frac{1}{M} \left[\mathsf{E}_{\boldsymbol{W}_{\mathrm{M}}} \left\{ \log \det(\boldsymbol{I}_{N_{\mathrm{M}}} + \boldsymbol{H}_{\mathrm{M}} \boldsymbol{P} \boldsymbol{H}_{\mathrm{M}}^{\mathsf{H}}) \right\} - \mathsf{E}_{\boldsymbol{W}_{\mathrm{E}}} \left\{ \log \det(\boldsymbol{I}_{N_{\mathrm{E}}} + \boldsymbol{H}_{\mathrm{E}} \boldsymbol{P} \boldsymbol{H}_{\mathrm{E}}^{\mathsf{H}}) \right\} \right]^{+}, \tag{3}$$

where $[\cdot]^{+} = \max\{0, \cdot\}$. Note here the difference to [12], where quasi-static fading scenario was considered.

For practical reasons, covariance matrix $\boldsymbol{P}$ is assumed to be designed based on the long-term *statistical* CSI, namely, $\{\rho_{\mathrm{M}}, \rho_{\mathrm{E}}, \boldsymbol{T}_{\mathrm{M}}, \boldsymbol{T}_{\mathrm{E}}, \boldsymbol{R}_{\mathrm{M}}, \boldsymbol{R}_{\mathrm{E}}\}$. Note, however, that in order to construct proper wiretap codes, Alice must have access to the *instantaneous* CSI, $\{\boldsymbol{H}_{\mathrm{M}}, \boldsymbol{H}_{\mathrm{E}}\}$. Thus, the obtained result is regarded as a computationally efficient lower bound on the achievable secrecy rates.

By choosing the proper covariance matrix $\boldsymbol{P}$, one can maximize the achievable secrecy rate of the wiretap channel (1). The corresponding optimization problem is formulated as

$$\begin{aligned} \max_{\boldsymbol{P}} \quad & R_{\mathrm{s}} \\ \mathrm{s.t.} \quad & \mathrm{tr}\{\boldsymbol{P}\} \leq M \\ & \boldsymbol{P} \succeq \mathbf{0}_{M}. \end{aligned} \tag{4}$$

Unfortunately, the objective function of the above problem has no explicit expression. To evaluate it, one has to perform averaging over the distribution of $\boldsymbol{W}_{\mathrm{M}}$ and $\boldsymbol{W}_{\mathrm{E}}$ using, *e.g.*, Monte-Carlo simulation. This approach is, however, quite time-consuming and inefficient. Therefore, a new approach has to be applied to maximize the ergodic secrecy rate. In the following section, we present an asymptotic expression for the ergodic secrecy rate in the limit where dimensions of the channel matrix grow infinitely large.

3   Achievable Ergodic Secrecy Rate

In this section, we provide the large-system approximation for the ergodic secrecy rate of a finite-antenna wiretap channel. We start with the following definition.

Definition 1. *Given the wiretap channel (1), the* large-system limit *(LSL) is defined as a regime, where*

$$N_M = \beta_M M \to \infty, \qquad\qquad \beta_M = \text{const}, \qquad\qquad (5)$$

$$N_E = \beta_E M \to \infty, \qquad\qquad \beta_E = \text{const}. \qquad\qquad (6)$$

That is, the numbers of antennas on each side of the channels grow large without bound at constant ratios.

Based on the above definition, the following proposition presents the large-system approximation for the ergodic MI.

Proposition 1. *In the LSL, the following holds*

$$R_s - [I_M(\rho_M) - I_E(\rho_E)]^+ \to 0, \qquad\qquad (7)$$

where

$$I_M(\rho_M) = \frac{1}{M} \log \det \left(\boldsymbol{I}_M + \beta_M e_M \boldsymbol{T}_M \boldsymbol{P} \right) + \frac{1}{M} \log \det \left(\boldsymbol{I}_{N_M} + \delta_M \boldsymbol{R}_M \right) - \frac{\beta_M}{\rho_M} \delta_M e_M \tag{8a}$$

$$I_E(\rho_E) = \frac{1}{M} \log \det \left(\boldsymbol{I}_M + \beta_E e_E \boldsymbol{T}_E \boldsymbol{P} \right) + \frac{1}{M} \log \det \left(\boldsymbol{I}_{N_E} + \delta_E \boldsymbol{R}_E \right) - \frac{\beta_E}{\rho_E} \delta_E e_E, \tag{8b}$$

and sets of parameters $\{e_M, \delta_M\}$ and $\{e_E, \delta_E\}$ form the unique solutions to the following two systems of equations

$$e_M = \frac{\rho_M}{N_M} \text{tr} \left\{ \boldsymbol{R}_M \left(\boldsymbol{I}_{N_M} + \delta_M \boldsymbol{R}_M \right)^{-1} \right\}, \tag{9a}$$

$$\delta_M = \frac{\rho_M}{M} \text{tr} \left\{ \boldsymbol{T}_M^{1/2} \boldsymbol{P} \boldsymbol{T}_M^{1/2} \left(\boldsymbol{I}_M + \beta_M e_M \boldsymbol{T}_M^{1/2} \boldsymbol{P} \boldsymbol{T}_M^{1/2} \right)^{-1} \right\}, \tag{9b}$$

$$e_E = \frac{\rho_E}{N_E} \text{tr} \left\{ \boldsymbol{R}_E \left(\boldsymbol{I}_{N_E} + \delta_E \boldsymbol{R}_E \right)^{-1} \right\}, \tag{10a}$$

$$\delta_E = \frac{\rho_E}{M} \text{tr} \left\{ \boldsymbol{T}_E^{1/2} \boldsymbol{P} \boldsymbol{T}_E^{1/2} \left(\boldsymbol{I}_M + \beta_E e_E \boldsymbol{T}_E^{1/2} \boldsymbol{P} \boldsymbol{T}_E^{1/2} \right)^{-1} \right\}, \tag{10b}$$

Proof. The proof is based on the concept of a deterministic equivalent [23,24]. Consider a matrix of the following type

$$\boldsymbol{B} = \boldsymbol{R}^{1/2} \boldsymbol{W} \boldsymbol{T} \boldsymbol{W}^{\mathsf{H}} \boldsymbol{R}^{1/2}, \tag{11}$$

where W is a random matrix consisting of i.i.d. entries with zero mean and variance $1/M$, while T and R are Hermitian non-negative definite of bounded normalized trace. The latter are assumed to be generated by tight sequences [25]. Moreover, we assume that $\exists\, b > a > 0$, such that

$$a < \liminf_N \beta < \limsup_N \beta < b, \tag{12}$$

where $\beta \triangleq N/M$. As shown in Corollary 1 in [24], when N and M grow large without bound at ratio β, the following holds

$$m(-x) - m^\circ(-x) \to 0 \tag{13}$$

almost surely, where $m(-x)$ is the Stieltjes transform of B for $x > 0$ and

$$m^\circ(-x) = \frac{1}{M}\mathrm{tr}\left\{(I_N + \delta R)^{-1}\right\}, \tag{14}$$

where e and δ form a unique solution of the following system of fixed-point equations

$$e = \frac{1}{N}\mathrm{tr}\left\{\frac{1}{x}R\left(I_N + \delta R\right)^{-1}\right\}, \tag{15a}$$

$$\delta = \frac{1}{M}\mathrm{tr}\left\{\frac{1}{x}T\left(I_M + \beta e T\right)^{-1}\right\}, \tag{15b}$$

which, according to Proposition 1 therein, could be solved *via* an iterative algorithm always converging to a unique fixed point.

Meanwhile, from Theorem 2 in [24] it follows that under the aforementioned assumptions and some additional constraints on spectral radius of matrices T and R, the Shannon transform [26] of B satisfies

$$\mathcal{V}(-x) - \mathcal{V}^\circ(-x) \to 0 \tag{16}$$

almost surely, where

$$\mathcal{V}^\circ(-x) = \frac{1}{M}\log\det\left(I_M + \beta e T\right) + \frac{1}{M}\log\det\left(I_N + \delta R\right) - x\beta\delta e. \tag{17}$$

The above Shannon transform represents the asymptotic behavior of the mean MI in the LSL. Thus, having computed (17) at $x = 1/\rho$, with parameters satisfying (15a), we can evaluate the ergodic MI of each MIMO channel within our wiretap model (viz., the main and eavesdropper's channels). To address the influence of the transmit covariance matrix, it suffices to consider $TP^{1/2}$ instead of T for both channels. This leads us exactly to (8), (9) and (10), thereby completing the proof.

4   Transmit Covariance Optimization

Based upon the asymptotic analysis carried out in the previous section, here we address the problem of transmit covariance optimization (4). As mentioned before, working directly with (3) is prohibitive due to expectation operators therein. Moreover, as we have seen from the previous section, the influence of the random parts of the channels $\boldsymbol{W}_\mathrm{M}$ and $\boldsymbol{W}_\mathrm{E}$ vanishes in the LSL. Thus, the objective function of the corresponding optimization problem simplifies to

$$r_\mathrm{s}(\boldsymbol{P}) = \frac{1}{M}\left[\log\det\left(\boldsymbol{I}_M + \beta_\mathrm{M} e_\mathrm{M} \boldsymbol{T}_\mathrm{M} \boldsymbol{P}\right) - \log\det\left(\boldsymbol{I}_M + \beta_\mathrm{E} e_\mathrm{E} \boldsymbol{T}_\mathrm{E} \boldsymbol{P}\right) \right]^+. \quad (18)$$

Note that here, we consider e_M and e_E as independent of the optimization variable $\boldsymbol{P}$ due to the following reason. The optimal solution of the optimization problem has to satisfy the KKT conditions, which require that $\nabla_{\boldsymbol{P}} r_\mathrm{s}(\boldsymbol{P}) = \boldsymbol{0}$. When taking into account the dependence of e_M and e_E on $\boldsymbol{P}$, one has to take the derivatives of $r_\mathrm{s}(\boldsymbol{P})$ w.r.t. the former. However, it can be verified that those are zero, and hence interdependence between e_M, e_E and $\boldsymbol{P}$ does not play any role in the optimization.

Unfortunately, since the problem is non-convex, finding the optimal covariance of $\boldsymbol{x}$ is difficult. Hence, we will provide several suboptimal solutions that give a lower bound on the secrecy capacity of the ergodic MIMO wiretap channel.

4.1   Water-Filling over the Main Channel

Isotropic transmission is the simplest strategy Alice can perform. However, it is not capacity achieving even for a generic MIMO channel. Instead, based on the statistical CSI of the main channel, $\{\boldsymbol{T}_\mathrm{M}, \boldsymbol{R}_\mathrm{M}\}$, Alice can perform SVD $\beta_\mathrm{M} e_\mathrm{M} \boldsymbol{T}_\mathrm{M} = \boldsymbol{U}\boldsymbol{\Sigma}\boldsymbol{V}^\mathsf{H}$, where $\boldsymbol{U}$ and $\boldsymbol{V}$ are orthonormal matrices. Then, optimal transmit covariance is given by the *water-filling* (WF) solution as follows

$$\boldsymbol{P}_\mathrm{WF}^\star = \boldsymbol{V}\boldsymbol{\Sigma}_{\boldsymbol{P}}\boldsymbol{V}^\mathsf{H}, \quad (19)$$

where $[\boldsymbol{\Sigma}_{\boldsymbol{P}}]_{m,m} = \left[\mu^{-1} - [\boldsymbol{\Sigma}]_{m,m}^{-1}\right]^+$, and μ is chosen to satisfy the power constraint. In this case Alice acts as if Eve did not exist, achieving the ergodic capacity of the main channel. However, in the presence of an eavesdropper this strategy may be quite inefficient, as we shall see later on.

4.2   GSVD-Based Precoder

Consider the scenario where the transmitter performs GSVD on the matrices related to channels (1a) and (1b). Although the solution based on this assumption is suboptimal, it is advantageous, as compared to the isotropic precoding. Moreover, it takes into account the presence of the eavesdropper and can potentially increase the ergodic secrecy rate as compared to the WF precoder.

When applied to (18), the GSVD-based beamforming method is realized as follows. Based on the statistical CSI of both channels, $\{T_M, R_M, T_E, R_E\}$, Alice performs GSVD on matrices $\beta_M e_M T_M$ and $\beta_E e_E T_E$

$$\beta_M e_M T_M = U_M \Sigma_M V^H, \tag{20}$$

$$\beta_E e_E T_E = U_E \Sigma_E V^H, \tag{21}$$

where $\Sigma_M^T \Sigma_M + \Sigma_E^T \Sigma_E = I_M$. The above GSVD simultaneously diagonalizes T_M and T_E, converting those into a set of parallel subchannels. Then, the transmitted vector is constructed as $x = V^{-H}s$, where $s \sim \mathcal{CN}(0_M, P)$ and P is a positive semi-definite diagonal matrix representing the power allocation across the subchannels. For the above beamforming strategy, the optimal power allocation was derived in [12] (here we have corrected the minor typo therein)

$$[P_{GSVD}^\star]_{i,i} = \frac{1}{2}\left[\text{sign}(\sigma_{M,i} - \sigma_{E,i}) + 1\right]\left[\frac{-1 + \sqrt{1 - 4\sigma_{M,i}\sigma_{E,i} + \frac{4(\sigma_{M,i} - \sigma_{E,i})\sigma_{M,i}\sigma_{E,i}}{\log(2)\mu v_i}}}{2\sigma_{M,i}\sigma_{E,i}}\right]^+, \tag{22}$$

where $\sigma_{M,i}$, $\sigma_{E,i}$ and v_i are the ith diagonal entries of $\Sigma_M^T \Sigma_M$, $\Sigma_E^T \Sigma_E$ and $V^{-1}V^{-H}$, respectively, and μ is chosen to satisfy the power constraint at the transmitter.

5   Numerical Results

In this section, we provide results based on numerical simulations along with some discussion. As seen from the objective function (18), spatial correlation at the receiver side has no effect on the precoding design. Hence, for the sake of simplicity, we assume that $R_M = I_{N_M}$ and $R_E = I_{N_E}$. Meanwhile, correlation at the transmitter side is assumed to be generated by a uniform linear antenna array with *Gaussian power azimuth spectrum* [27], so that the entries of correlation matrices T_M and T_E) are obtained by

$$[T]_{a,b} = \frac{1}{2\pi\delta^2}\int_{-\pi}^{\pi} e^{2\pi j d_\lambda(a-b)\sin(\phi) - \frac{(\phi - \theta)^2}{2\delta^2}}\, d\phi, \tag{23}$$

where d_λ is the relative antenna spacing (in wavelengths λ), θ is the mean angle and δ^2 is the mean-square angle spread.

First, we plot in Fig. 2, the dependence of the ergodic secrecy rate on the SNR. The transmit side correlation parameters are set as follows. The antenna numbers are set to $M = 6$, $N_M = 6$ and $N_E = 2$. The antenna spacing is set to one wavelength, the mean angles are set to $\theta_M = 40°$, $\theta_E = -10°$ and the root-mean-square angle spread is chosen for both channels to be $\delta_M = \delta_E = 5°$. From the figure, we see that the the results derived in the LSL (solid lines) match the simulations (markers) quite well even for relatively small numbers of antennas. Moreover, we also see that "statistical" water-filling over the main channel

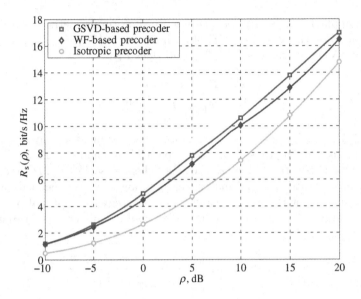

Fig. 2. Ergodic secrecy rate vs.SNR ($\rho_M = \rho_E = \rho$) for a MIMO wiretap channel with $M = 6$, $N_M = 6$ and $N_E = 2$ antennas. Transmit side correlation parameters: $d_\lambda = 1$, $\theta_M = 40°$, $\theta_E = -10°$, $\delta_M = \delta_E = 5°$. Solid curves denote analytic results, while markers denote simulated values averaged over 10 000 channel realizations.

performs well, approaching the performance of the GSVD-based precoding. The isotropic precoder also achieves quite high ergodic secrecy rates, which can be explained by a small number of antennas at the eavesdropper.

Figure 3 depicts similar dependence of the ergodic secrecy rate (3) on the SNR with different network parameters. The transmit side correlation parameters are chosen similar to the previous case, while the antenna numbers are set to $M = 2$, $N_M = 3$ and $N_E = 4$. From the figure we see that water-filling over the main channel is far from being optimal in this case. This can be explained by the fact that in this setting Eve has many antennas and is therefore quite powerful in terms of eavesdropping capabilities. Hence, maximizing the data rate of the main channel, while ignoring the eavesdropper, is a poor strategy in this case. The same observation applies to isotropic precoding, which performs even worse. On the other hand, "statistical" GSVD-based beamforming proves the most efficient among the considered strategies.

To emphasize the advantage of the GSVD we plot the ergodic secrecy rate as a function of the number of antennas at Eve's receiver, N_E, in Fig. 4. We fix $d_\lambda = 1$ and keep the same parameters as in the previous figure. From Fig. 4 we see that both the isotropic precoding and water-filling cannot provide strictly positive ergodic secrecy rates when N_E grows large. At the same time we observe that GSVD-based precoding allows to efficiently allocate the power to achieve strictly positive ergodic secrecy rates even when N_E becomes much larger than M and N_M.

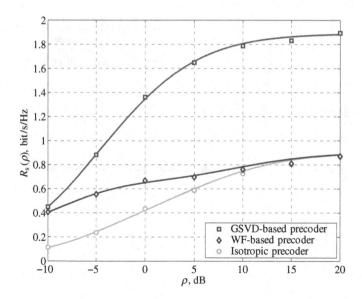

Fig. 3. Ergodic secrecy rate *vs.*SNR ($\rho_M = \rho_E = \rho$) for a MIMO wiretap channel with $M = 2$, $N_M = 3$ and $N_E = 4$ antennas. Transmit side correlation parameters: $d_\lambda = 1$, $\theta_M = 40°$, $\theta_E = -10°$, $\delta_M = \delta_E = 5°$. Solid curves denote analytic results, while markers denote simulated values averaged over 10 000 channel realizations.

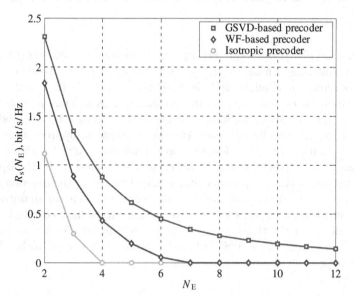

Fig. 4. Ergodic secrecy rate *vs.*number of Eve's antennas N_E for a MIMO wiretap channel with $M = N_M = 4$ antennas in the main channel. Transmit side correlation parameters: $d_\lambda = 1$, $\theta_M = 40°$, $\theta_E = -10°$, $\delta_M = \delta_E = 5°$. SNR is set to $\rho_M = \rho_E = 0$ dB. Solid curves denote analytic results, while markers denote simulated values averaged over 10 000 channel realizations.

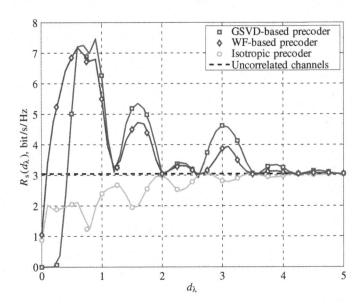

Fig. 5. Ergodic secrecy rate *vs.*antenna spacing d_λ for a MIMO wiretap channel with $M = 4$, $N_M = 4$ and $N_E = 2$ antennas. Transmit side correlation parameters: $\theta_M = 40°$, $\theta_E = -10°$, $\delta_M = \delta_E = 5°$. SNR is set to $\rho_M = \rho_E = 0$ dB. Solid curves denote analytic results, while markers denote simulated values averaged over 10 000 channel realizations.

In Fig. 5, we plot the ergodic secrecy rate R_s against the spacing between the neighboring antennas within the array. The rest of the transmit-side correlation parameters remain unchanged and the SNR is set to $\rho = 0$ dB. Firstly, we note that the achievable ergodic secrecy rates are non-convex and non-monotone functions of the antenna spacing. Similar behavior was previously observed in [28] and, moreover, the results obtained *via* the asymptotic approximation (solid lines) are confirmed with the Monte-Carlo simulation results (markers). Nevertheless, quite interestingly, it can be observed that at low SNR, the optimized secrecy rates are significantly higher than those obtained by the isotropic precoding. Moreover, those are even higher than the secrecy capacity of an uncorrelated wiretap channel, meaning that it can be advantageous to have correlation at low SNR, provided that the transmit covariance is optimized. Finally, we point out that again, as expected, the GSVD-based beamforming reveals to be the most efficient among other choices.

6   Conclusions

In the present paper, we have studied the ergodic secrecy rate of a multi-antenna wiretap channel. Using the theory of deterministic equivalents, we have obtained the large-system approximation of the achievable ergodic secrecy rate, which holds when the numbers of antennas at each terminal grow very large at constant ratios. The approximation proved accurate even for small numbers of antennas, thereby simplifying the computationally demanding problem of transmit covariance optimization. First, not only the objective function of the corresponding optimization problem has closed-form expression, but it has interesting properties attributed to log-det expressions. Secondly, the objective depends only on the correlation matrices of the channels, which can be known at the transmitter by the widely adopted statistical CSI assumption. Once the approximation was obtained, we were able to use some existing algorithms for the covariance optimization. In particular, we have shown that GSVD-based beamforming performs well, compared to, *e.g.*, water-filling over the main channel.

References

1. Wyner, A.D.: The wire-tap channel. Bell Syst. Tech. J. **54**(8), 1334–1387 (1975)
2. Foschini, G., Gans, M.: On limits of wireless communications in a fading environment when using multiple antennas. Wirel. Pers. Commun. **6**(3), 311–335 (1998)
3. Telatar, E.: Capacity of multi-antenna gaussian channels. Eur. Trans. Telecommun. **10**(6), 585–595 (1999)
4. Oggier, F., Hassibi, B.: The secrecy capacity of the MIMO wiretap channel. IEEE Trans. Inf. Theory **57**(8), 4961–4972 (2011)
5. Shafiee, S., Liu, N., Ulukus, S.: Towards the secrecy capacity of the Gaussian MIMO wire-tap channel: the 2-2-1 channel. IEEE Trans. Inf. Theory **55**(9), 4033–4039 (2009)
6. Liu, T., Shamai, S.: A note on the secrecy capacity of the multiple-antenna wiretap channel. IEEE Trans. Inf. Theory **55**(6), 2547–2553 (2009)
7. Khisti, A., Wornell, G.: Secure transmission with multiple antennas II: the MIMOME wiretap channel. IEEE Trans. Inf. Theory **56**(11), 5515–5532 (2011)
8. Bloch, M., Barros, J., Rodrigues, M., McLaughlin, M.: Wireless information-theoretic security. IEEE Trans. Inf. Theory **54**(6), 2515–2534 (2008)
9. Wong, T., Bloch, M., Shea, J.M.: Secret sharing over fast-fading MIMO wiretap channels. EURASIP J. Wirel. Commun. Network. **2009**, 506 973/1–506 973/17 (2009)
10. Gursoy, M.: Secure communication in the low-SNR regime: a characterization of the energy-secrecy tradeoff. In: Proceedings of IEEE International Symposium on Information Theory (ISIT) (2009)
11. Li, J. Petropulu, A.: Optimal input covariance for achieving secrecy capacity in gaussian mimo wiretap channels. In: IEEE International Conference Acoustical Speech Signal Processing (ICASSP), pp. 3362–3365 (2010)
12. Fakoorian, S.A., Swindlehurst, A.L.: Optimal power allocation for GSVD-based beamforming in the MIMO Gaussian wiretap channel. In: Proceedings of IEEE International Symposium on Information Theory (ISIT), pp. 2321–2325 (2012)
13. Loyka, S., Charalambous, C.D.: Further results on optimal signaling over secure MIMO channels. In: Proceedings of International Symposium on Inforamtion Theory (ISIT) (2013)
14. Liang, Y., Poor, H.V., Shamai, S.: Secure communication over fading channels. IEEE Trans. Inf. Theory **54**(6), 2470–2492 (2008)
15. Gopala, P., Lai, L., El Gamal, H.: On the secrecy capacity of fading channels. IEEE Trans. Inf. Theory **54**, 4687–4698 (2008)

16. Khisti, A., Wornell, G.: Secure transmission with multiple antennas I: the MISOME wiretap channel. IEEE Trans. Inf. Theory **56**(7), 3088–3104 (2010)
17. Li, J., Petropulu, A.P.: On ergodic secrecy rate for Gaussian MISO wiretap channels. IEEE Trans. Wirel. Commun. **10**(4), 1176–1187 (2011)
18. Van Nguyen, T., Shin, H.: Power allocation and achievable secrecy rates in MIS-OME wiretap channels. IEEE Commun. Lett. **15**(11), 1196–1198 (2011)
19. Lin, S.-C. Lin, P.-H.: On secrecy capacity of fast fading MIMOME wiretap channels with statistical CSIT. arXiv:1309.1516 (2013)
20. Lin, S.-C., Lin, P.-H.: On secrecy capacity of fast fading multiple-input wiretap channels with statistical CSIT. IEEE Trans. Inf. Forensics Secur. **8**(2), 414–419 (2013)
21. Couillet, R., Debbah, M.: Random Matrix Methods for Wireless Communications. Cambridge University Press, New York (2011)
22. Chizhik, D., Rashid-Farrokhi, F., Ling, J., Lozano, A.: Effect of antenna separation on the capacity of BLAST in correlated channels. IEEE Commun. Lett. **4**(11), 337–339 (2000)
23. Hachem, W., Loubaton, P., Najim, J.: Deterministic equivalents for certain functionals of large random matrices. Ann. Appl. Probab. **17**(3), 875–930 (2007)
24. Couillet, R., Debbah, M., Silverstein, J.W.: A deterministic equivalent for the analysis of correlated MIMO multiple access channels. IEEE Trans. Inf. Theory **57**(6), 3493–3514 (2011)
25. Billingsley, P.: Probability and Measure. Wiley, New York (2008)
26. Tulino, A.M., Verdú, S.: Random Matrix Theory and Wireless Communications. Now Publishers Inc., vol. 1: 1–82 (2004)
27. Wen, C.-K., Wong, K.-K.: Asymptotic analysis of spatially correlated MIMO multiple-access channels with arbitrary signaling inputs for joint and separate decoding. IEEE Trans. Inf. Theory **53**(1), 252–268 (2007)
28. Moustakas, A.L., Simon, S.H., Sengupta, A.M.: Statistical mechanics of multi-antenna communications: replicas and correlations. Acta Phys. Pol. **36**(9), 2719–2732 (2005)

Information Theoretic Security for Encryption Based on Conditional Rényi Entropies

Mitsugu Iwamoto[1][✉] and Junji Shikata[2]

[1] Center for Frontier Science and Engineering,
The University of Electro-Communications, Tokyo, Japan
`mitsugu@uec.ac.jp`
[2] Graduate School of Environment and Information Sciences,
Yokohama National University, Yokohama, Japan
`shikata@ynu.ac.jp`

Abstract. In this paper, information theoretic cryptography is discussed based on conditional Rényi entropies. Our discussion focuses not only on cryptography but also on the definitions of conditional Rényi entropies and the related information theoretic inequalities. First, we revisit conditional Rényi entropies, and clarify what kind of properties are required and actually satisfied. Then, we propose security criteria based on Rényi entropies, which suggests us deep relations between (conditional) Rényi entropies and error probabilities by using several guessing strategies. Based on these results, unified proof of impossibility, namely, the lower bounds on key sizes are derived based on conditional Rényi entropies. Our model and lower bounds include the Shannon's perfect secrecy, and the min-entropy based encryption presented by Dodis, and Alimomeni and Safavi-Naini at ICITS2012. Finally, a new optimal symmetric key encryption protocol achieving the lower bounds is proposed.

Keywords: Information theoretic cryptography · (Conditional) Rényi entropy · Error probability in guessing · Impossibility · Symmetric-key encryption

1 Introduction

Motivation and Related Works. How to measure the quantities of information is an important issue not only in information theory, but also in cryptography because information measures in cryptography tell us not only the coding efficiency but also security level in terms of equivocation of secret information. Historically, Shannon entropy [2] is the measure of information theoretic cryptography. On the other hand, it is also important to evaluate the cardinality of

---

The full version of this paper is available at the IACR ePrint Archive [1].

C. Padró (Ed.): ICITS 2013, LNCS 8317, pp. 103–121, 2014.
DOI: 10.1007/978-3-319-04268-8_7, © Springer International Publishing Switzerland 2014

a set in which a random variable takes values, i.e., Hartley entropy [3]. Further-more, min-entropy [4] is also considered to be an important quantity in *guessing* the secret in the context of cryptography.

For instance, consider the case of symmetric-key encryption. As is well known by Shannon's seminal work [5], the perfect secrecy in symmetric-key encryp-tion is formalized as $H(M) = H(M|C)$, where M and C are random variables which take values in sets of plaintexts and ciphertexts, respectively; and then, symmetric-key encryption with perfect secrecy implies the lower bound on secret-keys $H(K) \geq H(M)$ (Shannon's bound, Shannon's impossibility, [5]). Similarly, we also know that the number of key candidates can be no less than the cardinal-ity of the set of plaintexts. Furthermore, Dodis [6] recently showed that the sim-ilar bound also holds with respect to min-entropy, namely, $R_\infty(K) \geq R_\infty(M)$, for symmetric-key encryption with perfect secrecy. Also, Alimomeni and Safavi-Naini [7] introduced the *guessing secrecy*, formalized by $R_\infty(M) = R_\infty(M|C)$, and under which they derived the bound $R_\infty(K) \geq R_\infty(M)$, where $R_\infty(\cdot)$ and $R_\infty(\cdot|\cdot)$ are the min-entropy and the conditional min-entropy, respectively. Here, it is worth noting that the above results are proved utilizing *totally* different techniques. This fact is very interesting from the *theoretical* viewpoint, and it must be fruitful not only for cryptography but also for information theory if we can *unify* the above proofs and derive them as corollaries. In order to unify them, Rényi entropy [8] might be useful since it is considered to be a generalization of Shannon, min, and several other kinds of entropies as well as the cardinality.

Starting from the above motivation, we develop fundamental results about conditional Rényi entropies, and propose security criteria based on conditional Rényi entropies which is inspired by adversaries' guessing. Through these results, we finally show a unified framework of Shannon's impossibility via (conditional) Rényi entropies. Specifically, our contribution of this paper is as follows:

Conditional Rényi Entropies, Revisited (Sects. 2 and 3). As we described, we aim to show a unified framework of Shannon's impossibility via (conditional) Rényi entropies. Unfortunately, however, we cannot expect Rényi entropies to satisfy rich properties like Shannon entropies, since Rényi entropies are obtained axiomatically from several relaxed postulates for Shannon entropy. Due to this fact, *subadditivity* does not hold for Rényi entropy although it is very fundamen-tal property of Shannon entropy.

In considering the conditional Rényi entropies, we should refer to the result [9] which analyzed the relations among exiting conditional Rényi entropies. How-ever, their analyses are not sufficient in the following aspects. First, they do not consider the Rényi entropies from axiomatic point of view. Recalling that Rényi entropies are originally discovered axiomatically [8], it is important to discuss conditional Rényi entropies from axiomatic and/or technological view-points. Second, the analysis in [9] did not include two important conditional Rényi entropies due to Arimoto [10] and Hayashi [11] denoted by $R_\alpha^A(X|Y)$ and $R_\alpha^H(X|Y)$, respectively. To the best of our knowledge, they are first intro-duced in information theoretic [10] and cryptographic contexts [11], respectively. Third, cryptographically important conditional min-entropies are not sufficiently analyzed in [9] since they cannot be not obtained from the conditional Rényi entropies discussed in [9].

Based on the above considerations, we will discuss what kind of properties should be investigated in this paper from the axiomatic, information theoretic, and cryptographic viewpoints. Our analysis also includes $R_\alpha^A(X|Y)$ and $R_\alpha^H(X|Y)$. In Sect. 2.3, we start our discussion from the postulates required for Shannon and Rényi entropies, and discuss what kind of properties should be required and/or are interested in. As a result, we conclude that non-negativity, monotonicity, conditioning reduces entropy (CRE), data processing inequality (DPI) are hopefully required, but the chain rule might not be satisfied. Then, we consider the relation between conditional Rényi entropies and conditional min-entropies. We clarify that the cryptographically useful conditional min-entropies are obtained from the conditional Rényi entropies $R_\alpha^A(X|Y)$ and $R_\alpha^H(X|Y)$ as special cases.

Sections 3.1–3.3 are devoted to show that the above inequalities actually hold. Furthermore, we show an extension of Fano's inequality [12] for conditional Rényi entropies in Sect. 3.4, which will be useful in the forthcoming discussion as well as the inequalities discussed in Sects. 3.1–3.3.

Proposal of Security Criteria Based on Conditional Rényi Entropies (Sect. 4). In this paper, we propose security criteria based on conditional Rényi entropies $R_\alpha^A(X|Y)$ and $R_\alpha^H(X|Y)$. Our motivation and significance for proposing it lies in the following two points.

The first point lies in realistic significance which is deeply related to guessing probability by adversaries. Owing to theoretical results about the conditional Rényi entropies in Sects. 2 and 3, we will show that conditional Rényi entropies, $R_\alpha^A(X|Y)$ and $R_\alpha^H(X|Y)$, play an important role to derive a lower bound on failure probability of guessing by adversaries, and it turns out that our security criteria is a sufficient condition to make it reasonably large enough. Our way of thinking of this is deeply related to the approach to show the converse of channel coding theorem by Shannon [2] and the recent one to show the converse of channel coding theorem in finite blocklength regime [13,14] in information theory. The second point lies in mathematical importance for generalizing Shannon's impossibility (or Shannon's bounds) $H(K) \geq H(M)$ in symmetric-key encryption with perfect secrecy. For details about this contribution, see below.

Generalizing Shannon's Impossibility in Encryption (Sect. 5). One of our main purpose in this paper is to generalize Shannon's impossibility (or Shannon's bound) in perfectly secure symmetric-key encryption so that all known bounds (i.e., the Shannon's, Dodis's, and Alimomeni and Safavi-Naini's bounds) are captured in our generic bound. By utilizing information-theoretic results about conditional Rényi entropies obtained in Sects. 2 and 3, we extend Shannon's impossibility result for encryption by a generic and unified proof technique, and it turns out that our new bound includes all the bounds mentioned above as special cases.

In this paper, several proofs of theorems are omitted due to the space limitation. See the full version of this paper [1] for the omitted proofs.

2   Conditional Rényi Entropies, Revisited

2.1   Preliminaries: Rényi Entropies and α-Divergence

Definition 1 (Rényi entropy, [8]). *Let X be a random variable taking values on a finite set $\mathcal{X}$. For a real number $\alpha \geq 0$, the Rényi entropy of order α is defined by*[1] $R_\alpha(X) := \frac{1}{1-\alpha} \log \sum_{x \in \mathcal{X}} P_X(x)^\alpha$.

It is well known that many information measures such as Hartley entropy, Shannon entropy, collision entropy, and min-entropies are special cases of Rényi entropy. Namely, they are respectively obtained by $R_0(X) = \log|\mathcal{X}|$, $R_1(X) := \lim_{\alpha \to 1} R_\alpha(X) = H(X)$, $R_2(X) = -\log \Pr\{X = X'\}$, and $R_\infty(X) := \lim_{\alpha \to \infty} R_\alpha(X) = \min_{x \in \mathcal{X}}\{-\log P_X(x)\}$, where X and X' are independently and identically distributed (i.i.d.) random variables, and we define $H(X) := -\sum_{x \in \mathcal{X}} P_X(x) \log P_X(x)$ as Shannon entropy.

Definition 2 (α-divergence). *Let X and Y be random variables taking values on a finite set $\mathcal{X}$. For a real number $\alpha \geq 0$, the α-divergence is defined by* $D_\alpha(X\|Y) = D_\alpha(P_X\|P_Y) = \frac{1}{\alpha-1} \log \sum_{x \in \mathcal{X}} P_X(x)^\alpha / P_Y(x)^{\alpha-1}$.

The α-divergence is considered as an generalization of Kullback-Leibler divergence defined by $D(X\|Y) := \sum_{x \in \mathcal{X}} P_X(x) \log(P_X(x)/P_Y(x))$ since it holds that $\lim_{\alpha \to 1} D_\alpha(X\|Y) = D(X\|Y)$. Note that the α-divergence is nonnegative for all $\alpha \geq 0$, and it is equal to 0 if and only if $P_X(\cdot) = P_Y(\cdot)$, similarly to Kullback-Leibler divergence.

2.2   Definitions of Conditional Rényi Entropies

Similarly to Shannon entropy, it is natural to consider the *conditional* Rényi entropies. However, several definitions of conditional Rényi entropies have been proposed, e.g., [10,11,15–18]. In particular, relations and properties are discussed in [9] among three kinds of conditional Rényi entropies such as $R_\alpha^C(X|Y) := \sum_{y \in \mathcal{Y}} P_Y(y) R_\alpha(X|Y = y)$, $R_\alpha^{JA}(X|Y) := R_\alpha(XY) - R_\alpha(Y)$, and $R_\alpha^{RW}(X|Y) := \frac{1}{1-\alpha} \max_{y \in \mathcal{Y}} \log \sum_{x \in \mathcal{X}} P_{X|Y}(x|y)^\alpha$, defined in [15–18], respectively. The definitions $R_\alpha^C(X|Y)$ and $R_\alpha^{JA}(X|Y)$ can be interpreted as extensions of conditional Shannon entropy since they are analogues of $H(X|Y) := \sum_{y \in \mathcal{Y}} P_Y(y) H(X|Y = y)$ and $H(X|Y) := H(XY) - H(Y)$, respectively. The third definition $R_\alpha^{RW}(X|Y)$ is obtained by letting $\varepsilon = 0$ of the conditional smooth Rényi entropy [18].

---

[1] Throughout of the paper, the base of logarithm is e. Note that the base of logarithm is not essential since the same arguments hold for arbitrary base of logarithm. We also define $0^0 := 0$ for $\alpha = 0$.

In addition to the above, two conditional Rényi entropies are known. They are introduced in [10,11], and defined as

$$R_\alpha^A(X|Y) := \frac{\alpha}{1-\alpha} \log \sum_{y \in \mathcal{Y}} P_Y(y) \left\{ \sum_{x \in \mathcal{X}} P_{X|Y}(x|y)^\alpha \right\}^{1/\alpha} \tag{1}$$

$$R_\alpha^H(X|Y) := \frac{1}{1-\alpha} \log \sum_{y \in \mathcal{Y}} P_Y(y) \sum_{x \in \mathcal{X}} P_{X|Y}(x|y)^\alpha \tag{2}$$

respectively. Both of these conditional Rényi entropies are outside the scope of [9]. $R_\alpha^H(X|Y)$ is defined in [11] to derive an upper bound of leaked information in universal privacy amplification. $R_\alpha^A(X|Y)$ is used in [10] to show the strong converse of channel coding theorem. We also note that $R_\alpha^A(X|Y)$ is implicitly used even in cryptographic contexts. In [19], $R_{1+s}^A(X|Y) = -((1+s)/s)\phi(s/(1+s)|X|Y)$ is used to bound an average security measure of privacy amplification, where $\phi(t|X|Y) := \log \sum_y (\sum_x P_{XY}(x,y)^{\frac{1}{1-t}})^{1-t}$.

Not only the conditional Rényi entropies discussed in [9] but also $R_\alpha^A(X|Y)$ and $R_\alpha^H(X|Y)$ are non-negative and are bounded by $\log|\mathcal{X}|$ from above. Furthermore, note that the following fundamental relation holds.

Proposition 1. *For a fixed real number $\alpha \geq 0$, the probability distribution P_Y, and the conditional probability distribution $P_{X|Y}$, it holds that*

$$R_\alpha^H(X|Y) \leq R_\alpha^A(X|Y). \tag{3}$$

Note that $R_\alpha^H(X|Y) \leq R_\alpha^A(X|Y)$ for $\alpha > 1$ was proved in Lemma 7 of [19]. In addition, Proposition 1 means that: it holds even for $0 < \alpha < 1$ and its proof is simply shown by Jensen's inequality; and the cases of $\alpha = 0, 1$ are meant to take the limits at $\alpha = 0, 1$ (see Theorem 1).

2.3   Fundamental Requirements for Conditional Rényi Entropies

Here, we discuss fundamental properties required to conditional Rényi entropies from axiomatic, information theoretic, and cryptographic viewpoints. In this section, Rényi entropies are not restricted to each definition, and hence, it is denoted by $R_\alpha(X|Y)$.

Axiomatic Consideration. Recall that Rényi entropy is axiomatically obtained, namely, Rényi entropy is the unique quantity (up to a constant factor) that satisfies weakened postulates for Shannon entropy [8]. According to [8], the postulates that characterize the Shannon entropy are, (a) $H(X)$ is a symmetric function with respect to each probability in a probability distribution P_X; (b) $H(X)$ is a continuous function of P_X; (c) $H(X) = 1$ if X is a uniform binary random variable, and; (d) the *chain rule*, i.e., $H(XY) = H(Y) + H(X|Y)$ holds[2], where

---

[2] This form of the chain rule is inductively obtained by using the postulate (d) in [8, p. 547].

$H(X|Y) := \sum_y H(X|Y = y) = -\sum_{x,y} P_{XY}(x,y) \log P_{X|Y}(x|y)$. Then, Rényi entropy is obtained by (a)–(c) and, instead of (d), $H(XY) = H(X)+H(Y)$ if X and Y are statistically independent.

Based on this derivation, it might be acceptable to require conditional Rényi entropies to satisfy (a)–(c) with conditioned random variables. Namely,

- $R_\alpha(X|Y)$ is symmetric with respect to $\{P_{X|Y}(x|y)\}_{x \in \mathcal{X}}$ for each $y \in \mathcal{Y}$, and $\{P_Y(y)\}_{y \in \mathcal{Y}}$.
- $R_\alpha(X|Y)$ is a continuous function with respect to $P_{XY}(\cdot, \cdot)$.
- $R_\alpha(X|Y) = 1$ if a binary random variable X is uniformly distributed for given Y, i.e., $P_{X|Y}(1|y) = P_{X|Y}(0|y) = 1/2$ for all $y \in \operatorname{supp} Y$, where $\operatorname{supp} Y :=$ $\{y \in \mathcal{Y} \mid P_Y(y) > 0\}$.

All conditional Rényi entropies in this paper satisfy the above properties although we omit their proof.

Since the postulate (d) is replaced with $H(XY) = H(X)+H(Y)$, it is natural that Rényi entropies do not satisfy the chain rule. Actually, it is pointed out in [9, Theorem 5] that $R_\alpha^C(X|Y)$ and $R_\alpha^{RW}(X|Y)$ do not satisfy the chain rule for arbitrary $\alpha \neq 1$[3]. Similarly, the chain rule holds for neither $R_\alpha^A(X|Y)$ nor $R_\alpha^H(X|Y)$ as well. See the full version of this paper [1] for the numerical examples that do not satisfy the chain rule.

Instead, we consider several fundamental properties related to chain rule. Note that, *monotonicity*, i.e., $H(XY) \geq H(X)$ is derived from the chain rule since *non-negativity* holds for conditional Shannon entropies. Hence, the non-negativity for conditional Rényi entropies and monotonicity for Rényi entropies are important. In fact, it is known that the monotonicity holds for Rényi entropies. Hence, we are interested in the monotonicity for the conditional Rényi entropies. Namely, it is desirable to satisfy that $R_\alpha(X|Z) \leq R_\alpha(XY|Z)$ for random variables X, Y, and Z. This inequality for conditional Shannon entropies are introduced in [20, (13.9) in Lemma 13.6] as a useful one. Hence, we will investigate the following properties:

- (Non-negativity) $R_\alpha(X|Y) \geq 0$ for all random variables X and Y.
- (Conditioned monotonicity) $R_\alpha(X|Z) \leq R_\alpha(XY|Z)$ for random variables X, Y, and Z, where the equality holds if $Y = f(X, Z)$ for some (deterministic) mapping f.

It is also known that Rényi entropies *do not satisfy* the *subadditivity* since only the additivity for independent random variables is required instead of the postulate (d) for Rényi entropies. Subadditivity for Shannon entropy is written as $H(XY) \leq H(X) + H(Y)$, which is equivalent to $H(X|Y) \leq H(X)$. This inequality is called as "*Conditioning reduces entropy*" [21], CRE for short. Note that CRE states that the entropy of random variable X decreases if some information Y related to X is revealed. On the other hand, monotonicity implies that the entropy of X increases if some information is added.

---

[3] In the case of $\alpha = 1$, conditional Rényi entropies coincide with conditional Shannon entropy, and hence, chain rule is of course satisfied. In addition, it is obvious that $R_\alpha^{JA}(X|Y)$ also satisfies the chain rule since it is defined to satisfy the chain rule.

Furthermore, we can consider an inequality $I(X; Z|Y) \geq 0$, which is a direct consequence of CRE, i.e., $H(X|YZ) \leq H(X|Y)$. This property is often used in proving information theoretic inequality, e.g., see Proof I in Sect. 5.2. Also, combining this inequality with the chain rule, we can prove that Shannon entropy is a *polymatroid* [22]. In the case of Shannon entropy, $I(X; Z|Y) = 0$ holds when X, Y, and Z form a *Markov chain* in this order [21], in symbols $X \leftrightarrow Y \leftrightarrow Z$. Moreover, we note that stronger inequality than $H(X|YZ) \leq H(X|Y)$ is known for Shannon entropy if $X \leftrightarrow Y \leftrightarrow Z$. In this case, it holds that $H(X|Z) \leq H(X|Y)$, which is equivalent to $I(X; Z) \geq I(X; Y)$, called *Data processing inequality* (DPI).

Summarizing, we will investigate the following properties:

- (CRE) $R_\alpha(X|Y) \leq R_\alpha(X)$ for random variables X and Y, where the equality holds if X and Y are independent.
- (DPI) If $X \leftrightarrow Y \leftrightarrow Z$ is satisfied, it holds that $R_\alpha(X|Y) \geq R_\alpha(X|Z)$, where the equality holds if there exists a surjective mapping $f : \mathcal{Y} \to \mathcal{Z}$.

Relation to Other Entropies. Rényi entropy is an extension of many information measures such as Shannon entropy, min-entropy, and Hartley entropy, collision entropy, etc. In particular, from a cryptographic viewpoint, Shannon and min-entropies are prominently important. Hence, it is better if $R_\alpha(X|Y)$ satisfies the following properties:

(i) $\lim_{\alpha \to 1} R_\alpha(X|Y) = H(X|Y)$.
(ii) Conditional Rényi entropy of order α converges to conditional min-entropies if $\alpha \to \infty$.

Similarly to conditional Rényi entropies, it is known that we can find several definitions of conditional min-entropies. Among them, the average conditional min-entropy

$$R_\infty^{\mathsf{avg}}(X|Y) := -\log \mathbb{E}_Y \left[\max_x P_{X|Y}(x|Y) \right] \tag{4}$$

proposed in [23] is important from a cryptographic viewpoint, e.g.,[23–27]. Also, *worst case* conditional min-entropy can be found in the cryptographic context (e.g., in the analysis of physically unclonable functions (PUFs), see [28]).

$$R_\infty^{\mathsf{wst}}(X|Y) := -\log \max_{\substack{x \in \mathcal{X} \\ y \in \mathrm{supp}\, Y}} P_{X|Y}(x|y). \tag{5}$$

Here we note that the conditional Rényi entropies $R_\alpha^{\mathsf{C}}(X|Y)$, $R_\alpha^{\mathsf{JA}}(X|Y)$, and $R_\alpha^{\mathsf{RW}}(X|Y)$ do not satisfy either (i) or (ii) shown above. Namely, it is pointed out in [9] that,

- $\lim_{\alpha \to \infty} R_\alpha^{\mathsf{RW}}(X|Y) = R_\infty^{\mathsf{wst}}(X|Y)$ but $\lim_{\alpha \to 1} R_\alpha^{\mathsf{RW}}(X|Y) \neq H(X|Y)$,
- For $\mathsf{N} \in \{\mathsf{C}, \mathsf{JA}\}$, $\lim_{\alpha \to 1} R_\alpha^{\mathsf{N}}(X|Y) = H(X|Y)$ but $\lim_{\alpha \to \infty} R_\alpha^{\mathsf{N}}(X|Y) \neq R_\infty^{\mathsf{avg}}(X|Y)$, $R_\infty^{\mathsf{wst}}(X|Y)$.

In the above sense, $R_\alpha^N(X|Y)$, $N \in \{C, JA, RW\}$ do not satisfy our requirements for conditional Rényi entropies. In addition, note that (4) is not sufficiently analyzed in [9] since the conditional Rényi entropies corresponding to $R_\infty^{avg}(X|Y)$ is not provided in the literature while it plays important roles in many cryptographic applications.

One of the reasons why we focus on $R_\alpha^A(X|Y)$ and $R_\alpha^H(X|Y)$ missing in [9] is that they actually bridge the conditional Shannon entropy and the conditional min-entropy appeared in cryptography as shown below. The proof of $\lim_{\alpha \to 1} R_\alpha^A(X|Y) = H(X|Y)$ is provided in [10]. For the rest of the proofs, see the full version [1]. Therefore, in this paper, we will mainly focus on the properties of conditional Rényi entropies $R_\alpha^A(X|Y)$ and $R_\alpha^H(X|Y)$.

Theorem 1. *For random variables X and Y, following relations are satisfied:*

(i) $\lim_{\alpha \to 1} R_\alpha^A(X|Y) = \lim_{\alpha \to 1} R_\alpha^H(X|Y) = H(X|Y)$.

(ii) $\lim_{\alpha \to \infty} R_\alpha^A(X|Y) = R_\infty^{avg}(X|Y)$, *and* $\lim_{\alpha \to \infty} R_\alpha^H(X|Y) = R_\infty^{wst}(X|Y)$.

3   Information Theoretic Inequalities for Rényi Entropies

3.1   Conditioning Reduces Entropy

First, we discuss "*conditioning reduces entropy*" (CRE, [21]), which is formulated as, in the case of Shannon entropies $H(X) \geq H(X|Y)$ for random variables X and Y. However, it is pointed out in [9] that $R_\alpha^C(X|Y)$, $R_\alpha^{JA}(X|Y)$, and $R_\alpha^{RW}(X|Y)$ provided in Sect. 2.1 *do not satisfy* CRE in general[4]. Fortunately, however, $R_\alpha^A(X|Y)$ and $R_\alpha^H(X|Y)$, which are outside the scope of [9], satisfy CRE in general. Since CRE for $R_\alpha^A(X|Y)$ is proved in [10,29], we will focus on CRE with respect to $R_\alpha^H(X|Y)$ hereafter:

Theorem 2 (Conditioning reduces entropy). *Let X and Y be random variables taking values on $\mathcal{X}$ and $\mathcal{Y}$, respectively. For all $\alpha \geq 0$, it holds that*

$$R_\alpha^H(X|Y) \leq R_\alpha(X), \tag{6}$$

where the equality holds if X and Y are statistically independent.

From this result and [10,29], it is immediately seen that $R_\infty^{avg}(X|Y)$ and $R_\infty^{wst}(X|Y)$ also satisfy CRE, though it is possible to show it directly.

Theorem 2 is immediately obtained by recalling CRE for $R_\alpha^A(X|Y)$ and the relation given by (3) in Proposition 1. Namely, it holds that $R_\alpha^H(X|Y) \leq R_\alpha^A(X|Y) \leq R_\alpha(X)$. However, this proof does not tell us the difference between both sides of (6). To see this gap, we introduce a conditional α-divergence defined by the same idea with $R_\alpha^H(X|Y)$ in the following form.

---

[4] We can show that CRE is satisfied by $R_\alpha^{RW}(X|Y)$ in the case of $\alpha > 1$.

Definition 3 ([14]). *Let X_1 and X_2 be random variables taking values on $\mathcal{X}$, and Y be a random variable on $\mathcal{Y}$. Then, for a real number $\alpha \geq 0$, the conditional α-divergence between X_1 and X_2 given Y is defined as $D_\alpha(X_1\|X_2|Y) := D_\alpha(P_{X_1|Y}\|P_{X_2|Y}|P_Y) = \frac{1}{\alpha-1}\log\sum_{x,y}\frac{P_{X_1|Y}(x|y)^\alpha}{P_{X_2|Y}(x|y)^{\alpha-1}}P_Y(y)$.*

Then, the following relation holds, which can be seen as an alternative proof for Theorem 2 owing to $D_\alpha(P_{Y|X}\|P_Y|P_{X_\alpha}) \geq 0$. Moreover, the condition for the equality of (6) is easily derived by recalling that $D_\alpha(P_{Y|X}\|P_Y|P_{X_\alpha}) = 0$ if X and Y are statistically independent.

Theorem 3. *Let X, Y, and Z be random variables taking values on finite sets $\mathcal{X}$, $\mathcal{Y}$ and $\mathcal{Z}$, respectively. For all $\alpha \geq 0$, it holds that*

$$R_\alpha(X) - R_\alpha^{\mathsf{H}}(X|Y) = D_\alpha(P_{Y|X}\|P_Y|P_{X_\alpha}) \tag{7}$$

where $P_{X_\alpha}(x) := P_X(x)^\alpha / \sum_{\tilde{x}} P_X(\tilde{x})^\alpha$ for $x \in \mathcal{X}$.

This relation (7) is an analogue of the well-known definition of the mutual information, namely, $I(X;Y) := H(X) - H(X|Y)$ since the mutual information can be written as $I(X;Y) = D(P_{XY}\|P_X P_Y) = D(P_{Y|X}\|P_Y|P_X) = \sum_{x,y} P_Y(x)P_{Y|X}(y|x)\log\frac{P_{Y|X}(y|x)}{P_Y(y)}$.

Hence, it is natural to define a *mutual information of order α* by $I_\alpha^{\mathsf{H}}(X;Y) := R_\alpha(X) - R_\alpha^{\mathsf{H}}(X|Y)$, which is similar to the Arimoto's mutual information of order α defined by $I_\alpha^{\mathsf{A}}(X;Y) := R_\alpha(X) - R_\alpha^{\mathsf{A}}(X|Y)$, in the context of describing channel coding theorem in a general setting [10] .

Remark 1. *Note that $I_\alpha^{\mathsf{H}}(X;Y)$ and $I_\alpha^{\mathsf{A}}(X;Y)$ are not symmetric, i.e., it holds that $I_\alpha^{\mathsf{H}}(X;Y) \neq I_\alpha^{\mathsf{H}}(Y;X)$ and $I_\alpha^{\mathsf{A}}(X;Y) \neq I_\alpha^{\mathsf{A}}(Y;X)$ in general. In addition, it is seen that $I_\alpha^{\mathsf{A}}(X;Y) \leq I_\alpha^{\mathsf{H}}(X;Y)$ in general, since $R_\alpha^{\mathsf{H}}(X|Y) \leq R_\alpha^{\mathsf{A}}(X|Y)$.*

3.2   Data Processing Inequality

The data processing inequality (DPI, [21]) tells us that $I(X;Y) \geq I(X;Z)$ holds if $X \leftrightarrow Y \leftrightarrow Z$. We can extend Theorem 2, in the following way.

Theorem 4 (Data processing inequality). *Let X, Y, and Z be random variables taking on finite sets $\mathcal{X}$, $\mathcal{Y}$, and $\mathcal{Z}$, respectively, and assume that $X \leftrightarrow Y \leftrightarrow Z$. Then it holds that $I_\alpha^{\mathsf{A}}(X;Y) \geq I_\alpha^{\mathsf{A}}(X;Z)$ and $I_\alpha^{\mathsf{H}}(X;Y) \geq I_\alpha^{\mathsf{H}}(X;Z)$ for arbitrary $\alpha \geq 0$. The equality holds if and only if there exists a surjective mapping $f : \mathcal{Y} \to \mathcal{Z}$.*

Remark 2. *DPI is very useful since it implies that the quality of information degenerates by processing the information. It is worth noting that DPI generally holds only if we use $R_\alpha^{\mathsf{A}}(X|Y)$ and $R_\alpha^{\mathsf{H}}(X|Y)$ since DPI is extension of CRE.*

3.3   Conditioned Monotonicity

Here, we show an extended monotonicity for conditional Rényi entropy, which is also useful in cryptographic applications. In the case of Shannon entropy, this results is easily verified by subadditivity, while this fact is presented in [20, (13.9) in Lemma 13.6].

Theorem 5. *Let X, Y, and Z be random variables taking values on finite sets $\mathcal{X}$, $\mathcal{Y}$, and $\mathcal{Z}$, respectively. Then, for $\mathsf{N} \in \{\mathsf{A}, \mathsf{H}\}$, we have:*

(i) $R_\alpha^\mathsf{N}(X|Z) \leq R_\alpha^\mathsf{N}(XY|Z)$,
(ii) $R_\alpha^\mathsf{N}(X|Z) = R_\alpha^\mathsf{N}(XY|Z)$ if and only if $Y = f(X, Z)$ for some (deterministic) mapping f.

3.4   Fano's Inequality

We derive upper-bounds for $R_\alpha^\mathsf{H}(X|Y)$ as follows, and they can be seen as extension of Fano's inequality (see Remark 3).

Theorem 6. *Let X and Y be random variables taking values in a finite set $\mathcal{X}$. Also, let $P_e := \Pr\{X \neq Y\}$ and $\bar{P}_e := 1 - P_e$. Then, for $\alpha \geq 0$, we have the following inequalities.*

(i) If $0 \leq \alpha \leq 1$ and $P_e \geq 1 - \frac{1}{|\mathcal{X}|}$, or $\alpha \geq 1$ and $0 \leq P_e \leq 1 - \frac{1}{|\mathcal{X}|}$, it holds that
$$R_\alpha^\mathsf{H}(X|Y) \leq \frac{1}{1-\alpha} \log\left[(|\mathcal{X}| - 1)^{1-\alpha} P_e^\alpha + \bar{P}_e^\alpha\right].$$
(ii) If $0 \leq \alpha \leq 1$ and $0 \leq P_e \leq 1 - \frac{1}{|\mathcal{X}|}$, or $\alpha \geq 1$ and $P_e \geq 1 - \frac{1}{|\mathcal{X}|}$, it holds that
$$R_\alpha^\mathsf{H}(X|Y) \leq \frac{1}{1-\alpha} \log\left[(|\mathcal{X}| - 1)^{1-\alpha} P_e^{\alpha-1}(1 - \bar{P}_e^{2-\alpha}) + \bar{P}_e\right].$$

Here, in the above inequalities the case $\alpha = 1$ is meant to take the limits at $\alpha = 1$, and the case $P_e = 0$ is meant to take the limits at $P_e = 0$.

Remark 3. *In Theorem 1 it is shown that $\lim_{\alpha \to 1} R_\alpha^\mathsf{H}(X|Y) = H(X|Y)$. On the other hand, by applying the L'Hospital's rule to the right hands of inequalities in Theorem 6, we obtain the following finite limits at $\alpha = 1$:*

(i) $\displaystyle \lim_{\alpha \to 1} \frac{1}{1 - \alpha} \log\left[(|\mathcal{X}| - 1)^{1-\alpha} P_e^\alpha + \bar{P}_e^\alpha\right] = P_e \log(|\mathcal{X}| - 1) + h(P_e),$
(ii) $\displaystyle \lim_{\alpha \to 1} \frac{1}{1 - \alpha} \log\left[(|\mathcal{X}| - 1)^{1-\alpha} P_e^{\alpha-1}(1 - \bar{P}_e^{2-\alpha}) + \bar{P}_e\right] = P_e \log(|\mathcal{X}| - 1) + h(P_e),$

where $h(\cdot)$ is the binary entropy function. Therefore, by taking the limit at $\alpha = 1$ for each of inequalities in Theorem 6, we obtain Fano's inequality as a special case. In this sense, our inequalities in Theorem 6 can be considered as extension of Fano's inequality.

Remark 4. *Note that Fano's inequality implies $H(X|Y) \to 0$ as $P_e \to 0$. Theorem 6 implies that, for any $\alpha \geq 0$, $R_\alpha^\mathsf{H}(X|Y) \to 0$ as $P_e \to 0$, as we would expect.*

4   Security Criteria Based on Conditional Rényi Entropies

As explained in Sect. 1, our motivation and significance for considering security criteria based on conditional Rényi entropies lies in two points.

The first point lies in realistic significance which is deeply related to guessing probability by adversaries. In Sect. 4.2, we show that (conditional) Rényi entropies play an important role to derive a lower bound on failure probability of guessing by adversaries.

The second point lies in mathematical importance for generalizing Shannon's impossibility (or Shannon's bounds) in information-theoretic cryptography. Specifically, for symmetric-key encryption protocols, there exist several known bounds on secret-keys including the Shannon's bounds (see Sect. 4.1). And, our purpose is to extend those bounds in a generic and unified manner by using security criteria based on conditional Rényi entropies.

4.1   Existing Lower Bounds on Secret-Keys

We describe well-known Shannon's bounds [5] for symmetric-key encryption and its extensions (or variants) by Dodis [6], and Alimomeni and Safavi-Naini [7]. To describe the bounds, we use the following notation: let K, M, and C be random variables which take values in finite sets $\mathcal{K}$, $\mathcal{M}$, and $\mathcal{C}$ of secret-keys, plaintexts, and ciphertexts, respectively. Informally, a symmetric-key encryption is said to meet *perfect correctness* if it has no decryption-errors; a symmetric-key encryption is said to meet *perfect secrecy* if it reveals no information about plaintexts from ciphertexts, which is formalized by $H(M|C) = H(M)$ (see Sect. 5 for the formal model of encryption protocols and its explanation).

Proposition 2 (Shannon's bound: [5]). *Let Π be a symmetric-key encryption such that both encryption and decryption algorithms are deterministic. If Π satisfies perfect correctness and perfect secrecy, we have $H(K) \geq H(M)$ and $|\mathcal{K}| \geq |\mathcal{M}|$.*

Proposition 3 (Dodis's bound: Th.3 in [6]). *Let Π be a symmetric-key encryption. If Π satisfies perfect correctness and perfect secrecy, we have $R_\infty(K) \geq R_\infty(M)$.*

Remark 5. *Note that a similar result with Proposition 3 is proved in [30] using information spectrum methods [31]. In [30, Theorem 5], it is clarified that the inf-spectral rate of the secret key is not less than that of the plaintext. Noticing the recent results [33] of smooth min-entropy [32], the asymptotic version of min-entropy is equivalent to the inf-spectral entropy. Hence, we can say that Proposition 3 is proved in an asymptotic setting. However, [6] directly proves $R_\infty(K) \geq R_\infty(M)$ in a non-asymptotic setup.*

Proposition 4 (Alimomeni and Safavi-Naini's bound: Th.2 in [7]). *Let Π be a symmetric-key encryption such that both encryption and decryption algorithms are deterministic. If Π satisfies both $R_\infty(M) = R_\infty^{\mathrm{avg}}(M|C)$ and perfect correctness, we have $R_\infty(K) \geq R_\infty(M)$.*

4.2   Lower Bounds on Failure Probability of Adversary's Guessing

We show that lower bounds on failure probability of adversary's guessing are given by conditional Rényi entropies, $R_\alpha^H(M|C)$ or $R_\alpha^A(M|C)$, in general.

Let $\alpha > 1$. Suppose that an adversary obtains a ciphertext C by observing a channel, and he chooses an arbitrary function g. Let $\hat{M} := g(C)$, $P_e := \Pr\{M \neq \hat{M}\}$, and $\bar{P}_e := 1 - P_e$. The purpose of the adversary is to maximize $\Pr\{M = \hat{M}\} = \bar{P}_e$ (or equivalently, to minimize P_e) by taking a guessing strategy g. Without loss of generality, we assume $\bar{P}_e \geq 1/|\mathcal{M}|$.

First, we derive a lower bound on P_e by using $I_\alpha^H(M;C)$ as follows. The proof is given in the full version [1] where DPI for $R_\alpha^H(X|Y)$ and our extension of Fano's inequality (i.e., Theorem 6) are effectively used.

Theorem 7. *The failure probability of adversary's guessing is lower-bounded by*

$$P_e \geq 1 - \exp\left\{\frac{1-\alpha}{\alpha}R_\alpha(M)\right\}\exp\left\{\frac{\alpha-1}{\alpha}I_\alpha^H(M;C)\right\}. \tag{8}$$

In particular, if P_M is the uniform distribution, we have

$$P_e \geq 1 - |\mathcal{M}|^{\frac{1-\alpha}{\alpha}}\exp\left\{\frac{\alpha-1}{\alpha}I_\alpha^H(M;C)\right\}. \tag{9}$$

If we impose security criteria $I_\alpha^H(M;C) \leq \epsilon$ for small ϵ (say, $\epsilon = 0$) for an encryption protocol (note that any other quantity $R_\alpha(M)$, $|\mathcal{M}|$ is independent of security of the protocol), the above lower bound can be large, and hence the adversary cannot guess a target plaintext from a ciphertext with reasonable probability even if he chooses a powerful guessing strategy g.

Remark 6. *The bound (8) is tight for $\alpha = 2$ and $\alpha = \infty$ in the following sense.*

- *Case of $\alpha = 2$: Consider the case that $I_2^H(M;C) = 0$ and P_M is the uniform distribution. Then, (9) implies that $P_e \geq 1 - \exp(-\frac{1}{2}R_2(M)) = 1 - \frac{1}{\sqrt{|\mathcal{M}|}}$, or equivalently $\bar{P}_e \leq \frac{1}{\sqrt{|\mathcal{M}|}}$. The equality of this bound is achievable, since it is the collision probability (i.e., an adversary can take a strategy which selects a plaintext according to P_M).*
- *Case of $\alpha = \infty$: Consider the case $I_\infty^H(M;C) = 0$. Then, (8) implies that $P_e \geq 1 - \exp(-R_\infty(M)) = 1 - \max_m P_M(m)$, or equivalently $\bar{P}_e \leq \max_m P_M(m)$. The equality of this bound is achievable, since an adversary can take a strategy $g(C) = \arg\max_m P_M(m)$.*

Secondly, we show a lower bound on P_e by using $I_\alpha^A(M;C)$. The proof is given in the full version [1] where DPI for $R_\alpha^A(X|Y)$ and the results in [10,14] are effectively used.

Proposition 5. *The failure probability of adversary's guessing is lower-bounded by*

$$P_e \geq 1 - |\mathcal{M}|^{\frac{1-\alpha}{\alpha}}\exp\left\{\frac{\alpha-1}{\alpha}I_\alpha^A(M_{1/\alpha};C)\right\}, \tag{10}$$

where $P_{M_{1/\alpha}}(m) = \frac{P_M(m)^{1/\alpha}}{\sum_{\tilde{m}} P_M(\tilde{m})^{1/\alpha}}$. In particular, if P_M is the uniform distribution, we have

$$P_e \geq 1 - |\mathcal{M}|^{\frac{1-\alpha}{\alpha}} \exp\left\{\frac{\alpha-1}{\alpha} I_\alpha^A(M;C)\right\}. \tag{11}$$

Remark 7. If P_M is the uniform distribution, the bound (9) is directly obtained from the bound (11) since $I_\alpha^A(M;C) \leq I_\alpha^H(M;C)$. However, it is not the case in general.

Therefore, $I_\alpha^H(M;C) \leq \epsilon$ or $I_\alpha^A(M;C) \leq \epsilon$ for an extremely small $\epsilon \in [0,1]$ is a sufficient condition to show that the failure probability of adversary's guessing is large enough (or equivalently, the success probability of adversary's guessing is small enough). Our security criteria based on conditional Rényi entropies is $I_\alpha^H(M;C) \leq \epsilon$ or $I_\alpha^A(M;C) \leq \epsilon$, which is equivalent to $R_\alpha(M) - R_\alpha^H(M|C) \leq \epsilon$ or $R_\alpha(M) - R_\alpha^A(M|C) \leq \epsilon$, and it is natural to consider the security criteria in terms of an adversary's guessing probability.

5   Generalizing Shannon's Impossibility in Encryption

In this section, we extend the bounds in Sect. 4.1 in a generic and unified manner by using security criteria based on conditional Rényi entropies.

5.1   The Model and Security Definition

We explain the traditional model of (symmetric-key) encryption protocols. In the following, let $\mathcal{M}$ (resp. $\mathcal{C}$) be a finite set of plaintexts (resp. a finite set of ciphertexts). Also, let M be a random variable which takes plaintexts in $\mathcal{M}$ and P_M its distribution. C denotes a random variable which takes ciphertexts $c \in \mathcal{C}$.

Let $\Pi = ([P_{ED}], \pi_{enc}, \pi_{dec})$ be an *encryption* protocol as defined below:

- Let P_{ED} be a probability distribution over $\mathcal{E} \times \mathcal{D}$ which is a finite set of pairs of encryption and decryption keys. $[P_{ED}]$ is a key generation algorithm, and it outputs $(e,d) \in \mathcal{E} \times \mathcal{D}$ according to P_{ED};
- π_{enc} is an encryption algorithm. It takes an encryption key $e \in \mathcal{E}$ and a plaintext $m \in \mathcal{M}$ on input, and it outputs a ciphertext $c \leftarrow \pi_{enc}(e,m)$, which will be sent via an authenticated channel;
- π_{dec} is a decryption algorithm. It takes on input a decryption key $d \in \mathcal{D}$ and a ciphertext $c \in \mathcal{C}$, and it outputs $\tilde{m} \leftarrow \pi_{dec}(d,c)$ where $\tilde{m} \in \mathcal{M}$.

If $\Pi = ([P_K], \pi_{enc}, \pi_{dec})$ (i.e., $[P_{ED}] = [P_{KK}]$ and $e = d$), Π is said to be a *symmetric-key encryption*.

In this paper, we do not require that π_{enc} is deterministic, namely, π_{enc} can be randomized. Also, we assume that Π meets *perfect correctness*, namely, it satisfies $\pi_{dec}(d, \pi_{enc}(e,m)) = m$ for any possible (e,d) and m. In addition, we consider the case where an encryption protocol Π is usable at most one time (i.e., the one-time model).

Let P_M be a distribution on $\mathcal{M}$, and we assume that it is fixed in the following discussion.

Definition 4 (Secrecy). *For $\alpha \geq 0$, let $R_\alpha(\cdot|\cdot)$ be any of $R_\alpha^H(\cdot|\cdot)$ and $R_\alpha^A(\cdot|\cdot)$. An encryption protocol Π is said to meet ϵ-secrecy with respect to $R_\alpha(\cdot|\cdot)$, if it satisfies $R_\alpha(M) - R_\alpha(M|C) \leq \epsilon$. In particular, Π meets perfect secrecy with respect to $R_\alpha(\cdot|\cdot)$, if $\epsilon = 0$ above.*

Note that the traditional notion of perfect secrecy (i.e., $H(M|C) = H(M)$) is equivalent to that of perfect secrecy with respect to $H(\cdot|\cdot) = R_1^H(\cdot|\cdot) = R_1^A(\cdot|\cdot)$ (i.e., $\alpha = 1$).

Also, ϵ-secrecy with respect to $R_\alpha^H(\cdot|\cdot)$ (resp., $R_\alpha^A(\cdot|\cdot)$) is equivalent to $I_\alpha^H(M;C)$ $\leq \epsilon$ (resp., $I_\alpha^A(M;C) \leq \epsilon$) (see Sect. 4.2).

5.2   Basic Idea for Generalization of Shannon's Impossibility

By Shannon's work [5], it is well known that we have $H(K) \geq H(M)$ for symmetric-key encryption with perfect secrecy (see Prop. 2), which is often called Shannon's impossibility. It will be natural to generalize or extend it to the Rényi entropy. However, there exist some difficulties to generalize it in a technical viewpoint, since in general conditional Rényi entropies do not always have rich properties like the conditional Shannon entropy as we have seen in Sects. 2 and 3. In this subsection, we briefly explain our idea of generalizing Shannon's impossibility to the Rényi entropy.

First, let's recall two proof techniques used for deriving $H(K) \geq H(M)$ below, where PS, PC, and CRE mean perfect secrecy, perfect correctness, and conditioning reduces entropy, respectively.

Proof I	Proof II
$\begin{aligned} H(M) &= H(M|C) \text{ (by PS)} \\ &= H(M|C) - H(M|KC) \\ &\quad \text{(by PC)} \\ &= I(M;K|C) \\ &= H(K|C) - H(K|MC) \\ &\leq H(K|C) \\ &\leq H(K) \text{ (by CRE)} \end{aligned}$	$\begin{aligned} H(M) &= H(M|C) \text{ (by PS)} \\ &\leq H(MK|C) \\ &\quad \text{(by conditioned monotonicity)} \\ &= H(K|C) + H(M|KC) \\ &\quad \text{(by chain rule)} \\ &= H(K|C) \text{ (by PC)} \\ &\leq H(K) \text{ (by CRE)} \end{aligned}$

In addition to PS and PC, the property commonly used in both proofs is CRE. From this point of view, it would be reasonable to consider a class of conditional Rényi entropies $R_\alpha^H(\cdot|\cdot)$ and $R_\alpha^A(\cdot|\cdot)$ which satisfy CRE.

In addition, in order to complete the proofs, the useful property of the mutual information (i.e., $I(X;Y) = I(Y;X)$) is used in Proof I, while the properties of conditioned monotonicity and chain rule are used in Proof II. At this point, one may think it hopeless to apply the technique in Proof I, since $I_\alpha^H(X;Y) \neq I_\alpha^H(Y;X)$ and $I_\alpha^A(X;Y) \neq I_\alpha^A(Y;X)$ in general; and also one may think it hopeless to apply the technique even in Proof II, since each of $R_\alpha^H(\cdot|\cdot)$ and

$R_\alpha^A(\cdot|\cdot)$ does not satisfy the (weak) chain rule in general. Nonetheless, our idea is to follow that of Proof II: our technical point is not to use the (weak) chain rule, but to successfully utilize the equality condition of conditioned monotonicity in the case of PC. Owing to our new results about conditional Rényi entropies in Sects. 2 and 3, we can prove extension of Shannon's impossibility in a highly simple and unified way compared to other ways used for the proofs in the bounds in Sect. 4.1, as will be seen in Sect. 5.3.

5.3   Lower Bounds

We newly derive a family of lower bounds on secret-keys with respect to (conditional) Rényi entropies in a comprehensive way. And, it will be seen that our new bounds include all the existing bounds in Sect. 4.1 as special cases.

Theorem 8. *For arbitrary $\alpha \geq 0$, let $R_\alpha(\cdot|\cdot)$ be any of $R_\alpha^H(\cdot|\cdot)$ and $R_\alpha^A(\cdot|\cdot)$. Let $\Pi = ([P_{ED}], \pi_{enc}, \pi_{dec})$ be an encryption protocol satisfying perfect correctness. Then, we have the following bounds.*

(i) (Lower bound on size of encryption-keys) If Π satisfies $R_\alpha(C) \leq R_\alpha(C|M) + \epsilon$ and π_{enc} is deterministic, we have $R_\alpha(E) \geq R_\alpha(C) - \epsilon$.

(ii) (Lower bound on size of decryption-keys) Suppose that Π satisfies $R_\alpha(M) \leq R_\alpha(M|C) + \epsilon$. Then, we have $R_\alpha(D) \geq R_\alpha(M) - \epsilon$.

(iii) (Lower bound on size of ciphertexts) It holds that $R_\alpha(C) \geq R_\alpha(M)$.

Proof. First, we can show (i) as follows.

$$R_\alpha(C) \leq R_\alpha(C|M) + \epsilon \overset{(a)}{\leq} R_\alpha(CE|M) + \epsilon \overset{(b)}{=} R_\alpha(E|M) + \epsilon \overset{(c)}{=} R_\alpha(E) + \epsilon,$$

where (a) follows from Theorem 5 (i), (b) follows from Theorem 5 (ii) since π_{enc} is deterministic, and (c) follows from that M and E are independent.

Secondly, we can show (ii) as follows.

$$R_\alpha(M) \leq R_\alpha(M|C) + \epsilon \overset{(a)}{\leq} R_\alpha(MD|C) + \epsilon \overset{(b)}{=} R_\alpha(D|C) + \epsilon \overset{(c)}{\leq} R_\alpha(D) + \epsilon,$$

where (a) follows from Theorem 5 (i), (b) follows from Theorem 5 (ii) since Π meets perfect correctness, and (c) follows from that both $R_\alpha^H(\cdot|\cdot)$ and $R_\alpha^A(\cdot|\cdot)$ satisfy CRE (see Theorem 2).

Finally, we show (iii). Let $\hat{K} := (E, D)$. Then, we get

$$R_\alpha(M) \overset{(a)}{=} R_\alpha(M|\hat{K}) \overset{(b)}{\leq} R_\alpha(MC|\hat{K}) \overset{(c)}{=} R_\alpha(C|\hat{K}) \overset{(d)}{\leq} R_\alpha(C),$$

where (a) follows from that $\hat{K}$ and M are independent, (b) follows from Theorem 5 (i), (c) also follows from Theorem 5 (ii) since Π meets perfect correctness, and (d) follows from that both $R_\alpha^H(\cdot|\cdot)$ and $R_\alpha^A(\cdot|\cdot)$ satisfy CRE (see Theorem 2). □

In particular, we obtain the following results for symmetric-key encryption protocols. The proof is straightforward by setting $E = D = K$ in Theorem 8.

Corollary 1. *For arbitrary $\alpha \geq 0$, let $R_\alpha(\cdot|\cdot)$ be any of $R_\alpha^H(\cdot|\cdot)$ and $R_\alpha^A(\cdot|\cdot)$. Let $\Pi = ([P_K], \pi_{enc}, \pi_{dec})$ be a symmetric-key encryption protocol which meets perfect correctness. Then, we have the following.*

(i) If Π satisfies $R_\alpha(M) \leq R_\alpha(M|C) + \epsilon$, it holds that $R_\alpha(K) \geq R_\alpha(M) - \epsilon$.
(ii) If Π satisfies $R_\alpha(C) \leq R_\alpha(C|M) + \epsilon$ and π_{enc} is deterministic, we have $R_\alpha(K) \geq R_\alpha(C) - \epsilon$ and $R_\alpha(C) \geq R_\alpha(M)$.

Corollary 2. *For arbitrary $\alpha \geq 0$, let $R_\alpha(\cdot|\cdot)$ be any of $R_\alpha^H(\cdot|\cdot)$ and $R_\alpha^A(\cdot|\cdot)$. Let $\Pi = ([P_K], \pi_{enc}, \pi_{dec})$ be a symmetric-key encryption protocol which meets perfect correctness and ϵ-secrecy with respect to $R_\alpha(\cdot|\cdot)$. Then, it holds that $R_\alpha(K) \geq R_\alpha(M) - \epsilon$.*

Interestingly, the following proposition shows that traditional perfect secrecy implies a family of lower bounds of the Rényi entropy $R_\alpha(\cdot)$ for all $\alpha \geq 0$. The proof follows from Corollary 1 by applying $\epsilon = 0$.

Corollary 3. *Let $\Pi = ([P_K], \pi_{enc}, \pi_{dec})$ be a symmetric-key encryption protocol which meets both perfect correctness and perfect secrecy. Then, for any $\alpha \geq 0$, it holds that $R_\alpha(K) \geq R_\alpha(M)$. In particular, if π_{enc} is deterministic, we have $R_\alpha(K) \geq R_\alpha(C) \geq R_\alpha(M)$.*

Remark 8. *Note that the Shannon's bounds (i.e., Proposition 2) are special cases of Corollary 3, since they are obtained by applying $\alpha = 0, 1$ in Corollary 3[5]. Also, Dodis's bound (i.e., Proposition 3) is a special case of Corollary 3, since it is obtained by applying $\alpha = \infty$ in Corollary 3. Furthermore, Alimomeni and Safavi-Naini's bound (i.e., Proposition 4) is a special case of Corollary 2, since it is obtained by applying $\epsilon = 0$ and $R_\infty^{avg}(\cdot|\cdot) = \lim_{\alpha \to \infty} R_\alpha^A(\cdot|\cdot)$ in Corollary 2[7]. Therefore, since Corollaries 2 and 3 are special cases of Theorem 8, all the bounds are special cases of ours in Theorem 8.*

5.4 Construction

We note that $H(M|C) = H(M)$ implies $R_\alpha(M|C) = R_\alpha(M)$ for all $\alpha \geq 0$, where $R_\alpha(\cdot|\cdot)$ is $R_\alpha^H(\cdot|\cdot)$ or $R_\alpha^A(\cdot|\cdot)$. Therefore, in this sense security criteria based on the Shannon entropy implies security criteria based on the Rényi entropy. However, the converse is not true in general. Actually, security criteria based on the min-entropy is strictly weaker than that of the Shannon entropy. Although in [7] it is not shown that the lower bound in Proposition 4 is tight for symmetric-key encryption protocols which do not meet perfect security, we can show that it is tight by considering the following simple construction.

Suppose $\mathcal{M} = \mathcal{C} = \mathcal{K} = \{0,1\}$ and $P_K(0) = P_M(0) = p$ with $1/2 < p < 1$. We consider the one-time pad for 1-bit encryption $\Pi_1 = ([P_K], \pi_{enc}, \pi_{dec})$, where $\pi_{enc}(k,m) = k \oplus m$ and $\pi_{dec}(k,c) = k \oplus c$. Then, the following proposition shows security and key-size of the above construction, and the proof is given in the full version [1] .

---

[5] Strictly speaking, our bounds are slightly more general than Shannon's bounds and Alimomeni and Safavi-Naini's one, since we have removed the assumption that π_{enc} and π_{dec} are deterministic

Proposition 6. *The above protocol Π_1 does not meet perfect secrecy, and Π_1 satisfies perfect secrecy with respect to $R_\infty^{\mathrm{avg}}(\cdot|\cdot)$, or equivalently $I_\infty^{\mathsf{A}}(M;C) = 0$. Furthermore, it holds that $R_\infty(K) = R_\infty(M)$ in Π_1.*

Remark 9. *In the above construction Π_1, we note that $\lim_{\alpha\to\infty} R_\alpha^{\mathsf{H}}(M|C) = R_\infty^{\mathrm{wst}}(M|C) < R_\infty(M)$. Therefore, Π_1 does not meet perfect secrecy with respect to $R_\infty^{\mathrm{wst}}(\cdot|\cdot)$. Also, Π_1 illustrates $I_\infty^{\mathsf{A}}(M;C) \neq I_\infty^{\mathsf{A}}(C;M)$, while Π_1 meets $I_\infty^{\mathsf{H}}(M;C) = I_\infty^{\mathsf{H}}(C;M)(\neq 0)$.*

In general, for any sufficiently large $\alpha \geq 0$, the following construction shows that the lower bound in Corollary 2 for symmetric-key encryption protocols is tight in an asymptotic sense.

Suppose $\mathcal{M} = \mathcal{C} = \mathcal{K} = \{0,1\}$ and $P_M(0) = p$ and $P_K(0) = q$ such that $p = \frac{1}{2}(1 + \delta_1)$, $q = p + \delta_2$, and $0 < \delta_i$ and $\delta_i = o(1/\alpha)$ for $i = 1, 2$. We consider the one-time pad for 1-bit encryption $\Pi_2 = ([P_K], \pi_{enc}, \pi_{dec})$, where $\pi_{enc}(k, m) = k \oplus m$ and $\pi_{dec}(k, c) = k \oplus c$. Then, the following proposition is shown, and the proof is given in the full version [1] .

Proposition 7. *For a sufficiently large $\alpha \geq 0$, the above protocol Π_2 does not meet perfect secrecy, and Π_2 meets ϵ-secrecy with respect to $R_\alpha^{\mathsf{H}}(\cdot|\cdot)$, or equivalently $I_\alpha^{\mathsf{H}}(M;C) = \epsilon$, with $\epsilon = o(1/\alpha)$. Furthermore, it holds that $R_\alpha(K) = R_\alpha(M) - o(1/\alpha)$ in Π_2.*

Remark 10. *The above construction Π_2 meets ϵ-secrecy with respect to $R_\alpha^{\mathsf{A}}(\cdot|\cdot)$, or equivalently $I_\alpha^{\mathsf{A}}(M;C) = \epsilon$, with $\epsilon = o(1/\alpha)$. This fact directly follows from Proposition 7 and the inequality $I_\alpha^{\mathsf{A}}(M;C) \leq I_\alpha^{\mathsf{H}}(M;C)$. Also, by calculation we can see that Π_2 illustrates $I_\alpha^{\mathsf{H}}(M;C) \neq I_\alpha^{\mathsf{H}}(C;M)$ (see the full version [1]).*

Acknowledgments. The authors would like to thank the anonymous referees for their helpful comments. Mitsugu Iwamoto is supported by JSPS KAKENHI Grant No. 23760330. Junji Shikata is supported by JSPS KAKENHI Grant No. 23500012.

References

1. Iwamoto, M., Shikata, J.: Information theoretic security for encryption based on conditional Renyi entropies. IACR Cryptology ePrint Archive, 2013/440 (2013)
2. Shannon, C.: A mathematical theory of communication. Bell Syst. Tech. J. **27**(3), 379–423 (1948)
3. Hartley, R.V.L.: Transmission of information. Bell Syst. Tech. J. **7**(3), 535–563 (1928)
4. Håstad, J., Impagliazzo, R., Levin, L.A., Luby, M.: A pseudorandom generator from one-way function. SIAM J. Comput. **22**, 1364–1396 (1994)
5. Shannon, C.E.: Communication theory of secrecy systems. Bell Tech. J. **28**, 656–715 (1949)
6. Dodis, Y.: Shannon impossibility, revisited. In: Smith, A. (ed.) ICITS 2012. LNCS, vol. 7412, pp. 100–110. Springer, Heidelberg (2012)
7. Alimomeni, M., Safavi-Naini, R.: Guessing secrecy. In: Smith, A. (ed.) ICITS 2012. LNCS, vol. 7412, pp. 1–13. Springer, Heidelberg (2012)

8. Rényi, A.: On measures of information and entropy. In: Proceedings of the 4th Berkeley Symposium on Mathematics, Statistics and Probability, pp. 547–561 (1961)
9. Teixeira, A., Matos, A., Antunes, L.: Conditional Rényi entropies. IEEE Trans. Inf. Theory **58**(7), 4273–4277 (2012)
10. Arimoto, S.: Information measures and capacity of order α for discrete memoryless channels. Colloquia Mathematica Societatis János Bolyai, 16. Topics in Information Theory 41–52 (1975)
11. Hayashi, M.: Exponential decreasing rate of leaked information in universal random privacy amplification. IEEE Trans. Inf. Theory **57**(6), 3989–4001 (2011)
12. Fano, R.M.: Class notes for transmission of information (course 6.574). Technical report, MIT, Cambridge. (1952)
13. Polyanskiy, Y., Poor, V., Verdú, S.: Channel coding rate in the finite blocklength regime. IEEE Trans. Inf. Theory **56**(5), 2307–2359 (2010)
14. Polyanskiy, Y., Verdú, S.: Arimoto channel coding converse and Rényi divergence. In: Forty-Eighth Annual Allerton Conference, pp. 1327–1333 (2010)
15. Cachin, C.: Entropy measures and unconditional security in cryptography. Ph.D. thesis, Swiss Federal Institute of Technology, Zürich, Switzerland (1997)
16. Jizba, P., Arimitsu, T.: Generalized statistics: yet another generalization. Phys. A **340**, 110–116 (2004)
17. Jizba, P., Arimitsu, T.: The world according to Rényi: thermodynamics of multi-fractal systems. Ann. Phys. **312**, 17–59 (2004)
18. Renner, R.S., Wolf, S.: Simple and tight bounds for information reconciliation and privacy amplification. In: Roy, B. (ed.) ASIACRYPT 2005. LNCS, vol. 3788, pp. 199–216. Springer, Heidelberg (2005)
19. Hayashi, M.: Tight exponential analysis of universally composable privacy amplification and its applications. arXiv:1010.1358 (2010)
20. Stinson, D.R.: Cryptography: Theory and Practice, 3rd edn. Chapman & Hall/CRC, Boca Raton (2005)
21. Cover, T.M., Thomas, J.A.: Elements of Information Theory, 2nd edn. Wiley and Interscience, Hoboken (2006)
22. Fujishige, S.: Polymatroidal dependence structure of a set of random variables. Inf. Control **39**, 55–72 (1978)
23. Dodis, Y., Reyzin, L., Smith, A.: Fuzzy extractors: how to generate strong keys from biometrics and other noisy data. In: Cachin, C., Camenisch, J.L. (eds.) EUROCRYPT 2004. LNCS, vol. 3027, pp. 523–540. Springer, Heidelberg (2004)
24. Dodis, Y., Katz, J., Reyzin, L., Smith, A.: Robust fuzzy extractors and authenticated key agreement from close secrets. In: Dwork, C. (ed.) CRYPTO 2006. LNCS, vol. 4117, pp. 232–250. Springer, Heidelberg (2006)
25. Dodis, Y., Katz, J., Reyzin, L., Smith, A.: Fuzzy extractors: how to generate strong keys from biometrics and other noisy data. SIAM J. Comput. **38**(1), 97–139 (2008)
26. Dodis, Y., Katz, J., Reyzin, L., Smith, A.: Robust fuzzy extractors and authenticated key agreement from close secrets. In: Dwork, C. (ed.) CRYPTO 2006. LNCS, vol. 4117, pp. 232–250. Springer, Heidelberg (2006)
27. Dodis, Y., Yu, Y.: Overcoming weak expectations. In: Sahai, A. (ed.) TCC 2013. LNCS, vol. 7785, pp. 1–22. Springer, Heidelberg (2013)
28. Katzenbeisser, S., Kocabaş, U., Rozić, V., Sadeghi, A.-R., Verbauwhede, I., Wachsmann, C.: PUFs: myth, fact or busted? a security evaluation of physically unclonable functions (PUFs) cast in silicon. In: Prouff, E., Schaumont, P. (eds.) CHES 2012. LNCS, vol. 7428, pp. 283–301. Springer, Heidelberg (2012)

29. Arikan, E.: An inequality on guessing and its application to sequential decoding. IEEE Trans. Inf. Theory **42**(1), 99–105 (1996)

30. Koga, H.: New coding theorems for fixed-length source coding and Shannon's cipher system with a general source. In: ISITA2008, pp. 251–256, December 2008

31. Han, T.S.: Information-Spectrum Methods in Information Theory. Springer-Verlag, Heidelberg (2003)

32. Renner, R., Wolf, S.: Smooth Rényi entropy and its applications. In: ISIT2004, p. 232, June–July, 2004

33. Tomamichel, M., Hayashi, M.: A hierarchy of information quantities for finite block length analysis of quantum tasks. arXiv:1208.1478 (2012)

Insider-Proof Encryption with Applications for Quantum Key Distribution

Matthew McKague[1]([✉]) and Lana Sheridan[2]

[1] Department of Physics, University of Otago, Dunedin, New Zealand
matthew.mckague@otago.ac.nz
[2] Centre for Quantum Technologies, National University of Singapore,
3 Science Drive 2, Singapore 117543, Singapore
lana.s.sheridan@gmail.com

Abstract. We introduce insider-proof private channels which are private channels that additionally allow for security even when the key is correlated with the message. This prevents an insider, who has access to secret keys and the capability of choosing messages to be sent on the channel, from signalling to someone who can read the ciphertexts. We give a construction for approximately insider-proof private channels using 2-universal hash functions.

Quantum key distribution (QKD) offers the promise of information-theoretically secure communication, provided a number of assumptions are met. Ideally, the number of these assumptions required in a protocol should be reduced to a minimum. This is the motivation behind device independent QKD (DIQKD) protocols which use an adversarial model for the quantum devices. However, a previous report [3] pointed out that current protocols for DIQKD can leak key to an outside adversary when devices are used repeatedly. We show how to use the insider-proof private channel to allow DIQKD protocols to reuse devices any desired number of times without leaking information.

1 Introduction

We consider the use of private channels within quantum key distribution protocols in order to protect against attacks in certain scenarios where a minimal number of assumptions are made.

1.1 Private Channels

The one-time pad is probably the best known information-theoretically secure cryptographic primitive, which has many applications. The one-time pad is a particular realization of a *private channel*, which transmits messages between two parties without any information leaking two any third party. The one-time pad takes two resources, a shared private key and a public authenticated channel, and uses them to produce a private channel by adding the key k to the message

C. Padró (Ed.): ICITS 2013, LNCS 8317, pp. 122–141, 2014.
DOI: 10.1007/978-3-319-04268-8_8, © Springer International Publishing Switzerland 2014

m to produce the ciphertext $c = k \oplus m$ which is sent over the public channel. The shared key must be strictly uncorrelated with any adversaries or the message.

Now consider a scenario in which we break this last assumption. Suppose that an adversary is working in a secure lab and has access to the shared secret keys and can choose messages to send via the one-time pad. Further, there is some secret data d which the adversary wishes to communicate to an outside partner. Knowing k, the adversary chooses a message $m = k \oplus d$. The resulting ciphertext, sent via the public channel, is $k \oplus m = d$, from which the outside partner trivially obtains the secret data.

To protect against this scenario we define *insider-proof private channels* which are defined to be secure even if the messages are chosen adversarially with knowledge of any shared private keys. A concrete goal, then, is to find a realization of such a channel.

1.2   QKD

Quantum key distribution protocols [5] allow two distant parties who share some small initial key to grow new shared randomness by making measurements on quantum systems. In entanglement-based quantum key distribution schemes [8], such as we consider here, the key growth is accomplished by distributing two quantum systems in an entangled state between Alice and Bob (for example, via pairs of entangled photons) which they measure using quantum devices. (An entangled state is one that, even over physically separated systems, can not be decomposed as a tensor product of local states on the systems.) They then discuss their correlated measurement data via a public channel, performing error correction and privacy amplification to obtain a final key.

The security of entanglement-based schemes results from the fact that if Alice and Bob's states are highly entangled then their joint state is almost in a product state with Eve (this property of quantum mechanics is called *monogamy of entanglement* [7]). When product states are measured in any bases the classical outcomes are uncorrelated. Hence classical data obtained by measuring Alice and Bob's states will be uncorrelated with Eve. Furthermore, Alice and Bob can decide whether they share an entangled state by checking for certain correlations in their measurement data [8].

DIQKD. Proofs of security [15,16] for these protocols make assumptions about the behaviour of the devices that Alice and Bob use, usually by specifying a particular measurement to be made. Additional required assumptions are that Alice and Bob's devices are shielded within their labs so that they can only accept signals from outside - they do not signal to Eve - that quantum mechanics is valid, and that Alice and Bob can each generate randomness locally which is uncorrelated with Eve or their devices. Alice and Bob must also share a small initial key for authentication and communicate over an insecure public channel. If Eve tampers with the public channel (beyond passively listening), or the entangled states then QKD schemes can detect this and either abort or apply privacy amplification to eliminate Eve's knowledge of the final key.

Device-independent quantum key distribution (DIQKD) [1, 2, 12] is a concept for protocols that makes fewer assumptions. In particular they make no assumptions about how Alice and Bob's devices operate. Some assumptions are replaced with testable requirements, in particular that the measurement devices should have a very high efficiency to eliminate the "detection loophole." Also, typical security proofs for QKD make no mention of the fact that the devices should not signal to Eve - it is built into the model of the devices, but needs to be made explicit for DIQKD. In some DIQKD proofs the testable requirement for high detector efficiency is replaced with a "fair sampling" assumption since current devices are not capable of reaching high enough efficiencies. Note, however, that normal QKD schemes can also be broken if the fair sampling assumption is violated [10].

DIQKD protocols have the important advantage over traditional protocols in that even if the measurement devices do not operate as specified in security proofs the protocols can still certify whether a generated key is secure.

The Problem. Here we are interested in removing even more assumptions about the operation of the measurement devices than in the current proofs of security for device-independent protocols. Typically, DIQKD security proofs analyse security for a single round only. Instead we consider the possibility of reusing the devices over many rounds and we allow that they may have an internal memory which can store arbitrary amounts of quantum or classical information. As usual in the DIQKD scenario we treat the devices adversarially: we consider the worst possible case consistent with the assumptions and data gathered.

In this very untrusting model, usual DIQKD protocols face a problem which is that certain messages exchanged between Alice and Bob over a public channel are determined by the measurement devices via their outputs. Although this is known not to cause a problem (in certain protocols at least [4, 13]) for the *current* round of key generation, information about keys generated in previous rounds may leak if the measurement devices bias their outputs in some way [3]. We can think of Alice and Bob's quantum devices as Eve's inside agents who attempt to signal information to her over whatever channels are available.

In this paper we address this problem of reusing the same devices across multiple rounds of DIQKD, but do not consider how DIQKD might be accomplished in a single round of a protocol using adversarial devices with memory. See [13] for a proposal for such a protocol.

1.3   Results

Our main contribution is to describe, and prove the security of, an encryption scheme, the *insider-proof private channel*, which allows Alice and Bob to communicate securely in the presence of an inside agent who knows their shared keys and may choose some messages for them. In particular it is not possible for the agent to manipulate the ciphertext sent over the public channel so as to leak any information about Alice's private data; neither the message itself nor any other data is leaked to Eve.

Security and Construction. The security of our scheme is defined in terms of an ideal functionality which simply gives Alice's message to Bob and sends a random string to Eve consistent with the length of the message. (The length of the ciphertext forms an upper bound on the amount of information in the message, so Eve will always gain at least this much information about the message, but note that in our scheme, it is always possible to securely pad the encrypted message with a random string, resulting in fixed length strings transmitted from Alice to Bob.) This is similar to the usual ideal functionality of a private channel except that in our definition we allow the message, any other private data, *and the secret key* to be correlated in an arbitrary way. We show that our protocol simulates the ideal functionality to within any desired error. This gives an information-theoretic proof of security for our protocol.

Our construction is entirely classical, making use of 2-universal hash functions [6] and a local source of trusted randomness which is independent of Eve and the measurement devices. Such a source of randomness is already a requirement for DIQKD. Our proof makes use of the quantum leftover hashing lemma [17], giving security against quantum adversaries.

Application to DIQKD. In the context of DIQKD the insider-proof private channel allows Alice and Bob to exchange data (such as information for error correction and parameter estimation) which is determined by the devices across a public channel without leaking information from the devices to Eve. The encryption remains secure even if the devices have complete information about Alice and Bob's shared secret keys (generated in previous rounds of the protocol) and even if the devices have complete control over the message sent.

Our encryption protocol, when used within a DIQKD scheme, provides security in the case where Alice and Bob do not announce whether they abort or not (which is known to be another channel over which information may leak to Eve.) There is a linear penalty in terms of net secure key rate, and the security parameters also increase by a constant factor. However, for low error rates the secure key rate approaches 1 and the security parameters can be chosen so that the devices can be reused any desired number of times before they must be securely destroyed. Note that even the most trusting QKD schemes can only be used a finite number of times before they need to be rekeyed. Besides the lower secure key rate there is no penalty, asymptotically, for using our scheme.

In terms of initial key, Alice and Bob must share enough key to authenticate their messages and perform encryption for a single round of key generation, after which they use key generated in past rounds for encryption and authentication. If the error rate is low the required amount of initial key is much smaller than the amount generated in a single round.

Other Applications. The usefulness of our scheme is not limited to DIQKD. It can be used in any context, classical or quantum, in which there is some agent which may choose messages and has at least some information on the secret keys which are used for encryption. As an example, one might protect systems against trojan horses which attempt to collect data from the system and signal to Eve without being detected. If the only channel available is encrypted, and sending unencrypted data would be detected, then the trojan horse might attempt to bias the cihpertexts of the encrypted channel. Our scheme would protect against such signalling.

1.4 Organization of the Paper

The layout of this paper is as follows. In the next section, we describe what an ideal private channel consists of and introduce a new cryptographic concept: the ϵ-insider proof channel. This channel allows the secure transmission of a message, even if the message is chosen adversarially. In Part 2.2 of this section we give a recipe for implementing this channel and in Part 2.3 demonstrate the channel does allow secure message transmission except with probability ϵ.

In Sect. 3.1, we begin to look at applying the ϵ-insider proof channel to quantum key distribution and we specify and motivate the security model we are working in. Following that, we outline the modifications to a DIQKD protocol in Sect. 3.2, and in Sect. 3.3 it is shown that the DIQKD protocol is still secure with the modifications that use the new channel. The composition of repeated DIQKD rounds is considered in Sect. 3.4. Section 3.5 gives the asymptotic key rate achieved by these bounds. Further details of the proof of security in the DIQKD setting and a discussion of how protocol aborts need to be managed and the composability implications are given in the appendices.

2 The Private Channel

We first describe the scenario and define the ideal insider-proof private channel. We then give a protocol and prove that it approximates the ideal channel. The proof relies on 2-universal hashing and the quantum leftover hashing lemma [17].

2.1 The Ideal Channel

Let us define a situation where Alice wishes to privately communicate some information to Bob in the presence of a quantum eavesdropper, Eve, who wishes to obtain access to some of Alice's data. Further, there is an insider A' who has access to Alice's private keys and data, and who can choose some messages to be sent to Bob. That is, there will be some encrypted channel from Alice to Bob and A' can choose some inputs to the channel. However, A' has no other means of communicating with Eve. Alice and Bob's task is to complete their private communication in such a way that Eve cannot gain any information about Alice's data or the message.

Definitions. To begin, let us describe the registers we will use. A contains the message Alice will send, while B is the register which will hold the final message for Bob. C is the ciphertext, or otherwise contains all the raw information leaked to Eve during the protocol. For example, if the channel is implemented using a public channel then C contains all information sent over the channel. D contains secret information that Alice does not want to leak. Finally, E contains Eve's quantum side information. We assume that the length of A, B and C are public.

Definition 1. *The* ideal private channel *between A and B is defined as*

$$\Phi_{AB}^{IPC}(\rho) = \sum_{x,y} \left(|x\rangle\langle x|_A \otimes |x\rangle\langle y|_B \right) \rho \left(|x\rangle\langle x|_A \otimes |y\rangle\langle x|_B \right) \tag{1}$$

So, the ideal private channel erases B and copies the contents of A into it.

Definition 2. *A channel Φ_{ABC} is an ϵ-insider-proof private channel from A to B if there exists a channel Ψ_{CE} such that for all CCCCQ states ρ_{ABCDE},*

$$\left\| \Phi_{AB}^{IPC} \otimes I_D \otimes \Psi_{CE}(\rho) - \Phi_{ABC} \otimes I_{DE}(\rho) \right\|_1 \leq \epsilon \tag{2}$$

Furthermore, if this is true for $\epsilon = 0$ then we say that Φ is an insider-proof private channel.

This definition essentially says that we consider a channel secure if we can approximate it with the ideal channel, along with some simulator that generates a transcript for Eve without referring to the secret data.

Although we have not explicitly stated that the insider can choose the message, this is built into the fact that we allow *any* ρ, and hence this covers the cases where the insider has deliberately correlated the registers A, D and its memory A', possibly using some quantum measurement on half of an entangled $A'E$ state.

Finally, in the case where we wish to implement such a channel using some additional resources, such as a shared key or private randomness, we may extend ρ with additional registers and add conditions as necessary to specify the form of the resources. In keeping with the spirit of the definition, we will only consider resources where the insider has access to any stored data, including shared private keys.

It is interesting to note that, compared with the usual definition of a private channel, the only difference is that the private key is allowed to be correlated with the message.

2.2   The Channel

In order to achieve our goal, we must use some additional resources in the form of a shared private key and a true random number generator on Alice's side. The shared key is in register K while Alice's private random string is held in R. The initial state must satisfy $\rho_{KRBCDE} = U_K^{(n)} \otimes U_R^{(n)} \otimes \rho_{BCDE}$ and $\rho_{RABCDE} = U_R^{(n)} \otimes \rho_{ABCDE}$, where $U^{(n)}$ is the completely mixed state on n qubits. Note that the message can be correlated with the shared key, but the rest of the state cannot. As well, the private randomness is uncorrelated with all other registers. Our protocol is summarized as follows.

Protocol 1. *Input for Alice: strings a, k. Input for Bob: string k.*

1. *Alice chooses a string r uniformly at random.*
2. *Alice calculates $c = a \oplus \left[(k \cdot r) \mod 2^\ell\right]$ and discards k.*
3. *Alice broadcasts (c, r) and then discards them.*
4. *Bob reconstructs $a = c \oplus \left[(k \cdot r) \mod 2^\ell\right]$ and then discards k, r and c.*

2.3 Security of the Channel

We first sketch the proof, then provide the technical details. The insider A' chooses some message A with full knowledge of the shared key K. Hence the message can be correlated with K. However, we will use a K of length more than twice that of $|A|$ ($|K| > 2|A|$) so that there are still $> |A|$ bits of randomness in K, even conditioned on A. Now when we produce the encryption key K' by combining K with R, we produce a K' of length $|A|$. The leftover hashing lemma (stated below) then says that K' is almost completely random, even conditioned on A and R. The ciphertext is then also completely random, even conditioned on A and R, and Eve will not be able to figure out anything about A from R and the ciphertext.

In order to prove that Protocol 1 produces an ϵ-insider-proof private channel we first introduce 2-universal hash functions.

2-Universal Hash Functions. 2-universal hash functions are in fact families of functions which, given a random seed, produce a very uniform output.

Definition 3. *A 2-universal family of functions $\mathcal{F}$ is a family of functions $f : \mathcal{X} \to \mathcal{Y}$ such that, when f is drawn uniformly at random from $\mathcal{F}$, for every $x_1, x_2 \in \mathcal{X}$*

$$P(f(x_1) = f(x_2)) = \frac{1}{|\mathcal{Y}|} \tag{3}$$

Protocol 1 uses the following 2-universal family of hash functions introduced in [6].

Lemma 1. *The family of functions given by $f_r(k) = k \cdot r \mod 2^\ell$ is 2-unversal.*

Proof. Let $x_1 \neq x_2$ be given. We wish to count the r for which

$$(r \cdot x_1) = (r \cdot x_2) \mod 2^\ell. \tag{4}$$

Taking the expression $\mod 2^\ell$, i.e. taking the ℓ least significant bits of the string, can be expressed as taking the expression $\mod b$ for some element[1] b in $GF(2^n)$. Hence we can rewrite this as

$$r \cdot (x_1 \oplus x_2) = 0 \mod b. \tag{5}$$

---

[1] In particular, the element x^ℓ in the usual polynomial representation.

Since the multiplication is over a field, $r = 0 \mod b$ and there is one solution for every member of the equivalence class of 0, of which there are $2^{n-\ell}$ members. Hence the fraction of strings r that are solutions is $2^{n-\ell}/2^n = 2^\ell$ and the family of functions is 2-universal.   □

Note that the family is symmetric in the roles of r and k, so we can use k as the seed instead of r and the family is still 2-universal. The distinction becomes important in the following lemma, which gives a useful approximation of how uniform the output of the hash function is.

Lemma 2 (Quantum leftover hashing lemma [17]). *Let X and E be random variables. Let $\mathcal{F}$ be a family of 2-universal hash functions, indexed by a seed R such that $f_R \in \mathcal{F}$, that take an input $X \in \{0,1\}^n$, and output $Z \in \{0,1\}^\ell$. Then averaged over f_R, the distribution on Z has the property:*

$$\Delta(Z|ER) \le \epsilon' + \frac{1}{2}\sqrt{2^{\ell-H^{\epsilon'}_{\min}(X|E)}}, \tag{6}$$

where the distance from uniform, Δ, is given by

$$\Delta(A|B)_\rho = \min_{\sigma_B} \frac{1}{2}\|\rho_{AB} - \omega_A \otimes \sigma_B\|_1. \tag{7}$$

Proof of Security.

Theorem 2. *Let ℓ and $n > 2\ell$ be given. Then Protocol 1 implements an ϵ-insider-proof secure channel where*

$$\epsilon = \sqrt{2^{2\ell-n}} \tag{8}$$

Proof. We begin by reducing to an equivalent protocol by noting that, so long as Bob completes the protocol before interacting with outside parties, his operations commute with Eve's. Hence we may assume that Eve receives her copy of (c, r) after Bob has completed the protocol. This solves certain notational problems where we need to trace out registers in the proper sequence in order to obtain valid bounds. Also, in this version of the protocol, we make explicit the movement of registers between different parties.

Protocol 3. *Input for Alice: Registers A and K. Input for Bob: Register J.*

1. Alice uses her random number generator to initialize R with a uniformly random string.
2. Alice calculates $K' = (K \cdot R) \mod 2^\ell$, then discards K and sends R to Bob.
3. Bob calculates $J' = (J \cdot R) \mod 2^\ell$, then discards J.
4. Alice calculates $C = K' \oplus A$ and then discards K' and sends C to Bob.
5. Bob calculates $B = C \oplus J'$ and then discards J.
6. Bob passes C and R to Eve.

Here K contains the private shared key, of which J is Bob's copy.

Next we make a further reduction. At the end of step 5, Bob's state consists solely of B, which is a copy of A. Hence we can instead simply apply Φ_{AB}^{IPC} at the end of the protocol and remove all of Bob's operations, as well as J. Then Alice can simply send C and R directly to Eve. Hence we arrive at the following protocol

Protocol 4. *Input for Alice: Registers A and K.*

1. *Alice uses her random number generator to initialize R*
2. *Alice calculates $K' = (K \cdot R) \mod 2^\ell$ and discards K.*
3. *Alice calculates $C = A \oplus K'$ and discards K'.*
4. *Alice sends C and R to Eve.*
5. *Alice and Bob apply Φ_{AB}^{IPC}*

Now we proceed with the security proof. Let $\ell = |A|$ and $n = |K| = |R|$. For notational convenience we assume that C is created in step 3, and B is created in step 5, so we need not keep track of them beforehand. Let the quantum state just after step t be $\rho^{(t)}$ and the ϵ-smooth min-entropy be H_{min}^ϵ. We suppose for the moment that the key in register K is perfectly independent from Eve.

After step 1, since K is secret from Eve, $H_{min}^0(K|DE)_{\rho^{(1)}} = n$. By the chain rule for smooth entropies [15], we also have

$$H_{min}^0(K|ADE)_{\rho^{(1)}} \geq n - \ell. \tag{9}$$

In step 2 we apply the 2-universal hash given in Lemma 1, tracing out K and producing encryption key K' of length ℓ. Using the leftover hashing lemma we find

$$\Delta(K'|ADER)_{\rho^{(2)}} \leq \frac{1}{2}\sqrt{2^{2\ell-n}} = \epsilon_{hash} \tag{10}$$

and hence there exists a σ_{ADER} such that

$$\left\| \rho_{K'ADER}^{(2)} - U_{K'} \otimes \sigma_{ADER} \right\|_1 \leq \epsilon_{hash}. \tag{11}$$

Since for $U_{K'} \otimes \sigma_{ADER}$ A is independent of K', we can XOR them together in step 3 to obtain the ciphertext C which is again independent. We trace out K' and then C and R are sent to Eve in step 4. We find

$$\left\| \rho_{CADER}^{(4)} - U_C \otimes \sigma_{ADER} \right\|_1 \leq \epsilon_{hash}. \tag{12}$$

Next we want to approximate σ_{ADER}. Tracing out the C register, the above inequality becomes $\left\| \rho_{ADER}^{(4)} - \sigma_{ADER} \right\| \leq \epsilon_{hash}$. Since $\rho_{ADER}^{(4)} = \rho_{ADER}^{(1)} = \rho_{ADE} \otimes U_R$ we then obtain

$$\left\| U_C \otimes \sigma_{ADER} - U_C \otimes \rho_{ADE}^{(0)} \otimes U_R \right\| \leq \epsilon_{hash}. \tag{13}$$

Now $U_C \otimes \rho_{ADE} \otimes U_R$ is a state that Eve can create by herself by operating only on her registers by simply appending C and R distributed uniformly. Let us call this operation Ψ. Using the triangle inequality to combine (12) and (13),

$$\left\| \rho_{ACDER}^{(4)} - I_{AD} \otimes \Psi_{CER}(\rho^{(0)}) \right\|_1 \leq 2\epsilon_{hash} = \epsilon . \tag{14}$$

We now introduce register B and after step 5, this becomes

$$\left\| \rho_{ABCDER}^{(5)} - \Phi_{AB}^{IPC} \otimes I_D \otimes \Psi_{CER}(\rho^{(0)}) \right\|_1 \leq \epsilon . \tag{15}$$

Hence the protocol implements a $2\epsilon_{hash}$-insider-proof private channel. $\square$

3   Application to DIQKD

We now consider the application of the ϵ-insider proof channel to DIQKD in the context of reused devices with memory.

3.1   The Model

Alice and Bob share some private randomness and would like to grow more key from it using a shared quantum state. However, they do not trust their measuring devices or the state; in fact, they assume that Eve has built the devices and distributes the quantum state. Let us assume that it is possible for them to complete a device-independent quantum key distribution (DIQKD) protocol securely in this setting. There is some recent work that supports this assumption [4,13,14]. They successfully grow some new key on which Eve's knowledge is bounded to be less than ϵ, quantified using standard trace distance metrics [15]. After this, they would like to *reuse their devices* to grow more key in another round, but the malicious devices are allowed to have memories. As well, all shared randomness used in the protocol will be taken from the previously generated keys, and hence is also shared with the devices.[2] We would like to know whether Alice and Bob can grow new key in this situation.

We make the standard assumptions of DIQKD. We are working in the limit of long keys for each run of the protocol. We assume that the untrusted devices can be isolated within Alice and Bob's laboratories, such that they can receive arbitrary quantum signals from Eve, but can signal only to Alice and Bob and not directly to Eve. We also assume that Alice and Bob can both generate trusted randomness locally. Additionally, we assume Alice and Bob can perform classical processing privately from the untrusted measuring devices in their labs.

This model was first introduced in [3], where the authors argue that in standard protocols Alice and Bob cannot grow further key using the same devices. Particularly, they highlight the issue of whether the protocols are composable. We show how to modify standard DIQKD protocols to eliminate side channels related to Alice and Bob's public discussion and show that they can still grow new secret key. We comment on the issue of composability in Appendix B.

---

[2] At the very least, the devices can know the raw keys from previous rounds, and hence are strongly correlated with the final keys.

3.2   The Protocol

The modifications we propose are restricted to the classical post-processing portions of the protocol. The goal of the changes is to prevent the device from having a communication channel back to Eve within the protocol itself. To this end, we make use of an ϵ-insider-proof channel to send all information between Alice and Bob that the untrusted devices may have influenced. (We assume no other side channels.)

Our modification applies to DIQKD protocols with standard classical post-processing [15]. Importantly, with standard post-processing the only information communicated between Alice and Bob which depends on the quantum devices are the parameter estimation data, the error correction data, and the abort flag.

1. Eve distributes an entangled state ρ_{ABE} to the devices in Alice and Bob's labs. Alice and Bob supply random (and independent) lists of basis choices to the devices for the series of measurements and the devices output the results.
2. Alice announces her basis selections publicly to Bob. Where they have chosen the same basis, the measurement result bit should be correlated for Alice and Bob and can become part of the key. When they have chosen different bases, they can check for CHSH violation or perform other parameter estimations.
3. Alice must send to Bob a subset of her outcomes of size ℓ. To do this, they use Protocol 1 to implement an ϵ-insider-proof private channel, which must not leak information about previously grown keys (or other private data), d. The message string $a = a(k, d)$ is passed from Alice to Bob, encrypted. To do this, she generates a random string r ($|r| = n$) and chooses a string k ($|k| = n$) from her store of previously generated keys. She uses the type of 2-universal hash function introduced in Lemma 1 to create ciphertext $c = a \oplus (k \cdot r)$ mod 2^ℓ. She sends this to Bob along with r. Bob uses r and k to recover a.
4. Bob performs parameter estimation. He sends a similarly encrypted message to Alice containing a flag bit indicating abort or not, and if not, a second encrypted message containing the detected bit error rate Q, the observed parameters, and an appropriate error correction function, along with his parity check bits. Bob pads this communication with randomness, so it is *always of fixed length*. If they instead will abort, Bob sends the abort flag and a random message instead of the error correction information.
5. Alice uses the information to correct her string to Bob's.
6. Using a publicly chosen hash function they perform privacy amplification to reduce Eve's knowledge of the final key below a chosen bound. They discard the session encryption key k used in the protocol.

We now show the security of this protocol.

3.3   Security of DIQKD Using an Insider-Proof Channel

Here we give an overview of the proof of security. For full details refer to Appendix A.

Referring to Fig. 1, in step 1 of the protocol we begin with some state shared between Alice, Bob and Eve which is ϵ_0 away from the ideal state where Eve is in a product state with Alice and Bob. Step 2 can reveal no information about Alice's private data since the message sent to Bob comes from locally generated randomness which is independent of ρ_{ABE}. Hence there is no need to encrypt this information.

In step 3 Alice sends some measurement outcomes to Bob. Since these depend on Alice's device they must be encrypted using the insider-proof private channel. If the ideal channel were used then this would cause no further deviation from the ideal situation. In particular, no information would be revealed to Eve and Bob receives the required data for continuing the usual DIQKD protocol. Since we use the ϵ-insider-proof private channel instead the use of this channel moves the shared state ϵ further away from ideal. Step 4 similarly moves the state a further 2ϵ away from idea, since we use the ϵ-insider-proof private channel twice, once for the error correction data and once for the abort flag. Note that steps 3 and 4 are the only steps which are different from the usual DIQKD procedure.

Steps 5 and 6 cause further deviation from the ideal by ϵ_{qkd} due to the usual post-processing done in the DIQKD protocol.

3.4   Composing Rounds of the New Protocol

In the previous section, we saw that reusing untrusted devices in a new round of QKD using the new protocol caused an increase in the security parameter of the new and old keys by $3\epsilon + \epsilon_{qkd}$. For comparison, if the devices were trusted, and the original DIQKD protocol was used, this parameter would only have grown by ϵ_{qkd}.

Then composing s rounds of successful key growth together,

$$\left|\left| \Phi_{\text{prot}}^{\circ s}(U_K \otimes \sigma_D \otimes \tau_E) - \Phi_{\text{ideal}}^{\circ s}(U_K \otimes \sigma_D \otimes \tau_E) \right|\right|_1 \le 3\epsilon + \epsilon_{\text{qkd}} \; . \qquad (16)$$

where $\Phi^{\circ s}$ means the channel Φ applied s times. Again using the data processing inequality for s applications of Φ_{prot} on Eq. (31) and then the triangle inequality with Eq. (16) gives

$$\left|\left| \Phi_{\text{prot}}^{\circ s}(\rho_{KDE}) - \Phi_{\text{ideal}}^{\circ s}(U_K \otimes \sigma_D \otimes \tau_E) \right|\right|_1 \le \epsilon_0 + 3s\epsilon + s\epsilon_{\text{qkd}} \; . \qquad (17)$$

This shows that each additional round can add at most $3\epsilon + \epsilon_{\text{qkd}}$ to Eve's information on the previously grown keys.

Notice that if an abort occurs in round i, the new key is not obtained for that round, so the length of the final key string will depend on the number of aborts as well as the error rates. However, Alice and Bob still sent two encrypted messages to each other in an aborted round, in order to learn that their error rate was above threshold. Therefore, they still must add 3ϵ for that round, though not ϵ_{qkd}. This means that the security parameter will grow even on aborted rounds.

In practice, Alice and Bob should choose a maximum tolerated security loss of all of their keys ϵ_{sec}. This will determine the number of rounds they would be able to grow key in. They should agree to this number of rounds when they begin

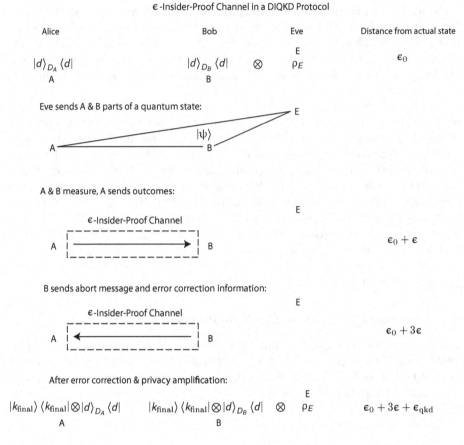

Fig. 1. Use of the insider-proof channel in a device independent quantum key distribution protocol.

to use their devices, then stop using and securely destroy the devices after that many rounds. They do not wish to leak information to Eve about the number of rounds that have aborted. (See Appendix B for further discussion.)

Note that this growth of the security parameter with the number of rounds is also seen in the standard trusted-device QKD models when some of the grown key is used for authentication in subsequent rounds. This means that even in the simplest form of QKD with authentication in which the most assumptions are made, there are only a finite number of rounds that Alice and Bob can compose before they exceed their security tolerance. At that point, they must re-key through some other means. This means that the results given here, which only achieve a finite number of uses of the devices, are the best that can be hoped for. Furthermore, in practice, all physical security devices have only a finite lifespan.

3.5   Asymptotic Secret Key Rate

The application key rates achievable with this protocol modification will depend on the key rate of the underlying DIQKD protocol used, and n the number of bits of the generated key that need to be used as the session keys for Alice and Bob's encrypted messages in the next round, and therefore cannot be used in other applications.

Since we do not know the details of which DIQKD protocol can be used when the devices have memories, we remain agnostic about the exact rate, however, we can assume it would take a form:

$$r \geq f(S_{\mathrm{obs}}) - H(A|B) \tag{18}$$

for some function f with S_{obs} an observed parameter (eg. a Bell-inequality violation) which is what is achieved by current protocols against memoryless devices [9,11].

In this new protocol, we do not need to remove the amount of communication $H(A|B)$ required for error correction, since this is encrypted. However, we will remove the amount of key required to encrypt the next round's communication. We now consider how much key this requires. From Theorem 2, we have:

$$\epsilon = \sqrt{2^{2\ell-n}} = \frac{1}{2^{(n-2\ell)/2}}, \tag{19}$$

Then $n - 2\ell = O(-\log \epsilon)$, so for a constant security parameter ϵ, the key length, n, needs only exceed twice the message length, 2ℓ, by a constant number of bits.

Now we must determine how large the total amount of encrypted information sent between Alice and Bob must be asymptotically. Suppose the sifted key length in one round is N. The parameter estimation message from Alice to Bob must contain the bit values of an $O(\log N)$-size subset of this string in order to achieve an estimation error approaching zero. As $N \to \infty$ the fraction of signals this represents goes to zero. Bob must send to Alice his error correction function results, the size of which will depend on the error rate. The amount of communication required will be $H(A|B) + f(\epsilon_{\mathrm{EC}})$ bits, where $f(\epsilon_{\mathrm{EC}})$ is a function of the security parameter for the error correction that does not depend on N, so that as $N \to \infty$ it also is negligible. Finally, Bob's abort flag requires a constant sized key.

In total, asymptotically, the amount of key needed to implement the insider-proof channels in the protocol depends only on the size of the error correction information to be shared. Since we have $n \geq 2\ell + c$ where c is a constant, the amount of key required is just twice the error rate: $2H(A|B)$.

Then we can see how the asymptotic key rate will change as compared with the original version of the protocol,

$$r \geq f(S_{\mathrm{obs}}) - 2H(A|B). \tag{20}$$

Notice that asymptotically the key rate does not fall as aborts occur, since in an abort, Bob will send the encoded abort flag, but will not encode the $H(A|B)$ bits of error correction information and rather save his key by sending a string output by his random number generator instead. In the finite key regime however, it is clear that aborts will reduce the amount of generated key that can be used in other applications. (See Appendix B for details of how to treat aborted rounds.)

4   Conclusions

We have introduced the concept of an insider-proof channel. We hope that it will have applications, particularly in device-independent schemes where untrusted devices can be assumed not to have direct communication to the adversary, but may be malicious. We construct an explicit example of such a channel that will allow trusted parties to communicate, even about information that the untrusted devices may have generated. We also show how this can be used to reuse untrusted devices for many rounds of QKD.

The model of DIQKD assumed here gives a lot of power to the eavesdropper, since Eve is allowed to prepare Alice and Bob's measuring devices. It is more restrictive to Alice and Bob than other models currently used to describe untrusted device scenarios, where their devices may have manufacturing flaws, but are assumed not to be outright malicious. Those models more realistically represent most cryptographic scenarios today, wherein perhaps a user does not understand the cryptography implemented by his web browser, but he downloaded an authenticated copy from a legitimate business. The business may not have correctly implemented the security, and this is what DIQKD would try to protect against, but it also does not benefit from gaining a reputation for selling users' credit card information to Eve.

However, this less-trusting model is interesting, first, because it provides bounds for what is possible in other more-trusting DI scenarios, and second, because despite its restrictions, QKD can still be performed without much loss of performance. We have introduced a small modification to a DIQKD protocol that allows untrusted and malicious devices to be used in repeated round of secure key growth. It is interesting to note that the only part of the protocol that requires modification is the classical post-processing. This suggests that perhaps existing QKD protocols could be adapted to other new models readily, simply by considering this portion carefully.

There remain some open questions. Are there other applications for insider-proof channels? More specifically, are there other contexts where messages may be chosen maliciously and with knowledge of private data? It also may be possible to improve the bounds presented here in order to get a higher asymptotic key rate. It would also be nice to fit this type of protocol into a composability framework, although it is not clear how to do that in existing frameworks. Additionally, there may be other modifications that could be made to existing protocols that accomplish this same task more efficiently.

Acknowledgements. We thank Marco Tomamichel for a helpful discussion and Roger Colbeck for his comments about composability. This work is funded by the Centre for

Quantum Technologies, which is funded by the Singapore Ministry of Education and the Singapore National Research Foundation, by the University of Otago through a University of Otago Research Grant and the Performance Based Research Fund, and by the Jack Dodd Centre for Quantum Technology.

A Security of DIQKD Using an Insider-Proof Channel

In order to complete a QKD protocol Alice and Bob will require a series of communication channels back and forth which they have authenticated. When the devices in Alice and Bob's labs may have some sensitive information in their memories, then some of these channels must be private channels, in order to show security.

Again, let the quantum state just after step t be $\rho^{(t)}$. At first, let us analyze the protocol assuming we start with a perfect key so that $p^{(0)} = U_K^{(3n)} \otimes \sigma_D \otimes \tau_E$. After step 1, Alice and Bob share with Eve the state ρ_{ABE}. They pick measurements and get outcomes in registers A' and B', so that their shared state becomes $\rho^{(1)}$, where

$$\rho^{(1)} = U_K^{(3n)} \otimes \sigma_D \otimes \sum_{o_{m_A}, o'_{m_B}} p(o_{m_A}, o'_{m_B}) |o_{m_A}\rangle_{A'} \langle o_{m_A}|$$

$$\otimes |o'_{m_B}\rangle_{B'} \langle o'_{m_B}| \otimes \rho_E^{(o_{m_A}, o'_{m_B})} . \tag{21}$$

Now in step 2, Alice uses a public channel to send Bob her measurement choices m_A and Bob can also use a public channel to send Alice his choices m_B. Alice will prepare a private message for Bob that includes a subset a of her outcomes o_{m_A}. She then implements (in step 3) an insider-proof quantum channel to Bob, according to Protocol 4.

We can alter Φ_{ABC} to take the string in register K as part of the input state rather than a parameter that defines Φ_{ABC}. In all other respects, the channel is unchanged. Let the new channel be Φ'_{ABC}. Then from Definition 2,

$$\left\| \mathrm{Tr}_K \, \Phi_{AB}^{IPC} \otimes I_D \otimes \Psi_{CE}(U_K \otimes \rho) - \mathrm{Tr}_K \, \Phi'_{ABC} \otimes I_{DE}(U_K \otimes \rho) \right\|_1 \le \epsilon . \tag{22}$$

Let the register A contain the subset of outcomes (so a is a function of o_{m_A}. Then after an ideal private channel the state will be $\rho^{(3)}$ such that:

$$\left\| \rho^{(3)} - \xi^{(3)} \right\|_1 \le \epsilon . \tag{23}$$

where

$$\xi^{(3)} := U_K^{(2n)} \otimes \sigma_D \otimes \sum_{o_{m_A}, o'_{m_B}} p(o_{m_A}, o'_{m_B}) |a\rangle_A \langle a| \otimes |o_{m_A}\rangle_{A'} \langle o_{m_A}|$$

$$\otimes |a\rangle_B \langle a| \otimes |o'_{m_B}\rangle_{B'} \langle o'_{m_B}| \otimes \rho_E^{(o_{m_A}, o'_{m_B})} \otimes I_{C,R} . \tag{24}$$

Bob will also have to reply in step 4, again using an insider-proof channel twice. First he sends a one-bit message about whether to abort and second he sends the error correction information. For an ideal private channel:

$$\left\|\rho^{(4)} - \xi^{(4)}\right\|_1 \leq 3\epsilon . \tag{25}$$

where

$$\xi^{(4)} := \sigma_D \otimes \sum_{o_{m_A}, o'_{m_B}} p(o_{m_A}, o'_{m_B}) |b\rangle_A \langle b| \otimes |o_{m_A}\rangle_{A'} \langle o_{m_A}|$$

$$\otimes |b\rangle_B \langle b| \otimes |o'_{m_B}\rangle_{B'} \langle o'_{m_B}| \otimes \rho_E^{(o_{m_A}, o'_{m_B})} \otimes (I_{C,R})^{\otimes 3} . \tag{26}$$

At this point, they arrive at identical raw keys with probability $1 - \epsilon_{EC}$, where Alice and Bob can choose ϵ_{EC} arbitrarily small. Then,

$$\left\|\rho^{(5)} - \xi^{(5)}\right\|_1 \leq 3\epsilon + \epsilon_{EC} + \epsilon_{PE} , \tag{27}$$

defining

$$\xi^{(5)} := \sigma_D \otimes \sum_{o_{m_A}, o'_{m_B}} p(o_{m_A}, o'_{m_B}) |k_{\text{raw}}\rangle_{A'} \langle k_{\text{raw}}| \otimes |k_{\text{raw}}\rangle_{B'} \langle k_{\text{raw}}| \otimes \rho_E^{(o_{m_A}, o'_{m_B})} ,$$

$$\tag{28}$$

where we dropped the C and R registers for convenience, and k_{raw} still depends on o_{m_A} and o'_{m_B}. They then implement a privacy amplification hash in step 6 and let us define $\epsilon_{\text{qkd}} = \epsilon_{EC} + \epsilon_{PE} + \epsilon_{PA}$. So now we are left with a state $\rho_{A'B'CDER}^{(6)}$ such that:

$$\left\|\rho_{A'B'CDER}^{(6)} - \mathcal{U}_{A'B'} \otimes \sigma_D \otimes \tau'_{CER}\right\|_1 \leq 3\epsilon + \epsilon_{\text{qkd}} . \tag{29}$$

where $\mathcal{U}_{A'B'}$ is the normalized uniform distribution over all strings of a given length and we have followed the standard analysis (see eg. [15]) for the overheads of a single round of QKD. We can write this instead as

$$\|\Phi_{\text{prot}}(U_K \otimes \sigma_D \otimes \tau_E) - \Phi_{\text{ideal}}(U_K \otimes \sigma_D \otimes \tau_E)\|_1 \leq 3\epsilon + \epsilon_{\text{qkd}} . \tag{30}$$

where Φ_{prot} is the action of the entire modified QKD protocol and Φ_{ideal} is an ideal protocol that shares key between Alice and Bob while leaking nothing to Eve.

Now let us relax the assumption of a perfect key. Instead, assume that Alice and Bob have already successfully grown some key using a DIQKD protocol, secure against malicious devices with memory. Before step 1, we assume that Eve has bounded correlations with these keys:

$$\|\rho_{KDE} - U_K \otimes \sigma_D \otimes \tau_E\|_1 \leq \epsilon_0 . \tag{31}$$

We can apply Φ_{prot} to both states in the above bound. Then using the data processing inequality, we have

$$||\Phi_{\mathrm{prot}}(\rho_{KDE}) - \Phi_{\mathrm{prot}}(U_K \otimes \sigma_D \otimes \tau_E)||_1 \le \epsilon_0 \ . \tag{32}$$

We can use the triangle inequality on Eqs. (30) and (32), to finally obtain

$$||\Phi_{\mathrm{prot}}(\rho_{KDE}) - \Phi_{\mathrm{ideal}}(U_K \otimes \sigma_D \otimes \tau_E)||_1 \le \epsilon_0 + 3\epsilon + \epsilon_{\mathrm{qkd}} \ . \tag{33}$$

Now, let us back up a minute and consider what happens if Alice and Bob need to abort in step 4. Implementing the insider-proof channel uses up their store of private key. Asymptotically, the largest amount of key will be used to send the error correction information. However, if they abort, there is no need to send this. By using separate applications of the channel, after sending the signal to abort, Bob is free to not use the insider-proof channel and instead send a random string. This is fine, since referring to Protocol 1 the contents of R are uniformly random, and, looking at Eq. (12), the contents of C cannot be distinguished from a uniform string by the adversary, except with probability ϵ. Therefore, in the case of an abort, the largest share of the cost of establishing a insider-proof channel can be avoided by breaking up Bob's messages in this way.

Notice also that extending each state in the norm in Eq. 33 to a larger Hilbert space by tensor product with a state corresponding to a uniformly random n-bit string $2^{-n} \sum_x |x\rangle\langle x|$ will not increase the trace distance. Therefore, all encoded messages sent from Alice can be assumed to have a fixed length and remain secure.

B Aborts

It may happen that on some rounds Alice and Bob must abort the protocol. However, since the devices that Alice and Bob use can cause an abort even on a "good" state $\rho_{A'B'E}$, they can use this as a pretext to signal to Eve, as was observed in [3]. Therefore, Alice and Bob must hide aborts when they occur. As explained in Sect. 3.2, they can do this since they have encrypted the parameter estimation bits and will also encrypt Bob's signal as to whether or not to abort. If they abort, they pretend to continue the protocol, but instead of exchanging encrypted information to perform error correction, they send random strings. In this round they do not gain any additional key, but also Eve does not learn that they aborted.

Another concern is that it is possible for the boxes to conduct a denial-of-service attack until Alice and Bob run out of key. If this should occur before the number of rounds that Alice and Bob had agreed to use the devices for, this would also constitute a signal to Eve. They must hide this also, so should it occur, Alice and Bob should simulate the remaining rounds of key growth (sending each other random strings) and then destroy the adversarial boxes securely. This is not a foolproof solution however, since in the meantime Alice and Bob may need to communicate privately. Thus at some point they will be forced to re-key and there is no reason to assume Eve will not notice this. Therefore, it is conceivable that she may gain some information from the fact that this has happened and it seems there is no way to completely avoid that, though Alice and Bob could keep a piece of their initial authentication key from before the first round against this eventuality. (This is similar to the case in trusted-device QKD when Eve executes repeated denial-of-service attacks on Alice and Bob until they run out of key.)

It appears that in this model we cannot think about each run of the device independent protocol as a stand-alone element in a universal composability scheme, in which it is public information how much key they have at any given time. Alice and Bob certainly do not want to output on each round whether they succeeded or failed in obtaining key. This may lead to additional considerations. For example, the adversary may expect Alice and Bob to send a one-time-pad encoded message at a particular time during the multi-round life of the devices when they do not have key available to devote to the purpose. If this occurs they can still avoid leaking information to the adversary by sending a random string of the appropriate length instead. (However, this does not accomplish the communication task Alice and Bob presumably wished to accomplish.) Note that in this case, Alice and Bob have to consider their quantum key distribution in the wider setting in which it is employed to avoid leaking information. Nevertheless, when key is generated in the DIQKD scheme, the resulting key is secure under the trace distance definition given in [15].

References

1. Acín, A., Brunner, N., Gisin, N., Massar, S., Pironio, S., Scarani, V.: Device-independent security of quantum cryptography against collective attacks. Phys. Rev. Lett. **98**, 230501 (2007)
2. Acin, A., Gisin, N., Masanes, L.: From Bell's theorem to secure quantum key distribution. Phys. Rev. Lett. **97**(12), 120405 (2006)
3. Barrett, J., Colbeck, R., Kent, A.: Prisoners of their own device: trojan attacks on device-independent quantum cryptography. arXiv:1201.4407v3 (2012)
4. Barrett, J., Colbeck, R., Kent, A.: Unconditionally secure device-independent quantum key distribution with only two devices. Phys. Rev. A **86**, 062326 (2012)
5. Bennett, C.H., Brassard, G.: Quantum cryptography: public-key distribution and coin tossing. In: Proceedings of IEEE International Conference on Computers, Systems and Signal Processing, pp. 175–179. IEEE, New York (1984)
6. Carter, J.L., Wegman, M.N.: Universal classes of hash functions. J. Comput. Syst. Sci. **18**(2), 143 (1979)
7. Coffman, V., Kundu, J., Wootters, W.K.: Distributed entanglement. Phys. Rev. A **61**, 052306 (2000)
8. Ekert, A.K.: Quantum cryptography based on Bell's theorem. Phys. Rev. Lett. **67**(6), 661–663 (1991)
9. Hanggi, E., Renner, R.: Device-independent quantum key distribution with commuting measurements. arXiv:1009.1833v2 (2010)
10. Makarov, V., Anisimov, A., Skaar, J.: Effects of detector efficiency mismatch on security of quantum cryptosystems. Phys. Rev. A **74**(2), 022313 (2006)

11. Masanes, L., Pironio, S., Acín, A.: Secure device-independent quantum key distribution with causally independent measurement devices. Nat. Commun. **2**, 238 (2011)
12. Pironio, S., Acín, A., Brunner, N., Gisin, N., Massar, S., Scarani, V.: Device-independent quantum key distribution secure against collective attacks. New J. Phys. **11**, 045021 (2009)
13. Reichardt, B.W., Unger, F., Vazirani, U.: Classical command of quantum systems via rigidity of CHSH games. arXiv:1209.0449 (2012)
14. Reichardt, B.W., Unger, F., Vazirani, U.: A classical leash for a quantum system: command of quantum systems via rigidity of CHSH games. arXiv:1209.0448 (2012)
15. Renner, R.: Security of quantum key distribution. Int. J. Quant. Inf. **6**, 1 (2008)
16. Shor, P.W., Preskill, J.: Simple proof of security of the BB84 quantum key distribution protocol. Phys. Rev. Lett. **85**, 441–444 (2000)
17. Tomamichel, M., Schaffner, C., Smith, A., Renner, R.: Leftover hashing against quantum side information. IEEE Trans. Inf. Theory **57**, 5524 (2011)

Superposition Attacks
on Cryptographic Protocols

Ivan Damgård[1,2]([✉]), Jakob Funder[1], Jesper Buus Nielsen[1], and Louis Salvail[1]

[1] Department of Computer Science, Aarhus University, Aarhus, Denmark
[2] Université de Montreal, Montreal, Canada
ivan@cs.au.dk

Abstract. Attacks on cryptographic protocols are usually modeled by allowing an adversary to ask queries to an oracle. Security is then defined by requiring that as long as the queries satisfy some constraint, there is some problem the adversary cannot solve, such as compute a certain piece of information. Even if the protocol is quantum, the queries are typically classical. In this paper, we introduce a new model of quantum attacks on protocols, where the adversary is allowed quantum access to the primitive, i.e., he may ask several classical queries in quantum superposition. This is a strictly stronger attack than the standard one, and we consider the security of several primitives in this model. We show that a secret-sharing scheme that is secure with threshold t in the standard model is secure against superposition attacks if and only if the threshold is lowered to $t/2$. This holds for all classical as well as all known quantum secret sharing schemes. We then consider zero- knowledge and first show that known protocols are not, in general, secure in our model by designing a superposition attack on the well-known zero-knowledge protocol for graph isomorphism. We then use our secret-sharing result to design zero-knowledge proofs for all of NP in the common reference string model. While our protocol is classical, it is sound against a cheating unbounded quantum prover and computational zero-knowledge even if the verifier is allowed a superposition attack. Finally, we consider multiparty computation and give a characterization of a class of protocols that can be shown secure, though not necessarily with efficient simulation. We show that this class contains non-trivial protocols that cannot be shown secure by running a classical simulator in superposition.

The first three authors acknowledge support from the Danish National Research Foundation and The National Science Foundation of China (under the grant 61061130540) for the Sino-Danish Center for the Theory of Interactive Computation, within which part of this work was performed; and also from the CFEM research center (supported by the Danish Strategic Research Council) within which part of this work was performed.
Louis Salvail is supported by Quebec's INTRIQ, Canada's NSERC strategic program FREQUENCY, and Canada's NSERC discovery grant.

C. Padró (Ed.): ICITS 2013, LNCS 8317, pp. 142–161, 2014.
DOI: 10.1007/978-3-319-04268-8_9, © Springer International Publishing Switzerland 2014

1 Introduction

Attacks on cryptographic protocols are usually modeled by allowing an adversary to query an oracle that represents the primitive he attacks, for instance the adversary specifies a message he wants to have signed, a challenge he wants a prover to answer, or a subset of players he wants to corrupt Security is then defined by requiring that as long as the queries satisfy some constraint, there is some problem the adversary cannot solve, such as compute a certain piece of information.

Several previous works consider what happens to security of classical protocols if we allow the adversary to be quantum. The model usually considered is that the adversary is now a quantum machine, but otherwise plays exactly the same game as in a normal attack, i.e., he still communicates classically with the protocol he attacks. One example of this is the work of Watrous [Wat06], showing that a large class of zero-knowledge protocols are also zero-knowledge against a quantum verifier.

In this paper, we introduce a new model of quantum attacks on classical as well as quantum cryptographic protocols, where the adversary is allowed to ask several classical queries to the oracle in quantum superposition. In more concrete terms, we ask, for multiparty protocols: what happens if the adversary can be in superposition of having corrupted several different subsets? or, for zero-knowledge protocols: what happens if a quantum verifier can be in superposition of having issued several different challenges to the prover, and receive the responses in superposition? As we will argue below, we believe such superposition attacks to be a valid physical concern, but they also form a very natural generalization from a theory point of view: in the literature on black-box quantum computing, quantum black-box access to a function is usually defined by extending classical black-box access such that queries are allowed to contain several inputs in superposition. Our superposition attacks extend conventional attacks in the same way.

There is recent work [BDF+11, Zha12b] that considers the random oracle model and shows security of various schemes even if the adversary has quantum access to the random oracle. These result are quite different from ours in that they are concerned with allowing everything "in the adversary's brain" to be quantum, rather than considering his communication with the rest of the world as we do. To the best of our knowledge our work is the first to consider adversaries that have quantum access to the cryptographic primitive or protocol under attack[1] but we emphasize that in independent work [BZ12, Zha12a] superposition attacks are also considered, on pseudorandom functions and message authentication codes.

At first sight, superposition attacks may seem rather exotic. However, it is not hard to see that in several scenarios, it is very natural to consider these attacks:

---

[1] A preliminary announcement of some of our results was made in an invited talk by one of the authors at the ICITS 2011 conference.

Consider first protocols that handle quantum data, such as in several previous works on quantum secret sharing and multiparty computation (e.g., Ben-Or et al. [BCG+05]). Such a protocol requires players to communicate quantum information and keep throughout the game a joint entangled quantum state that involves all the players. If the players can do this, we should assume that the adversary can do something of similar technological difficulty. It therefore seems fair to allow the adversary to be in superposition of having interacted with different subsets of players. Note here that "interacting with a player" does not have to be a macroscopic process: the adversary could attempt to communicate with the player in a way that is physically different from what the implementation of the protocol expected, and in this way get more information about the private state of the player than he was supposed to. For instance, the effect of sending on a different frequency or a different number of particles than expected may be hard to predict and may depend heavily on the way the protocol is implemented. Several known attacks on quantum key distribution work in this way. Now, if the communication defined by the protocol is quantum in the first place, we see no reason why such an attack cannot be performed in superposition against different players.

Second, what about classical protocols? One might think that here, super-position attacks cannot be mounted. The argument would be that since honest players are classical, they would "automatically" do a measurement of anything they receive, thus forcing a collapse of any quantum state they are given. However, this may be a dangerous assumption in the future, considering the fact that classical computing equipment becomes smaller and approaches the quantum limit. If an adversary captures such a device containing a secret key, he may be able to cool it down, for instance, and get some quantum effects to happen during communication. On top of this, even honest players may in the future use quantum computing and communication, but may sometimes need to execute a classical protocol. Having to always do this on separate classical hardware would be an unpleasant limitation.

So if we cannot be sure that hardware always behaves classically, perhaps an easy solution would be to require explicitly in the protocol that every incoming message is measured? However, such an idea seems problematic from a practical point of view: an instruction to measure an incoming message makes little sense to someone implementing the protocol on a classical machine, so we have to trust that someone else responsible for the physical implementation will put equipment in place to do the measurement. Moreover, making sure the measurement is actually done is not as straightforward as one might think: most physicists today subscribe to an interpretation of quantum mechanics where the belief is that the wave function never actually collapses even when a measurement is done. Instead, information is transferred to (a part of) the environment and this is experienced as a collapse to a party who does not have access to the environment. In our case, this means that if the adversary were to get access to this environment, then from his point of view no measurement took place. Hence, equipment that seeks to enforce that a measurement is done from the adversary's point of view must in some sense keep information away from the adversary, and this may be non-trivial if we are dealing with microscopic equipment.

In the face of these problems, we believe the most natural and elegant solution is to ask for protocols that are secure regardless of whether any measurement is performed on incoming messages, which exactly means we need security even if the adversary has quantum access to the primitive.

Contributions of the paper. We first show that any classical secret-sharing scheme that is perfectly secure with threshold t in the standard model is perfectly secure against superposition attacks if and only if the adversary's superposition is constrained to contain subsets of size at most $t/2$. If this condition is not satisfied, not only does perfect security fail, we show examples where the adversary may even learn the secret with certainty. We also consider quantum secret sharing schemes and show that the same results hold for a large class of schemes derived from classical linear secret sharing, this includes essentially all known schemes.

We then consider (classical) zero-knowledge protocols and first give strong evidence that known protocols are not, in general, secure against superposition attacks. We give such an attack on the well-known graph isomorphism protocol, showing how to extract from the prover the number of fixed points of the prover's secret permutation. A simple reduction shows that if this attack could be simulated, then there is an efficient quantum algorithm computing the isomorphism between two graphs, as long as the isomorphism is unique. Thus the protocol can only be zero-knowledge if graph isomorphism in most cases is easy on a quantum computer.

We then use our result on classical secret-sharing to construct zero-knowledge proofs for all of NP in the common reference string (CRS) model. While our protocol is classical, it is sound against a cheating unbounded quantum prover and computational zero-knowledge against a quantum verifier, even if the verifier is allowed a superposition attack[2]. Since our simulation is straight-line, the protocol is also secure under concurrent composition. We stress that our construction does not make assumptions beyond what we need to protect against standard attacks, nor is it less efficient than known constructions. Therefore this construction is an affirmative answer to our question above: we can indeed have protocols that are secure, regardless of whether incoming messages are measured or not.

Finally, we consider classical multiparty computation and we define a UC-style model for static and passive superposition attacks on classical MPC protocols. Given our result on secret-sharing schemes, it is natural to speculate that classical MPC protocols that are secure against t corruptions, are secure

---

[2] Since we use the CRS model, the reader may ask why we do not use existing protocols for non-interactive zero-knowledge (NIZK), where the prover just sends a single message to the verifier. In this way, the adversary would not get a chance to do a superposition attack. However, the most general assumption under which NIZK is known to be possible with an efficient prover is existence of one-way trapdoor permutations. They in turn are only known to be realizable under assumptions that are easily broken by a quantum adversary, such as factoring. Therefore we do not consider NIZK a satisfactory solution.

against superposition attacks corrupting $t/2$ players. The situation turns out to be more complicated, however: We show that for the model that gives the adversary the most power (and hence is the most hostile to the simulator), simulation based security is not possible at all. However, putting a natural constraint on the adversary, we are able to give a characterization of a class of protocols that can be shown secure, though not necessarily with efficient simulation. We show that this class contains non-trivial protocols, where by non-trivial, we mean that although the protocol is secure against a classical attack, we can show that it cannot be proved secure against a superposition attack by simply running the classical simulator in superposition. The simulator that does exist is in some sense "more quantum".

Whether more general positive results hold in this constrained model remains an open question. Likewise, the very natural question of security of *quantum* multiparty computation protocols against superposition attacks remains open. Note, however, that existing work on quantum multiparty computation is typically based on quantum secret sharing, where the adversary's choice of subset to corrupt is classical. The negative part of our result on secret sharing described above shows that such protocol are not necessarily secure against superposition attacks as they stand.

2   Preliminaries

We will model players in protocols in two different ways: when we are not interested in computational limitations on parties, a player will be specified by a series of unitary transforms where the ith transform is done on all qubits available to the party, after the ith message has been received (in the form of a quantum register), and then some designated part of the storage is sent as the next outgoing message. We are limiting ourselves to perfect unitary transformation of the party's register because we are exactly considering the situation where an attacker manages to prevent coupling between the party and the environment.

In cases where we want to bound the computational complexity of a player, we consider players to be an infinite family of interactive quantum circuits, as in the model from [FS09], and then the complexity is the circuit size.

2.1   Running Functions in Superposition

Consider any function, $f : X \to Y$ and a register of qubits, $|\psi\rangle = \sum_x \alpha_x |x\rangle |0\rangle \in \mathcal{H}_X \otimes \mathcal{H}_Y$, where $\dim(\mathcal{H}_X) = |X|$ and $\dim(\mathcal{H}_Y) = |Y|$. To *run* f on $|\psi\rangle$ means to apply the unitary transformation, U_f, such that $U_f \sum_x \alpha_x |x\rangle |0\rangle = \sum_x \alpha_x |x\rangle |f(x)\rangle$. In general the register in $\mathcal{H}_Y$, called the *response register*, can contain any superposition of values, not just 0. In this case, we have that, $U_f \sum_{x,a} \alpha_{x,a} |x\rangle |a\rangle = \sum_{x,a} \alpha_{x,a} |x\rangle |f(x) \oplus a\rangle$ where $\oplus$ is the bitwise xor.

3   Secret Sharing

In (classical) secret sharing n parties are sharing some secret value $s \in \mathbb{S}$ using randomness $r \in \mathcal{R}$, where $\mathbb{S}$ and $\mathcal{R}$ are the sets of possible secrets and randomness. We name the parties $P_1, \ldots, P_n$. Let $[n] = \{1, \ldots, n\}$. Each party, P_i, receives a *share* $v_i(s, r) \in \{0, 1\}^k$, also called his *private view* . That is, $v_i : \mathbb{S} \times \mathcal{R} \to \{0, 1\}^k$.

For $A \subset [n]$, let $v_A(s, r) = \{v_i(s, r)\}_{i \in A}$ be the string containing the concatenation of views for parties P_i with $i \in A$. For convenience in the following we assume that each such string is padded, so that they have the same length regardless of the size of A. That is, $v_A : \mathbb{S} \times \mathcal{R} \to \{0, 1\}^t$. An *adversary structure* G is a family of subsets $G \subset 2^{[n]}$. A secret sharing scheme is perfectly secure against classical G-attacks if for any $A \in G$, the distribution of $v_A(s, r)$ does not depend on s. The adversary structure of the secret sharing scheme is the maximal $F \subseteq 2^{[n]}$ for which the scheme is perfectly secure against F attacks. We will only consider so-called *perfect* secret-sharing schemes, where it holds for all $A \notin G$ that $v_A(s, r)$ uniquely determines the secret s. I.e., in a perfectly secure, perfect secret-sharing scheme a set of shares either carry no information on the secret or fully determines the secret.

We will model any passive attack on the scheme as a one-time query to an *corruption oracle*. The corruption oracle for a specific run of a secret sharing scheme $O(s, r, A) = v_A(s, r)$ is the function that for a specific choice of secret, randomness and set of parties, returns the private view of those parties. That is, $O : \mathbb{S} \otimes \mathcal{R} \otimes F \to \{0, 1\}^t$.

3.1   Two-Party Bit Sharing Example

Before we present the full model for secret sharing we start with a small example. We consider the case of 2 parties sharing a single bit, $b \in \{0, 1\}$, using a random bit, $r \in \{0, 1\}$. Here $[n] = \{1, 2\}$, $F = \{(1), (2)\}$, $v_1(b, r) = b \oplus r$, $v_2(b, r) = r$.

This scheme is of course secure against a classical attack, which we can model by giving an adversary one-time access to an oracle that will return one share (r or $r \oplus b$) on request. However, it is well known from the Deutch-Jozsa algorithm that given quantum access to such an oracle, one can compute the xor of the two bits from only one query. Hence the scheme is not secure against a superposition attack. In the following we consider what happens in the general case.

3.2   Model for Secret Sharing

We will now give the full technical description of the model for superposition attacks on general secret sharing. To do this we first consider the state spaces needed to run the protocol and the attack on the protocol. First is the space that contains the shares for all the parties, $\mathcal{H}_{\text{parties}}$. The state in the register for this space is unchanged throughout the attack and is

$$|parties\rangle_{\mathsf{p}} = \sum_{s \in \mathbb{S}, r \in \mathcal{R}} \sqrt{p_s} \sqrt{p_r} |s, r, v_{[n]}(s, r)\rangle_{\mathsf{p}} = \sum_{s \in \mathbb{S}, r \in \mathcal{R}} \sqrt{p_s} \sqrt{p_r} |s, r\rangle \bigotimes_{i=1}^{n} |v_i(s, r)\rangle,$$

where $|s, r\rangle$ is the purification of the secret and randomness choice. This is purely for technical reasons and does not matter for the adversary as he never sees it (and hence they might as well be considered measured). Secondly is the space for the environment, $\mathcal{H}_{env}$, which the adversary can use to choose his query and use as potential auxiliary register. The initial state for the environment is a general (pure) state,

$$|\psi\rangle_e = \sum_x \alpha_x |x\rangle_e \in \mathcal{H}_{env} ,$$

where x is in some set of arbitrary, but finite size. We will omit this for readability. Finally is the space holding the adversary's query to the corruption oracle, $\mathcal{H}_{query}$. This is initially a 'blank' state,

$$|\omega\rangle_q = |0, 0\rangle_q \in \mathcal{H}_{query}.$$

The space for the entire model is hence, $\mathcal{H}_{total} = \mathcal{H}_{parties} \otimes \mathcal{H}_{env} \otimes \mathcal{H}_{query}$, and the initial state is,

$$|init\rangle_t = \sum_{s \in \mathbb{S}, r \in \mathcal{R}} \sqrt{p_s}\sqrt{p_r}|s, r, v_{[n]}(s, r)\rangle_p \otimes \sum_x \alpha_x |x\rangle_e \otimes |0, 0\rangle_q \in \mathcal{H}_{total} .$$

The attack will be defined by two operations and an adversary structure, F. First the adversary needs to construct his query for the oracle. This includes choosing the superposition of subsets he will corrupt and associated values for the response registers. This is an arbitrary unitary operation. We will denote it, $U_{QUERY}^{ADV,F}$,

$$U_{QUERY}^{ADV,F} : \mathcal{H}_{env} \otimes \mathcal{H}_{query} \to \mathcal{H}_{env} \otimes \mathcal{H}_{query} .$$

After this unitary operation the state is

$$
\begin{aligned}
|query\rangle_t &= U_{QUERY}^{ADV,F}|init\rangle_t \\
&= \sum_{s \in \mathbb{S}, r \in \mathcal{R}} \sqrt{p_s}\sqrt{p_r}|s, r, v_{[n]}(s, r)\rangle_p \otimes \sum_{x, A \in F, a \in \{0,1\}^t} \alpha_{x,A,a}|x\rangle_e \otimes |A, a\rangle_q
\end{aligned}
$$

where we assume it is the identity on $\mathcal{H}_{parties}$. Next the oracle, $O(s, r, A)$, is run. Let

$$U_O : \mathcal{H}_{parties} \otimes \mathcal{H}_{query} \to \mathcal{H}_{parties} \otimes \mathcal{H}_{query}$$

denote the unitary applying this function. The state afterwards is $U_O|query\rangle_t$, which equals

$$\sum_{s \in \mathbb{S}, r \in \mathcal{R}} \sqrt{p_s}\sqrt{p_r}|s, r, v_{[n]}(s, r)\rangle_p \otimes \sum_{x, A \in F, a \in \{0,1\}^t} \alpha_{x,A,a}|x\rangle_e \otimes |A, a \oplus v_A(s, r)\rangle_q$$

where we assume U_O is padded with appropriate identities. Consider the final state the adversary sees for a specific secret, s,

$$\rho_s^{ADV,F} = \sum_{r \in \mathcal{R}} p_r \left|\psi_r^{ADV,F}\right\rangle\!\left\langle\psi_r^{ADV,F}\right| ,$$

where $|\psi_r^{ADV,F}\rangle = \sum_{x, A \in F, a \in \{0,1\}^t} \alpha_{x,A,a}|x\rangle_e \otimes |A, a \oplus v_A(s, r)\rangle_q.$

Definition 1. *A secret sharing scheme S is perfectly secure against superposition F-attacks if, and only if, for all unitary matrices, $U_{\text{QUERY}}^{\text{ADV},F} : \mathcal{H}_{\text{env}} \otimes \mathcal{H}_{\text{query}} \rightarrow \mathcal{H}_{\text{env}} \otimes \mathcal{H}_{\text{query}}$ and all possible pairs of inputs, $s, s' \in S$ it holds that $\rho_s^{\text{ADV},F} = \rho_{s'}^{\text{ADV},F}$.*

3.3 (In)security Against Superposition Attacks on Classical Secret-Sharing

For an adversary structure F, we define $F^2 = \{A \mid \exists B, C \in F : A = B \cup C\}$.

Theorem 1. *Let G be the classical adversary structure for S. S is perfectly secure against superposition F-attacks if and only if $F^2 \subseteq G$.*

Proof. For the forward direction, consider the adversary's final state,

$$\rho_s^{\text{ADV}} = \sum_{r \in \mathcal{R}} p_r \, |\psi_r^{\text{ADV}}\rangle\langle\psi_r^{\text{ADV}}|,$$

which equals

$$\sum_{r,x,x',A,A',a,a'} p_r \alpha_{x,A,a} \alpha_{x',A',a'}^* |x\rangle_e \langle x'|_e \otimes |A, a \oplus v_A(s,r)\rangle_q \langle A', a' \oplus v_{A'}(s,r)|_q \, .$$

Now, for any fixed A, A', a, a' and s, consider the matrix

$$\sum_{r \in \mathcal{R}} p_r |A, a \oplus v_A(s,r)\rangle_q \langle A', a' \oplus v_{A'}(s,r)|_q.$$

The crucial observation now is that this matrix is in 1-1 correspondence with the joint distribution of $v_A(s,r)$ and $v_{A'}(s,r)$. Namely, its entries are indexed by pairs of strings (α, β), where α, β are strings of the same length. And furthermore the (α, β)'th entry is the probability that the events $v_A(s,r) = \alpha \oplus a$ and $v_{A'}(s,r) = \beta \oplus a'$ occur simultaneously, where the probability is taken over a random r. Now, if $F^2 \subseteq G$, we have that S is perfectly secure against classical F^2-attacks. Therefore the joint distribution of $v_A(s,r)$ and $v_{A'}(s,r)$ does not depend on s, consequently each matrix

$$\sum_{r \in \mathcal{R}} p_r |A, a \oplus v_A(r,s)\rangle_q \langle A', a' \oplus v_{A'}(s,r)|_q$$

is independent of s as well. Hence $\forall s, s' \in S : \rho_s^{\text{ADV},F} = \rho_{s'}^{\text{ADV},F}$ as required.

For the only-if part, assume for contradiction that $F^2 \not\subseteq G$, i.e., there exist A_0, A_1 such that $A_0 \cup A_1 \notin G$. It follows that a secret shared using S is uniquely determined from shares in $A_0 \cup A_1$. Then consider the query $|\omega_a\rangle = (|A\rangle|0\rangle + |A'\rangle|0\rangle)/\sqrt{2}$. By the same computation as above, we see that ρ_s^{ADV} contains a submatrix of form $\sum_{r \in \mathcal{R}} |a_A \oplus v_A(s,r)\rangle\langle a_{A'} \oplus v_{A'}(s,r)|$, that corresponds to the joint distribution of shares in A and A'. But since the secret is uniquely determined from these shares, it follows that this submatrix is different for different secrets, and hence we get that there exists a measurement with non-zero bias towards the secret, and so $\mathcal{S}$ is not perfectly secure against superposition F-attacks. This is exactly the result we saw in the small example in Sect. 3.1.   □

Alternative models for secret sharing. Here we take a closer look at how the response register in handled during a superposition attack: When the adversary runs a classical component in superposition, and sends it a message, then the reply will in general be a superposition, nevertheless the reply might be computed in different ways. In general quantum information processing, the standard assumption is that the result is xor'ed into a response register a supplied along with the input, e.g., if the component computes a function f, then on input $|x\rangle|a\rangle$, the output is $|x\rangle|a \oplus f(x)\rangle$. This ensures that the components acts unitarily when the input is quantum. We call this the *supplied response register* model.

When considering the case of an adversary attacking a protocol one may be able to argue that the adversary will not have enough control to be able to decide the *a priori* content of the response register. It may be more reasonable to assume that the component the adversary talks to will create the response register and return it to the adversary. We model this setting of *created response registers* by restricting the more general setting by allowing only $a = 0$, in which case the adversary will always receive $|x\rangle|f(x)\rangle$. Note that Theorem 1 applies in this setting as well.

3.4 Attacks on Secret Sharing

Theorem 1, tells us that we cannot have perfect security if the condition $F^2 \subseteq G$ is violated, but nothing about how much information the adversary can actually gain on the secret in this case. Of course, if $F \not\subseteq G$, the adversary can trivially learn the secret. But if $F \subseteq G$ one might hope that the adversary only learns a small amount of information, and even that this could become negligible by increasing the amount of randomness used to create the shares. However, in the lemma below we show that, under a simple assumption on the secret sharing scheme, an attacker can distinguish between two possible secrets with considerable bias. The attack works even in the restricted setting of created response registers. The proof is found in the full paper [DFNS11].

Lemma 1. *Let G be the classical adversary structure for $\mathcal{S}$. If there exist two subsets, A_0, $A_1 \in G$ such that (1) $A_0 \cup A_1 \notin G$ and (2) any secret, $s \in \mathbb{S}$, combined with the shares in A_0 (A_1) uniquely determine the choice of randomness, $r \in \mathcal{R}$, then the following holds.*
For any two secrets $s, s' \in \mathbb{S} : s \neq s'$, there exists a query (with $a = 0$) that will allow an adversary to distinguish between s and s' with probability p_{guess}, where $p_{guess} \geq \frac{3}{4}$.

An example of such a scheme is a Shamir secret sharing scheme that is classically secure against t corrupted players. Here any subset of t players combined with the secret will give $t + 1$ points on a polynomial of degree at most t and hence uniquely determine the choice of randomness.

4   Quantum Secret Sharing

In this section we study the security of *quantum* secret sharing against superposition attacks. The situation turns out to be more complicated than for the classical case, and security depends on the exact model for what the adversary is allowed to do.

The model we will use for quantum secret sharing is that a secret is a quantum state $|sec\rangle = \sum_{s \in \mathbb{S}} \alpha_s |s\rangle$, i.e., some superposition over the possible classical choices of secret. The secret sharing scheme is then a unitary transform that maps each basis state $|s\rangle$ plus an ancilla of appropriate size to a state

$$|\Phi_s\rangle = \sum_{v_1,\ldots,v_n \in \{0,1\}^k} \alpha_{v_1,\ldots,v_n} |v_1\rangle \cdots |v_n\rangle ,$$

where we think of the content of the i'th register as the share of the i'th player. A quantum secret sharing scheme is secure against adversary structure F, if any subset of shares corresponding to a subset $A \in F$ contains no information on the secret state, but any subset of shares B where $B \notin F$ allows reconstruction of the secret. It follows from the no-cloning theorem that security can only hold if F has the property that for any $B \notin F$, the complement $\bar{B}$ is in F.

An example of quantum secret sharing can be derived from Shamir's secret sharing scheme. Here we assume that $n = 2t + 1$, and the adversary structure contains all subsets of size at most t, and $\mathbb{S} = \mathbb{F}_p$ for the finite field $\mathbb{F}_p$. We then define $|\Phi_s\rangle = \frac{1}{\sqrt{M}} \sum_{f \in P_s} |f(1)\rangle \cdots |f(n)\rangle$, where P_s is the set of polynomials of degree at most t with $f(0) = s$, and M the number of such polynomials.

There are several ways to define what it means that an adversary gets access to some of the shares. The simplest form of attack we consider is called a *share capture attack*, where the adversary essentially steals a subset of the shares (or subsets of shares in superposition). Since it seems natural to assume that some evidence of the absence of shares would be left after this, we assume that the players whose shares are captured are left with erasure symbols $\perp$ instead of shares. Some notation to describe this more formally: we will let $\mathbf{v} = v_1, \ldots, v_n$ in the following, and $|\mathbf{v}_A\rangle$ will stand for the basis state $|\mathbf{v}_A\rangle = |w_1\rangle \cdots |w_n\rangle$, where $w_i = v_i$ if $i \in A$ and $w_i = \perp$ otherwise. Likewise, for the Shamir based example, we let $|f(A)\rangle = |u_1\rangle \cdots |u_n\rangle$ where $u_i = f(i)$ if $i \in A$ and $u_i = \perp$ otherwise.

In an F-share capture attack, a query $\sum_{A \in F} \alpha_A |A\rangle |\perp\rangle \cdots |\perp\rangle$ is prepared, where the last part of the register will contain the captured shares. Then a unitary transform U is executed on the shares and the adversary's query. U is specified by the following action on basis states for shares and player subsets:

$$U(|v_1\rangle \cdots |v_n\rangle |A\rangle |\perp\rangle \cdots |\perp\rangle) = |\mathbf{v}_{\bar{A}}\rangle |A\rangle |\mathbf{v}_A\rangle .$$

We define U to act as the identity on all basis vectors not involved in the above expression. This clearly makes U be unitary. In the actual attack,

$$U(|\Phi_s\rangle \sum_{A \in F} \alpha_A |A\rangle |\bot\rangle \cdots |\bot\rangle)$$

is computed and the adversary is given the last two registers, containing the corrupted set(s) and the captured shares. We say that the scheme is secure against F-share capture attacks if it always holds that the state the adversary gets is independent of $|s\rangle$. By linearity, security trivially extends to superpositions over different $|s\rangle$'s.

Proposition 1. *Any quantum secret sharing scheme that is secure for adversary structure F is also secure against F-share capture attacks.*

The proof is straightforward and is found in the full paper [DFNS11].

A more interesting result emerges if we allow the adversary slightly more power. We will consider what we call a *capture-and-replace attack*. Here, the adversary prepares a query as before and U is executed. Now, the adversary does some local computation. For convenience and without loss of generality for our result, we assume that a unitary transform V is applied by the adversary to the shares captured $|v_A\rangle_a$ (where a denotes the registers held by the corrupted players) together with an ancilla in state $|0\rangle_z$: $V|v_A\rangle_a|0\rangle_z = |\phi_A\rangle_{az}$. Finally, the adversary keeps register Z before U is executed again on the remaining registers. Note that $U = U^\dagger$, so the second transformation *puts the shares back in place*. It seems hard to argue that the adversary would be limited to only one application of U, so there is good motivations to consider this attack. We talk about *F-capture-and-replace attacks* in the same way as above. It is easy to see that capture attacks are a special case of capture-and-replace attacks. In this more general case however, it turns out that superposition attacks help the adversary, and for the Shamir based scheme, we get a result similar to what we have for classical secret sharing.

Theorem 2. *Let G be the adversary structure containing sets of at most t, for which the Shamir based quantum secret sharing scheme is perfectly secure. Then, the scheme is perfectly secure against F-capture-and-replace attacks in superposition if and only if $F^2 \subseteq G$.*

The proof is similar to the proof of Theorem 1 and can be found in the full paper [DFNS11]. The theorem generalizes easily to any quantum secret sharing scheme derived from a classical linear scheme. We conjecture it generalizes to any quantum scheme. However, the only other quantum schemes we are aware of are schemes that use quantum shares for classical data. For instance, the 4 Bell-states can be used to share 2 classical bits among two players who receive only one qubit each. This scheme can also be broken under a superposition attack.

5   Zero-Knowledge

5.1   An Attack Against the Graph Isomorphism Protocol

Consider the well-known protocol for proving graph isomorphism: The common input is two graphs (G_0, G_1) on n nodes, where the prover P knows a permutation π such that $\pi(G_0) = G_1$. P will send to the verifier V a graph $H = \sigma(G_0)$ where σ is a random permutation on n nodes. V sends a random bit b, and P returns the permutation $\rho = \pi^b \sigma^{-1}$. Finally V checks that $\rho(H) = G_b$.

This protocol is perfect zero-knowledge against a classical as well as a quantum verifier, but in the quantum case the proof assumes that the verifier is limited to sending a classical bit b as challenge to the prover (see [Wat06] for a precise definition of zero-knowledge when the verifier is quantum). We consider what happens if a superposition attack is allowed, and we give a concrete attack that allows to extract non-trivial information from the prover. We will only consider input graphs for which the permutation π is uniquely defined from G_0, G_1. This is mostly for simplicity, but note also that it is well-known that deciding whether the permutation is unique is equivalent to deciding graph isomorphism in the *general* case. Hence, assuming the latter is hard, algorithms trying to compute an isomorphism between G_0 and G_1 are unlikely to have an easier time when the permutation is unique.

To analyze what happens, we need to assume a concrete way in which P communicates his permutation to V in the final message. We will assume a natural method, namely to send ρ, P sends $\rho(0), \ldots, \rho(n-1)$ in the classical case. We generalize this to the quantum case in the standard way: V supplies a register $|b\rangle |i_0\rangle_0 \cdots |i_{n-1}\rangle_{n-1}$ and $|b\rangle |i_0 + \rho_b(0) \bmod n\rangle_0 \cdots |i_{n-1} + \rho_b(n-1) \bmod n\rangle_{n-1}$, in returned, where ρ_b is the correct answer to b. By adding the answer into the response register, we ensure that the operation of P is unitary.

The proof of the theorem below works by first constructing a concrete attack that the verifier might execute and concluding that this attack would allow to decide if the prover's secret permutation has a fixed point or not. Then, if a simulator existed for such a verifier, a simple reduction[3] allows us to get the full isomorphism between the graphs in all cases where the permutation in question is unique:

Theorem 3. *If the graph isomorphism protocol is zero-knowledge against superposition attacks, then graph isomorphism can be computed efficiently by a quantum algorithm for all inputs where the permutation in question is uniquely defined by the input graphs.*

Proof. We describe the attack a verifier might execute. We first specify the state we will send to P:

$$\frac{1}{\sqrt{2}} \left(|0\rangle + |1\rangle \right) F_n(|1 + r \bmod n\rangle_0) F_n(|1\rangle_1) \cdots F_n(|1\rangle_{n-1}) ,$$

---

[3] We are grateful to Elad Verbin for pointing this reduction out to us.

where F_n is the quantum Fourier transform over $\mathbb{Z}_n$ and r is a random non-zero value in $\mathbb{Z}_n$. The state can also be written as

$$\frac{1}{\sqrt{2}} \left(|0\rangle F_n(|1 + r \bmod n\rangle_0) \; F_n(|1\rangle_1) \cdots F_n(|1\rangle_{n-1}) + \right.$$
$$\left. |1\rangle F_n(|1 + r \bmod n\rangle_0) \; F_n(|1\rangle_1) \cdots F_n(|1\rangle_{n-1}) \right) .$$

To see what happens to this state under the operation done by P, consider the k'th register of those where F_n is applied, in the summand corresponding to challenge bit b. Before P's operation, it is in state

$$F_n(|i_k\rangle_k) = \sum_{j=0}^{n-1} \omega_n^{i_k j} |j\rangle_k ,$$

where ω_n is the principal n'th root of unity and $i_0 = 1 + r \bmod n$ and $i_k = 1$ otherwise. After the operation, we have the new state

$$\sum_{j=0}^{n-1} \omega_n^{i_k j} |j + \rho_b(k)\rangle_k = \sum_{j'=0}^{n-1} \omega_n^{i_k(j' - \rho_b(k))} |j'\rangle_k$$
$$= \omega_n^{-i_k \rho_b(k)} \sum_{j'=0}^{n-1} \omega_n^{i_k j'} |j'\rangle_k = \omega_n^{-i_k \rho_b(k)} F_n(|i_k\rangle_k) ,$$

by a simple substitution of variables. Plugging this into the above overall state, we get that the state P returns can be written as

$$\frac{1}{\sqrt{2}} \cdot \left(|0\rangle \; \omega_n^{-(1+r)\rho_0(0)} F_n(|1 + r \bmod n\rangle) \omega_n^{-\rho_0(1)} F_n(|1\rangle) \cdots \omega_n^{-\rho_0(n-1)} F_n(|1\rangle) \right.$$
$$\left. + |1\rangle \; \omega_n^{-(1+r)\rho_1(0)} F_n(|1 + r \bmod n\rangle) \omega_n^{-\rho_1(1)} F_n(|1\rangle) \cdots \omega_n^{-\rho_1(n-1)} F_n(|1\rangle) \right) .$$

Collecting some terms, we get

$$\frac{1}{\sqrt{2}} \cdot \left(|0\rangle \; \omega_n^{-r\rho_0(0) - \sum_k \rho_0(k)} F_n(|1 + r \bmod n\rangle) F_n(|1\rangle) \cdots F_n(|1\rangle) \right.$$
$$\left. + |1\rangle \; \omega_n^{-r\rho_1(0) - \sum_k \rho_1(k)} F_n(|1 + r \bmod n\rangle) F_n(|1\rangle) \cdots F_n(|1\rangle) \right) .$$

Note that since ρ_0, ρ_1 are permutations, we have

$$\sum_k \rho_0(k) = \sum_k \rho_1(k) = n(n-1)/2.$$

Using this and the fact that $\rho_0 = \sigma^{-1}, \rho_1 = \pi\sigma^{-1}$, we get that our state is of form

$$\frac{1}{\sqrt{2}} \omega_n^{-n(n-1)/2 - r\sigma^{-1}(0)} \left(|0\rangle + \omega_n^{r(\sigma^{-1}(0) - \pi(\sigma^{-1}(0)))} |1\rangle \right) \otimes$$
$$F_n(|1 + r \bmod n\rangle) F_n(|1\rangle) \cdots F_n(|1\rangle) .$$

In the final step, we measure the first bit of the state in the basis

$$(|0\rangle + |1\rangle)/\sqrt{2}, (|0\rangle - |1\rangle)/\sqrt{2}.$$

Call the measurement results 0 respectively 1.

Let us consider the distribution we can expect of the measurement result: $\sigma^{-1}(0)$ is uniform in $\mathbb{Z}_n$. Furthermore, it is clear that $r(\sigma^{-1}(0) - \pi(\sigma^{-1}(0)))$ is 0 if $\sigma^{-1}(0)$ is a fixed point of π and uniform in $\mathbb{Z}_n^*$ otherwise. It follows that the distribution of the final measurement result depends only on the number of fixed points of P's secret π.

Furthermore, if $\sigma^{-1}(0)$ is a fixed point of π, we will measure 0 with probability 1, if not, we get result 1 with non-negligible probability. It follows by a Chernoff bound that in a polynomial number of queries we can decide except with negligible error probability whether π has a fixed point or not. In fact, it is not hard to see that the distribution of the measurement result for different numbers of fixed points have non-negligible statistical distance, so in a polynomial number of queries one can even get a reliable estimate of the number of fixed points of π.

Now, if the protocol was zero-knowledge in our model, a simulator would exist that on input any two isomorphic graphs would create a state indistinguishable from the state our attack creates with the help of the prover. Thus, running the simulator a sufficient number of times followed by the measurements described above, we get an oracle that tells us whether the permutation that takes one graph to the other has a fixed point.

Using such an oracle, we can compute the permutation: let $G' = \theta(G_1)$ for a random permutation θ and ask the oracle if the permutation mapping G_0 to G' has a fixed point. If the answer is no, we know that, e.g., $\theta(\pi(0)) \neq 0$ or equivalently $\pi(0) \neq \theta^{-1}(0)$. Since we know θ, we can exclude one possibility for $\pi(0)$. Repeating this, we eventually find $\pi(0)$ and can compute other values of π in the same way. This terminates in polynomial time since a random permutation has no fixed points with constant probability (about $1/e$), and if this happens, the value we can exclude is uniform among the potential values.   □

5.2   A Superposition-Secure Zero-Knowledge Protocol

In this section, we present a zero-knowledge proof for any NP problem in the common reference string model. The proof is sound for an unbounded prover (quantum or not) and is computationally zero-knowledge for a polynomially bounded quantum verifier, even if superposition attacks are allowed.

For the protocol, we need a commitment scheme with special properties: we require a *keyed* commitment scheme $\mathtt{Commit}_{\mathtt{pk}}$, where the corresponding public key $\mathtt{pk}$ is generated by one of two possible key-generation algorithms: $\mathcal{G}_{\mathrm{H}}$ or $\mathcal{G}_{\mathrm{B}}$. For a key $\mathtt{pkH}$ generated by $\mathcal{G}_{\mathrm{H}}$, the commitment scheme $\mathtt{Commit}_{\mathtt{pkH}}$ is perfectly hiding, whereas the other generator, $\mathcal{G}_{\mathrm{B}}$, produces a key $\mathtt{pkB}$, such that $\mathtt{Commit}_{\mathtt{pkB}}$ is unconditionally binding. Furthermore, we require that keys $\mathtt{pkH}$ and $\mathtt{pkB}$ produced by the two generators are computationally indistinguishable, for any family of polynomial size quantum circuits. We call such a commitment scheme a *dual-mode* commitment scheme. As a candidate for implementing such a system, we can use a construction proposed in [DFS04]. That construction can be based on any decision problem for which there is a perfect honest-verifier zero-knowledge Σ-protocol, and where it is hard (for a quantum adversary) to distinguish yes-instances from no-instances. A plausible candidate for such a problem is the code equivalence problem (see [DFS04] for more details)[4].

5.3   The Model

We now describe the framework for our protocol: the proof system is specified w.r.t. a language L, and we have a prover P and a verifier V, both are assumed classical (when playing honestly). They get as input a common reference string CRS chosen with a prescribed distribution σ and a string x. P and V interact and at the end V outputs *accept* or *reject*. The first two properties we require are standard: *Completeness:* if $x \in L$ and P, V follow the protocol, V outputs *accept* with probability 1. *Soundness:* if $x \notin L$ (but CRS is chosen according to σ) then for any prover P^*, V outputs *accept* with probability negligible (in the length of x) when interacting with P^* on input x and CRS.

For zero-knowledge, we extend the capabilities of a cheating verifier V^* so it may do a superposition attack. For simplicity, we give our definition of superposition zero-knowledge only for 3-move public-coin protocols, i.e., conversations are assumed to have the form (a, e, z), where e is a random challenge issued by the verifier. It is not hard to extend the definition but the notation becomes more cumbersome. First, V^* is assumed to be a quantum machine, and the protocol is executed as follows: V^* receives x, CRS and P's first message a. Now, instead of sending a classical challenge e, V^* is allowed to send a query $\sum_{e,y} \alpha_{e,y} |e\rangle |y\rangle$. We assume the prover will process the query following his normal algorithm in superposition, so the verifier will get the same two registers back, in state $\sum_{e,y} \alpha_{e,y} |e\rangle |y + z(x, e, \rho)\rangle$, where $z(x, e, \rho)$ is P's response to challenge e on input x and internal randomness ρ. Finally, V^* outputs 0 or 1. Let $p_{real}(x)$ be the probability that 1 is output. We say that the proof system is *superposition zero-knowledge* if there exists a polynomial time quantum machine, the simulator S, such that the following holds for any cheating verifier V^* and $x \in L$: S interacts with V^* on input x, and we let $p_{\text{SIM}}(x)$ be the probability that V^* outputs 1. Then $|p_{real}(x) - p_{\text{SIM}}(x)|$ is negligible (in the length of x).

Note that, as usual in the CRS model, S only gets x as input and may therefore generate the reference string itself.

---

[4] An alternative construction can be derived from the public-key encryption scheme of Regev [Reg05], which is based on a worst-case lattice assumption. However, the resulting commitment scheme in unconditional hiding mode is only statistically secure (rather than perfect). To use this scheme in our protocol we would need a version of Theorem 1 that holds for secret-sharing schemes with statistical security. We believe such a result is true, but do not have a proof at the time of writing.

5.4   The Protocol

We now describe the basic ideas behind our protocol: we will let the CRS contain the following: $pkB, c = \mathtt{Commit}_{pkB}(0), pkB'$, where the public keys are both generated by $\mathcal{G}_B$. Then, using a standard trick, we will let P show that either $x \in L$ or c contains a 1. Since of course the latter statement is false, P still needs to convince us that $x \in L$. The simulator, on the other hand, can construct a reference string where c does contain 1 and simulate by following the protocol. The CRS will look the same to the verifier so we just need that the change of witness used is not visible in the proof, i.e., the proof should be so-called *witness indistinguishable*. In this way, we can simulate without rewinding, and this allows V^* to be quantum.

However, standard techniques for witness indistinguishability are not sufficient to handle a superposition attack. For this, we need to be more specific about the protocol: a first attempt (which does not give us soundness) is that P will secret-share his witness w (where for the honest prover, w will be a witness for $x \in L$), to create shares $s_1, \ldots, s_n$ where we assume the scheme has t-privacy. Then P's first message is a set of commitments $a = (\mathtt{Commit}_{pkB'}(s_1, r_1), \ldots, \mathtt{Commit}_{pkB'}(s_n, r_n))$. The verifier's challenge e will point out a random subset of the commitments, of size $t/2$, and the prover opens the commitments requested. Intuitively, this is zero-knowledge by Theorem 1: since we limit the number of shares the verifier can ask for to half the threshold of the secret sharing scheme, the state V^* gets back contains no information on the secret w.

On the other hand, this protocol is of course not sound, the verifier cannot check that the prover commits to meaningful shares of anything. To solve this, we make use of the "MPC in the head" technique from [IKOS09]: Here, we make use of an n-party protocol in which the witness w is secret-shared among the players, and a multiparty computation is done to check whether w is correct with respect to the claim on the public input, namely in our case $x \in L$ or the c from the CRS contains 1. Finally all players output *accept* or *reject* accordingly. It is assumed that the protocol is secure against active corruption of t players where t is $\Theta(n)$. We will call this protocol $\pi_{L,CRS}$ in the following. Several examples of suitable protocols can be found in [IKOS09]. In their construction, the prover emulates an execution of π in his head, and we let $v_{\pi_{L,CRS}}(i, \rho)$ denote the view of virtual player i, where ρ is the randomness used. The prover then commits to $v_{\pi_{L,CRS}}(i, \rho)$, for $i = 1, \ldots, n$ and the verifier asks the prover to open t randomly chosen views that are checked for consistency and adherence to $\pi_{L,CRS}$. It is shown in [IKOS09] that if no valid witness exists for the public input, then the verifier will detect an error with overwhelming probability.

Now, observe that the process of emulating π can be thought of as a secret sharing scheme, where the prover's witness w is shared and each $v_\pi(i, \rho)$ is a share: indeed any t shares contain no information on w by t-privacy of the protocol. Therefore combining this with our rudimentary idea from before gives us the solution.

Superposition-Secure Zero-Knowledge Proof for any *NP*-Language L.
The public input is x, of length k bits. The distribution σ generates the common
reference string as $\text{pkB}, c = \text{Commit}_{\text{pkB}}(0), \text{pkB}'$, where the public keys are both
generated by $\mathcal{G}_{\text{B}}$ on input 1^k.

1. The prover P emulates $\pi_{L,CRS}$ to generate $v_{\pi_{L,CRS}}(i, \rho)$ and sends to the
   verifier V: $\text{Commit}_{\text{pkB}'}(v_{\pi_{L,CRS}}(i, \rho), r_i)$, for $i = 1, \ldots, n$.
2. V sends a challenge e designating a random subset of the commitments of
   size $t/2$.
3. P opens the commitments designated by e, V checks the opened views according to the algorithm described in [IKOS09], and accepts or rejects according
   to the result.

Theorem 4. *If $(\mathcal{G}_{\text{B}}, \mathcal{G}_{\text{H}}, \text{Commit})$ form a secure dual-mode commitment scheme,
then the above protocol is complete, sound and superposition zero-knowledge.*

Proof. Completeness is trivial by inspection of the protocol. Soundness follows
immediately from the soundness proof in [IKOS09], we just have to observe
that the fact that the prover opens $t/2$ and not t views makes no difference, in
fact the proof holds as long as $\Theta(n)$ views are opened. For zero-knowledge, we
describe a simulator S: It will generate a common reference string as $\text{pkH}, c = \text{Commit}_{\text{pkH}}(1), \text{pkH}'$ where both public keys are generated by $\mathcal{G}_{\text{H}}$ on inout 1^k. It
then plays the protocol with V^*, answering its quantum queries by following the
protocol. This is possible since c now contains a 1, so S knows a valid witness.
To show that V^* cannot distinguish the simulation from the protocol, we define
series of games

Game 0 The protocol as described above, but where P talks to V^* doing a
superposition attack.
Game 1 As Game 0, but the CRS is generated as $\text{pkH}, c = \text{Commit}_{\text{pkH}}(0), \text{pkH}'$,
where both public keys are generated by $\mathcal{G}_{\text{H}}$.
Game 2 As Game 1, but the CRS is generated as $\text{pkH}, c = \text{Commit}_{\text{pkH}}(1), \text{pkH}'$.
Game 3 As Game 2, but P uses as witness the fact that c contains a 1.

Now, Game 0 and Game 1 are computationally indistinguishable by assumption
on the dual-mode commitment scheme. Game 1 and Game 2 are perfectly indistinguishable by the fact that commitments done using pkH are perfectly hiding.
Game 2 and Game 3 are perfectly indistinguishable by Theorem 1 and the fact
that commitments done using pkH' are perfectly hiding. More concretely, note
that if you take a secret-sharing scheme meeting the conditions of Theorem 1
and you augment each share with a commitment, under a perfectly hiding commitment scheme, to all the other shares, then you obtain a secret-sharing scheme
that still meets the conditions of Theorem 1 Then you note that the protocol can
be seen as using such an augmented secret-sharing scheme where the prover's
witness is the secret, so we can apply Theorem 1 to conclude that Games 2 and
3 cannot be distinguished. Finally, note that Game 3 is exactly the same game
as the simulation.   □

6 Multiparty Computation

We give a short summary of our results on multiparty computation. The details can be found in the full paper [DFNS11]. To consider the security of multiparty computation under superposition attacks we define a UC-style model that captures security under static and passive attacks. We use a notion where the environment chooses inputs to and gets outputs from the parties, and also attacks the protocol, i.e., he may issue a query $|q\rangle$ where he asks to corrupt a subset of players, possibly several in superposition. In the real process, he gets directly $|q\rangle$ back where the views of the corrupted players have been added in, including their inputs and outputs, their randomness and all messages sent and received. In the ideal process, the query goes to a simulator, who sends it to an ideal functionality. The functionality only adds in the inputs and outputs of corrupt players and the simulator must patch in views that match. Finally the environment gets the patched view back, and we now demand that its final states in the real and the ideal process are indistinguishable. Again we can make a distinction between *created response registers*, where the views are returned in newly created registers, and *supplied response registers*, where the environment provides the registers in which the (patched) views should be returned. This gives rise to two distinct MPC models, which we call the *CRR model* and the *SRR model* below.

Our first result is that in the SRR model, one can construct settings where simulation seems to be impossible for purely technical reasons. Consider the dummy 4-party function $d(x_1, x_2, x_3, x_4) = (\lambda, \lambda, \lambda, \lambda)$, where λ is the empty string, i.e., the function which gives no outputs on any of its inputs. Consider protocol δ, where parties P_2, P_3, P_4 runs as follows: On input x_i, output λ and terminate, and where P_1 runs as follows: On input x_1, create a random secret sharing $(s_1, \ldots, s_4)$ of x_1, send s_i to P_i and then output λ and terminate. If we pick a secret sharing scheme which classically tolerates 2 corrupted parties, then the secret sharing scheme is secure against corruption of 1 party under superposition attacks. We would therefore expect the protocol δ to be a secure implementation of d against corruption of 1 party under superposition attacks. It turns out that δ is *not* a secure implementation of d against 1 corruption in the SRR model. The reason is that the environment can put the supplied register in a uniform superposition over all values. Then when the inputs and outputs are added to the register by the ideal functionality it will have the same state regardless of x_1. So the simulator gets no information on x_1 when P_1 is corrupted and hence cannot simulate the shares that P_1 sends. The simulator could try to process the supplied register to get rid of the problem, but for every simulator there exists an environment that can anticipate what the simulator will do and can invert its operation. The details are in the full paper [DFNS11].

We then show that in the CRR model, δ *is* indeed a secure evaluation of d against corruption of 1 player, as we would expect; The details are in the full paper [DFNS11]. Together, these results suggest that the "correct" model is the CRR model.

We then proceed to investigate general feasibility of secure function evaluation against superposition attacks in the CRR model. This problem, however,
turns out to be far from trivial. As an example of this, suppose the protocol
in question is classically secure against corruptions of sets of size t. Now, since
the protocol is a classical process that in our model is run in superposition over
the inputs, one could expect that we could get a simulator for a superposition
attack with $t/2$ corruptions by running the classical simulator in superposition.
This turns out to be false. Specifically, we show that even though the above
protocol δ is a classical secure implementation of d against $t = 2$ corruptions, it
cannot be proven superposition attack secure against $t/2 = 1$ corruptions using
a simulator which consists of running a classical simulator in superposition. The
problem seems to come from the fact that in the MPC model, also the dealer,
P_1, may be corrupted[5], which can be used to force the way to simulate the shares
of different corrupt subsets to be inter-consistent, which in turn is the same as
being able to simultaneously simulate a corruption of all other players than the
dealer. But this is impossible, as they have three shares, which is sufficient to
determine x_1. The details are in the full paper [DFNS11].

Not all hope is lost, however. The fact that simple classical simulation in
superposition is insufficient to prove superposition attack security does not rule
out simulators which are "more quantum" than this. And, indeed, we can show
that a large class of protocols can in fact be proven superposition attack secure,
although the simulator may not always be efficient. For deterministic functions
f we give, in classical terms, a complete characterization of the class of classical
MPC protocols which securely evaluate f under superposition attack.

The characterization goes as follows. Let f be a deterministic function, let
π be a protocol, let $A \subseteq \{1, \ldots, n\}$ denote a subset of corrupted parties, let
$s = (s_1, \ldots, s_n)$ denote a vector of inputs for π and let $\mathbb{S}$ denote the set of
possible input vectors. For two input vectors s and s' let $F_{s,s'} = \{A \in F | s_A = s'_A \wedge f_A(s) = f_A(s')\}$ be the subset of allowed corruptions where the corrupted
parties have the same inputs and outputs in f. Finally, let $r = (r_1, \ldots, r_n)$
denote a vector of random inputs for π and let $\mathcal{R}$ denote the space of such
vectors. Then it holds that the protocol π is a perfectly secure evaluation of f
against superposition F-attacks in the CRR model iff it is correct and there exist
a family of permutations, $\{\pi_{s,s',A} : \mathcal{R} \to \mathcal{R}\}_{s,s' \in \mathbb{S}, A \in F_{s,s'}}$ with the following two
properties,

1. $\forall s, s' \in \mathbb{S}, \forall A \in F_{s,s'}, \forall r \in \mathcal{R} : |v_A(s, \pi_{s,s',A}(r))\rangle = |v_A(s', \pi_{s',s,A}(r))\rangle$.
2. $\forall s, s', s'' \in \mathbb{S}, \forall A \in F_{s,s'}, A' \in F_{s,s''} :$
$$\sum_{r \in \mathcal{R}} |v_A(s, r)\rangle \langle v_{A'}(s, r)| = \sum_{r \in \mathcal{R}} |v_A(s, \pi_{s,s',A}(r))\rangle \langle v_{A'}(s, \pi_{s,s'',A'}(r))|.$$

(The proof is in the full paper [DFNS11]) Note that property (1) is exactly
the statement that a (not necessarily efficient) simulator exists in the classical
model.

---

[5] (This is in contrast to the pure secret-sharing model where only shareholders can be
corrupted.)

References

[BCG+05] Ben-Or, M., Crépeau, C., Gottesman, D., Hassidim, A., Smith, A.: Secure multiparty quantum computation with (only) a strict honest majority. In: 46th Annual IEEE Symposium on Foundations of Computer Science (FOCS), pp. 249–260 (2005)

[BDF+11] Boneh, D., Dagdelen, O., Fischlin, M., Lehmann, A., Schaffner, C., Zhandry, M.: Random oracles in a quantum world. In: Lee, D.H., Wang, X. (eds.) ASIACRYPT 2011. LNCS, vol. 7073, pp. 41–69. Springer, Heidelberg (2011)

[BZ12] Boneh, D., Zhandry, M.: Quantum-secure message authentication codes. Electron. Colloquium. Comput. Complex. 19:136, 1–27 (2012)

[CJW04] Chefles, A., Jozsa, R., Winter, A.: On the existence of physical transformations between sets of quantum states. Int. J. Quant. Inf. $2(1)$, 11–21 (2004). http://arxiv.org/abs/quant-ph/0307227

[DFNS11] Damgård, I., Funder, J., Nielsen, J. B., Salvail, L.: Superposition attacks on cryptographic protocols. Cryptology ePrint archive, report 2011/421. http://eprint.iacr.org/ (2011)

[DFS04] Damgård, I.B., Fehr, S., Salvail, L.: Zero-knowledge proofs and string commitments withstanding quantum attacks. In: Franklin, M. (ed.) CRYPTO 2004. LNCS, vol. 3152, pp. 254–272. Springer, Heidelberg (2004)

[FS09] Fehr, S., Schaffner, C.: Composing quantum protocols in a classical environment. In: Reingold, O. (ed.) TCC 2009. LNCS, vol. 5444, pp. 350–367. Springer, Heidelberg (2009)

[IKOS09] Ishai, Y., Kushilevitz, E., Ostrovsky, R., Sahai, A.: Zero-knowledge proofs from secure multiparty computation. SIAM J. Comput. $39(3)$, 1121–1152 (2009)

[KN08] Kol, G., Naor, M.: Cryptography and game theory: designing protocols for exchanging information. In: Canetti, R. (ed.) TCC 2008. LNCS, vol. 4948, pp. 320–339. Springer, Heidelberg (2008)

[PVW08] Peikert, C., Vaikuntanathan, V., Waters, B.: A framework for efficient and composable oblivious transfer. In: Wagner, D. (ed.) CRYPTO 2008. LNCS, vol. 5157, pp. 554–571. Springer, Heidelberg (2008)

[Reg05] Regev, O.: On lattices, learning with errors, random linear codes, and cryptography. In: 37th Annual ACM Symposium on Theory of Computing (STOC), pp. 84–93 (2005)

[Wat06] Watrous, J.: Zero-knowledge against quantum attacks. In: 38th Annual ACM Symposium on Theory of Computing (STOC), pp. 296–305, http://www.cs.uwaterloo.ca/watrous/papers.html (2006)

[Zha12a] Zhandry, M.: How to construct quantum random functions. In: FOCS, pp. 679–687 (2012)

[Zha12b] Zhandry, M.: Secure identity-based encryption in the quantum random oracle model. In: Safavi-Naini, R., Canetti, R. (eds.) CRYPTO 2012. LNCS, vol. 7417, pp. 758–775. Springer, Heidelberg (2012)

Overcoming Weak Expectations via the Rényi Entropy and the Expanded Computational Entropy

Yanqing Yao[1,2]([✉]) and Zhoujun Li[1,3]

[1] State Key Laboratory of Software Development Environment, Beihang University,
Beijing 100191, China
[2] Department of Computer Science, New York University, New York 10012, USA
[3] Beijing Key Laboratory of Network Technology, Beihang University, Beijing, China
yaoyanqing1984@sina.com, lizj@buaa.edu.cn

Abstract. In the ideal world, cryptographic models take for granted that the secret sources (e.g. secret keys and other secret randomness) are derived from uniform distribution. However, in reality, we may only obtain some 'weak' random sources guaranteed with high unpredictability (e.g. biometric data, physical sources, and secrets with partial leakage). Formally, the security of cryptographic models is measured by the expectation of some function, called 'perfect' expectation in the ideal model and 'weak' expectation in the real model respectively. We propose some elementary inequalities which show that the 'weak' expectation is not much worse than the 'perfect' expectation. Instead of discussing the results based on the min-entropy and collision entropy by Dodis and Yu [TCC 2013], we present how to overcome weak expectations dependent on the Rényi entropy and the expanded computational entropy. We achieve these results via employing the discrete form of the Hölder inequality. We also use some techniques to guarantee that the expanded computational entropy is useful in the security model. Thus our results are more general, and we also obtain some results from a computational perspective. The results apply to all 'unpredictability' applications and some indistinguishability applications including CPA-secure symmetric-key encryption schemes, weak Pseudorandom Functions and Weaker Computational Extractors.

Keywords: Weak secret sources · The rényi entropy · Computational entropy · Symmetric-key encryption schemes · Weak pseudorandom functions · Computational extractors

1 Introduction

Traditionally, if a cryptographic system is secure, it means that it can be formally proved that it's secure in a certain security model, which usually takes for granted that the secret is perfectly random. Unfortunately, in the real world the secret

C. Padró (Ed.): ICITS 2013, LNCS 8317, pp. 162–178, 2014.
DOI: 10.1007/978-3-319-04268-8_10, © Springer International Publishing Switzerland 2014

may only be obtained from non-uniform distribution. For example, if the secret source is biometric data [8,11], physical sources [3,4], secrets with partial leakage or group elements from Diffie-Hellman key exchange [16,22], then it can't satisfy perfect randomness.

Recently, there has been some interest in basing cryptographic primitives on weak secrets, where the only information about the secret is some non-trivial amount of entropy. Formally, the (T, ε)–security (in the real model) of a cryptographic application P essentially requires that for any adversary A with resource T and non-uniform distribution R, the expectation of $f(R)$, which we call 'weak expectation' is upper bounded by ε, where the function $f(r)$ denotes A′s advantage conditioned on secret key being r. In the ideal model, the non-uniform distribution R is replaced with uniform distribution. Dodis and Yu [13] have discovered an elementary inequality that upper bounds the weak expectation of $f(R)$ by a product of two terms: the first term only depends on the entropy deficiency (i.e. the difference between m = length(R) and the amount of entropy it has), and the second is essentially the 'variance' of f under uniform distribution U_m. However, in [13], only min-entropy is considered for some applications and collision entropy is considered for some other applications. It's well known that as a measure of the diversity, uncertainty, or randomness of a system, the Rényi entropy [24] is the most general notion, which includes the Shannon entropy, the min-entropy, and the collision entropy. The advantage of the Rényi entropy compared with collision entropy was proposed by Hayashi [18,19]. We'll study the upper bound of the 'weak expectation' from the most general perspective of the entropy–the Rényi entropy. When the Rényi entropy is converted into min-entropy and collision entropy, the corresponding results are the same as those of [13]. Moreover, in [13], the entropy is information-theoretic. In reality, it's infeasible to information-theoretically measure the 'weak source'.

The discovery [6,17,25] that simple computational assumptions (namely the existence of one-way functions) make the computational and information-theoretic notions completely different has been one of the most fruitful results in computer science history, with impact on cryptography, complexity theory and computational learning theory. Two of the fundamental papers [17,25] found it natural to extend information theory more generally to the computational setting, and attempt to define its most fundamental notion of entropy. The most used is due to Håstad, Impagliazzo, Levin, and Luby [17] (called HILL entropy). In this paper, we'll use an expanded version of the HILL entropy to study how to overcome 'weak' expectations.

APPLICATIONS. Firstly, we capitalize on the inequalities via the Rényi entropy and expanded computational entropy to all unpredictability[1] applications (e.g. one-way functions, MACs and digital signatures). Secondly, the inequalities dependent on the Rényi entropy can be applied to

---

[1] "unpredictability" means the adversary's unpredictable property in the security game.

indistinguishability[2] applications including CPA-secure symmetric-key encryption schemes, weak Pseudorandom Functions, Extractors and Non-Malleable Extractors similar to the results of [13] that depend on collision entropy. Thirdly, for some indistinguishability applications, such as CPA-secure symmetric key encryption schemes and weak pseudorandom functions (PRF), we obtain some results based on the expanded computational entropy, while those [13] that depend on collision entropy are already greatly improved results as compared to state-of-the-art [23] with much simpler proofs. We also introduce the concept of weaker computational extractors, whose input is a source of sufficiently high computational entropy, while the output is close to a uniform distribution under the computational distance. Then we show a construction of a weaker computational extractor from any weak PRF.

OUR CONTRIBUTION AND TECHNIQUES. We employ the discrete form of the Hölder inequality, so that the weak expectation can be upper bounded by a product of two terms, the first of which is determined by the Rényi entropy, while the second only depends on the expectation of some function of f under uniform distribution. More formally, we get two main results:

Result 1. *If an unpredictability application P is $(T, \varepsilon)-secure in the ideal model, then P is $(T, (2^d \cdot \varepsilon)^{\frac{1}{\alpha'}})-secure in the $(m - d)-real_\alpha$ model where $\alpha \in (1, \infty)$ and $\frac{1}{\alpha} + \frac{1}{\alpha'} = 1$.*

Result 2. *Let $\alpha, \alpha' \in (1, \infty)$ and $\frac{1}{\alpha} + \frac{1}{\alpha'} = 1$. If an indistinguishability application P is $(T', \varepsilon)-secure and $(T', \tilde{T}, \gamma)$-simulatable, then*

(1) *If $1 < \alpha' < 2$, we have that P is (T, σ)-α'th power secure, where $\sigma \leq (\frac{\varepsilon + \gamma}{2})^{\frac{\alpha'}{2}}$. In particular, P is $(T, [2^d \cdot (\frac{\varepsilon + \gamma}{2})^{\frac{\alpha'}{2}}]^{\frac{1}{\alpha'}})-secure in the $(m - d)-real_\alpha$ model.*

(2) *If $\alpha' \geq 2$, we have that P is (T, σ)-α'th power secure, where $\sigma \leq \frac{\varepsilon + \gamma}{2}$. In particular, P is $(T, (2^d \cdot \frac{\varepsilon + \gamma}{2})^{\frac{1}{\alpha'}})-secure in the $(m - d)-real_\alpha$ model.*

Compared to previous results, our results are more general, since in previous literature [13], only $\alpha = \infty$ (i.e. the min entropy) and $\alpha = 2$ (i.e. the collision entropy) are considered.

Though Barak and Dodis et al. [2,13] proposed a double-run trick to study the connection between the security model and the square-security model for indistinguishability applications, it seems impossible to directly expand this trick to find the relationship between the security model and the βth power security model in the ideal world. Fortunately, we find that if the Hölder inequality is employed, then we can adopt the square-security model as a bridge between the security model and the βth power security model. Consequently, Result 2 can be obtained.

In [13], the randomness of a distribution is measured by its entropy which is information-theoretic. In reality, it's infeasible to information-theoretically measure the 'weak source'. Thus in this paper, we extend these objective measures to

---

[2] "indistinguishability" means the adversary's indistinguishable property in the security game.

the computational case. By employing the Rényi entropy, we expand the computational entropy in [17] and study how to overcome the 'weak' expectation. We discover that if the attacker's advantage circuit size is chosen to be the circuit size in the concept of expanded computational entropy, then this kind of computational entropy is useful in overcoming the 'weak' expectation, and some results similar to Result 1 and 2 can be obtained. We also show some indistinguishability applications including CPA-secure symmetric-key encryption schemes, weak Pseudorandom Functions and Weaker Computational Extractors.

ORGANIZATION. The rest of the paper is organized as follows. In the following section, we recall some concepts and notations to be used in the paper. In Sect. 3, we present how to overcome Weak Expectations via the Rényi Entropy. In Sect. 4, we use an expanded version of the HILL entropy to study how to overcome 'weak' expectations. Section 5 concludes the paper.

2 Preliminaries

In this section, we present some notations and definitions that will be used later.

Definition 2.1. ([24]) *The Rényi entropy of order α of a random variable X is defined as*

$$H_\alpha(X) = \frac{1}{1-\alpha} \log(\sum_x Pr(X = x)^\alpha),$$

where $\alpha \geq 0$ and $\alpha \neq 1$.

Remark 2.1. If $\alpha \to 1$, $H_\alpha(X)$ converges to the Shannon entropy [9]:

$$H_1(X) = -\sum_x Pr(X = x) \log Pr(X = x).$$

If $\alpha = 2$, $H_\alpha(X)$ is called the collision entropy of X:

$$H_2(X) = -\log \sum_x Pr(X = x)^2.$$

If $\alpha \to \infty$, $H_\alpha(X)$ converges to the min entropy:

$$H_\infty(X) = -\log \max_x Pr(X = x).$$

It's very natural to extend the average (aka conditional) collision entropy and min-entropy in [13] to the average (aka conditional) Rényi entropy, which is as follows.

Definition 2.2. *The average (aka conditional) Rényi entropy of a random variable X conditioned on another random variable Z is defined as follows.*

$$H_\alpha(X|Z) = \frac{1}{1-\alpha} \log(\mathbb{E}_{z \leftarrow Z}[\sum_x Pr(X = x|Z = z)^\alpha]),$$

where $z \leftarrow Z$ is denoted as sampling an element z according to distribution Z, $\alpha \geq 0$ and $\alpha \neq 1$.

If $\alpha = 2(resp.\infty)$, $H_\alpha(X|Z)$ is the same as the definition of average (aka conditional) collision entropy (resp. min-entropy) in [13]. The difference between average (aka conditional) Rényi entropy (when $1 < \alpha \leq 2$) and collision entropy was discussed in [18,19].

The advantage of a circuit C in distinguishing the random variables X, Y is denoted as $\Delta_C(X,Y) = |Pr(C(X) = 1) - Pr(C(Y) = 1)|$. The statistical distance between two random variables X, Y is defined by $\mathsf{SD}(X,Y) = \frac{1}{2}\sum_x |Pr(X = x) - Pr(Y = x)| = \max_C \Delta_C(X,Y)$. Given a circuit D, define the computational distance δ^D between X and Y as $\delta^D(X,Y) = |\mathbb{E}[D(X)] - \mathbb{E}[D(Y)]|$. We write $\Delta_C(X,Y|Z)$(resp. $\mathsf{SD}(X,Y|Z)$, $\delta^D(X,Y|Z)$) as shorthand for $\Delta_C((X,Z),(Y,Z))$(resp. $\mathsf{SD}((X,Z),(Y,Z))$, $\delta^D((X,Z),(Y,Z))$).

Let $\mathcal{D}_s^{det,\{0,1\}}$ (resp. $\mathcal{D}_s^{det,[0,1]}$) be the set of all deterministic circuits of size s with binary output in $\{0,1\}$ (resp. $[0,1]$), and let $\mathcal{D}_s^{rand,\{0,1\}}$ (resp. $\mathcal{D}_s^{rand,[0,1]}$) as the set of probabilistic circuits with output in $\{0,1\}$ (resp. $[0,1]$).

HILL computational entropy is parameterized by quality (how distinguishable is X from a variable Z that has true entropy) and quantity (how much true entropy is there in Z). Formally, it's defined as follows.

Definition 2.3. ([5,17]) *A distribution X has HILL entropy at least k, denoted $H_{\varepsilon,s}^{HILL}(X) \geq k$ if there exists a distribution Y where $H_\infty(Y) \geq k$, such that $\forall D \in \mathcal{D}_s^{det,[0,1]}$, $\delta^D(X,Y) \leq \varepsilon$.*

Definition 2.4. ([21]) *Let (X,Y) be a pair of random variables. X has conditional HILL entropy at least k conditioned on Y, denoted $H_{\varepsilon,s}^{HILL}(X|Y) \geq k$, if there exists a collection of distributions Z_y for each $y \in Y$, giving rise to a joint distribution (Z,Y), such that $H_\infty(Z|Y) \geq k$ and $\forall D \in \mathcal{D}_s^{rand,[0,1]}$, $\delta^D((X,Y),(Z,Y)) \leq \varepsilon$.*

As shown in [15], HILL entropy (resp. conditional HILL entropy) drawing D from $\mathcal{D}_s^{det,\{0,1\}}$, $\mathcal{D}_s^{det,[0,1]}$, $\mathcal{D}_s^{rand,\{0,1\}}$, $\mathcal{D}_s^{rand,[0,1]}$ is essentially equivalent. However, the above definition is only limited to the min-entropy. It's natural to expand it to the Rényi entropy. The expanded version is as follows.

Definition 2.5. *A distribution X has Expanded HILL entropy at least k, denoted $H_{\alpha,\varepsilon,s}^{EHILL}(X) \geq k$ if there exists a distribution Y where $H_\alpha(Y) \geq k$, such that $\forall D \in \mathcal{D}_s^{det,[a,b]}$, $\delta^D(X,Y) \leq \varepsilon$, where $a < b$ and $\alpha \geq 0$ and $\alpha \neq 1$.*

Definition 2.6. *Let (X,Y) be a pair of random variables. X has conditional EHILL entropy at least k conditioned on Y, denoted $H_{\alpha,\varepsilon,s}^{EHILL}(X|Y) \geq k$, if there exists a collection of distributions Z_y for each $y \in Y$, giving rise to a joint distribution (Z,Y), such that $H_\alpha(Z|Y) \geq k$ and $\forall D \in \mathcal{D}_s^{rand,[a,b]}$, $\delta^D((X,Y),(Z,Y)) \leq \varepsilon$, where $a < b$ and $\alpha \geq 0$ and $\alpha \neq 1$.*

Similar to [15], Expanded $HILL$ entropy (resp. conditional EHILL entropy) drawing D from $\mathcal{D}_s^{det,\{a,b\}}$, $\mathcal{D}_s^{det,[a,b]}$, $\mathcal{D}_s^{rand,\{a,b\}}$, $\mathcal{D}_s^{rand,[a,b]}$ is essentially equivalent.

ABSTRACT SECURITY GAMES. The security of an application P is defined via an interactive game between a probabilistic attacker A and a probabilistic challenger $\mathsf{C}(r)$, where C is fixed by the definition of P, and where the particular secret key r used by C is derived from U_m in the 'ideal' setting, and from some distribution R in the 'real' setting. The game can have an arbitrary structure, but at the end $\mathsf{C}(r)$ should output a bit, with output 1 indicating that A 'won' the game and 0 otherwise.

Given a particular key r, we define the advantage $f_{\mathsf{A}}(r)$ of A or r (against particular C fixed by P) as follows. For unpredictability games, denote $f_{\mathsf{A}}(r)$ as the expected value of $\mathsf{C}(r)$ taken over the internal coins of A and C; and for indistinguishability games, $f_{\mathsf{A}}(r)$ is the expectation of $\mathsf{C}(r) - \frac{1}{2}$, thus $f_{\mathsf{A}}(r) = Pr_{\mathsf{C},r}(\mathsf{A}\ wins) - \frac{1}{2}$. f_{A} is called A's advantage circuit.

Let U_m be the uniformly random distribution over $\{0,1\}^m$. Denote $|\mathbb{E}(f_{\mathsf{A}}(U_m))|$ as the advantage of A (in the ideal model). For $c \geq 0$ and $c \neq 1$ and all distributions R with $H_c(R) \geq m - d$, denote $\max_R |\mathbb{E}(f_{\mathsf{A}}(R))|$ as the advantage of A in the $(m - d)-$real$_c$ model instead of limiting c to be ∞ or 2 in [13]. Similarly, for $\alpha \geq 0$ and $\alpha \neq 1$, denote $\max_R |\mathbb{E}(f_{\mathsf{A}}(R))|$, taken over all distributions R with $H_{\alpha,\varepsilon,s}^{EHILL}(R) \geq m - d$, as the advantage of A in the $(m - d)-$real$_{\alpha,\varepsilon,s}^{EHILL}$ model[3].

Definition 2.7. ([13]) *An application P is $(T, s, \varepsilon)-$secure (in the ideal model) if the advantage of any $T-$bounded A with the advantage circuit size s is at most ε.*

For $c \geq 0$ and $c \neq 1$, an application P is $(T', \varepsilon')-$secure in the $(m - d)-$real$_c$ model if the advantage of any $T'-$bounded A in the $(m - d)-$real$_c$ model is at most ε'.

Definition 2.8. *For $\alpha \geq 0$ and $\alpha \neq 1$, an application P is $(T', s', \varepsilon')-$secure in the $(m - d)-$real$_{\alpha,\varepsilon_0,s'}^{EHILL}$ model if the advantage of any $T'-$bounded A with the advantage circuit size s' in the $(m - d)-$real$_{\alpha,\varepsilon_0,s'}^{EHILL}$ model is at most ε'.*

3 Overcoming Weak Expectations via the Rényi Entropy

Since the unavailability of perfect random secret sources, it's valuable to discover the connection between the advantages $|\mathbb{E}(f_{\mathsf{A}}(U_m))|$ (in the ideal model) and $\max_R |\mathbb{E}f_{\mathsf{A}}(R)|$ (in the $(m-d)-$real$_c$ model) where $c \geq 0$ and $c \neq 1$. Unfortunately, existing results [13] only considered the min-entropy for unpredictability applications and the collision entropy for indistinguishability applications. In the following, based on the Rényi Entropy and the discrete form of the Hölder inequality, we'll present an inequality which unify the corresponding connection in both unpredictability and indistinguishability applications. Then we present its applications and discuss its form when side information exists.

---

[3] The difference between the model here and that in [13] is that the 'weak' secret source here is measured by expanded HILL entropy while it's measured by collision entropy or min-entropy in [13].

Lemma 3.1. ([1]) *Let* $\alpha, \alpha' \in (1, \infty)$ *and* $\frac{1}{\alpha} + \frac{1}{\alpha'} = 1$, *then for all* $(x_1, x_2, \cdots, x_n), (y_1, y_2, \cdots, y_n) \in \mathbb{R}^n$, *we have*

$$\sum_{k=1}^{n} |x_k y_k| \leq (\sum_{k=1}^{n} |x_k|^{\alpha})^{1/\alpha} (\sum_{k=1}^{n} |y_k|^{\alpha'})^{1/\alpha'},$$

which is the discrete form of the Hölder inequality.

Theorem 3.1. *Let* $\alpha, \alpha' \in (1, \infty)$ *and* $\frac{1}{\alpha} + \frac{1}{\alpha'} = 1$, *then for any (deterministic) real-valued function* $f : \{0, 1\}^m \to \mathbb{R}$ *and any random variable* R *with* $H_\alpha(R) \geq m - d$, *we have*

$$|\mathbb{E}[f(R)]| \leq (2^d \cdot \mathbb{E}[|f(U_m)|^{\alpha'}])^{\frac{1}{\alpha'}}.$$

Proof. From Definition 2.1, $\sum_r Pr(R = r)^\alpha = 2^{(1-\alpha)H_\alpha(R)}$. According to Lemma 3.1, we have

$$|\mathbb{E}[f(R)]| = |\sum_r Pr(R = r)f(r)| \leq \sum_r |Pr(R = r)f(r)|$$

$$\leq [\sum_r Pr(R = r)^\alpha]^{\frac{1}{\alpha}} \cdot [\sum_r |f(r)|^{\alpha'}]^{\frac{1}{\alpha'}}$$

$$= [2^{(1-\alpha)H_\alpha(R)}]^{\frac{1}{\alpha}} \cdot [\frac{1}{2^m} \cdot \sum_r |f(r)|^{\alpha'}]^{\frac{1}{\alpha'}} \cdot (2^m)^{\frac{1}{\alpha'}}$$

$$= [2^{(1-\alpha)H_\alpha(R)}]^{\frac{1}{\alpha}} \cdot \{2^m \cdot \mathbb{E}[|f(U_m)|^{\alpha'}]\}^{\frac{1}{\alpha'}}$$

$$\leq 2^{\frac{(1-\alpha)(m-d)}{\alpha}} \cdot \{2^m \cdot \mathbb{E}[|f(U_m)|^{\alpha'}]\}^{\frac{1}{\alpha'}}$$

$$= (2^d \cdot \mathbb{E}[|f(U_m)|^{\alpha'}])^{\frac{1}{\alpha'}}.$$

Remark 3.1.

- If $\alpha \to \infty$, we get $|\mathbb{E}[f(R)]| \leq 2^d \mathbb{E}[|f(U_m)|]$. Furthermore, if f is non-negative function, the result of Theorem 3.1 degenerates into the result of Lemma 3.1 in [13]. It was mentioned that when the value of f can be negative, the result in Corollary 3.1 of [13] (i.e. $\mathbb{E}[f(R)] \leq 2^d \mathbb{E}[f(U_m)]$) is generally false, while our result shows that if the absolute value operation is added to both sides of the inequality, then the inequality holds.

- If $\alpha = 2$, the result of Theorem 3.1 degenerates into the result of Lemma 3.2 in [13].

- If $\alpha \to 1$, using L'Hôpital's rule, we get

$$\lim_{\alpha' \to \infty} \{2^d \cdot \mathbb{E}[|f(U_m)|^{\alpha'}]\}^{\frac{1}{\alpha'}} = \lim_{\alpha' \to \infty} [\sum_r |f(r)|^{\alpha'}]^{\frac{1}{\alpha'}}$$

$$= e^{\lim_{\alpha' \to \infty} \frac{\ln(\sum_r |f(r)|^{\alpha'})}{\alpha'}} = e^{\lim_{\alpha' \to \infty} \frac{\sum_r |f(r)|^{\alpha'} \ln |f(r)|}{\sum_r |f(r)|^{\alpha'}}} = \max_r |f(r)|.$$

On the other hand, we can easily get that $|\mathbb{E}[f(R)]| \leq \max_r |f(r)|$ irrespective of the Rényi entropy. Thus it's meaningless to discuss the result under Shannon entropy.

Corollary 3.1. *Let $\alpha, \alpha' \in (1, \infty)$ and $\frac{1}{\alpha} + \frac{1}{\alpha'} = 1$, then for any (deterministic) real-valued function $f : \{0,1\}^m \to [0,1]$ and any random variable R with $H_\alpha(R) \geq m - d$, we have*

$$\mathbb{E}[f(R)] \leq (2^d \cdot \mathbb{E}[|f(U_m)|^{\alpha'}])^{\frac{1}{\alpha'}} \leq (2^d \cdot \mathbb{E}[|f(U_m)|])^{\frac{1}{\alpha'}}.$$

Corollary 3.2. *If an unpredictability application P is $(T, \varepsilon)-$secure in the ideal model, then P is $(T, (2^d \cdot \varepsilon)^{\frac{1}{\alpha'}})-$secure in the $(m - d)-$real$_\alpha$ model where $\alpha \in (1, \infty)$ and $\frac{1}{\alpha} + \frac{1}{\alpha'} = 1$.*

Remark 3.2. The above corollary shows a upper bound about the advantage of an adversary in the $(m - d)-$real$_\alpha$ model, though the upper bound is not tight. Since $\lim\limits_{\alpha \to \infty} (2^d \cdot \varepsilon)^{\frac{1}{\alpha'}} = \lim\limits_{\alpha' \to 1} (2^d \cdot \varepsilon)^{\frac{1}{\alpha'}} = 2^d \cdot \varepsilon$, we have that the above corollary degenerates into Corollary 3.1 of [13].

Corollary 3.2 can be applied to all "unpredictability" applications such as one-way functions, MACs and digital signatures. It shows that if the secret sources are derived from the real world only guaranteeing high Rényi entropy, then the unpredictable cryptosystems in ideality have not to be redesigned in the real model, and the security levels in reality can be measured by that in ideality and the Rényi entropy of the 'weak' random secret sources.

Definition 3.1. *Consider $\beta > 1$. An application P is $(T, \sigma) - \beta$th power secure if for any $T-$bounded adversary A, we have $\mathbb{E}[|f(U_m)|^\beta] \leq \sigma$, where $f(r)$ denotes A's advantage conditioned on key being r.*

Corollary 3.3. *If an indistinguishability application P is $(T, \sigma) - \alpha'$th power secure in the ideal model, then P is $(T, (2^d \cdot \sigma)^{\frac{1}{\alpha'}})-$secure in the $(m - d)-$real$_\alpha$ model where $\alpha, \alpha' \in (1, \infty)$ and $\frac{1}{\alpha} + \frac{1}{\alpha'} = 1$.*

Though the min-entropy can be generalized to the Rényi entropy for all unpredictability applications, it appears very difficult to connect $\mathbb{E}[|f(U_m)|^{\alpha'}]$ and $\mathbb{E}[f(U_m)]$ for indistinguishability applications. The reason is that for indistinguishability applications, the range of the function $f(r)$ is $[-\frac{1}{2}, \frac{1}{2}]$, thus the absolute value operation on the right hand side of the inequality in Theorem 3.1 can't be deleted. Fortunately, Dodis et al. [13] proposed the Double-Run Trick to connect $\mathbb{E}[f_B(U_m)]$ and $\mathbb{E}[f_A(U_m)^2]$ where A and B are two adversaries in the same kind of attack game with different number of oracle queries. We'll adopt this technique and find the relationship between $\mathbb{E}[f_A(U_m)^2]$ and $\mathbb{E}[|f_A(U_m)|^{\alpha'}]$ with $\alpha' > 1$.

Dodis et al. [13] introduced the concept of simulatability about an indistinguishability application P and obtain the following Lemma (Lemma 3.2) via using the Double-Run Trick.

Lemma 3.2. (*see* [13]) *Assume P is $(T', \varepsilon)-$secure and (T', T, γ)-simulatable[4], then P is (T, σ)-square secure, where $\sigma \leq \frac{\varepsilon + \gamma}{2}$.*

In particular, P is $(T, \sqrt{2^{d-1}(\varepsilon + \gamma)})$-secure in the $(m - d)$-real$_2$ model.

In the above lemma, only collision entropy is considered. We'll amplify it to the Rényi entropy. Divesh Aggarwal observed that the following lemma can be employed to make the amplification.

Lemma 3.3. *Consider $1 < \beta < 2$. For any (deterministic) real-valued function $f : \{0,1\}^m \to [-\frac{1}{2}, \frac{1}{2}]$, we have*

$$\mathbb{E}[|f(U_m)|^\beta] \leq \{\mathbb{E}[|f(U_m)|^2]\}^{\frac{\beta}{2}}.$$

The proof of Lemma 3.3 is given in Appendix B.

Theorem 3.2. *Let $\alpha, \alpha' \in (1, \infty)$ and $\frac{1}{\alpha} + \frac{1}{\alpha'} = 1$. Assume an indistinguishability application P is $(T', \varepsilon)-$secure and (T', T, γ)-simulatable, then*

(1) *If $1 < \alpha' < 2$, we have that P is (T, σ)-α'th power secure, where $\sigma \leq (\frac{\varepsilon + \gamma}{2})^{\frac{\alpha'}{2}}$. In particular, by Corollary 3.3, P is $(T, [2^d \cdot (\frac{\varepsilon + \gamma}{2})^{\frac{\alpha'}{2}}]^{\frac{1}{\alpha'}})-$secure in the $(m - d)-$real$_\alpha$ model.*

(2) *If $\alpha' \geq 2$, we have that P is (T, σ)-α'th power secure, where $\sigma \leq \frac{\varepsilon + \gamma}{2}$. In particular, by Corollary 3.3, P is $(T, (2^d \cdot \frac{\varepsilon + \gamma}{2})^{\frac{1}{\alpha'}})-$secure in the $(m - d)-$real$_\alpha$ model.*

Proof. By Lemma 3.2, we have that P is (T, σ')-square secure, where $\sigma' \leq \frac{\varepsilon + \gamma}{2}$.
    (1) If $1 < \alpha' < 2$, from Lemma 3.3, we obtain that

$$\mathbb{E}[|f_A(U_m)|^{\alpha'}] \leq \{\mathbb{E}[|f_A(U_m)|^2]\}^{\frac{\alpha'}{2}} \leq (\frac{\varepsilon + \gamma}{2})^{\frac{\alpha'}{2}}.$$

Therefore, P is (T, σ)-α'th power secure, where $\sigma \leq (\frac{\varepsilon + \gamma}{2})^{\frac{\alpha'}{2}}$.
    (2) If $\alpha' \geq 2$, then $\mathbb{E}[|f_A(U_m)|^{\alpha'}] \leq \mathbb{E}[|f_A(U_m)|^2]$ according to $f_A(r) \in [-\frac{1}{2}, \frac{1}{2}]$ for all $r \in \{0,1\}^m$. Therefore, P is (T, σ)-α'th power secure, where $\sigma \leq \frac{\varepsilon + \gamma}{2}$.

Remark 3.3. Dodis et al. [13] enumerated the applications of Lemma 3.2 to CPA-secure symmetric-key encryption schemes, weak Pseudorandom Functions, Extractors and Non-Malleable Extractors. If the weak random sources are measured by the Rényi entropy instead of the collision entropy, we can obtain similar results via Theorem 3.2.

In some settings, the weak secret sources are derived using some procedure, during which the attacker gets some side information S about the secret sources. Therefore, it's valuable to extend the inequality of Theorem 3.1 into the average (aka. conditional) setting. Then it can be employed similarly to study the relationship between the average-case ideal security quantity and real security quantity. The inequality is as follows.

---

[4] For space limitation, this definition is in Appendix A.

Theorem 3.3. *Let* $\alpha, \alpha' \in (1, \infty)$ *and* $\frac{1}{\alpha} + \frac{1}{\alpha'} = 1$, *then for any real-valued function* $f(z, s)$ *and any random variables* (Z, S), *where* $|Z| = m$ *and* $H_\alpha(Z|S) \geq m - d$, *we have*

$$|\mathbb{E}[f(Z, S)]| \leq \{2^d \cdot \mathbb{E}[|f(U_m, S)|^{\alpha'}]\}^{\frac{1}{\alpha'}}.$$

- *If* $\alpha \to \infty$ *and* f *is a non-negative function, the above result degenerates into the result of Lemma 3.5 (a) in [13].*
- *If* $\alpha = 2$, *the above result degenerates into the result of Lemma 3.5 (b) in [13].*

Proof. From Definition 2.2, we have

$$\sum_s Pr[S = s] \sum_z Pr[Z = z|S = s]^\alpha = 2^{(1-\alpha)H_\alpha(Z|S)}.$$

Therefore, from Lemma 3.1, we have

$$|\mathbb{E}[f(Z, S)]| = |\sum_{s,z} Pr[S = s] \cdot Pr[Z = z|S = s] \cdot f(z, s)|$$

$$= 2^m \cdot |\sum_{s,z} [(\frac{1}{2^m})^{\frac{1}{\alpha}} \cdot Pr[S = s]^{\frac{1}{\alpha}} \cdot Pr[Z = z|S = s]] \cdot [(\frac{1}{2^m})^{\frac{1}{\alpha'}} \cdot Pr[S = s]^{\frac{1}{\alpha'}} \cdot f(z, s)]|$$

$$\leq 2^m \cdot \sqrt[\alpha]{\sum_{s,z} \frac{1}{2^m} \cdot Pr[S = s] \cdot Pr[Z = z|S = s]^\alpha} \cdot \sqrt[\alpha']{\sum_{s,z} \frac{1}{2^m} \cdot Pr[S = s] \cdot |f(z, s)|^{\alpha'}}$$

$$= 2^m \cdot \sqrt[\alpha]{\frac{1}{2^m} \cdot 2^{(1-\alpha) \cdot H_\alpha(Z|S)}} \cdot \sqrt[\alpha']{\mathbb{E}[|f(U_m, S)|^{\alpha'}]}$$

$$\leq 2^{\frac{(1-\alpha)(m-d)}{\alpha}} \cdot \{2^m \cdot \mathbb{E}[|f(U_m, S)|^{\alpha'}]\}^{\frac{1}{\alpha'}}$$

$$= \{2^d \cdot \mathbb{E}[|f(U_m, S)|^{\alpha'}]\}^{\frac{1}{\alpha'}}.$$

4 Overcoming Weak Expectations via the Expanded Computational Entropy

Dodis and Yu [13] found some elegant results about overcoming weak expectations based on the min-entropy and the collision entropy, which are information-theoretic. In reality, the 'weak source' may only be measured by efficient algorithms. Thus, computational entropy may be a more valuable tool to study how to overcoming weak expectation. Two papers [17, 25] extended information theory more generally to the computational setting, and attempted to define its most fundamental notion of entropy. Due to the most usefulness of HILL entropy introduced by Håstad, Impagliazzo, Levin, and Luby [17], in this section, we'll use an expanded version of the HILL entropy (EHILL entropy) to study how to overcome 'weak' expectations. We choose the attacker's advantage circuit size as the circuit size in the concept of expanded computational entropy, and obtain an inequality via the EHILL entropy. Then we present the relationship between the ideal security quantity and real security quantity via the EHILL entropy in all unpredictability applications and some indistinguishability applications. We also show some concrete indistinguishability applications. Finally, we discuss its form when side information exists.

Theorem 4.1. Let $\alpha, \alpha' \in (1, \infty)$ and $\frac{1}{\alpha} + \frac{1}{\alpha'} = 1$, then for any (deterministic) real-valued function $f : \{0,1\}^m \to [a,b]$ with size s and any random variable R with $H_{\alpha,\varepsilon_0,s}^{EHILL}(R) \geq m - d$, we have $|\mathbb{E}[f(R)]| \leq \{2^d \cdot \mathbb{E}[|f(U_m)|^{\alpha'}]\}^{\frac{1}{\alpha'}} + \varepsilon_0$.

Proof. Since $H_{\alpha,\varepsilon_0,s}^{EHILL}(R) \geq m - d$, we get that there exists a distribution Y where $H_\alpha(Y) \geq m - d$, such that $\forall D \in \mathcal{D}_s^{det,[a,b]}$, $\delta^D(R,Y) \leq \varepsilon_0$.

From Theorem 3.1, we have that $\mathbb{E}[f(Y)] \leq \{2^d \cdot \mathbb{E}[|f(U_m)|^{\alpha'}]\}^{\frac{1}{\alpha'}}$. Since $f \in \mathcal{D}_s^{det,[0,1]}$, we have that $|\mathbb{E}[f(R)] - \mathbb{E}[f(Y)]| \leq \varepsilon_0$. Thus

$$|\mathbb{E}[f(R)]| \leq \{2^d \cdot \mathbb{E}[|f(U_m)|^{\alpha'}]\}^{\frac{1}{\alpha'}} + \varepsilon_0.$$

Corollary 4.1. Let $\alpha, \alpha' \in (1, \infty)$ and $\frac{1}{\alpha} + \frac{1}{\alpha'} = 1$. For any (deterministic) real-valued function $f : \{0,1\}^m \to [0,1]$ with size s and any random variable R with $H_{\alpha,\varepsilon_0,s}^{EHILL}(R) \geq m - d$, we have

$$\mathbb{E}[f(R)] \leq \{2^d \cdot \mathbb{E}[f(U_m)^{\alpha'}]\}^{\frac{1}{\alpha'}} + \varepsilon_0 \leq \{2^d \cdot \mathbb{E}[f(U_m)]\}^{\frac{1}{\alpha'}} + \varepsilon_0.$$

Corollary 4.2. If an unpredictability application P is $(T, \varepsilon) - secure$ in the ideal model, then P is $(T, (2^d \cdot \varepsilon)^{\frac{1}{\alpha'}} + \varepsilon_0) - secure$ in the $(m-d) - real_{\alpha,\varepsilon_0,s}^{EHILL}$ model where $\alpha \in (1, \infty)$ and $\frac{1}{\alpha} + \frac{1}{\alpha'} = 1$.

The above corollary shows that if the secret sources are derived from the real world only guaranteeing high expanded computational entropy, then the unpredictable cryptosystems in ideality have not to be redesigned in the real model, and the security levels in reality can be measured by that in ideality and the expanded computational entropy of the 'weak' random secret sources.

For indistinguishability applications, since $f(r) \in [-\frac{1}{2}, \frac{1}{2}]$, we can't get the inequality like Corollary 4.1. We'll instead introduce the following definition.

Definition 4.1. Consider $\beta > 1$. An application P is $(T, s, \sigma) - \beta th$ power secure if for any $T-$bounded adversary A with the advantage circuit size s, we have $\mathbb{E}[|f(U_m)|^\beta] \leq \sigma$, where $f(r)$ denotes $A's$ advantage conditioned on key being r.

Applying this definition to Theorem 4.1, we get that α'th power security implies real model security as follows.

Corollary 4.3. If an application P is $(T, s, \sigma) - \alpha'$th power secure, then P is $(T, s, (2^d \cdot \sigma)^{\frac{1}{\alpha'}} + \varepsilon_0) - secure$ in the $(m - d) - real_{\alpha,\varepsilon_0,s}^{EHILL}$ model where $\alpha \in (1, \infty)$ and $\frac{1}{\alpha} + \frac{1}{\alpha'} = 1$.

In the following we'll obtain the relationship between the ideal security quantity and real security quantity.

Theorem 4.2. *Let $\alpha, \alpha' \in (1, \infty)$ and $\frac{1}{\alpha} + \frac{1}{\alpha'} = 1$. Assume P is a (T', s', ε)−secure and $((T', s'), (T, s), \gamma)$−simulatable[5], then*

(1) If $1 < \alpha' < 2$, we have that P is (T, s, σ)-α'th power secure, where $\sigma \leq (\frac{\varepsilon + \gamma}{2})^{\frac{\alpha'}{2}}$. In particular, by Corollary 4.3, P is $(T, s, [2^d \cdot (\frac{\varepsilon + \gamma}{2})^{\frac{\alpha'}{2}}]^{\frac{1}{\alpha'}} + \varepsilon_0)$−secure in the $(m - d)$−$real_{\alpha, \varepsilon_0, s}^{EHILL}$ model.

(2) If $\alpha' \geq 2$, we have that P is (T, s, σ)-α'th power secure, where $\sigma \leq \frac{\varepsilon + \gamma}{2}$. In particular, by Corollary 4.3, P is $(T, s, (2^d \cdot \frac{\varepsilon + \gamma}{2})^{\frac{1}{\alpha'}} + \varepsilon_0)$−secure in the $(m - d)$−$real_{\alpha, \varepsilon_0, s}^{EHILL}$ model.

Proof. From Theorem 3.2, we get this result.

In the following, we show that the above result can be successfully applied to CPA-secure symmetric-key encryption schemes, weak Pseudorandom Functions and Weaker Computational Extractors.

Theorem 4.3. *Let $\alpha, \alpha' \in (1, \infty)$ and $\frac{1}{\alpha} + \frac{1}{\alpha'} = 1$. Assume P is a $((2t, 2q), s', 0)$− CPA secure symmetric-key encryption scheme in the ideal model. Then*

(1) If $1 < \alpha' < 2$, then P is $((t, q), s, [2^d \cdot (\frac{\varepsilon}{2})^{\frac{\alpha'}{2}}]^{\frac{1}{\alpha'}} + \varepsilon_0)$−secure in the $(m - d)$−$real_{\alpha, \varepsilon_0, s}^{EHILL}$ model.

(2) If $\alpha' \geq 2$, then P is $((t, q), s, (2^d \cdot \frac{\varepsilon}{2})^{\frac{1}{\alpha'}} + \varepsilon_0)$−secure in the $(m - d)$−$real_{\alpha, \varepsilon_0, s}^{EHILL}$ model.

Proof. From Theorem 4.2, we get this result.

Definition 4.2. *A family $\mathcal{H}$ of functions $\{h_r : \{0, 1\}^n \to \{0, 1\}^l | r \in \{0, 1\}^m\}$ is $((t, q), s, \delta)$−secure weak PRF, if for any t−bounded attacker A with the advantage circuit size s, and random $x, x_1, \cdots, x_{q-1} \leftarrow U_n$ and $r \leftarrow U_m$, we have*

$$\Delta_A(h_r(x), U_l | x, x_1, h_r(x_1), \cdots, x_{q-1}, h_r(x_{q-1})) \leq \delta.$$

The concept of weak PRF here is essentially equivalent to the one in [13], as the definition here is produced via adding the parameter s to the one in [13]. Just like CPA-secure symmetric-key encryption schemes, weak PRFs are easily seen to be $(((2t, 2q), s'), ((t, q), s), 0)$−simulatable. By Theorem 4.2, we have

Theorem 4.4. *Let $\alpha, \alpha' \in (1, \infty)$ and $\frac{1}{\alpha} + \frac{1}{\alpha'} = 1$. Assume P is a $((2t, 2q), s', \delta)$−secure weak PRF in the ideal model. Then*

(1) If $1 < \alpha' < 2$, we have that P is $((t, q), s, \sigma)$-α'th power secure, where $\sigma \leq (\frac{\varepsilon + \gamma}{2})^{\frac{\alpha'}{2}}$. In particular, P is $((t, q), s, [2^d \cdot (\frac{\varepsilon + \gamma}{2})^{\frac{\alpha'}{2}}]^{\frac{1}{\alpha'}} + \varepsilon_0)$−secure in the $(m - d)$−$real_{\alpha, \varepsilon_0, s}^{EHILL}$ model.

---

[5] For space limitation, this definition is in Appendix A.

(2) If $\alpha' \geq 2$, we have that P is $((t,q), s, \sigma)-\alpha'$th power secure, where $\sigma \leq \frac{\varepsilon+\gamma}{2}$. In particular, P is $((t,q), s, (2^d \cdot \frac{\varepsilon+\gamma}{2})^{\frac{1}{\alpha'}} + \varepsilon_0)-secure$ in the $(m-d)-real_{\alpha,\varepsilon_0,s}^{EHILL}$ model.

Extractors have many applications such as key generation, leakage-resilient encryption and derandomization of BPP and IP, but its existence is still not enough under computational perspective. Therefore, we introduce an expanded definition of Extractors.

Definition 4.3. (Weaker Computational Extractors) *We say that an efficient function $E_{wc} : \{0,1\}^m \times \{0,1\}^n \rightarrow \{0,1\}^l$ is a $(k, H_{\alpha,\varepsilon_0,s}^{EHILL}, \varepsilon)-weaker$ computational extractor, if for all R (over $\{0,1\}^m$) with $H_{\alpha,\varepsilon_0,s}^{EHILL}(R) \geq k$, for random S (uniform over $\{0,1\}^n$), and $\forall D \in \mathcal{D}_s^{ran,[0,1]}$, we get*

$$\delta^D(E_{wc}(R;S), U_l|S) \leq \varepsilon$$

where $\alpha \geq 0$, $\alpha \neq 1$, and $S \leftarrow U_n$ is the random seed of E_{wc}. The value $L = k - l$ is called the entropy loss of E_{wc}.

Remark 4.1. It should be noticed that computational extractors and weak computational extractors have been studied in [10]. Essentially, computational extractors are efficient functions that map a source of sufficiently high min-entropy to an output, requiring that the joint distribution of output and seed be computationally indistinguishable from uniform. A weak computational extractor is defined similarly, but only requiring that the output of the function (without the seed) be indistinguishable from uniform. While in this paper, it only requires the computational distance between the uniform distribution and the joint distribution of output and seed be upper bounded by ε, in this sense, the output of the function is further relaxed.

Corollary 4.4. *Let $\alpha, \alpha' \in (1, \infty)$ and $\frac{1}{\alpha} + \frac{1}{\alpha'} = 1$. If $\mathcal{H} \overset{def}{=} \{h_r : \{0,1\}^n \rightarrow \{0,1\}^l | r \in \{0,1\}^m\}$ is $((2t,2), s', \delta)-secure$ weak PRF in the ideal model, then*

(1) *If $1 < \alpha' < 2$, then $E_{wc}(r;z) \overset{def}{=} h_r(z)$ is $((t,1), s, [2^d \cdot (\frac{\varepsilon+\gamma}{2})^{\frac{\alpha'}{2}}]^{\frac{1}{\alpha'}} + \varepsilon_0)-secure$ in the $(m-d)-real_{\alpha,\varepsilon_0,s}^{EHILL}$ model. Hence, $E_{wc}(r;z)$ is a $(m-d, H_{\alpha,\varepsilon_0,s}^{EHILL}, [2^d \cdot (\frac{\varepsilon+\gamma}{2})^{\frac{\alpha'}{2}}]^{\frac{1}{\alpha'}} + \varepsilon_0)-weaker$ computational extractor.*

(2) *If $\alpha' \geq 2$, then $E_{wc}(r;z) \overset{def}{=} h_r(z)$ is $((t,1), s, (2^d \cdot \frac{\varepsilon+\gamma}{2})^{\frac{1}{\alpha'}} + \varepsilon_0)-secure$ in the $(m-d)-real_{\alpha,\varepsilon_0,s}^{EHILL}$ model. Hence, $E_{wc}(r;z)$ is a $(m-d, H_{\alpha,\varepsilon_0,s}^{EHILL}, (2^d \cdot \frac{\varepsilon+\gamma}{2})^{\frac{1}{\alpha'}} + \varepsilon_0)-weaker$ computational extractor.*

In the following, we study how to extend the inequality of Theorem 3.1 into the average (aka. conditional) setting. It's as follows.

Theorem 4.5. *Let $\alpha, \alpha' \in (1, \infty)$ and $\frac{1}{\alpha} + \frac{1}{\alpha'} = 1$, then for any real-valued function $f(r,s)$ with size s_0 and any random variables (R,S), where $|R| = m$ and $H_{\alpha,\varepsilon_0,s_0}^{EHILL}(R|S) \geq m - d$, we have*

$$|\mathbb{E}[f(R,S)]| \leq \{2^d \cdot \mathbb{E}[|f(U_m, S)|^{\alpha'}]\}^{\frac{1}{\alpha'}} + \varepsilon_0.$$

Proof. Since $H^{EHILL}_{\alpha,\varepsilon_0,s_0}(R|S) \geq m - d$, we have that there exists a joint distribution (Z, S), such that $H_\infty(Z|S) \geq m - d$ and for $\forall D \in \mathcal{D}_s^{ran,[0,1]}$, $\delta^D((R, S), (Z, S)) \leq \varepsilon_0$.

According to Theorem 3.3, we have $|\mathbb{E}[f(Z, S)]| \leq \{2^d \cdot \mathbb{E}[|f(U_m, S)|^{\alpha'}]\}^{\frac{1}{\alpha'}}$. Since $f \in \mathcal{D}_s^{ran,[a,b]}$, we have $|\mathbb{E}[f(Z, S)] - \mathbb{E}[f(R, S)]| \leq \varepsilon_0$. Thus,

$$|\mathbb{E}[f(R, S)]| \leq |\mathbb{E}[f(Z, S)]| + \varepsilon_0 \leq \{2^d \cdot \mathbb{E}[|f(U_m, S)|^{\alpha'}]\}^{\frac{1}{\alpha'}} + \varepsilon_0.$$

5   Conclusion

In the ideal world, a cryptographic system is considered to be secure, if it can be formally proved that it's secure in certain security model, which takes for granted the secret is perfectly random. However, in the real world, the secret may only be obtained from non-uniform distribution with some non-trivial amount of entropy. The security of cryptographic models is measured by the expectation of some function, with called 'perfect' expectation in the ideal model and 'weak' expectation in the real model respectively. We propose some elementary inequalities via the Rényi entropy and the expanded computational entropy, which show that the 'weak' expectation is not much worse than the 'perfect' expectation. The results apply to all 'unpredictability' applications and some indistinguishability applications including CPA-secure symmetric-key encryption schemes, weak Pseudorandom Functions and Weaker Computational Extractors. Compared to the results based on the min-entropy and collision entropy by Dodis and Yu [TCC 2013], our results are more general, and we also obtain some results from a computational perspective.

Acknowledgments. We would like to thank Yevgeniy Dodis and Divesh Aggraval for helpful discussions. In particular, Divesh showed us Lemma 3.3 and how to prove it. We also wish to thank the anonymous reviewers for useful comments. This work is supported by the Natural Science Foundation of China (60973105, 61370126, 61170189, and 61170107), the Fund for the Doctoral Program of Higher Education of China (20111102130003 and20101303110004), the Fund of the State Key Laboratory of Software Development Environment (SKLSDE-2013ZX-19, SKLSDE-2012ZX-11), the Innovation Foundation of Beihang University for Ph.D. Graduates under Grant No. 2011106014, the Fund of the Scholarship Award for Excellent Doctoral Student granted by Ministry of Education under Grant No.400618, and the Fund for CSC Scholarship Programme under Grant No. 201206020063.

A   Definitions

Definition 1. (see [13]) *We say that an indistinguishability application P is $((T', T, \gamma)$-simulatable, if for any secret key r and any legal, T-bounded attacker A, there exists a (possibly illegal!) $T'-$bounded attacker B (for some $T' \geq T$) such that:*

(1) The execution between B and 'real' $C(r)$ defines two independent executions between a copy A_i of A and a 'simulated' challenger $C_i(r)$, for $i = 1, 2$. In particular, except reusing the same r, A_1, $C_1(r)$, A_2, $C_2(r)$ use fresh and independent randomness, including independent challenge bits b_1 and b_2.

(2) The challenge b used by 'real' $C(r)$ is equal to the challenge b_2 used by 'simulated' C_2.

(3) Before making its guess b' of the challenge bit b, B learns the values b_1, b'_1 and b'_2.

(4) The probability of B violating the failure predicate F is at most γ.

Definition 2. *We say that an indistinguishability application P is $((T', s'), (T, s), \gamma)-$simulatable, if for any secret key r and any legal, T-bounded attacker A with the advantage circuit size s, there exists a (possibly illegal!) $T'-$bounded attacker B (for some $T' \geq T$) with the advantage circuit size s' such that it satisfies items (1)-(4) of Definition 1.*

Remark. The definition here is essentially equivalent to Definition 1, as the definition here is obtained via adding the parameters s and s' to Definition 1.

B   Proof

Proof. Since $1 < \beta < 2$, we have $\frac{2}{\beta} > 1$. From the Hölder inequality, we have

$$\sum_{r \in \{0,1\}^m} [|f(r)^\beta| \cdot 1] \leq [\sum_{r \in \{0,1\}^m} |f(r)^\beta|^{\frac{2}{\beta}}]^{\frac{\beta}{2}} \cdot (\sum_{r \in \{0,1\}^m} 1)^{1-\frac{\beta}{2}}$$

$$= [\sum_{r \in \{0,1\}^m} |f(r)|^2]^{\frac{\beta}{2}} \cdot 2^{m \cdot (1-\frac{\beta}{2})}.$$

Therefore,

$$\mathbb{E}[|f(U_m)|^\beta] = \frac{1}{2^m} \sum_{r \in \{0,1\}^m} |f(r)^\beta|$$

$$\leq (2^m)^{\frac{\beta}{2}} \cdot [\frac{1}{2^m} \cdot \sum_{r \in \{0,1\}^m} |f(r)|^2]^{\frac{\beta}{2}} \cdot 2^{m \cdot (-\frac{\beta}{2})}$$

$$= \{\mathbb{E}[|f(U_m)|^2]\}^{\frac{\beta}{2}}.$$

References

1. Abualrub, M.S., Sulaiman, W.T.: A note on Hölder's inequality. Int. Math. Forum 4(40), 1993–1995 (2009)
2. Barak, B., Dodis, Y., Krawczyk, H., Pereira, O., Pietrzak, K., Standaert, F.-X., Yu, Y.: Leftover hash lemma, revisited. In: Rogaway, P. (ed.) CRYPTO 2011. LNCS, vol. 6841, pp. 1–20. Springer, Heidelberg (2011)
3. Barak, B., Halevi, S.: A model and architecture for pseudo-random generation with applications to /dev/random. In: Proceedings of the 12th ACM Conference on Computer and Communication Security, pp. 203–212 (2005)
4. Barak, B., Shaltiel, R., Tromer, E.: True random number generators secure in a changing environment. In: Proceedings of the 5th Cryptographic Hardware and Embedded Systems, pp. 166–180 (2003)
5. Barak, B., Shaltiel, R., Wigderson, A.: Computational analogues of entropy. In: Arora, S., Jansen, K., Rolim, J., Sahai, A. (eds.) RANDOM 2003 and APPROX 2003. LNCS, vol. 2764, pp. 200–215. Springer, Heidelberg (2003)
6. Blum, M., Micali, S.: How to generate cryptographically strong sequences of pseudo-random bits. SIAM J. Comput. 13(4), 850–864 (1984)
7. Boneh, D., Shoup, V.: A graduate Course in Applied Cryptography. http://cs.nyu.edu/courses/fall12/CSCI-GA.3210-001/index.html
8. Boyen, X., Dodis, Y., Katz, J., Ostrovsky, R., Smith, A.: Secure remote authentication using biometric data. In: Cramer, R. (ed.) EUROCRYPT 2005. LNCS, vol. 3494, pp. 147–163. Springer, Heidelberg (2005)
9. Bromiley, P.A., Thacker, N.A., Bouhova-Thacker, E., Shannon Entropy, Rényi Entropy, and Information (2004)
10. Dachman-Soled, D., Gennaro, R., Krawczyk, H., Malkin, T.: Computational extractors and pseudorandomness. In: Cramer, R. (ed.) TCC 2012. LNCS, vol. 7194, pp. 383–403. Springer, Heidelberg (2012)
11. Dodis, Y., Ostrovsky, R., Reyzin, L., Smith, A.: Fuzzy extractors: how to generate strong keys from biometrics and other noisy data. SIAM J. Comput. 38(1), 97–139 (2008)
12. Dodis, Y., Ristenpart, T., Vadhan, S.P.: Randomness condensers for efficiently samplable, seed-dependent sources. In: 9th Theory of Cryptography Conference, pp. 618–635 (2012)
13. Dodis, Y., Yu, Y.: Overcoming weak expectations. In: Sahai, A. (ed.) TCC 2013. LNCS, vol. 7785, pp. 1–22. Springer, Heidelberg (2013)
14. Fuller, B., O'Neill, A., Reyzin, L.: A unified approach to deterministic encryption: new constructions and a connection to computational entropy. In: Cramer, R. (ed.) TCC 2012. LNCS, vol. 7194, pp. 582–599. Springer, Heidelberg (2012)
15. Fuller, B., Reyzin, L.: Computational entropy and information leakage. Technical report, IACR Cryptology e-Print Archive http://eprint.iacr.org/2012/466.pdf (2012)
16. Gennaro, R., Krawczyk, H., Rabin, T.: Secure hashed diffie-hellman over non-DDH groups. In: Cachin, C., Camenisch, J.L. (eds.) EUROCRYPT 2004. LNCS, vol. 3027, pp. 361–381. Springer, Heidelberg (2004)
17. Håstad, J., Impagliazzo, R., Levin, L.A., Luby, L.M.: A pseudorandom generator from any one-way function. SIAM J. Comput. 28(4), 1364–1396 (1999)
18. Hayashi, M.: Exponential decreasing rate of leaked information in universal random privacy amplification. IEEE Trans. Inf. Theory 57(6), 3989–4001 (2011)

19. Hayashi, M.: Tight exponential evaluation for universal composablity with privacy amplification and its applications. Accepted in IEEE Trans. Inf. Theory (arXiv:1010.1358) (2010)
20. Holenstein, T., Maurer, U.M., Sjödin, J.: Complete classification of bilinear hardcore functions. In: Franklin, M. (ed.) CRYPTO 2004. LNCS, vol. 3152, pp. 73–91. Springer, Heidelberg (2004)
21. Hsiao, C.-Y., Lu, C.-J., Reyzin, L.: Conditional computational entropy, or toward separating pseudoentropy from compressibility. In: Naor, M. (ed.) EUROCRYPT 2007. LNCS, vol. 4515, pp. 169–186. Springer, Heidelberg (2007)
22. Krawczyk, H.: Cryptographic extraction and key derivation: the HKDF scheme. In: Rabin, T. (ed.) CRYPTO 2010. LNCS, vol. 6223, pp. 631–648. Springer, Heidelberg (2010)
23. Pietrzak, K.: A leakage-resilient mode of operation. In: Joux, A. (ed.) EUROCRYPT 2009. LNCS, vol. 5479, pp. 462–482. Springer, Heidelberg (2009)
24. Rényi, A.: On measures of information and entropy. In: Proceedings of the 4th Berkeley Symposium on Mathematics, Statistics and Probability, pp. 547–561 (1960)
25. Yao Andrew, C.: Theory and applications of trapdoor functions. In: Proceedings of 23rd FOCS, pp. 80–91. IEEE (1982)

Modulus Computational Entropy

Maciej Skórski$^{(\boxtimes)}$

Cryptology and Data Security Group, University of Warsaw, Warsaw, Poland
maciej.skorski@gmail.com

Abstract. The so-called *leakage-chain rule* is a very important tool used in many security proofs. It gives an upper bound on the entropy loss of a random variable X in case the adversary who having already learned some random variables $Z_1, \ldots, Z_\ell$ correlated with X, obtains some further information $Z_{\ell+1}$ about X. Analogously to the information-theoretic case, one might expect that also for the *computational* variants of entropy the loss depends only on the actual leakage, i.e. on $Z_{\ell+1}$. Surprisingly, Krenn et al. have shown recently that for the most commonly used definitions of computational entropy this holds only if the computational quality of the entropy deteriorates exponentially in $|(Z_1, \ldots, Z_\ell)|$. This means that the current standard definitions of computational entropy do not allow to fully capture leakage that occurred "in the past", which severely limits the applicability of this notion.

As a remedy for this problem we propose a slightly stronger definition of the computational entropy, which we call the *modulus computational entropy*, and use it as a technical tool that allows us to prove a desired chain rule that depends only on the actual leakage and not on its history. Moreover, we show that the modulus computational entropy unifies other, sometimes seemingly unrelated, notions already studied in the literature in the context of information leakage and chain rules. Our results indicate that the modulus entropy is, up to now, the weakest restriction that guarantees that the chain rule for the computational entropy works. As an example of application we demonstrate a few interesting cases where our restricted definition is fulfilled and the chain rule holds.

1 Introduction

Entropy is the most fundamental concept in Information Theory. First introduced in this context by Shannon [Sha48], as a measure of the uncertainty associated with a probability distribution, it has been generalized in many ways. The commonly used generalization of Shannon Entropy is Rényi Entropy, defined for any arbitrary nonnegative order, which includes Shannon Entropy as a special case of order 1. Informally, a reasonable entropy measure indicates for a given distribution how much randomness it contains. According to this intuition, distributions uniform over large sets should have very high entropy, in opposite to

This work was partly supported by the WELCOME/2010-4/2 grant founded within the framework of the EU Innovative Economy Operational Programme.

C. Padró (Ed.): ICITS 2013, LNCS 8317, pp. 179–199, 2014.
DOI: 10.1007/978-3-319-04268-8_11, © Springer International Publishing Switzerland 2014

distributions which has small support or hit a small set with high probability, being easy to predict.

Indistinguishability and entropy. The notion of entropy has been generalized also for the purpose of Computational Complexity Theory and Cryptography, to take *computational* aspects into account. The reader might wish to refer to [Rey11] for a short survey. Historically computational entropy was first introduced in [Yao82] and, basing on a different concept, in [HILL99]. This last approach, based on the notion of *indistinguishability*, is the one we follow in this work. Let us try to give some intuitions here (the precisely definitions will be given in Sect. 2). To define computational entropy of X, one relaxes the requirement that X should have entropy itself. Instead, we assume that X is only close to a distribution Y which has suitable information-theoretic entropy. We have to specify two things: (a) the notion of entropy we use and (b) what does it mean "being close". To give a rigorous formulation of (b), one uses the concept of *distinguishing*, borrowed from convex analysis and topology. Function D separates (*distinguishes*) a set $\mathbb{X}$ from another set $\mathbb{Y}$ with *advantage* at least ϵ if $D(x) - D(y) \geqslant \epsilon$ for every $x \in \mathbb{X}$, $y \in \mathbb{Y}$. In turn, for a predefined class $\mathcal{D}$ of functions, two sets are said to be $(\mathcal{D}, \epsilon)$-indistinguishable, if there is no $D \in \mathcal{D}$ that can distinguish between these two sets with advantage greater than ϵ. The smaller ϵ and the wider class $\mathcal{D}$ we take, the stronger indistinguishability we obtain. Especially, indistinguishability applied to two probability distributions (as one-element sets) and all boolean functions (as distinguishers), where acting D on a distribution $\mathbf{P}_X$ is defined by $D(\mathbf{P}_X) = \mathbf{E}_{x \leftarrow X} D(x)$, yields the definition of the statistical distance. In applications involving computational complexity, one usually use circuits of bounded size as a class of distinguishers.

Leakage Lemma and Chain Rule. Leakage lemma is the term commonly used in referring to various generalizations of the observation which, saying less formally, states that min-entropy of a distribution X conditioned on another distribution Z distributed over $\{0,1\}^m$ decreases, with respect to min-entropy of X, by at most m (the number of bits in the string encoding Z). The name comes from security-related applications, where one considers entropy of a distribution conditioned on information that might have been revealed to the adversary. The larger difference between entropy of a distribution and entropy of the corresponding conditioned distribution, the larger leakage is; such an approach, based on computational entropy, was used first by Dziembowski and Pietrzak [DP08]. In turn, the term leakage chain rule is used to state the same principle for the case when we are given entropy of X conditioned on Z_1, and observing some further leakage Z_2 ask for the entropy of X conditioned on $Z_1 Z_2$. Such conditioning of an already conditioned distribution refers to the so called "leakage-after-leakage" scenario. The name "Leakage Chain Rule" comes from the fact that we think of Z_1 and Z_2 as information about X that "leaked" subsequently to the adversary.

For commonly used information-theoretic notions of conditional entropy, the chain rule is known to be true, i.e. the loss in entropy depends on $|Z_2|$ and not on Z_1. The problems appear in the case of computational generalizations of entropy. The computational leakage lemma [DP08, FR12], turned out not to give rise naturally to the leakage chain rule at least for important indistinguishability based definitions of conditional computational entropy and was addressed as an open problem [FOR12]. The computational leakage chain rule was proved only for specific scenarios, either by adding strong assumptions to definitions [FR12,CKLR11], or by changing definitions (see [Rey11] for the discussion of computational relaxed entropy based on Leakage Lemma [GW10]). Recently, a counterexample to the chain rule for computational min entropy has been found [KPW13]. It shows that the computational entropy of $X|Z_1 Z_2$ can decrease dramatically with respect to the entropy of $X|Z_1$, even if Z_2 is just a one bit.

Our contribution. Interested in establishing the (possibly) weakest condition to make the leakage chain rule work for the 'standard' computational entropy (i.e. defined using indistinguishability and the min-entropy), we define the modulus computational entropy and show that its definition is satisfied by technical assumptions which have been used by other authors to obtain a chain rule: the decomposable entropy introduced by Fuller and Reyzin [FR12] and the samplability assumption used by Chung et al. in [CKLR11]. Interestingly, it is implied by the "squared-indistinguishability" introduced in [DY13]. Furthermore, we investigate three cases that has not been considered yet: (a) when computational entropy is almost maximal, (b) the existence of an **NP** oracle over the domain of X to which distinguishers are given access[1], and (c) when the leakage is relatively short. In all these cases our definition is fulfilled and the chain rule works. Summing up, we reduce already known necessary conditions to the one simpler concept and show a few new non-trivial cases where the chain rule works.

Our techniques. We observe that to ensure the chain rule, one need to control *the conditional advantages of distinguishers*, i.e. advantages calculated conditionally on appropriate events. The same concept appears in [DY13]. This elementary technique leads to quite non-trivial results and we believe that its application can be of independent interest.

Outline of the work. Section 2 deals with some preliminary concepts, conventions and notations. In Sect. 3 we explain basic definitions and terminology related to the computational entropy, and discuss the positive and negative results related to the leakage chain rule problem. In Sect. 4 we introduce our main tool– the modulus entropy and show that the leakage chain rule holds for this notion. Section 5 contains a brief summary of the most important consequences of our results - estimating the cost of conversions to the modulus entropy from several technical assumptions. Section 6 provides their proofs.

2   Preliminaries

Throughout this work we assume that all random variables are defined on some finite probability space and they take values in $\{0,1\}^*$. If X is a random variable

---

[1] We stress that this is a non-trivial result, as the computational entropy X given Z is calculated by distinguishers on $\{0,1\}^{n+m}$, thus it might happen that even circuits of size 2^n are not able to break it.

then $\mathbf{P}_X$ will be its distribution. Writing $X \in S$ we mean that X takes its values in the set S. By $|S|$ we denote the cardinality of S. For two random variables X, Z by $X|Z = z$ we denote the distribution of X conditioned on $Z = z$ and (X, Z) means the concatenation of X and Z. For every n, by U_n we denote the uniform distribution over $\{0, 1\}^n$. By $(\det\{0, 1\}, s)$ and $(\det[0, 1], s)$ we mean the class of all deterministic circuits of size at most s, with output in the set $\{0, 1\}$ and $[0, 1]$ respectively. Similarly, we denote by $(\operatorname{rand}\{0, 1\}, s)$ the set of all randomized boolean circuits of size at most s. All logarithms are taken to the base 2. For $D : \mathcal{X} \to [0, 1]$ and $k \leq \log |\mathcal{X}|$ we denote by $\operatorname{Max}_D^k \subseteq \mathcal{X}$ a set of cardinality 2^k such that for every $x \in \operatorname{Max}_D^k$ and every $x' \notin \operatorname{Max}_D^k$ we have $D(x) \geqslant D(x')$. For a boolean function D, we write $|D| = \sum_{x \in \mathcal{X}} D(x)$.

2.1   Min Entropy

We start with recalling information-theoretic notions.

Definition 1 (Min Entropy). *A random variable X has at least k bits of min-entropy, denoted by $\mathbf{H}_\infty (X) \geqslant k$, if and only if $\max_x \mathbf{P}_X (x) \leqslant 2^{-k}$.*

The *conditional* min-entropy can be defined in two ways, both compatible with the above definition. The first one is given below.

Definition 2 (Worst-Case Conditional Min-Entropy). *Given a pair of random variables (X, Z) we say that X conditioned on Z has the min-entropy at least k and denote it by $\mathbf{H}_\infty(X|Z) \geqslant k$, if and only if for every z we have*

$$\max_x \mathbf{P}_{X|Z=z} (x) \leqslant 2^{-k}.$$

It is called the *worst-case* because it requires X to have high min-entropy when it is conditioned on the event "$Z = z$" for *every* z. The alternative definition requires this fact to hold *on average*:

Definition 3 (Average Conditional Min-Entropy [DORS08]). *Given a pair of random variables (X, Z) we say that X conditioned on Z has the average min-entropy at least k and denote $\widetilde{\mathbf{H}}_\infty (X|Z) \geqslant k$, if and only if*

$$\mathbf{E}_{z \leftarrow Z} \left[\max_x \mathbf{P}_{X|Z=z} (x) \right] \leqslant 2^{-k}.$$

Usually it is not so important which one of these definitions is used, as one can convert the average conditional min entropy into the worst-case variant.

Lemma 1 (See [DORS08], Lemma 2.2). *Suppose that $\widetilde{\mathbf{H}}_\infty (X|Z) \geqslant k$. Then holds $\mathbf{H}_\infty (X|Z = z) \geqslant k - \log \frac{1}{\delta}$ with probability at least $1 - \delta$ over $z \leftarrow Z$.*

2.2   Indistinguishability

Below we outline the concept of *indistinguishability*, being a key point in defining computational entropy.

Definition 4. *Let* X *and* Y *be subsets of some set* P. *Given* $\epsilon > 0$ *we say that a function* $F : P \to [0,1]$ *distinguishes between* X *and* Y *with advantage at least* ϵ *if for every* $x \in X$ *and every* $y \in Y$ *we have* $|F(x) - F(y)| \geqslant \epsilon$.

Definition 5. *Let* X *and* Y *be as in Definition 4. Given a class* $\mathcal{F}$ *of* $[0,1]$-*valued functions on* P, *we say that* X *and* Y *are* $(\mathcal{F}, \epsilon)$-*indistinguishable if there is no* $F \in \mathcal{F}$ *that can distinguish between* X *and* Y *with advantage greater than* ϵ.

In this paper we are mostly interested in the case when P is equal to the set of all probability distributions over some finite space Ω. In this case, every function $D : \Omega \to [0,1]$ gives rise to a distinguisher $F_D : P \to [0,1]$ defined as $F_D(\mu) = \mathbf{E}_{x \leftarrow \mu} D(x)$. Thus, we will overload the notation and say that D *distinguishes between* X *and* Y *with advantage at least* ϵ if the corresponding function F_D distinguishes between X and Y with advantage at least ϵ. We note that D can also be a *randomized* function, which receives an additional input R chosen independently at random. The expectation $\mathbf{E}D(\cdot)$ is then taken also over R.

3   Computational Entropy and Leakage - Previous Works

As mentioned before, computational entropy can be obtained by generalizing entropy notions in many ways. We follow the approach based on indistinguishability as it seems to be the most standard way and was originally used for studying leakage [DP08] as well as in further leakage-related works [CKLR11, FR12, GW10].

3.1   Defining Computational Entropy

Three-layer definition. There are three key points, essential for defining computational entropy via indistinguishability:

(a) specify, for every k, what it means that a distribution "has (non-computational) entropy at least k",
(b) model the adversary, in particular define his computational power, and determine his maximal acceptable success probability, and
(c) define the measure of the "computational distance" between a given distribution and the set of distributions with entropy at least k (in the sense of (a)).

In (a) one usually uses information-theoretic notion of entropy, most often the min-entropy[2]. For (b) one uses a pair $(\mathcal{D}, \epsilon)$ within the framework described

---

[2] We use only min-entropy in this work. See, however, [VZ12] for a similar definition based on Shanon Entropy.

in Sect. 2.2. Finally, a rigorous formulation of (c) can be given in two ways, traditionally called the "HILL" or the "Metric" version. In the HILL version, defining entropy of a random variable X, we require X to be indistinguishable from *one single* distribution with high entropy (in the sense of (a)), whereas in the definition of the Metric Entropy we require X to be indistinguishable from the set of *all* of high-entropy distributions, which is a bit *weaker* assumption. The formal definitions below are provided for the conditional versions of both notions. The unconditional versions, denoted $\mathbf{H}^{\mathrm{HILL},\mathcal{D},\epsilon}(X)$ and $\mathbf{H}^{\mathrm{Metric},\mathcal{D},\epsilon}(X)$, are special cases obtained by fixing in the definitions below Z to be constant.

Definition 6 (HILL Computational Conditional Entropy [HLR07]). *Let X, Z be random variables taking values in $\{0,1\}^n$ and $\{0,1\}^m$ respectively. Given $\epsilon > 0$ and a class of distinguishers $\mathcal{D}$, we say that X conditioned on Z has at least k bits of computational HILL entropy against $(\mathcal{D}, \epsilon)$ and denote by $\tilde{\mathbf{H}}^{\mathrm{HILL},\mathcal{D},\epsilon}(X|Z) \geqslant k$, if there exists a random variable $Y \in \{0,1\}^n$ satisfying $\tilde{\mathbf{H}}_\infty(Y|Z) \geqslant k$, such that (X,Z) is $(\mathcal{D}, \epsilon)$-indistinguishable from (Y,Z) .*

Definition 7 (Metric Computational Conditional Entropy [HLR07]). *With $\epsilon, \mathcal{D}, X$ and Z as in Definition 6, we say that X conditioned on Z has at least k bits of computational metric entropy against $(\mathcal{D}, \epsilon)$, denoting $\tilde{\mathbf{H}}^{\mathrm{Metric},\mathcal{D},\epsilon}(X|Z) \geqslant k$, if (X,Z) is $(\mathcal{D}, \epsilon)$-indistinguishable from the set of all distributions (Y,Z), satisfying $\tilde{\mathbf{H}}_\infty(Y|Z) \geqslant k$.*

Usually one formulates both definitions more explicitly without using the very general notion of indistinguishability (as in Definition 5)

> Definition 6: $\tilde{\mathbf{H}}^{\mathrm{HILL},\mathcal{D},\epsilon}(X|Z) \geqslant k$ if there exists a random variable $Y \in \{0,1\}^n$, $\tilde{\mathbf{H}}_\infty(Y|Z) \geqslant k$ satisfying $|\mathbf{E}D(X,Z) - \mathbf{E}D(Y,Z)| \leqslant \epsilon$ for all $D \in \mathcal{D}$.
>
> Definition 7: $\tilde{\mathbf{H}}^{\mathrm{Metric},\mathcal{D},\epsilon}(X|Z) \geqslant k$ if for every $D \in \mathcal{D}$ there exists a random variable $Y \in \{0,1\}^n$, $\tilde{\mathbf{H}}_\infty(Y|Z) \geqslant k$ and $|\mathbf{E}D(X,Z) - \mathbf{E}D(Y,Z)| \leqslant \epsilon$.

However, our, more general, definitional approach appears to be more useful for the applications presented in the sequel. The definitions of the HILL Computational *Worst*-Case Conditional Entropy $\mathbf{H}^{\mathrm{HILL},\mathcal{D},\epsilon}(X|Z)$ and the Metric Computational *Worst*-Case Conditional Entropy $\mathbf{H}^{\mathrm{Metric},\mathcal{D},\epsilon}(X|Z)$ are obtained by replacing $\tilde{\mathbf{H}}_\infty(Y|Z) \geqslant k$ in Definitions 6 and 7 (resp.) with $\mathbf{H}_\infty(Y|Z) \geqslant k$.

The equivalence between the HILL and Metric-type Entropy. It has been observed that the Metric Entropy is more convenient for proving leakage-related results and, in fact, appears in all such proofs more or less implicitly. Fortunately, there exists a conversion from the Metric Entropy (against real-valued circuits) to HILL Entropy [BSW03]. This result in its full generality can be stated as follows:

Theorem 1 (Generalization of [BSW03], Theorem 5.2). *Let $\mathcal{P}$ be the set of all probability measures over Ω. Suppose that we are given a class $\mathcal{D}$ of $[0,1]$-valued functions on Ω, with the following property: if $D \in \mathcal{D}$ then $D^c =^{\mathrm{def}}$*

$1 - D \in \mathcal{D}$. For $\delta > 0$, let $\mathcal{D}'$ be the class consisting of all convex combinations of length $\mathcal{O}\left(\frac{\log|\Omega|}{\delta^2}\right)$ over $\mathcal{D}$. Let $\mathcal{C} \subset \mathcal{P}$ be any arbitrary convex subset of probability measures and $X \in \mathcal{P}$ be a fixed distribution. Consider the following statements:

(a) X is $(\mathcal{D}, \epsilon + \delta)$ indistinguishable from some distribution $Y \in \mathcal{C}$
(b) X is $(\mathcal{D}', \epsilon)$ indistinguishable from the set of all distribution $Y \in \mathcal{C}$

Then (b) implies (a).

This more general statement follows by inspection of the original proof.

Remark 1. By choosing $\Omega = \{0,1\}^{n+m}$, a random variable $Z \in \{0,1\}^m$ and $\mathcal{C}$ to be the set of all distributions (Y, Z) satisfying $\mathbf{H}_\infty(Y|Z) \geqslant k$ or alternatively $\widetilde{\mathbf{H}}_\infty(Y|Z) \geqslant k$, we obtain the conversion from Metric Conditional Entropy to HILL Conditional Entropy, for both: the worst and average case variants.

3.2   Leakage Rules

We are now ready to state the leakage chain rule for conditional min-entropy and compare it with its known generalizations to computational case. Generally, we are interested in the following problem:

> Suppose we have a pair of random variables (X, Z_1) and we know the conditional entropy of X given Z_1. What is the lower bound on the entropy of X given (Z_1, Z_2), where Z_2 is some other (possibly correlated) random variable?

In the information-theoretic case we have the following result (cf. [DORS08], Lemma 2.2)

Lemma 2 (Leakage Chain Rule). Let X, Z_1, Z_2 be random variables over $\{0,1\}^n, \{0,1\}^{m_1}, \{0,1\}^{m_2}$ respectively. Then

$$\widetilde{\mathbf{H}}_\infty(X|Z_1, Z_2) \geqslant \widetilde{\mathbf{H}}_\infty(X|Z_1) - m_2 \tag{1}$$

In the computational framework, the first leakage-related result appeared in [DP08] and (formulated in a different way) in [RTTV08]. The parameters were improved next in [FR12].

Lemma 3 (Leakage Lemma [FR12]). Let X and Z be random variables over $\{0,1\}^n$ and $\{0,1\}^m$, resp. Then

$$\widetilde{\mathbf{H}}^{\text{Metric},(\det[0,1],s'),\epsilon'}(X|Z) \geqslant \mathbf{H}^{\text{Metric},(\det[0,1],s),\epsilon}(X) - m$$

where $s' = s + \mathcal{O}(1)$, $\epsilon' = 2^m \epsilon$ and $(\det[0,1], s)$ stands for the class of circuits (as defined in Sect. 2).

Let us observe, at least under assumption that there exists an exponentially secure pseudorandom generator, that both losses: in quantity (by m bits) and security measured as s/ϵ (by factor almost equal to 2^m) can appear simultaneously[3] - see Theorem 10 in Appendix A.

Leakage Chain Rule for Computational Entropy - negative and positive results. It is a natural question to ask if the Leakage Chain Rule (Lemma 2) can be "translated" into the computational version. In particular, one might be tempted to conjecture that for X, Z_1 and Z_2 as in Lemma 2 it holds that

$$\widetilde{\mathbf{H}}^{\text{Metric},[0,1],s',\epsilon'} (X|Z_1, Z_2) \geqslant^? \widetilde{\mathbf{H}}^{\text{Metric},[0,1],s,\epsilon} (X|Z_1) - m_2, \qquad (2)$$

with the security loss of factor 2^{m_2} or $\text{poly}(2^{m_2}, 1/\epsilon)$ for the above stated in terms of HILL entropy, where by the security loss we mean $\frac{s'}{\epsilon'}/\frac{s}{\epsilon}$ (reduces to ϵ/ϵ' if $s' \approx s$). Unfortunately, this conjecture is false in general [KPW13]. On the positive side, some progress towards proving it for restricted definitions of entropy has been recently made [FR12, CKLR11, Rey11, GW10]. In [FR12], the authors use an assumption called *decomposability*:

Definition 8 ([FR12]). *Let X, Z be as in Lemma 3. Given the parameter s, we say that the decomposable metric-entropy of X conditioned on Z is at least k and denote $\widetilde{\mathbf{H}}^{\text{Metric}-d,[0,1],s,\epsilon} (X|Z) \geqslant k$, if for every z*

$$\widetilde{\mathbf{H}}^{\text{Metric},[0,1],s,\epsilon(z)} (X|Z = z) \geqslant k(z)$$

where $\epsilon(z), k(z)$ are some numbers satisfying $\mathbf{E}\left[2^{-k(Z)}\right] = 2^{-k}$ and $\mathbf{E}\left[\epsilon(Z)\right] \leqslant \epsilon$.

Using this definition they are able to prove the following.

Theorem 2 ([FR12]). *Let X, Z_1, Z_2 be as in Lemma 2. Then for $s' \approx s$, and $\epsilon' = 2^{m_2}\epsilon$, we have*

$$\widetilde{\mathbf{H}}^{\text{Metric}-d,[0,1],s',\epsilon'} (X|Z_1, Z_2) \geqslant \widetilde{\mathbf{H}}^{\text{Metric}-d,[0,1],s,\epsilon} (X|Z_1) - |Z_2|$$

In the other approach [CKLR11], the authors use some *samplability* assumptions.

Theorem 3 ([CKLR11]). *Let X, Z_1, Z_2 be as above. Suppose that there exists a random variable Y' with the following properties: (a) $\mathbf{H}_\infty(Y'|Z_1) \geqslant k$, the pair $(Y', Z_1), (X, Z_1)$ is (s, ϵ) indistinguishable and (b) there exists a randomized circuit Γ of complexity s_Γ, which receives on its input $z \in \text{supp}(Z_1)$ and return samples of $Y'|Z_1 = z_1$. Then for $s' = \Omega(s \cdot 2^{-m_2}\delta - s_\Gamma), \epsilon' \approx \epsilon + \delta$ we have*

$$\mathbf{H}^{\text{Metric},[0,1],s',\epsilon'} (X|Z_1, Z_2) \geqslant \mathbf{H}^{\text{Metric},[0,1],s,\epsilon}(X|Z_1) - |Z_2| - \log(1/\delta).$$

Finally, there is yet another result related to the chain rule problem, due to [GW10]. The authors prove a version of 3 for using a *nonstandard definition* of Metric Conditional Min-Entropy, which they call the *relaxed computational*

---

[3] The question whether it can happen was raised in [FR12]

entropy. The difference is in Layer (a) of the definition: they require (X, Z), to be indistinguishable from all distribution (Y, Z') satisfying $\mathbf{H}_\infty (Y|Z') \geqslant k$, where– in comparison to Definition 6– Z' is *not necessarily* equal to Z. As observed in [Rey11], one can easily generalize their approach to prove an "efficient" computational version of 2 for this definition, with a loss of a factor at most poly $(2^{m_2}, \epsilon^{-1})$ in security. It seems however, that in the context of leakage Definitions 7 and 6 are more suitable, because Z can be what an adversary might have learned about X [CKLR11]; see also the conclusions in [KPW13]. Being interested in applications in leakage cryptography, we follow the standard definition of the computational entropy in this paper.

4   Modulus Entropy

Our definition is a bit different than Definition 8.

Definition 9 (Modulus Metric Entropy). *Let $X \in \{0,1\}^n$ and $Z \in \{0,1\}^m$ be random variables. Given $\epsilon > 0$ and a class of deterministic boolean functions $\mathcal{D}$, we say that X conditioned on Z has modulus entropy at least k against $(\mathcal{D}, \epsilon)$, and denote it by $\widetilde{\mathbf{H}}^{|\mathrm{Metric}|, \mathcal{D}, \epsilon} (X|Z) \geqslant k$, if for any $D \in \mathcal{D}$ there exists a random variable $Y \in \{0,1\}^n$, satisfying $\widetilde{\mathbf{H}}_\infty(Y|Z) \geqslant k$, such that*

$$\mathbf{E}_{z \leftarrow Z} \left| \mathbf{E}_{x \leftarrow (X|Z=z)} D(x, z) - \mathbf{E}_{x \leftarrow (Y|Z=z)} D(x, z) \right| \leqslant \epsilon \tag{3}$$

The definition above, formulated for the average-case conditional entropy, can be stated also for the worst-case version, by replacing $\widetilde{\mathbf{H}}_\infty$ with $\mathbf{H}_\infty$. Using Lemma 1 we obtain immediately a conversion (with some loss) between them:

Lemma 4. *Suppose that $\widetilde{\mathbf{H}}^{|\mathrm{Metric}|, \mathcal{D}, \epsilon} (X|Z) \geqslant k$. Then $\mathbf{H}^{|\mathrm{Metric}|, \mathcal{D}, \epsilon+\delta} (X|Z) \geqslant k - \log(1/\delta)$.*

Intuitions and motivations behind modulus entropy. The only difference between Definition 7 and Definition 9 is that they differ in order of the expectation and absolute value signs. Thus, by the triangle inequality, the Modulus Entropy is smaller than Metric Entropy. However, they are not necessarily equal in general. Indeed, for D distinguishing between (X, Z) and (Y, Z) with the advantage no greater than ϵ, contributions to this advantage from particular values of z, given by the expressions $\epsilon_D(z) = \mathbf{E}_{x \leftarrow X|Z=z} D(x, z) - \mathbf{E}_{x \leftarrow Y|Z=z} D(x, z)$ can differ in signs. For a few values z we can "flip" the output of $D(\cdot, z)$ as to ensure that all their contributions are of the same sign; this is however not possible if Z is to long, unless we lose much in efficiency. Thus $|\mathbf{E}_{z \leftarrow Z} \epsilon_D(z)| \leqslant \epsilon$ does not imply $\mathbf{E}_{z \leftarrow Z} |\epsilon_D(z)| \leqslant \epsilon$, which is required by inequality (3). In comparison to Definition 8, our approach is far more general as allow $\epsilon(z)$ and $k(z)$ to be dependent on a chosen D.

We stress that condition 3 is not unnatural. Its purpose is to give much more control over the particular contributions to the advantage, corresponding to the outcomes of Z. For instance, Dodis et al. in [DY13] control the average square of the contributions to the advantage (by the inequality $\mathbf{E}_{z \leftarrow Z} |\epsilon_D(z)|^2 \leqslant \epsilon$), defining "squared indistinguishability".

4.1   Leakage Chain Rule for Modulus Entropy

We now show how modulus entropy allows us to prove a leakage chain rule. We start with the reformulation of the leakage lemma proved in [FR12].

Lemma 5 (Corollary from [FR12], Proof of Lemma 3.5). *Let D be a boolean function, (X, Z) as in Lemma 3. Suppose $|\mathbf{E}_{x \leftarrow X} D(x) - \mathbf{E}_{x \leftarrow Y} D(x)| \leqslant \epsilon$, where $\mathbf{H}_\infty(Y) \geqslant k$. Then for any $z \in \mathrm{supp}(Z)$ there exist a distribution Y'_z such that $\mathbf{H}_\infty(Y'_z) \geqslant k - \log(1/\mathbf{P}_Z(z))$ and $|\mathbf{E}_{x \leftarrow X|Z=z} D(x) - \mathbf{E}_{x \leftarrow Y'_z} D(x)| \leqslant \epsilon/\mathbf{P}(Z = z)$.*

Now we are in position to prove the following (tight) chain rule.

Theorem 4. *Let X, Z_1, Z_2 be as in Lemma 2 and $\mathcal{D}$ be a class of boolean functions. Suppose that $\widetilde{\mathbf{H}}^{|\mathrm{Metric}|, \mathcal{D}, \epsilon}(X | Z_1) \geqslant k$. Then $\widetilde{\mathbf{H}}^{|\mathrm{Metric}|, \mathcal{D}, 2^{m_2}\epsilon}(X | Z_1, Z_2) \geqslant k - m_2$.*

Proof. Fix a distinguisher $D = D(x, z_1, z_2)$. We will construct a distribution (Y, Z_1, Z_2) such that $\widetilde{\mathbf{H}}_\infty(Y | Z_1, Z_2) \geqslant k - m_2$ and D cannot distinguish (X, Z_1, Z_2) from (Y, Z_1, Z_2) with advantage better than $2^{m_2}\epsilon$. For any z_2, let (Y^{z_2}, Z_1) be a distribution corresponding to $D(\cdot, z_2)$ in the sense of Definition 9 (we write Y^{z_2} as this distribution depends also on z_2). More precisely, (Y^{z_2}, Z_1) is such that

$$\mathbf{E}_{z_1 \leftarrow Z_1} \underbrace{\left| \mathbf{E}_{x \leftarrow (X|Z_1=z_1)} D(x, z_1, z_2) - \mathbf{E}_{x \leftarrow (Y^{z_2}|Z_1=z_1)} D(x, z_1, z_2) \right|}_{\epsilon_D(z_1, z_2):=} \leqslant \epsilon \quad (4)$$

holds (cf. (3) in Definition 9). For every pair (z_1, z_2) let $\epsilon_D(z_1, z_2)$ denote the value within the first expected value sign, as indicated on (4). Now, Lemma 5 implies that for any z_1, z_2 there exists a distribution Y'_{z_1, z_2} such that

$$\left| \mathbf{E} D(X | Z_1 = z_1, Z_2 = z_2, z_1, z_2) - \mathbf{E} D(Y'_{z_1, z_2}, z_1, z_2) \right| \leqslant \frac{\epsilon_D(z_1, z_2)}{\mathbf{P}_{Z_2|Z_1=z_1}(z_2)} \quad (5)$$

and its min-entropy $\mathbf{H}_\infty(Y'_{z_1, z_2})$ is at least $k(z_1, z_2)$, where

$$k(z_1, z_2) \geqslant \mathbf{H}_\infty(Y^{z_2} | Z_1 = z_1) - \log(1/\mathbf{P}_{Z_2|Z_1=z_1}(z_2)) \quad (6)$$

Define (Y, Z_1, Z_2) by $(Y | Z_1 = z_1, Z_2 = z_2) \stackrel{d}{=} Y'_{z_1, z_2}$. Now we have

$$\overbrace{\mathbf{E}_{(z_1, z_2) \leftarrow (Z_1, Z_2)} \left| \mathbf{E}_{x \leftarrow X|Z_1=z_1, Z_2=z_2} D(x, z_1, z_2) - \mathbf{E}_{x \leftarrow Y'_{z_1, z_2}} D(x, z_1, z_2) \right|}^{\leqslant \frac{\epsilon_D(z_1, z_2)}{\mathbf{P}(Z_2=z_2|Z_1=z_1)} \text{ (by (5))}}$$

$$\leqslant \sum_{z_1, z_2} \mathbf{P}((Z_1, Z_2) = (z_1, z_2)) \cdot \frac{\epsilon_D(z_1, z_2)}{\mathbf{P}(Z_2 = z_2|Z_1 = z_1)}$$

$$= \sum_{z_1, z_2} \mathbf{P}(Z_1 = z_1) \epsilon_D(z_1, z_2) = \sum_{z_2} \mathbf{E}_{z_1 \leftarrow Z_1} \epsilon_D(z_1, z_2) \leqslant \sum_{z_2} \epsilon = 2^{m_2}\epsilon$$

where the last inequality follows from (4). It remains to prove that $\tilde{\mathbf{H}}_\infty (Y \,|Z_1, Z_2) \geqslant k - m_2$. We have:

$$\mathbf{E}_{(z_1,z_2)\leftarrow(Z_1,Z_2)}2^{-k(z_1,z_2)} \leqslant \mathbf{E}_{(z_1,z_2)\leftarrow(Z_1,Z_2)}\left[\frac{\max\limits_{x}\mathbf{P}\left[Y^{z_2} = x\big|\, Z_1 = z_1\right]}{\mathbf{P}_{Z_2|Z_1=z_1}(z_2)}\right]$$

$$= \sum_{z_1,z_2} \max_{x}\mathbf{P}\left[Y^{z_2} = x\big|\, Z_1 = z_1\right] \cdot \mathbf{P}_{Z_1}(z_1)$$

$$= \sum_{z_2}\mathbf{E}_{z_1\leftarrow Z_1}\left[\max_{x}\mathbf{P}\left[Y^{z_2} = x\big|\, Z_1 = z_1\right]\right] \leqslant 2^{m_2}\cdot 2^{-k}$$

where the first step follows from (6) and the last one from $\tilde{\mathbf{H}}_\infty \left(Y^{z_2}\big|\, Z_1\right) \geqslant k$.

Remark 2. Note that the entropy obtained after the leakage is again the Modulus Entropy. Thus, one can apply this theorem several times. The samplability restriction in Theorem 3 does not have this feature.

Chain Rule for entropy against different circuits classes. Theorem 4 deals only with entropy against boolean deterministic distinguishers $\mathcal{D}$. It is natural to ask if one could replace this class with a more general one, in particular, would the theorem still hold if, in its statement, $\mathcal{D}$ was equal to the class of randomized or real-valued distinguishers. We answer this question affirmatively in Lemma 6 below. To make its statement as strong as possible, in the assumption we use the Modulus Entropy against boolean deterministic circuits as the weakest option and the HILL Entropy as the strongest notion in the assertion.[4]

Lemma 6. *Let X, Z be as in Theorem 3. Suppose that $\tilde{\mathbf{H}}^{|\mathrm{Metric}|,s,\epsilon}(X|Z) \geqslant k$. Then $\mathbf{H}^{\mathrm{HILL},s',\epsilon'}(X|Z) \geqslant k'$, where $\epsilon' = \epsilon + 2\delta$, $s' = s\cdot\mathcal{O}\left(\frac{\delta^2}{n+m}\right)$, $k' = k - \log\frac{1}{\delta}$.*

Proof. If $\tilde{\mathbf{H}}^{|\mathrm{Metric}|,s,\epsilon}(X|Z) \geqslant k$ then $\tilde{\mathbf{H}}^{\mathrm{Metric},\det\{0,1\},s,\epsilon}(X|Z) \geqslant k$, as we pointed out in the discussion after Lemma 4. Lemma 4 yields $\mathbf{H}^{\mathrm{Metric},\det\{0,1\},s,\epsilon+\delta}(X|Z) \geqslant k - \log\frac{1}{\delta}$. Since for the Metric Worst-Case Entropy it makes no significant difference whether we use real-valued or boolean distinguishers (see Theorem 11 in Appendix B), we obtain $\tilde{\mathbf{H}}^{\mathrm{Metric},s',[0,1],\epsilon+\delta}(X|Z) \geqslant k - \log\frac{1}{\delta}$ where $s' = s + \mathcal{O}(1)$. The claim follows now from Theorem 1.

5 Passing to Modulus Entropy

While the modulus entropy, as shown in Theorem 4, solves the leakage chain rule problem, it keeps being rather a technical assumption. We will give some concrete examples where its definition is fulfilled, and thus admits the chain

---

[4] Recall that for the HILL Entropy all kinds of circuits: deterministic boolean, deterministic real valued, randomized boolean are equivalent [FR12] thus we can abbreviate the notation writing just $\mathbf{H}^{\mathrm{HILL},s',\epsilon'}(X|Z)$.

Table 1. Conversions to the modulus entropy

Additional assumptions on $\widehat{\mathbf{H}}^{\mathrm{Metric},\{0,1\},s,\epsilon}(X\|Z) \geqslant k$	Our conversion: $\widetilde{\mathbf{H}}^{\|\mathrm{Metric}\|,s',\epsilon'}(X\|Z) \geqslant k'$			
	k'	ϵ'	s'	
(a) Decomposable entropy [FR12]	k	ϵ	s	Theorem 5
(b) Samplability of $Y\|Z=z$ given z, where $(Y,Z) \sim^{\epsilon,s} (X,Z)$ [CKLR11]	$k - \mathcal{O}\left(\log\frac{1}{\epsilon}\right)$	$\mathcal{O}(\epsilon)$	$\mathcal{O}\left(s/\frac{1}{\epsilon^2}\right)$	Theorem 7
(c) Entropy against poly(n)-circuits, given an access to an **NP** oracle over $\{0,1\}^n$	$k - \mathcal{O}\left(\log\frac{1}{\epsilon}\right)$	$\mathcal{O}(\sqrt{\epsilon})$	$\mathcal{O}\left(s/\mathrm{poly}\left(n,\frac{1}{\epsilon}\right)\right)$	Theorem 8 (point b)
(d) Entropy very high, i.e. $k > n - \mathcal{O}\left(\log\frac{1}{\epsilon}\right)$	$k - \mathcal{O}\left(\log\frac{1}{\epsilon}\right)$	$\mathcal{O}(\sqrt{\epsilon})$	$\mathcal{O}\left(s/\frac{m+n}{\epsilon^3}\log\frac{1}{\epsilon}\right)$	Theorem 8 (point a)
(e) None	k	$2^t\epsilon$	$s - \mathcal{O}\left(2^{m-t}m\right)$	Theorem 6
(f) X is (ϵ,s) squared-indistinguishable from Y given Z, and $\widetilde{\mathbf{H}}_\infty(Y\|Z) \geqslant k$	k	$\sqrt{\epsilon}$	s	Theorem 9

rule. In comparison to the assertion of Theorem 4, they rely on some other assumptions added to the Metric Entropy of $X\|Z$. Conversion to the modulus entropy, with estimated loss in parameters, is summarized in Table 1.

As shown, some of these assumptions were already studied in the leakage literature. The proofs of conversions will be given in the next section.

5.1   Benefits of Using Modulus Entropy

To summarize, let us mention the three key features of the modulus entropy:

(a) it implies the metric entropy which is widely used in the leakage-resilient cryptography,
(b) it allows to apply the tight chain rule multiple times, and
(c) it can be obtained from the known assumptions that guarantee the chain rule (decomposability, samplability) and from other important or at least non-trivial cases (squared-indistinguishability, high pseudo-entropy, NP-oracle).

Modulus Entropy vs Samplability and Decomposability. Comparing the conversion results in the table with Theorems 2 and 3, we see that Modulus Entropy is a weaker restriction and still guarantees the chain rule with at least comparable quality. Starting from decomposability or samplability, converting to the Modulus Entropy first and applying the chain rule next (and possibly translating into the HILL entropy) yields the same loss as the direct use of that assumptions.

6   Proofs of Conversion Results

Throughout all the proofs in this section, X, Z are random variables over $\{0,1\}^n$ and $\{0,1\}^m$ respectively. The proofs are based on the following technical lemma.

Lemma 7. *Let X, Z be random variables over $\{0,1\}^n, \{0,1\}^m$. Suppose that D is such that for all distributions (Y, Z) with $\mathbf{H}_\infty(Y|Z) \geqslant k$ the following holds:*

$$\mathbf{E}_{z \leftarrow Z} \left| \mathbf{E}_{x \leftarrow X|Z=z} D(x, z) - \mathbf{E}_{x \leftarrow Y|Z=z} D(x, z) \right| \geqslant \epsilon. \tag{7}$$

Then either for $D' = D$ or for $D' = D^c$ we have that for all distributions (Y, Z) with $\mathbf{H}_\infty(Y|Z) \geqslant k$ the following is true:

$$\mathbf{P}_{(x,z) \leftarrow (X,Z)} \left[D'(x, z) - \mathbf{E}_{x \leftarrow Y|Z=z} D'(x, z) \geqslant \epsilon/4 \right] \geqslant \epsilon^2/16.$$

Proof. Consider the distribution (Y^+, Z) which minimizes the left-hand side of (7). Define $\epsilon(z) := \left| \mathbf{E}_{x \leftarrow X|Z=z} D(x, z) - \mathbf{E}_{x \leftarrow Y^+|Z=z} D(x, z) \right|$. Observe that

$$\min_{(Y,Z): \mathbf{H}_\infty(Y|Z) \geqslant k} \mathbf{E}_{z \leftarrow Z} \left| \mathbf{E}_{x \leftarrow X|Z=z} D(x, z) - \mathbf{E}_{x \leftarrow Y|Z=z} D(x, z) \right| =$$

$$= \mathbf{E}_{z \leftarrow Z} \left[\min_{Y_z: \mathbf{H}_\infty(Y_z) \geqslant k} \left| \mathbf{E}_{x \leftarrow X|Z=z} D(x, z) - \mathbf{E}_{x \leftarrow Y_z} D(x, z) \right| \right].$$

Therefore, for every distribution Y_z with min-entropy $\mathbf{H}_\infty(Y_z) \geqslant k$ we have

$$\left| \mathbf{E}_{x \leftarrow X|Z=z} D(x, z) - \mathbf{E}_{x \leftarrow Y|Z=z} D(x, z) \right| \geqslant \epsilon(z)$$

Note that if $\epsilon(z) > 0$ then either (a) $\mathbf{E}_{x \leftarrow X|Z=z} D(x, z) - \mathbf{E}_{x \leftarrow Y|Z=z} D(x, z) \geqslant \epsilon(z)$ or (b) $\mathbf{E}_{x \leftarrow X|Z=z} D(x, z) - \mathbf{E}_{x \leftarrow Y|Z=z} D(x, z) \leqslant -\epsilon(z)$ holds for all Y_z with $\mathbf{H}_\infty(Y_z) \geqslant k$. This follows from the convexity of the set of distributions $\mathbf{H}_\infty(Y_z) \geqslant k$, which in turn implies that all values of $\mathbf{E}_{x \leftarrow X|z=z} D(x, z) - \mathbf{E}_{x \leftarrow Y_z} D(x, z)$, over the choice of Y_z, form a convex set. Therefore

$$\mathbf{E}_{x \leftarrow X|z=z} D'(x, z) - \mathbf{E}_{x \leftarrow Y_z} D'(x, z) \geqslant \epsilon(z)$$

holds for all Y_z with $\mathbf{H}_\infty(Y_z) \geqslant k$, where D' is defined, depending on z, by

$$D'(x, z) := \begin{cases} D(x, z) & \text{in case (a)} \\ D^c(x, z) & \text{in case (b)} \\ 0 & \text{if } \epsilon(z) = 0. \end{cases} \tag{8}$$

Since $\epsilon(z) \geqslant \frac{\epsilon}{2}$ holds[5] with probability at least $\frac{\epsilon}{2}$ over $z \leftarrow Z$, we get

$$\mathbf{E}_{x \leftarrow X|Z=z} D'(x, z) - \max_{Y_z: \mathbf{H}_\infty(Y_z) \geqslant k} \mathbf{E}_{x \leftarrow Y|Z=z} D'(x, z) \geqslant \epsilon/2$$

---

[5] Throughout the proofs, we will make use of the simple Markov-style principle: let X be a non-negative random variable bounded by M. Then $X > \frac{1}{2M} \mathbf{E} X$ with probability at least $\frac{1}{2} \mathbf{E} X$.

with probability at least $\frac{\epsilon}{2}$ over $z \leftarrow Z$. For every such z we obtain

$$\mathbf{P}_{x \leftarrow X|Z=z}\left[D'(x,z) - \max_{Y_z : \mathbf{H}_\infty(Y_z) \geqslant k} \mathbf{E}_{x \leftarrow Y|Z=z}D'(x,z) \geqslant \frac{\epsilon}{4}\right] \geqslant \frac{\epsilon}{4}$$

Taking expectation over $z \leftarrow Z$ we conclude that

$$\mathbf{P}_{(x,z) \leftarrow (X,Z)}\left[D'(x,z) - \max_{Y_z : \mathbf{H}_\infty(Y_z) \geqslant k} \mathbf{E}D'(Y_z,z) \geqslant \frac{\epsilon}{4}\right] \geqslant \frac{\epsilon^2}{8}.$$

Therefore, either for $D' = D$ or $D' = D^c$ the probability on the left-hand side of the above inequality needs to be at least $\frac{1}{2} \cdot \frac{\epsilon^2}{8} = \frac{\epsilon^2}{16}$, which proves the claim.

6.1 Decomposable Entropy

We start by noticing that Definition 8 is stronger than our Definition 9.

Theorem 5. *Suppose* $\widetilde{\mathbf{H}}^{\mathrm{Metric}-d,s,\epsilon}(X|Z) \geqslant k$. *Then* $\widetilde{\mathbf{H}}^{|\mathrm{Metric}|,s,\epsilon}(X|Z) \geqslant k$.

Proof. Fix a distinguisher $D = D(x,z)$. According to Definition 8, for every z we have a distribution Y_z such that $\mathbf{H}_\infty(Y_z) \geqslant k(z)$ and $|\mathbf{E}D(X|Z=z) - \mathbf{E}D(Y_z)| \leqslant \epsilon(z)$. Consider a distribution (Y,Z) defined by $(Y|Z=z) \stackrel{d}{=} Y_z$. Since $\mathbf{E}_{z \leftarrow Z}\epsilon(z) \leqslant \epsilon$, we obtain inequality (3). In turn, the assumptions on $k(z)$ implies $\widetilde{\mathbf{H}}_\infty(Y|Z) \geqslant k$.

The following theorem converts Metric Entropy into Modulus Entropy (cf. case (e) in Table 1). Its principal significance is that the equivalence between both definitions is established, provided that Z is sufficiently short (grows at most logarithmically in the security parameters).

Theorem 6. *Suppose that* $\mathbf{H}^{\mathrm{Metric},\{0,1\},s,\epsilon}(X|Z) \geqslant k$. *Then* $\mathbf{H}^{|\mathrm{Metric}|,s',\epsilon'}(X|Z) \geqslant k$, *where* $\epsilon' = 2^t\epsilon$ *and* $s' = s - \mathcal{O}(2^{m-t}m)$.

Proof. For the sake of contradiction suppose that for some D of complexity s' and for every (Y,Z) such that $\mathbf{H}_\infty(Y|Z) \geqslant k$ we have that

$$\mathbf{E}_{z \leftarrow Z}\left|\mathbf{E}_{x \leftarrow X|Z=z}D(x,z) - \mathbf{E}_{x \leftarrow Y|Z=z}D(x,z)\right| \geqslant \epsilon'.$$

Applying the same reasoning as at the beginning of the proof of Lemma 7, we obtain that there exist a distinguisher D' (cf. (8)) such that for every distribution Y_z with $\mathbf{H}_\infty(Y_z) \geqslant k$ it holds that

$$\mathbf{E}_{x \leftarrow X|z=z}D'(x,z) - \mathbf{E}_{x \leftarrow Y_z}D'(x,z) \geqslant \epsilon'(z), \tag{9}$$

where $\mathbf{E}_{z \leftarrow Z}\epsilon'(z) \geqslant \epsilon'$. Thus, for every (Y,Z) such that $\mathbf{H}_\infty(Y|Z) \geqslant k$ we have

$$\mathbf{E}_{(x,z) \leftarrow (X,Z)}D'(x,z) - \mathbf{E}_{(x,z) \leftarrow (Y,Z)}D'(x,z) \geqslant \mathbf{E}_{z \leftarrow Z}\epsilon'(z) \geqslant \epsilon'.$$

Recall that in the proof of Lemma 7, the value $D'(x,z)$ is defined as equal to $D(x,z)$ or $D^c(x,z)$ or 0, depending on z. Instead, we can follow that construction with respect to only 2^{m-t} "heaviest" values z maximizing $\mathbf{P}(Z=z)\epsilon'(z)$ and setting $D' = 0$ for other z. The obtained circuit is of size at most $s' + \mathcal{O}(2^{m-t}m) = s$ and distinguishes with the advantage at least $2^{-t}\epsilon' = \epsilon$.

6.2 The Samplability Assumption

In the next theorem we deal with the samplability assumption used in [CKLR11].

Theorem 7. *Suppose that (X, Z) is (s, ϵ)-indistinguishable from a distribution (Y', Z), with the following properties (a) $\mathbf{H}_\infty(Y'|Z) \geqslant k$ and (b) there exists a randomized circuit Γ receiving on its input $z \in \mathrm{supp}(Z)$ and returning samples from the distribution $Y'|Z = z$. Then*

$$\mathbf{H}^{|\mathrm{Metric}|, s \cdot \frac{\epsilon^2}{64} - \mathrm{size}(\Gamma), 8\sqrt{\epsilon}}(X|Z) \geqslant k - 2\log(1/\epsilon) - 7.$$

Proof. Suppose that $\mathbf{H}^{|\mathrm{Metric}|, s', \epsilon'}(X|Z) < k'$, where $k' = k - 2\log(1/\epsilon) - 7$ and $\epsilon' = \epsilon^2/64$ and $s' = \epsilon^2 s/64 - \mathrm{size}(\Gamma)$. Thus, for some D of size s' and every (Y, Z) with $\mathbf{H}_\infty(Y|Z) \geqslant k'$ we have

$$\mathbf{E}_{z \leftarrow Z} \left| \mathbf{E}_{x \leftarrow X|Z=z} D(x, z) - \mathbf{E}_{x \leftarrow Y|Z=z} D(x, z) \right| \geqslant \epsilon'. \qquad (10)$$

Let D' be a distinguisher obtained from Lemma 7. Consider the following D'': on input (x, z), which comes either from (X, Z) or (Y', Z) do the following:

- for $i = 1$ to $\ell = \lceil \frac{64}{\epsilon^2} \rceil - 1$ sample $y_i \leftarrow Y'|Z = z$ using the circuit Γ,
- if $D'(x, z) > \max_{i=1,\dots,l} D'(y_i, z)$ — output 1, otherwise output 0.

Clearly D'' has complexity at most $(\ell + 1) \cdot (s' + \mathrm{size}(\Gamma)) = s$. We will show that it gives sufficient distinguishing advantage. We start with the following easy observation, used implicitly in [CKLR11] (the proof of Lemma 16).

Lemma 8. *For D be a $[0, 1]$-valued function. If Y^+ is distributed uniformly over Max_D^k, then for any Y with $\mathbf{H}_\infty(Y) \geqslant k + \log \frac{1}{\delta}$ we have*

$$\mathbf{P}_{x \leftarrow Y}[D(x) - \mathbf{E}_{x \leftarrow Y^+} D(x) > 0] < \delta.$$

The proof that D'' is indeed a good distinguisher consists of two steps

Claim. On input $(x, z) \leftarrow (X, Z)$ the circuit D'' outputs 1 w.p. at least $\epsilon'^2/32$.

Proof. Consider a distribution (Y^+, Z) such that for every z the distribution $Y^+|Z = z$ is uniform over $\mathrm{Max}_{D'(\cdot, z)}^k$. Since y_i are independent and distributed according to $Y'|Z = z$, it follows from Lemma 8 that $\mathbf{E}_{x \leftarrow Y^+|Z=z} D'(x) \geqslant \max_i D'(y_i, z)$ holds with probability at least $\left(1 - 2^{k'-k}\right)^\ell \geqslant 1 - \ell \cdot 2^{k'-k} \geqslant \frac{1}{2}$. Now, Lemma 7 yields $D'(x, z) > \mathbf{E}_{x \leftarrow Y^+|Z=z} D'(x)$ with probability at least $\frac{\epsilon'^2}{16}$ over (x, z). Since sampling y_i is independent from (X, Z), the claim follows.

Claim. On input $(y, z) \leftarrow (Y', Z)$ the circuit D'' outputs 1 w.p. at most $\epsilon'^2/64$.

Proof. Note that y and $y_1, \dots, y_\ell$ are all independent copies of the distributions $Y'|Z = z$. Therefore probability that $y > \max_{i=1,\dots,l} y_i$ is at most $\frac{1}{\ell+1} \leqslant \frac{\epsilon'^2}{64}$.

From the last two claims we get $\mathbf{P}(D''(X, Z) = 1) - \mathbf{P}(D''(Y', Z) = 1) \geqslant \epsilon'^2/64$, which completes the proof of Theorem 7.

6.3   Approximate Counting

It turns out that using a technique called the *approximate counting*, one can show a conversion from metric to modulus entropy. However, we need some additional assumptions to achieve both: high accuracy and efficiency in counting:

Theorem 8. *Suppose that one of the following is true:*

(a) $\mathbf{H}^{\text{Metric,rand}\{0,1\},s,\epsilon}(X|Z) \geqslant k$ *against circuits of size s,*
(b) $\mathbf{H}^{\text{Metric},\{0,1\},s,\epsilon}(X|Z) \geqslant k$ *against circuits of size $s = \text{poly}(n)$, with an access to an* **NP***-oracle.*

Then we have $\mathbf{H}^{|\text{Metric}|,s',\epsilon'}(X|Z) \geqslant k'$, *where* $\epsilon' = 8\sqrt{\epsilon}$, $k' = k - \log \frac{1}{\epsilon}$ *and* s' *given by* $s' = \mathcal{O}\left(s \cdot \frac{2^{k-n-2}\cdot\epsilon}{\log(1/\epsilon)}\right)$ *in case (a) or* $s' = \text{poly}(n,\epsilon)$ *in case (b).*

Note that to make the conversion in (a) efficient, we need the assumption that k is large as it is easy to see that if k is much smaller than n then, in the formula that gives the bound on s', the 2^{k-n-2} factor starts to dominate over ϵ.

Proof (Proof of Theorem 8). Suppose that $\mathbf{H}^{|\text{Metric}|,s',\epsilon'}(X|Z) < k'$. Then Lemma 7 implies that for all $Y \in \{0,1\}^n$ with $\mathbf{H}_\infty(Y|Z) \geqslant k'$ and some distinguisher D' of complexity $s'+1$ we have

$$\mathbf{P}_{(x,z)\leftarrow(X,Z)}\left[D'(x,z) - \mathbf{E}D'(Y|Z=z,z) \geqslant \epsilon'/4\right] \geqslant \epsilon'^2/16. \tag{11}$$

Since

$$\max_{Y_z:\mathbf{H}_\infty(Y_z)\geqslant k'} \mathbf{E}(Y_z,z) = \min\left(1, 2^{-k'}|D'(\cdot,z)|\right) \tag{12}$$

hence, combining this with (11), we obtain

$$\mathbf{P}_{(x,z)\leftarrow(X,Z)}\left[D'(x,z) - 2^{-k'}|D'(\cdot,z)| \geqslant \epsilon'/4\right] \geqslant \epsilon'^2/16. \tag{13}$$

We now show that there exists a randomized function h such that for every z

$$\mathbf{P}\left(\left|h(z) - 2^{-k'}|D'(\cdot,z)|\right| \leqslant \epsilon'/8\right) \geqslant 1 - \epsilon'^2/64, \tag{14}$$

and $h(z)$ is samplable for all z's satisfying $|D'(\cdot,z)| < 2^{k'}$. More precisely: there exists a randomized circuit of size $\mathcal{O}\left(s' \cdot \frac{2^{n-k}}{\epsilon^2}\log\frac{1}{\epsilon}\right) = s$, which computes $h(z)$ correctly for every such z. This is a corollary from the following claim.

Claim. Let D be a boolean circuit such that $|D| \leqslant 2^k$. Then for $\delta', \delta'' \in \left(0, \frac{1}{2}\right)$, $\ell > 4 \cdot 2^{n-k}\frac{1}{\delta'^2}\log\frac{1}{\delta''}$ and $(U_i)_{i=1,\ldots,\ell}$ being independent and uniform over $\{0,1\}^n$, the following inequality holds:

$$\mathbf{P}\left[\left|\ell^{-1}\sum_{i=1}^{\ell} D(U_i) - 2^{-n}|D|\right| \geqslant 2^{k-n}\delta'\right] \leqslant 2\delta''.$$

Proof. Define $g = \frac{1}{\ell} \sum_{i=1}^{\ell} D(U_i)$. The Chernoff Inequality[6] yields

$$\mathbf{P}\left[|g - \mathbf{E}D(U)| \geqslant \delta\right] \leqslant 2 \max\left(e^{-\frac{\delta^2 \ell^2}{4\sigma^2}}, e^{-\frac{\ell\delta}{2}}\right),$$

where $\sigma^2 = \mathrm{Var}\left(\sum_{i=1}^{\ell} D(U_i)\right)$. Since $\mathrm{Var}(D(U_i)) = 2^{k-n}(1 - 2^{k-n})$ we have $\sigma^2 = \ell \cdot 2^{k-n}(1 - 2^{k-n})$. By setting $2^{n-k}\delta = \delta'$ we get $\frac{\delta^2 \ell^2}{4\sigma^2} \geqslant \frac{2^{k-n}\ell\delta'^2}{4}$ and $\frac{\ell\delta}{2} \geqslant \frac{2^{k-n}\ell\delta'}{2}$. Since $\mathbf{E}D(U) = |D|/2^n$, choosing ℓ sufficiently large so that $2^{k-n}\ell\delta'^2 > 4\log(1/\delta'')$, we obtain $\mathbf{P}\left[|g \cdot 2^{n-k} - |D| \cdot 2^{-k}| \geqslant \delta'\right] \leqslant 2e^{-\log\frac{1}{\delta''}} < 2\delta''$.

It follows from the claim that $h(z) = \frac{2^{k-n}}{\ell} \sum_{i=1}^{\ell} D(U_i, z)$ is a required sampler. Consider the following distinguisher D'': on input (x, z), which comes either from (X, Z) or (Y, Z), return 1 iff $D'(x, z) > h(z) + \frac{\epsilon'}{8}$. We will prove that D'' distinguishes between (X, Z) and all (Y, Z) satisfying $\mathbf{H}_\infty(Y|Z) \geqslant k$. Note that if $D''(x, z) = 1$ then $h(z) < 1 - \frac{\epsilon'}{8}$ and hence $|D'(\cdot, z)| < 2^{k'}$. Especially, D'' is of complexity at most s. Now, inequalities (14) and (13) yield

$$\mathbf{P}_{(x,z)\leftarrow(X,Z)}\left[D'(x, z) > h(z) + \epsilon'/8\right] \geqslant$$
$$\mathbf{P}_{(x,z)\leftarrow(X,Z)}\left[D'(x, z) > 2^{-k'}|D'(\cdot, z)| + \epsilon'/4\right] - \epsilon'^2/64 \geqslant 3\epsilon'^2/64,$$

Let $k' = k + \log(\frac{1}{\delta})$ where $\delta = \frac{\epsilon'^2}{64}$. From (12), (13), (14) and Lemma 8, we obtain

$$\mathbf{P}_{(x,z)\leftarrow(Y,Z)}\left[D'(x, z) > h(z) + \epsilon'/8\right] \leqslant$$
$$\mathbf{P}_{(x,z)\leftarrow(Y,Z)}\left[D'(x, z) > 2^{-k'}|D'(\cdot, z)|\right] + \epsilon'^2/64 \leqslant \epsilon'^2/32.$$

Combining the last two estimates yields, if only $\mathbf{H}_\infty(Y|Z) \geqslant k'$, the inequality

$$\mathbf{P}\left[D'(X, Z) = 1\right] - \mathbf{P}\left[D'(Y, Z) = 1\right] \geqslant \epsilon'^2/64$$

which completes the proof for case (a). In case (b), we proceed in the same way but we compute numbers $h(z)$ using an **NP** oracle. The basic result we use can be stated as follows:

Lemma 9. *[OG09] There is a probabilistic algorithm which, given a boolean circuit D over $\{0,1\}^n$ of size* $\mathrm{poly}(n)$ *and a natural number M, decides, with success probability at least $\frac{3}{4}$, whether $\frac{1}{4}M < |D| < 4M$, in time* $\mathrm{poly}(n)$, *using an oracle for* **NP**.

---

[6] We use the following version: Let X_i be random variables satisfying $|X_i - \mathbf{E}X_i| \leqslant 1$ and $X = \sum_i X_i$. Then $\mathbf{P}\left[|X - \mathbf{E}X| \geqslant \lambda\sigma\right] \leqslant 2\min\left(e^{-\frac{\lambda^2}{4}}, e^{-\frac{\lambda\sigma}{2}}\right)$, where $\sigma = \mathrm{Var}(X)$

Let us make three important observations:

- The success probability $\frac{3}{4}$ can be amplified to $1-\delta$, by repeating the algorithm $\mathcal{O}\left(\log\frac{1}{\delta}\right)$ times and taking the majority answer.
- The factor 4 can be improved to $1+\gamma$, by running the algorithm on the circuit $D' = D_1 \wedge \ldots \wedge D_k$, where D_i for $i = 1, \ldots, k$ are copies of D and k is such that $(1+\gamma)^k \leqslant 4$.

Hence, there is an algorithm which, with probability at least $1 - \delta$, computes a value g such that $(1 - \gamma)M < |D| < (1+\gamma)M$, in time poly $\left(n, \frac{1}{\gamma}, \log\frac{1}{\delta}\right)$, using an oracle for **NP**. For every z, let $M(z)$ be a value obtained by applying this algorithm to the circuit $D'(\cdot, z)$ and $\gamma = \frac{\epsilon'}{16}$, $\delta = 1 - \frac{\epsilon'^2}{64}$. Define $h(z) := 2^{-k}M(z)$. If $|D'(\cdot, z)| < 2^{k'}$, then $|M(z) - |D'(\cdot, z)|| \leqslant 2 \cdot 2^{k'} \cdot \frac{\epsilon}{16}$ holds with probability at least $1 - \frac{\epsilon'^2}{64}$, and thus for such values z holds the same estimate as in (14). We proceed further with h as in the previous proof.

6.4   Squared Indistinguishability

Theorem 9. *We say that X is (s, ϵ) squared-indistinguishable from Y given Z, if for every circuit D of size s, $\mathbf{E}_{z \leftarrow}[\mathbf{E}D(X|Z = z, z) - \mathbf{E}D(Y|Z = z, z)]^2 \leqslant \epsilon$ (motivated by [DY13]). Suppose that $X|Z$ is (s, ϵ) squared-indistinguishable from Y given Z, and $\widetilde{\mathbf{H}}_\infty(Y|Z) \geqslant k$. Then $\mathbf{H}^{|\mathrm{Metric}|,s,\sqrt{\epsilon}}(X|Z) \geqslant k$.*

Proof. From the inequality between the first and the second moment we obtain:

$$\mathbf{E}_{z \leftarrow Z}|\mathbf{E}D(X|Z = z, z) - \mathbf{E}D(Y|Z = z, z)| \leqslant$$
$$\left(\mathbf{E}_{z \leftarrow Z}[\mathbf{E}D(X|Z = z, z) - \mathbf{E}D(Y|Z = z, z)]^2\right)^{\frac{1}{2}} \leqslant \sqrt{\epsilon}. \quad (15)$$

Acknowledgments. I would like to express special thanks to Stefan Dziembowski and Krzysztof Pietrzak, for their helpful suggestions and discussions.

A   Tightness of the Leakage Lemma

Lemma 10. *Let $X \in \{0, 1\}^n$ be a random variable, $f : \{0, 1\}^m \to \{0, 1\}^n$ be a deterministic circuit of size s and $\epsilon < \frac{1}{12}$. Then $\widetilde{\mathbf{H}}^{\mathrm{Metric},\det\{0,1\},s,\epsilon}(f(X)|X) < 3$.*

Proof. Consider the following distinguisher D: on the input (y, x), where $x \in \{0, 1\}^m$ and $y \in \{0, 1\}^n$, run $f(x)$ and return 1 iff $f(x) = y$. Then for every x we get $D(f(x), x) = 1$. Let Y be any random variable over $\{0, 1\}^n$ such that $\widetilde{\mathbf{H}}_\infty(Y|X) \geqslant 3$. Then by Lemma 1, with probability $\frac{2}{3}$ over $x \leftarrow X$ we have $\mathbf{H}_\infty(Y|X = x) \geqslant 3 - \log_2(3)$. Since $D(y, x) = 0$ if $y \neq x$, for any such x we have $\mathbf{E}_{y \leftarrow Y|X=x}D(y, x) \leqslant 2^{-(3-\log_2(3))} \leqslant \frac{3}{8}$, and thus, with probability $\frac{2}{3}$ over $x \leftarrow X$, we get $\mathbf{E}_{y \leftarrow f(X)|X=x}D(y, x) - \mathbf{E}_{y \leftarrow Y|X=x}D(y, x) \geqslant \frac{5}{8}$. Taking the expectation over $x \leftarrow X$ we obtain finally $\mathbf{E}D(f(X), X) - \mathbf{E}D(Y, X) \geqslant \frac{2}{3} \cdot \frac{5}{8} - \frac{1}{3} \cdot 1 = \frac{1}{12}$.

We use this lemma to show that the estimate in Lemma 3 cannot be improved:

Theorem 10 (Tightness of the estimate in Lemma 3). *Suppose that there exists an exponentially secure pseudorandom generator f. Then for every m and $C > 0$ we have $\mathbf{H}^{\mathrm{HILL},\mathrm{rand}\{0,1\},2^{\mathcal{O}(m)},\frac{1}{2^{\mathcal{O}(m)}}}(f(U_m)) \geqslant m + C$ and simultaneously $\widetilde{\mathbf{H}}^{\mathrm{Metric},\det\{0,1\},\mathrm{poly}(m),\frac{1}{\mathrm{poly}(m)}}(f(U_m)|U_m) \leqslant 3$.*

Proof. The first inequality follows from the definition of the exponentially secure pseudorandom generator. The second inequality is implied by Lemma 10. ∎

B Metric Entropy vs Different Kinds of Distinguishers

Below we prove the equivalence between boolean and real valued distinguishers

Theorem 11. *For any random variables X, Z over $\{0,1\}^n, \{0,1\}^m$ we have $\mathbf{H}^{\mathrm{Metric},\det[0,1],s',\epsilon}(X|Z) = \mathbf{H}^{\mathrm{Metric},\det\{0,1\},s,\epsilon}(X|Z)$, where $s' \approx s$.*

Proof. We only need to prove $\mathbf{H}^{\mathrm{Metric},\det[0,1],s',\epsilon}(X|Z) \geqslant \mathbf{H}_\infty^{\mathrm{Metric},\det\{0,1\},s,\epsilon}(X|Z)$ as the other direction is trivial (because the class $(\det[0,1], s)$ is larger than $(\det\{0,1\}, s)$). Suppose that $\mathbf{H}^{\mathrm{Metric},\det[0,1],s,\epsilon}(X|Z) < k$. Then for some D and all Y satisfying $\mathbf{H}_\infty(X|Z) \geqslant k$ we have $\left|\mathbf{E}_{(x,z)\leftarrow(X,Z)}D(x,z) - \mathbf{E}_{(x,z)\leftarrow(Y,Z)}D(x,z)\right| \geqslant \epsilon$. Applying the same reasoning as in Theorem 6 we can replace D with D', which is equal either to D or to D^c, obtaining for all distributions $\mathbf{H}_\infty(Y|Z) \geqslant k$, the following:

$$\mathbf{E}D'(X,Z) - \mathbf{E}D'(Y,Z) \geqslant \epsilon.$$

Consider the distribution (Y^+, Z) minimizing the left side of the above inequality. Equivalently, it maximizes the expected value of D' under the condition $\mathbf{H}_\infty(Y|Z) \geqslant k$. Since this condition means that $\mathbf{H}_\infty(Y^+|Z=z) \geqslant k$ for all z, we conclude that $Y^+|Z=z$, for fixed z, is distributed over 2^k values of x giving the greatest values of $D'(x,z)$. Calculating the expected values in the last inequality via integration of the tail yields

$$\int_{t\in[0,1]} \mathbf{P}_{(x,z)\leftarrow(X,Z)}\left[D(x,z) > t\right] \mathrm{d}t - \int_{t\in[0,1]} \mathbf{P}_{(x,z)\leftarrow(Y^+,Z)}\left[D(x,z) > t\right] \mathrm{d}t \geqslant \epsilon$$

therefore for some number $t \in (0,1)$, the following holds:

$$\mathbf{P}_{(x,z)\leftarrow(X,Z)}\left[D(x,z) > t\right] \geqslant \mathbf{P}_{(x,z)\leftarrow(Y^+,Z)}\left[D(x,z) > t\right] + \epsilon.$$

Let D'' be a $\{0,1\}$-distinguisher that for every (x,z) outputs 1 iff $D(x,z) > t$. Clearly D'' is of size $s + \mathcal{O}(1)$ and satisfies

$$\mathbf{E}_{(x,z)\leftarrow(X,Z)}D''(x,z) \geqslant \mathbf{E}_{(x,z)\leftarrow(Y^+,Z)}D''(x,z) + \epsilon.$$

We assumed that (Y, Z) maximizes $\mathbf{E}D'(Y, Z)$. Now we argue that (Y, Z) is also maximal for D''. We know that for every z the distribution Y_z is flat over the set $\text{Max}^k_{D'(\cdot,z)}$ of 2^k values of x corresponding to largest values of $D'(x,z)$. It is easy to see that $\text{Max}^k_{D'(\cdot,z)} = \text{Max}^k_{D''(\cdot,z)}$. Therefore, we have shown in fact that

$$\mathbf{E}_{(x,z)\leftarrow(X,Z)}D''(x,z) - \max_{(Y,Z):\,\mathbf{H}_\infty(Y|Z)\geqslant k} \mathbf{E}_{(x,z)\leftarrow(Y,Z)}D''(x,z) \geqslant \epsilon,$$

which means exactly that $\mathbf{H}^{\text{Metric},\{0,1\},s',\epsilon}(X|Z) < k$.

References

[BSW03] Barak, B., Shaltiel, R., Wigderson, A.: Computational analogues of entropy. In: Arora, S., Jansen, K., Rolim, J.D.P., Sahai, A. (eds.) RANDOM 2003 and APPROX 2003. LNCS, vol. 2764, pp. 200–215. Springer, Heidelberg (2003)

[CKLR11] Chung, K.-M., Kalai, T.Y., Liu, F.-H., Raz, R.: Memory delegation. Cryptol. ePrint Arch. **2011**, 273 (2011). http://eprint.iacr.org/

[DORS08] Dodis, Y., Ostrovsky, R., Reyzin, L., Smith, A.: Fuzzy extractors: how to generate strong keys from biometrics and other noisy data. SIAM J. Comput. **38**(1), 97–139 (2008)

[DP08] Dziembowski, S., Pietrzak, K.: Leakage-resilient cryptography in the standard model. IACR Cryptol. ePrint Arch. **2008**, 240 (2008)

[DY13] Dodis, Y., Yu, Y.: Overcoming weak expectations. In: Sahai, A. (ed.) TCC 2013. LNCS, vol. 7785, pp. 1–22. Springer, Heidelberg (2013)

[FOR12] Fuller, B., O'Neill, A., Reyzin, L.: A unified approach to deterministic encryption: new constructions and a connection to computational entropy. Cryptol. ePrint Arch. **2012**, 005 (2012). http://eprint.iacr.org/

[FR12] Fuller, B., Reyzin, L.: Computational entropy and information leakage. Cryptol. ePrint Arch. **2012**, 466 (2012). http://eprint.iacr.org/

[GW10] Gentry, C., Wichs, D.: Separating succinct non-interactive arguments from all falsifiable assumptions. Cryptol. ePrint Arch. **2010**, 610 (2010). http://eprint.iacr.org/

[HILL99] Hastad, J., Impagliazzo, R., Levin, L.A., Luby, M.: A pseudorandom generator from any one-way function. SIAM J. Comput. **28**(4), 1364–1396 (1999)

[HLR07] Hsiao, C.-Y., Lu, C.-J., Reyzin, L.: Conditional computational entropy, or toward separating pseudoentropy from compressibility. In: Naor, M. (ed.) EUROCRYPT 2007. LNCS, vol. 4515, pp. 169–186. Springer, Heidelberg (2007)

[KPW13] Krenn, S., Pietrzak, K., Wadia, A.: A counterexample to the chain rule for conditional HILL entropy. In: Sahai, A. (ed.) TCC 2013. LNCS, vol. 7785, pp. 23–39. Springer, Heidelberg (2013)

[OG09] O'Donnell, R., Guruswami, V.: An intensive introduction to computational complexity theory, University Lecture. http://www.cs.cmu.edu/~odonnell/complexity/ (2009)

[Rey11] Reyzin, L.: Some notions of entropy for cryptography. In: Fehr, S. (ed.) ICITS 2011. LNCS, vol. 6673, pp. 138–142. Springer, Heidelberg (2011)

[RTTV08] Reingold, O., Trevisan, L., Tulsiani, M., Vadhan, S.: Dense subsets of pseudorandom sets. In: Proceedings of the 2008 49th Annual IEEE Symposium on Foundations of Computer Science, FOCS '08, pp. 76–85. IEEE Computer Society, Washington (2008)

[Sha48]   Shannon, C.E.: A mathematical theory of communication. Bell Syst. Tech. J. **27**, 379–423 (1948)

[VZ12]   Vadhan, S., Zheng, C.J.: Characterizing pseudoentropy and simplifying pseudorandom generator constructions. In: Proceedings of the 44th Symposium on Theory of Computing, STOC '12, pp. 817–836. ACM, New York (2012)

[Yao82]   Yao, A.C.: Theory and application of trapdoor functions. In: Proceedings of the 23rd Annual Symposium on Foundations of Computer Science, SFCS '82, pp. 80–91. IEEE Computer Society, Washington (1982)

Broadcast (and Round) Efficient Verifiable Secret Sharing

Juan Garay[1], Clint Givens[2], Rafail Ostrovsky[3], and Pavel Raykov[4]([✉])

[1] AT&T Labs – Research, Florham Park, NJ, USA
`juan.a.garay@gmail.com`
[2] Maine School of Science and Mathematics, Limestone, MN, USA
`cgivens@gmail.com`
[3] Department of Computer Science and Department of Mathematics, UCLA,
Los Angeles, CA, USA
`rafail@cs.ucla.edu`
[4] ETH Zürich, Zürich, Switzerland
`pavel.raykov@inf.ethz.ch`

Abstract. Verifiable secret sharing (VSS) is a fundamental cryptographic primitive, lying at the core of secure multi-party computation (MPC) and, as the distributed analogue of a commitment functionality, used in numerous applications. In this paper we focus on unconditionally secure VSS protocols with honest majority.

In this setting it is typically assumed that parties are connected pairwise by authenticated, private channels, and that in addition they have access to a "broadcast" channel. Because broadcast *cannot* be simulated on a point-to-point network when a third or more of the parties are corrupt, it is impossible to construct VSS (and more generally, MPC) protocols in this setting without using a broadcast channel (or some equivalent addition to the model).

A great deal of research has focused on increasing the efficiency of VSS, primarily in terms of round complexity. In this work we consider a refinement of the round complexity of VSS, by adding a measure we term *broadcast complexity*. We view the broadcast channel as an expensive resource and seek to minimize the number of rounds in which it is invoked as well.

We construct a (linear) VSS protocol which uses the broadcast channel only *twice* in the sharing phase, while running in an overall constant number of rounds.

The unabridged version of this paper appears in [GGOR13].

Clint Givens is supported in part by NSF grants 0830803, 09165174, 1065276, 1118126 and 1136174, US-Israel BSF grant 2008411, OKAWA Foundation Research Award, IBM Faculty Research Award, Xerox Faculty Research Award, B. John Garrick Foundation Award, Teradata Research Award, and Lockheed-Martin Corporation Research Award. This material is based upon work supported by the Defense Advanced Research Projects Agency through the U.S. Office of Naval Research under Contract N00014-11-1-0392. The views expressed are those of the author and do not reflect the official policy or position of the Department of Defense or the U.S. Government.

C. Padró (Ed.): ICITS 2013, LNCS 8317, pp. 200–219, 2014.
DOI: 10.1007/978-3-319-04268-8_12, © Springer International Publishing Switzerland 2014

1   Introduction

Verifiable secret sharing (VSS) [CGMA85], where a *dealer* wishes to share a secret among a group of n parties, at most t of which (possibly including the dealer) may be actively malicious, is a fundamental cryptographic primitive, lying at the core of secure multi-party computation (MPC) [GMW87,BGW88, CCD88] and used in a myriad of applications. Our focus in this paper is on *unconditionally* (a.k.a. *information-theoretically*) secure VSS protocols (meaning that the security properties are guaranteed to hold even when the malicious parties are endowed with unbounded computational power) with honest majority ($t < n/2$).

In the unconditional setting, it is typically assumed that parties are connected pairwise by authenticated, private channels, and that in addition they have access to a "broadcast" channel. Broadcast allows one party to send a consistent message to all other parties, guaranteeing consistency even if the broadcaster is corrupted. Because broadcast cannot be simulated on a point-to-point network when more than a third of the parties are corrupt [LSP82], even probabilistically, it is impossible to construct VSS (or more generally, MPC) protocols in this setting without using a "physical broadcast channel" (that is, a black-box which securely implements broadcast), or some equivalent addition to the model. Further, it is known that in this regime ($n/3 \le t < n/2$), protocols are subject to some (negligibly small) error probability and cannot achieve so-called perfect security[CCD88,RB89,DDWY93], which is possible when $t < n/3$.

A great deal of research has focused on understanding the complexity as well as increasing the efficiency of VSS, primarily in terms of round complexity [GIKR02,FGG+06,KKK08,PCRR09,KPC10]. Indeed, given its typical applications, such as implementing a pre-processing phase, as well as the *share* phase in the general "share-compute-reveal" shape of an MPC protocol [GMW87], or its use during the *setup* phase of information-theoretic protocols when $t \ge n/3$ (e.g., [PW96,BTHR07,HR13]; see Related work), a fast execution—namely, a (small) constant number of rounds (some specific figures given later on)—is of utmost importance.

In this work we consider a refinement of the round complexity of VSS, by incorporating an additional measure which we term *broadcast complexity*. We view the broadcast channel as an expensive resource and seek to minimize the number of rounds in which it is invoked as well. Justifiably so, high-level descriptions of VSS (and, more generally, MPC) protocols tend to treat broadcast as a black-box. When $t < n/3$, this may be viewed simply as a convenient abstraction, since broadcast in any case can be simulated in a point-to-point network using Byzantine agreement[1].

However, when $t < n/2$, the black-box treatment of broadcast is (as described above) no longer a convenience but a **requirement**, and there are compelling

---

[1] Trouble comes, however, when analyzing round complexity: as observed in [KK07, Koo07,KKK08], Byzantine agreement is round-expensive, and the compilation from black-box broadcast to simulated broadcast blows up the number of rounds substantially.

reasons to consider it more expensive than "mere" secure channels. Indeed, while the latter can be realized for example via the physical exchange (using trusted couriers) of large one-time pads between every pair of players, which may be done in an asynchronous preprocessing phase and without any centrally trusted party, we see no equally straightforward approach to physically implement *broadcast* without a trusted party, and when the participants are geographically scattered. Hence it is only natural to treat physical broadcast as an expensive resource, and in particular to treat a protocol's *broadcast rounds* as (substantially) more expensive than ordinary rounds. In addition, the question of how many broadcast rounds does VSS require in the $t < n/2$ regime is compelling from a theoretical perspective.

Our results. Thus motivated to better understand the broadcast requirements of verifiable secret sharing when $t < n/2$, in this work we present new upper bounds on its broadcast and round complexity. Specifically, we show a constant-round, linear VSS protocol which only uses *two* broadcasts in the sharing phase and none in reconstruction—what we call a $(2, 0)$-broadcast VSS. The overall number of rounds is $(20, 1)$, again meaning 20 rounds in the sharing phase and 1 reconstruction round.

To our knowledge, the most efficient VSS protocol in terms of broadcast rounds for the settings with $t < n/2$ is the $(2, 2)$-broadcast, $(3, 2)$-round protocol of Kumaresan *et al.* [KPC10], which is exponential-time and not (apparently) linear. The same authors also give a $(3, 2)$-broadcast, $(4, 2)$-round VSS which is polynomial-time and linear (we believe—though the authors do not claim it here either), at the expense of an additional round in the sharing phase. Hence our $(2, 0)$-broadcast protocol improves the overall broadcast complexity (although it is not as round-efficient).

Considering linear, constant-round protocols which use zero broadcasts during reconstruction (which are more suitable for VSS applications such as [broadcast-efficient] MPC), the most broadcast-efficient VSS protocol we are aware of is the $(7, 0)$-broadcast protocol described in [RB89, Rab94]. Recently, Hirt and Raykov [HR13] presented an approach allowing to construct $(1, 0)$-broadcast VSS protocols for $t < n/2$, but the overall number of protocol rounds is *linear* in n, making it not ideally fit for the natural applications of VSS mentioned above.

We derive our $(2, 0)$-broadcast, constant-round VSS protocol in two stages.

1. In the first stage, we obtain a $(3, 0)$-broadcast, constant-round protocol which is inspired by the protocol in [Rab94], but leverages a number of novelties and optimizations to reduce the broadcast complexity from 7 to 3; its overall round complexity is $(9, 1)$. This is presented in Sect. 3.1.
2. In the second stage, we apply a transformation to the sharing phase of the above protocol such that it uses *two* rounds of broadcast instead of three. This optimization is in turn inspired by the one presented in [KK07], and the key method is what the authors called *moderated* protocols. This method is a generic transformation which given any protocol Π employing broadcast

channels, constructs a "moderated" version Π' of Π where all calls to broadcast channels are substituted with a special broadcast simulation subroutine controlled by a designated party (called *the moderator*).

A new key technical element in our construction is to show how using one round of physical broadcast (the first one in our stage-1 protocol) one can prepare a *setup* which allows to invoke sufficiently many broadcast simulation routines later on. This transformation yielding the final VSS protocol is presented in Sect. 3.2.

As our focus in this work is on reducing the overall number of broadcast *rounds*, rather than broadcast (or otherwise) *communication complexity*, we forgo explicit treatment of the latter. We do however note that protocols described herein can be compiled via generic techniques into significantly more communication-efficient versions; see work of Fitzi and Hirt [FH06], as well as recent work by Ben-Sasson *et al.* [BFO12].

Related work. We already mentioned above the most closely related work regarding unconditionally secure VSS for $t < n/2$ [Rab94,KPC10]. The role of broadcast in multiparty protocols has been studied in a number of other previous works. Katz *et al.* [KKK08,KK07,Koo07], seeking to improve overall round complexity when broadcast is simulated over point-to-point channels, construct constant-round protocols for VSS and MPC whose descriptions use only a single broadcast round. However, for $t < n/2$ they assume a PKI infrastructure (e.g., pseudosignatures [PW96]—more on this below) is already in place.

Fitzi *et al.* [FGMR02,FGH+02] , as well as Goldwasser and Lindell [GL05], consider broadcast and MPC protocols for $t < n$ which do not use physical broadcast at all (nor equivalent assumptions), but instead weaken the guarantees provided by the protocol. In particular these protocols are not robust and so may fail to deliver any output at all. On the other hand, the so-called *detectable broadcast* (and *detectable MPC*) protocols of [FGMR02,FGH+02] do achieve consistency among honest players: either the broadcast (MPC) succeeds and all honest parties receive output, or it fails, in which case all honest parties agree that it failed.

As mentioned above, unconditionally secure broadcast cannot be simulated on a point-to-point network when more than a third of the parties are corrupt. However, if there is a setup phase during which the parties enjoy access to a physical broadcast channel (but need not know their future inputs), Pfitzmann and Waidner [PW96] showed how to construct *pseudosignatures*, an information-theoretic authentication technique for multiparty protocols which can then be used to simulate future invocations of broadcast by running a so-called "authenticated" Byzantine agreement protocol [DS83]; this avoids any need for a physical broadcast channel during the main phase of the protocol. The number of broadcast rounds in the [PW96] setup construction is $O(n^2)$, and it works for an arbitrary number of corruptions ($t < n$). This was later improved to $O(n)$ broadcast rounds by Beerliová-Trubíniová *et al.* in [BTHR07], at the price of tolerating $t < n/2$ corruptions, and recently by Hirt and Raykov to just 1, as mentioned above. However, the overall round complexity of this construction (as well as that in [BTHR07]) is $O(n)$.

Minimizing the use of broadcast has also been considered in the related problem known as *secure message transmission by public discussion* (SMT-PD), where a Sender wants to send a message to a Receiver privately and reliably. Recall that in this problem, Sender and Receiver are connected by n channels, up to $t < n$ of which may be maliciously controlled by a computationally unbounded adversary, as well as one public channel, which is reliable but not private. SMT-PD was introduced in [GO08] as an important building block for achieving unconditionally secure MPC on sparse (i.e., not fully connected) networks. The motivation for this abstraction comes from the feasibility in partially connected settings for a subset of the nodes in the network to realize a broadcast functionality despite the limited connectivity [DPPU86, Upf92], which plays the role of the public channel. Such implementation of the public channel on point-to-point networks is costly and highly non-trivial in terms of rounds of computation and communication, as mentioned earlier. See, e.g., [GGO11] for further details.

We now turn to the presentation of the model, definitions and building blocks, followed by the new VSS protocol (Sect. 3). Due to space limitations, some of the auxiliary constructions and proofs appear in the full version of the paper [GGOR13].

2   Model, Definitions and Tools

We consider a complete, synchronous network of n players $P_1, \ldots, P_n$ who are pairwise connected by secure (private and authenticated) channels, and who additionally have access to a broadcast channel. Some of these players are corrupted by a centralized adversary $\mathcal{A}$ with *unbounded computing power*. The adversary is *active*, directing players under his control to deviate from the protocol in arbitrary ways. As noted, we consider only *static* rather than adaptive adversary in this work, meaning that he chooses which players to corrupt prior to the start of protocol execution. The computation evolves as a series of rounds. In a given round, honest players' messages depend only on information available to them from prior rounds; $\mathcal{A}$, however, is *rushing*, and receives all messages (and broadcasts) sent by honest players before deciding on the messages (and broadcasts) of corrupted players. Sometimes we refer to $\mathcal{A}$ thus defined as a *t-adversary*. We consider statistical security (since, as mentioned above, perfect security is unachievable in this setting), and let κ denote the error parameter, $\kappa \geq 2n$.

Information checking. An *information checking scheme (IC)* [RB89] is a triple of protocols (ICSetup, ICValidate, ICReveal) which achieves a limited signature-like functionality for three players: a *dealer D*, *intermediary I*, and *receiver R*. D holds as input a secret $s \in \mathbb{F}$, which he passes to I in ICSetup. ICValidate insures that even if D cheats, I knows a value which R will accept. In ICReveal, I sends s to R, together with some authenticating data, on the basis of which R accepts or rejects s as having originated from D. More formally, the scheme should satisfy the following guarantees:

CORRECTNESS: If D, I, and R are honest, then R will accept s in ICReveal.

NON-FORGERY: If D and R are honest, then R will reject any incorrect value $s^* \neq s$ passed to him in ICReveal, except with negligible probability.

COMMITMENT: If I and R are honest, then at the end of ICValidate I knows a value s such that R will accept s in ICReveal, except with negligible probability.

PRIVACY: If D and I are honest, then prior to ICReveal, a cheating R has no information on s.

We call an IC scheme *linear* if it meets the following additional condition.

LINEARITY: If D, I, and R have invoked ICSetup and ICValidate with respect to several secrets $\{s_i\}$, then I may (without further interaction) invoke ICReveal to authentically disclose any (public) linear combination of the s_i without revealing each s_i individually.

Our weak secret sharing and verifiable secret sharing protocols make use of a linear IC subprotocol based on that of [CDD+01], with some minor adjustments to increase broadcast efficiency. The protocol and its proof of security appear in the full version of the paper [GGOR13].

Weak secret sharing. An (n,t)-*weak secret sharing scheme (WSS)* is a pair of protocols (WSS-Share, WSS-Rec) for a set of players $\mathcal{P} = \{P_1, \ldots, P_n\}$, one of whom, the *dealer* D, holds input $s \in \mathbb{F}$. It must satisfy the following guarantees in the presence of an unbounded adversary corrupting up to t of the parties:

WEAK COMMITMENT: W.h.p., at the end of WSS-Share there exists a fixed value $s^* \in \mathbb{F} \cup \{\bot\}$, defined by the joint view of the honest parties, such that all honest parties will output the same value, either s^* or $\bot$, in WSS-Rec. If D is honest, then w.h.p. all honest parties will output $s^* = s$.

PRIVACY: If D is honest, then prior to WSS-Rec $\mathcal{A}$ gains no information on s (i.e., his view is statistically independent of s).

WSS is useful as an information-theoretic, distributed commitment for the dealer D. Thus, we may say that a dealer who completes WSS-Share has *committed* to his (effective) input s, and that upon completing WSS-Rec he *decommits* (if a proper value is reconstructed). We call a commitment to a value in $\mathbb{F}$ a *proper commitment* (regardless of whether it equals the dealer's actual input), and a commitment to $\bot$ an *improper* (or *garbage*) *commitment*. We will also need a slightly relaxed version of WSS called *WSS-without-agreement* (or *very weak secret sharing* [BPW91]), in which the Commitment property above is replaced by

WEAK COMMITMENT WITHOUT AGREEMENT: W.h.p., at the end of WSS-Share there exists a fixed value $s^* \in \mathbb{F} \cup \{\bot\}$, defined by the joint view of the honest parties, such that each honest party will output either s^* or $\bot$ in WSS-Rec (but some may output s^* and others $\bot$). If D is honest, then w.h.p. all honest parties will output $s^* = s$.

Furthermore, we will call a WSS(-without-agreement) *linear* if it satisfies the following in addition:

LINEARITY: If D has properly committed to several secrets $\{s^{(k)}\}$, then he may (without further interaction) invoke WSS-Rec to decommit to any (public) linear combination of the $s^{(k)}$. If some of the commitments are garbage, there still exists a fixed value $s^* \in \mathbb{F} \cup \{\bot\}$ which is reconstructed as the "linear combination" (w.h.p.).

We can slightly strengthen this requirement in the case of the sum of two values, to say that if one is properly committed and the other is garbage, their sum is garbage also (as opposed to any fixed value, which Linearity gives). We will use this property later on in the construction of VSS protocols.

PROPER + IMPROPER: If D has committed separately to $s \in \mathbb{F}$ and to $\bot$, then the reconstruction of the sum $s + \bot$ (or $\bot + s$) will yield $\bot$ (w.h.p.).

Our WSS(-without-agreement) protocol is presented in Sect. 3.1. It has a single sharing phase, which uses two broadcasts, and two different reconstruction phases: one which uses a single broadcast round and achieves ordinary WSS, and one which uses no broadcast but achieves only WSS-without-agreement.

Verifiable secret sharing. An (n,t)-*verifiable secret sharing scheme* [CGMA85] is a pair of protocols (VSS-Share, VSS-Rec) for a set of players $\mathcal{P} = \{P_1, \ldots, P_n\}$, one of whom, the *dealer* D, holds input $s \in \mathbb{F}$. In addition to the Privacy property above in the WSS case, VSS must satisfy the following, stronger guarantee in the presence of an unbounded adversary corrupting up to t of the parties:

COMMITMENT: W.h.p., at the end of VSS-Share there exists a fixed value $s^* \in \mathbb{F}$, defined by the joint view of the honest parties, such that all honest parties will output s^* in VSS-Rec. If D is honest, then $s^* = s$.

VSS strengthens WSS by guaranteeing that even when a cheating D does not cooperate in the Reconstruction phase, the honest players can still recover the value he committed to (which we now require to be a proper field element, not $\bot$). This makes possible a stronger variant of linearity, in which honest players can reconstruct linear combinations of secrets shared by *different dealers*. This strong linearity property is crucial for MPC applications of VSS.

We say that the parties *verifiably share* a secret s if each (honest) party maintains some state such that, when the honest parties invoke VSS-Rec on that joint state, they will reconstruct the value s (w.h.p.). Clearly, if a dealer D has just completed VSS-Share with effective input s, then the parties verifiably share s.

LINEARITY: If the parties verifiably share secrets $\{s^{(k)}\}$, then they also (without further interaction) verifiably share any (public) linear combination of the secrets.

We now turn to broadcast-type [LSP82] primitives over point-to-point channels (and slightly extended communication models; see below) which will become useful when further reducing the number of physical broadcasts (Sect. 3.2).

Gradecast. Graded broadcast (a.k.a. "gradecast") was introduced by Feldman and Micali [FM88]. It allows to broadcast a value among the set of recipients but with weaker consistency guarantees than in the case of standard broadcast, where all honest recipients are required to output the same value. In addition to the value v_i each recipient P_i also outputs a grade $g_i \in \{0, 1\}$.

Formally, a protocol achieves graded broadcast if it allows the dealer $D \in \mathcal{P}$ to distribute a value $v \in \mathcal{D}$ among parties $\mathcal{P}$ with every party P_i outputting a value $v_i \in \mathcal{D}$ with a grade $g_i \in \{0, 1\}$ such that:

VALIDITY: If the dealer D is correct, then every correct $P_i \in \mathcal{P}$ outputs $(v_i, g_i) = (v, 1)$.

GRADED CONSISTENCY: If a correct $P_i \in \mathcal{P}$ outputs (v_i, g_i) with $g_i = 1$, then every correct $P_j \in \mathcal{P}$ outputs (v_j, g_j) with $v_j = v_i$.

In [Fit03] gradecast is considered in different communication models. First, it is shown that gradecast is achievable from point-to-point channels if and only if $t < n/3$. Second, an extended communication model is considered where each player can broadcast to a (every) pair of other players. Such a primitive is called *2-cast*. A construction is then given which tolerates $t < n/2$ and achieves binary gradecast given 2-cast channels.

In this paper we will make use of a round-efficient gradecast protocol allowing *arbitrary* domains $\mathcal{D}$ based on that construction. Our construction works as follows: First, we construct a *weak broadcast* primitive (see next) given 2-cast; then, based on weak broadcast we build gradecast.

Weak broadcast. Weak broadcast (a.k.a. *Crusader agreement* [Dol82]) is another weak form of broadcast, where the recipients either decide on the value sent by the dealer or on a special symbol $\perp$ indicating that the dealer is malicious.

Formally, a protocol achieves weak broadcast if it allows the dealer D to distribute a value $v \in \mathcal{D}$ among parties $\mathcal{P}$ with every party P_i outputting a value $v_i \in \mathcal{D} \cup \{\perp\}$ such that:

VALIDITY: If the dealer D is correct, then every correct $P_i \in \mathcal{P}$ outputs $v_i = v$.
WEAK CONSISTENCY: If a correct $P_i \in \mathcal{P}$ outputs $v_i \neq \perp$, then every correct $P_j \in \mathcal{P}$ outputs $v_j \in \{v_i, \perp\}$.

The modifications to the gradecast and weak broadcast protocols in [Fit03] to allow for arbitrary domains $\mathcal{D}$, instead of just the binary domain, are presented in the full version of the paper [GGOR13].

3   A Broadcast- and Round-Efficient VSS Protocol

In this section we present our new $(2, 0)$-broadcast, constant-round VSS protocol for $t < n/2$. Its overall round complexity is $(20, 1)$. This is the first linear VSS protocol enjoying such a small number of broadcast rounds without trusted setup, while running in an overall constant number of rounds. We first obtain a $(3,0)$-broadcast, $(9,1)$-round protocol which, at a high level, is inspired by the $((7,0)$-broadcast) protocol in [RB89]; we then apply a moderated-protocol transformation to shave off one additional broadcast round.

3.1   A (3, 0)-Broadcast, Constant-Round VSS Protocol

Our VSS protocol's sharing phase uses a WSS protocol, which we now describe. Our WSS(-without-agreement) protocol uses two broadcasts in its sharing phase, and admits two different reconstruction phases: one which uses a single broadcast round and achieves ordinary WSS, and one which uses no broadcast but achieves only WSS-without-agreement. In turn, the protocol makes use of a linear IC subprotocol based on that in [CDD+01]. (Due to space limitations, the protocol appears in the full version of the paper [GGOR13].) The WSS protocol(s) is shown below. Since its sharing and reconstruction phases are invoked at different rounds of the VSS protocol's sharing phase, we specify them as separate protocols for convenience. The WSS protocol, with its two different reconstruction phases.

Protocol WSS-Share($\mathcal{P}, D, s$)

1. D chooses a random polynomial $f(x)$ of degree $\leq t$ such that $f(0) = s$, and sets $s_i := f(i)$; this will be P_i's share. For each pair $P_i, P_j \in \mathcal{P} - \{D\}$, run ICSetup($D, P_i, P_j, s_i$).
2–5. **2 x BROADCAST in 4,5:** For each $P_i, P_j \in \mathcal{P} - \{D\}$, run ICValidate($D, P_i, P_j, s_i$).

Protocol WSS-Rec($\mathcal{P}, D, s$)

1. For each pair $P_i, P_j \in \mathcal{P} - \{D\}$, run ICReveal($P_i, P_j, s_i$).
2. **BROADCAST:** D broadcasts the polynomial $f(x)$ which he used to share the secret. P_i broadcasts the list of pieces $\{(j, s_j)\}$ which he accepted in ICReveal in the previous step.
   Let HAPPY denote the set of players who accept at least $n - t$ pieces, and all of whose accepted pieces lie on the polynomial $f(x)$. If $|\text{HAPPY}| \geq n - t$, all players take $s = f(0)$ to be the secret, otherwise $\perp$.

Protocol WSS-Rec-NoBC($\mathcal{P}, D, s$)

1. For each pair $P_i, P_j \in \mathcal{P} - \{D\}$, run ICReveal($P_i, P_j, s_i$). If P_i accepts at least $n - t$ pieces, and all accepted pieces lie on a polynomial $f(x)$ of degree $\leq t$, then P_i takes $s = f(0)$ to be the secret, otherwise $\perp$.

Theorem 1. WSS = (WSS-Share, WSS-Rec) *is a linear weak secret sharing scheme secure against a static, unbounded adversary corrupting $t < n/2$ players. Furthermore,* WSS* = (WSS-Share, WSS-Rec-NoBC) *is a linear WSS-without-agreement scheme, secure against a static, unbounded adversary who corrupts $t < n/2$ players.*

Proof. COMMITMENT. First consider a cheating D. At the end of WSS-Share, an honest P_i holds s_i which all honest parties will accept (due to the Commitment property of the IC protocol). Now these pieces s_i held by the honest parties define a polynomial $f^*(x)$; if $\deg f^*(x) > t$, then each honest party will accept pieces not lying on the dealer's broadcast polynomial $f(x)$. Therefore we will have $|\mathsf{HAPPY}| < n - t$, and $\perp$ will be reconstructed. Note that this situation is precisely a garbage commitment.

Otherwise $\deg f^*(x) \leq t$ (and the commitment is proper). If the dealer's broadcast polynomial $f(x) \neq f^*(x)$ then again each honest party will accept pieces not on $f(x)$, and so $\perp$ will be reconstructed. If $f^*(x) = f(x)$ then it may be the case that $\perp$ is reconstructed (depending on the values honest parties accept from dishonest parties), or that $s^* = f(0) = f^*(0)$ is reconstructed. Regardless, there is only one non-$\perp$ value which may be reconstructed, and it is fixed by the joint view of the honest parties at the end of WSS-Share.

Now if D is honest, then by the IC Non-Forgery property no cheating party can fool an honest party into accepting a value other than s_i during ICReveal (except with negligible probability). It follows that each honest player will accept $\geq n - t$ pieces, and all their accepted values will lie on the dealer's polynomial $f(x)$. Thus $|\mathsf{HAPPY}| \geq n - t$ and the parties output $s = f(0)$.

PRIVACY. If D is honest, then by the IC Privacy property, the adversary has no information on any s_i value held by an honest player P_i prior to ICReveal. Hence the adversary learns only the t points on the polynomial $f(x)$ corresponding to dishonest players' shares, and in particular has no information on $f(0) = s$ prior to WSS-Rec.

COMMITMENT WITHOUT AGREEMENT. Define $f^*(x)$ as above, by the shares of the honest parties. As before if $\deg f^*(x) > t$, all honest parties will accept a set of pieces which do not lie on any degree t polynomial, and they will all output $\perp$.

If $\deg f^*(x) \leq t$, then honest party P_i will output $s^* = f^*(0)$ only if all the pieces he accepts from dishonest parties lie on $f^*(x)$; otherwise the set of pieces he accepts will lie on no polynomial of degree t, and he will output $\perp$.

For an honest D, the argument is the same as in the with-agreement case: Due to IC Non-Forgery, all honest parties will (w.h.p.) accept only values which lie on $f(x)$, and so all will output the correct value $s = f(0)$.

LINEARITY. Suppose D has properly committed to values $\{s^{(k)}\}$, using polynomials $f_k(x)$. Then for each value $s^{(k)}$, player P_i holds a share $s_i^{(k)}$. To commit to a linear combination of the $s^{(k)}$, in WSS-Rec P_i reveals the linear combination of his $s_i^{(k)}$ during ICReveal (in place of "s_i"), and D broadcasts the linear combination of these polynomials (in place of "$f(x)$"). Then the properties of commitment and privacy remain in place, since taking a linear combination of polynomials of degree at most t results in a new polynomial of degree at most t.

If some of the commitments were garbage, this means exactly that some of the polynomials (defined by the shares of the honest players) were of degree $> t$. Nevertheless, taking a linear combination of these polynomials results in a single, fixed polynomial whose free term is the only possible non-$\perp$ value which honest parties will reconstruct (and then only if the new polynomial has degree $\leq t$).

PROPER + IMPROPER. A proper commitment is associated with a polynomial of degree $\leq t$, and an improper commitment with one of degree $> t$. Thus the sum of the two has degree $> t$, corresponds to another improper commitment, and will yield $\perp$ (w.h.p.).

We are now ready to present $\mathsf{VSS_{3bc}}$, our $(3,0)$-broadcast, $(9,1)$-round VSS protocol, which uses the WSS protocol above in its sharing phase. Regarding the presentation of our protocol(s), many VSS protocol descriptions rely on a bivariate-polynomial approach; others are univariate-based. We opt for the latter, since we feel that this protocol's structure lends itself best to a univariate polynomial description. At a high level, the protocol is inspired by that of Rabin and Ben-Or [RB89], and has a similar structure. First D distributes shares of a t-degree polynomial f where $s := f(0)$ and of additional random t-degree polynomials g_k. Each player P_i commits to all shares via WSS. Then the parties jointly carry out a cut-and-choose process in which the players are challenged to reconstruct either g_k or $f + g_k$ for each k, which must be degree t. Players who complain of incompatible shares, or fail to participate, have their shares broadcast (and hence fixed) by D.

As mentioned earlier, Rabin and Ben-Or's VSS requires 7 broadcast rounds in the share phase. One novelty which allows us to reduce broadcast round complexity to 3 is that we require the *dealer* as well as the players to commit via WSS to the shares he distributed, which constrains the misbehavior of a cheating dealer. After all commitments are in place, the players broadcast a round of cut-and-choose challenges in step 7. In step 8, parties respond to the challenges by using WSS-without-agreement to reconstruct the shares of the appropriate polynomials. In the final step 9, a broadcast is used to confirm the results of the WSS-without-agreement; at the same time D has a chance (and is obligated) to broadcast shares of players for whom he did not reconstruct the correct share in step 8.

An additional trick which saves us a broadcast round can be seen in step 6, which is inserted between the last two rounds of the WSS share phase. In this step, the parties perform a *pre-broadcast* by sending each other player their intended WSS final-round broadcast on point-to-point channels. In step 7, they officially complete WSS by echoing the pre-broadcast. This forces a cheating player to "semi-commit" in step 6 to one of at most $n - t$ possible final-round broadcasts for WSS, since a majority (including at least one honest player) must confirm his pre-broadcast. Luckily, semi-commitment restricts cheaters' options enough that players are able to broadcast the cut-and-choose challenges in the *same round*—step 7—rather than waiting for full commitment and then using another broadcast. (Note that in the case of a non-rushing adversary, step 6 is unnecessary.)

Protocol VSS-Share$_{3bc}(\mathcal{P}, D, s)$

1. D chooses a random polynomial $f(x)$ of degree $\leq t$ such that $f(0) = s$, and sets $s_i := f(i)$. Also for $1 \leq k \leq \kappa n$, D chooses random polynomials $g_k(x)$ of degree $\leq t$, and sets $t_{ki} := g_k(i)$. D sends $(s_i, \{t_{ki}\}_k)$ to P_i.

2–5. **BROADCAST:** P_i and D will now each act as WSS dealers to commit to P_i's share s_i. We reserve s_i to denote the value D commits to, and let s_i^* denote that which P_i commits to (these may be different if D and/or P_i is dishonest). D and P_i act as dealer in steps 1–4 of WSS-Share (D, s_i), WSS-Share(P_i, s_i^*), WSS-Share(D, t_{ki}), and WSS-Share(P_i, t_{ki}^*) $(1 \leq k \leq \kappa n)$.

6. The parties have just completed WSS-Share step 4/ICValidate step 3. In the next step (corresponding to WSS-Share step 5/ICValidate step 4) the WSS/IC dealer will resolve conflicts. Instead of doing so immediately, let BC_i denote the broadcast which P_i would make. P_i first sends-to-all BC_i. Also, if D conflicted with any P_i in the previous step (namely in ICValidate step 3) then in the following round D will broadcast *all* the values $(s_i, \{t_{ki}\}_k)$. For now, D sends-to-all these values, which we call *public pieces*.

7. **BROADCAST:** Now P_i broadcasts BC_i, which completes WSS-Share step 5/ICValidate step 4, and D broadcasts the values $(s_i, \{t_{ki}\}_k)$ which he sent-to-all in the previous step. Of course each player broadcasts his view of the previous step; if it is not the case that at least $t + 1$ players agree that P_i's broadcast this round matches what he told them in the previous round, then P_i is disqualified.

   Additionally, each $P_i \neq D$ broadcasts a random challenge $C_i \in \{0,1\}^\kappa$ for D and for the other P_j's. The challenge indicates, for each index $k \in [\kappa n]$ assigned to P_i (κ such in total), whether:
   (1) D and P_j should reveal $f(x) + g_k(x)$, in which case set $v_{kj} = s_j + t_{kj}$ and $v_{kj}^* = s_j^* + t_{kj}^*$; or
   (2) D and P_j should reveal $g_k(x)$, in which case set $v_{kj} = t_{kj}$ and $v_{kj}^* = t_{kj}^*$.

8. $\forall k \in [\kappa n]$, $j \in [n]$, P_i participates in WSS-Rec-NoBC(D, v_{kj}) and WSS-Rec-NoBC(P_j, v_{kj}^*). P_i's outputs from these protocols are $v_{kj}^{(i)}$ and $v_{kj}^{*(i)}$, respectively.

9. **BROADCAST:** Each P_i broadcasts his view of the previous round— namely, the reconstructed shares $v_{kj}^{(i)}$ and $v_{kj}^{*(i)}$, for all k, j.

   If a majority of players agrees on a non-$\perp$ reconstructed value for v_{kj} (resp. v_{kj}^*), then such value is the *broadcast (BC) consensus* for the given commitment, and the players who agree *participate in the consensus*. If no BC consensus exists, or if the player who shared the value does not participate, then the sharing player is disqualified. Consequently, if D is not so disqualified, then there exists a BC consensus (which D endorses) for all v_{kj}. Assuming this is the case, then D is nevertheless disqualified if for any k, the set of shares $\{v_{kj}\}_j$, together with appropriate public pieces, does not lie on a polynomial of degree $\leq t$.

   In addition to broadcasting his view as described above, D also accuses player P_j, by publicly broadcasting the shares $(s_j, \{t_{kj}\}_k)$, if either of the following occurred:

(1) D output $\perp$ in any WSS-Rec-NoBC instance for which P_j was dealer; or
(2) D reconstructed an incorrect value for P_j's share of any challenge poly-
    nomial ($v_{kj}^{*(D)} \neq v_{kj}$).

If any such public pieces fail to lie on the appropriate degree-t polynomial,
or if D neglects to accuse P_j when there exists a BC consensus that $v_{kj}^* \neq v_{kj}$, then D is disqualified.

Let HAPPY denote the set of **non-disqualified** players who were **not
accused** by D. If $|\text{HAPPY}| < n - t$, then D is disqualified.

Protocol VSS-Rec$_{0bc}(\mathcal{P}, s)$

1. Each player $P_i \in$ HAPPY invokes WSS-Rec-NoBC(P_i, s_i).
   Each player $P_i \in \mathcal{P}$ creates a list of shares consisting of those s_j which he
   accepts from any WSS-Rec-NoBC(P_j, s_j) (including his own), together with
   all public pieces s_j. He takes any $t + 1$ shares from the list, interpolates a
   polynomial $f(x)$, and outputs $s := f(0)$ as the secret.

Theorem 2. *Protocol* VSS$_{3bc} = ($VSS-Share$_{3bc}$, VSS-Rec$_{0bc})$ *is a* $(3,0)$-*broadcast*,
$(9,1)$-*round, linear verifiable secret sharing scheme secure against an unbounded
adversary who corrupts $t < n/2$ players.*

The number of broadcast rounds, as well as total number of rounds, is easily
verified by inspection. In particular, broadcast is used in rounds 5, 7 and 9.
We will specifically reference these rounds in the next section, where we only
keep first and third broadcasts. The proof of Theorem 2 is broken up into three
lemmas, as follows.

Lemma 3. (PRIVACY) *If D is honest, then w.h.p. the adversary $\mathcal{A}$ gains no
information on s prior to* VSS-Rec$_{0bc}$.

Proof. The secret-sharing properties of degree-t polynomials assure that the joint
distribution of all shares handed by D to the corrupted parties in step 1, is
uniformly random, in particular independent of s.

By the privacy property of protocol WSS employed in steps 2–7, the individual shares $(s_i, \{t_{ki}\}_k)$ of any honest party remain independent of the adversary's
view. If in step 7 D broadcasts $(s_i, \{t_{ki}\}_k)$ for some P_i who conflicted with D
in an instance of ICValidate, then that P_i must have been corrupt and hence $\mathcal{A}$
already knew these values (as well as the fact that D would broadcast them).

In step 7, $\mathcal{A}$ learns the honest parties' random challenges, which are independent of s and its shares, and thus yield no additional information.

The values reconstructed in step 8 are, for each challenge, either $f(x) + g_k(x)$
or $g_k(x)$. The $g_k(x)$'s themselves were chosen uniformly at random, and until step
8 $\mathcal{A}$ knew nothing about them except for the shares held by corrupt parties, by
WSS Privacy. Hence, conditioned on $\mathcal{A}$'s view up to that point, the revealed
polynomial is uniformly random subject to consistency with the shares held by
corrupted parties. Since D is honest he will answer all challenges correctly, and
so $\mathcal{A}$ knows in advance that all honest parties will "accept" D's responses.

In step 9, $\mathcal{A}$ knows in advance what each honest party reconstructed from each WSS, so those broadcasts reveal nothing. Additionally, if D accuses P_j, then D output either $\perp$ or an incorrect value in some instance WSS-Rec-NoBC$(P_j, *)$. This implies w.h.p. that P_j was dishonest (WSS Commitment Without Agreement), in which case $\mathcal{A}$ learns nothing when D broadcasts the shares $(s_j, \{t_{kj}\}_k).$[2]

Lemma 4. (COMMITMENT) *With high probability, at the end of* VSS-Share$_{3bc}$ *there exists a fixed* $s^* \in \mathbb{F}$ *such that all honest players output* s^* *during* VSS-Rec$_{0bc}$. *If D is honest, then* $s^* = s$.

The proof of this lemma is presented in the full version of the paper [GGOR13].

Lemma 5. (LINEARITY) *If the parties verifiably share secrets* $\{s^{(k)}\}$, *then they also (without further interaction) verifiably share any (public) linear combination of the* $s^{(k)}$.

Proof. Consider the situation when parties verifiably share a secret s according to the protocol, for a dealer D who was not disqualified. By the Commitment proof, we know that w.h.p. D's WSS-commitment to s_i is proper for all i, and, further, that each happy player has properly WSS-committed to the same value. Since happy P_i have made proper WSS-commitments, the linearity of WSS-commitment implies that such P_i can reveal (and are committed to) any linear combination thereof.

Now consider secrets $s^{(k)}$ which are verifiably shared with shares $s_i^{(k)}$, interpolating polynomials $f_k(x)$ all of degree $\leq t$. (We ignore the "shares" of players who are disqualified in some execution of VSS-Share$_{3bc}$—such players must be corrupt and without loss of generality other players simply ignore their messages and shares during VSS-Rec$_{0bc}$.) Then any $t + 1$ of the summed shares $\sum_k s_i^{(k)}$ interpolate the polynomial $f(x) = \sum_k f_k(x)$, which is of degree $\leq t$ with free term $\sum_k s^{(k)}$.

For any given non-disqualified P_i each share $s_i^{(k)}$ associated with that player is (w.h.p.) either (1) properly WSS-shared among all parties; or (2) publicly known. If *all* the $s_i^{(k)}$ for P_i are publicly known, then other players simply use the public sum $\sum_k s_i^{(k)}$ as P_i's share during VSS-Rec$_{0bc}$. Otherwise, by the linearity property of WSS P_i can reveal any sum of $s_i^{(k)}$'s. In particular, he can reveal exactly the sum of those $s_i^{(k)}$'s which are not already public, and this is what he does when revealing his "share" in VSS-Rec$_{0bc}$. This is of course the functional equivalent of revealing the sum of all the $s_i^{(k)}$'s since the other players need only add the public values to the reconstructed value to obtain the "true" share $\sum_k s_i^{(k)}$ of $\sum_k s^{(k)}$. (And revealing the sum of all shares reveals exactly the same information as revealing the sum of the non-public shares.)

---

[2] As this discussion suggests, it may happen that D broadcasts an honest party's shares in step 9; this can only happen if $\mathcal{A}$ succeeds in an IC forgery attempt (hence with negligible probability). As a consequence, our protocol achieves statistical but not perfect privacy. On the other hand, privacy *is* perfect conditioned on the event that $\mathcal{A}$ is unsuccessful in all forgery attempts, as a failed forgery by itself reveals nothing about s.

3.2 Further Reducing the Number of Broadcast Rounds

We now show how to modify protocol VSS-Share$_{3bc}$ so that only *two* rounds of broadcast suffice. This improvement is inspired by the transformation presented in Sect. 3.3 of [KK07].

We execute the transformation in three steps. First, we show how using one round of physical broadcast one can prepare a *setup* (details below) which allows to simulate sufficiently many gradecast channels later on. Second, we consider a *moderated* version of VSS-Share$_{3bc}$ where the dealer acts as the moderator. Third, we instruct the players to use one more round of physical broadcast in order to agree on whether the moderator behaved correctly or not. The overall construction results in a constant-round share protocol which uses physical broadcast in two rounds only—one for gradecast setup generation and one for agreeing whether the dealer's moderation was honest.

First, we describe two additional building blocks used in our transformation.

Gradecast from setup. In [HR13], Hirt and Raykov recently showed how to prepare a *setup* allowing to simulate 2-cast channels (protocols Setup$_3$ and Broadcast$_3$ in [HR13]). The setup protocol Setup$_3$ takes 3 rounds, where in the first two rounds point-to-point channels are used and in the third round a physical broadcast is used. The protocol Broadcast$_3$ simulating 2-cast from the prepared setup uses point-to-point channels during 3 rounds.

Since gradecast is achievable from 2-cast channels in settings with $t < n/2$ (recall the description of gradecast in Sect. 2), we can interpret the setup for 2-cast channels as a setup for gradecast channels. Let the protocol SetupGradecast be defined to generate such a setup, i.e., SetupGradecast runs sufficiently many instances of Setup$_3$ for each triple of players in parallel. The following lemma summarizes the security achieved by the pair of protocols (SetupGradecast, Gradecast).

Lemma 6. *Protocol* Gradecast *is a 6-round protocol achieving gradecast from a setup and point-to-point channels tolerating $t < n/2$ malicious parties. Moreover, the setup used by protocol* Gradecast *is prepared using the 3-round protocol* SetupGradecast*, where in the first two rounds point-to-point channels are used and in the third round physical broadcast is used.*

Moderated VSS. In [KK06], Katz and Koo proposed a new primitive called *moderated VSS* which allows to execute VSS under the supervision of a designated party called *the moderator*. If the moderator is honest, then the resulting protocol actually achieves the security properties of VSS; otherwise no security is guaranteed.

Formally, a two-phase protocol for parties $\mathcal{P}$, where there is a distinguished dealer $D \in \mathcal{P}$ who holds an initial input s and a moderator $P^{**} \in \mathcal{P}$ (who may possibly be the dealer), is a moderated VSS protocol tolerating t malicious parties if the following conditions hold for any adversary controlling at most t parties:

- Each honest party P_i outputs a bit f_i at the end of the sharing phase, and a value s_i at the end of the reconstruction phase.
- If the moderator is honest during the sharing phase, then each honest party P_i outputs $f_i = 1$ at the end of this phase.
- If there exists an honest party P_i who outputs $f_i = 1$ at the end of the sharing phase, then the protocol achieves VSS; specifically: (1) if the dealer is honest then all honest parties output s at the end of the reconstruction phase, and the joint view of all the malicious parties at the end of the sharing phase is independent of s, and (2) the joint view of the honest parties at the end of the sharing phase defines a value s' such that all honest parties output s' at the end of the reconstruction phase.

Theorem 7 ([KK06]). *Assume there exists a constant-round VSS protocol Π, using a broadcast channel in the sharing phase only, which tolerates t malicious parties. Then there exists a constant-round moderated VSS protocol Π', using a gradecast channel and tolerating the same number of malicious parties.*

The compilation of Π into Π' is achieved by requiring the players to use a "moderated broadcast subroutine" to simulate broadcast. Each time players invoke the subroutine they update their flag f_i indicating whether the broadcast simulation has been successful. Players start executing Π' with f_i set to 1. The moderated subroutine Modercast for party P_i broadcasting a message m is defined as following.

Protocol Modercast$(\mathcal{P}, P^{**}, P_i, m)$

1. P_i gradecasts the message m.
2. The moderator P^{**} gradecasts the message he output in the previous step.
3. Let (m_j, g_j) and (m'_j, g'_j) be the outputs of party P_j in steps 1 and 2, respectively. Within the underlying execution of Π', party P_j will use m'_j as the message "broadcast" by P_i.
4. Furthermore, P_j sets $f_j := 0$ if (1) $g'_i \neq 1$, or (2) $m'_i \neq m_i$ and $g_i = 1$.[3]

We are now ready to show the enhanced VSS protocol.

A (2,0)-broadcast, constant-round VSS protocol. In order to reduce the number of rounds where physical broadcast is used we apply the following transformation to the protocol VSS-Share$_{3bc}$:

1. First, we generate gradecast setup using protocol SetupGradecast.
2. We then run a *moderated* version of the protocol VSS-Share$_{3bc}$, where the dealer acts as a moderator. The Modercast subroutine uses two sequential gradecast invocations that are simulated using the setup prepared by the protocol Gradecast.

---

[3] We note that in the description of the compilation from [KK06] gradecast with grades in $\{0, 1, 2\}$ is used. Here we use gradecast with grades in $\{0, 1\}$ because during the compilation it is only required to distinguish the maximal grade from all other grades (so we put maximal grade to 1 instead of 2).

3. Finally, each player broadcasts (using physical broadcast) his flag f_i indicating whether he trusts the moderator (who is also the dealer). If the number of players broadcasting 1 is greater than $n/2$ then the sharing phase was successful, otherwise the dealer is disqualified.

The second and the third steps of the transformation have been already proposed by Katz and Koo in [KK07], while in the first step they make use of a pre-distributed PKI acting as a setup for gradecast. In our transformation, instead of assuming a PKI we generate a setup for gradecast using the protocol SetupGradecast. We call the modified sharing phase VSS-Share$_{2bc}$.

Furthermore, in VSS-Share$_{2bc}$ we optimize the round complexity of the transformation by parallelizing the beginning and the end of the protocol VSS-Share$_{3bc}$ with the protocol SetupGradecast and broadcasting the flags, respectively.

Protocol VSS-Share$_{2bc}(\mathcal{P}, D, s)$

1-2. Players execute rounds 1 and 2 of the protocol SetupGradecast in parallel with rounds 1 and 2 of VSS-Share$_{3bc}$.

3-5. **BROADCAST:** Players execute round 3 of SetupGradecast and rounds 3-5 of VSS-Share$_{3bc}$. Each player broadcasts the concatenation of the values resulting from protocols SetupGradecast and VSS-Share$_{3bc}$.

6. Players execute round 6 of the protocol VSS-Share$_{3bc}$.

7-18. **MODERCAST:** Players execute round 7 of VSS-Share$_{3bc}$ where the Modercast subroutine is used instead of broadcast. The subroutine invokes two gradecast channels sequentially. Each call to the gradecast channel is simulated using the protocol Gradecast, which takes 6 rounds.

19. Players execute round 8 of the protocol VSS-Share$_{3bc}$.

20. **BROADCAST:** Players execute round 9 of VSS-Share$_{3bc}$. Each player additionally broadcasts flag f_i indicating whether Modercast was successful. If the number of $f_i = 1$ is greater than $n/2$, then the sharings generated by VSS-Share$_{3bc}$ are accepted; otherwise, the dealer is disqualified.

Theorem 8. *Protocol* VSS$_{2bc} = ($VSS-Share$_{2bc},$ VSS-Rec$_{0bc})$ *is a* $(2,0)$-*broadcast,* $(20,1)$-*round, linear verifiable secret sharing scheme secure against an unbounded adversary who corrupts* $t < n/2$ *players.*

Proof sketch. Due to Theorem 2, VSS$_{3bc} = ($VSS-Share$_{3bc},$ VSS-Rec$_{0bc})$ is a linear verifiable secret sharing scheme secure against an unbounded adversary who corrupts $t < n/2$ players. Hence, due to Theorem 7 the protocol VSS-Share$_{2bc}$ obtains a moderated VSS protocol when substituting broadcasts in VSS-Share$_{3bc}$ with Modercast. Finally, due to the definition of moderated VSS, if there exists at least one honest party with $f_i = 1$ then the moderated version of VSS-Share$_{3bc}$ achieves VSS. Hence, since $t < n/2$, if more than $n/2$ parties broadcast $f_i = 1$ then VSS-Share$_{2bc}$ achieves VSS; otherwise the dealer is corrupt and hence can be disqualified.

4   Summary and Open Problems

In the $t < n/2$, unconditional security regime, just because protocols treat broadcast as a black-box should not, from a theoretical perspective or otherwise, entitle us to consider it a *free resource*, as there are compelling reasons to consider it more expensive than "mere" secure channels. In this paper we proposed a refinement of the round complexity of VSS, by adding a measure we term *broadcast complexity*, and seeked to minimize the number of rounds in which it is invoked as well, presenting a $(2, 0)$-broadcast, constant-round VSS protocol for $t < n/2$. This is the first linear VSS protocol enjoying such a small number of broadcast rounds without trusted setup, while running in an overall constant number of rounds.

One drawback of our resulting VSS protocol is that it is only proved secure for static adversaries, since our WSS protocol, based on [CDD+01]'s, is not adaptively secure. It is possible that the VSS protocol is adaptively secure, even though the WSS protocol is not (per [Rab94, CDD+01]). We leave this corroboration for future work. We also leave open the question of whether $(1, 0)$-broadcast, constant-round VSS protocols exist.

References

[BFO12]   Ben-Sasson, E., Fehr, S., Ostrovsky, R.: Near-linear unconditionally-secure multiparty computation with a dishonest minority. In: Safavi-Naini, R., Canetti, R. (eds.) CRYPTO 2012. LNCS, vol. 7417, pp. 663–680. Springer, Heidelberg (2012)

[BGW88]   Ben-Or, M., Goldwasser, S., Wigderson, A.: Completeness theorems for non-cryptographic fault-tolerant distributed computation. In: Proceedings of the 20th Annual ACM Symposium of the Theory of Computation, pp. 1–10, May 1988

[BPW91]   Baum-Waidner, B., Pfitzmann, B., Waidner, M.: Unconditional byzantine agreement with good majority. In: Jantzen, M., Choffrut, C. (eds.) STACS 1991. LNCS, vol. 480, pp. 285–295. Springer, Heidelberg (1991)

[BTHR07]   Beerliová-Trubíniová, Z., Hirt, M., Riser, M.: Efficient Byzantine agreement with faulty minority. In: Kurosawa, K. (ed.) ASIACRYPT 2007. LNCS, vol. 4833, pp. 393–409. Springer, Heidelberg (2007)

[CCD88]   Chaum, D., Crépeau, C., Damgård, I.: Multiparty unconditionally secure protocols. In: Proceedings 20th Annual Symposium on Theory of Computing, STOC. Association for Computing Machinery, May 1988

[CDD+01]   Cramer, R., Damgård, I., Dziembowski, S., Hirt, M., Rabin, T.: Efficient multiparty computations secure against an adaptive adversary. In: Stern, J. (ed.) EUROCRYPT 1999. LNCS, vol. 1592, pp. 311–326. Springer, Heidelberg (1999)

[CGMA85]   Chor, B., Goldwasser, S., Micali, S., Awerbuch, B.: Verifiable secret sharing and achieving simultaneity in the presence of faults. In: Proceedings of Twenty Sixth IEEE Symposium in Foundations of Computer Science, pp. 383–395 (1985)

[DDWY93]   Dolev, D., Dwork, C., Waarts, O., Yung, M.: Perfectly secure message transmission. J. ACM 1(40), 17–47 (1993)

[Dol82]   Dolev, D.: The Byzantine generals strike again. J. Algorithms **3**, 14–30 (1982)

[DPPU86]   Dwork, C., Peleg, D., Pippenger, N., Upfal, E.: Fault tolerance in networks of bounded degree (preliminary version). In: Proceedings of the Eighteenth Annual ACM Symposium on Theory of Computing, STOC, Berkeley, California, USA, pp. 370–379, 28–30 May 1986

[DS83]   Dolev, D., Strong, H.: Authenticated algorithms for Byzantine agreement. SIAM J. Comput. **12**(4), 656–666 (1983)

[FGG+06]   Fitzi, M., Garay, J., Gollakota, S., Pandu Rangan, C., Srinathan, K.: Round-optimal and efficient verifiable secret sharing. In: Halevi, S., Rabin, T. (eds.) TCC 2006. LNCS, vol. 3876, pp. 329–342. Springer, Heidelberg (2006)

[FGH+02]   Fitzi, M., Gottesman, D., Hirt, M., Holenstein, T., Smith, A.: Detectable byzantine agreement secure against faulty majorities. In: Proceedings of the Twenty-First Annual Symposium on Principles of Distributed Computing, PODC '02, pp. 118–126. ACM, New York (2002)

[FGMR02]   Fitzi, M., Gisin, N., Maurer, U., von Rotz, O.: Unconditional Byzantine agreement and multi-party computation secure against dishonest minorities from scratch. In: Knudsen, L.R. (ed.) EUROCRYPT 2002. LNCS, vol. 2332, pp. 482–501. Springer, Heidelberg (2002)

[FH06]   Fitzi, M., Hirt, M.: Optimally efficient multi-valued Byzantine agreement. In: Proceedings of the Twenty-Fifth Annual ACM Symposium on Principles of Distributed Computing, PODC '06, pp. 163–168. ACM, New York (2006)

[Fit03]   Fitzi, M.: Generalized communication and security models in Byzantine agreement. Ph.D. thesis, ETH Zurich, March 2003; Reprint as vol. 4 of ETH Series in Information Security and Cryptography. Hartung-Gorre Verlag, Konstanz (2003). ISBN 3-89649-853-3

[FM88]   Feldman, P., Micali, S.: Optimal algorithms for Byzantine agreement. In: Proceedings of the Twentieth Annual ACM Symposium on Theory of Computing, STOC '88, pp. 148–161. ACM, New York (1988)

[GGO11]   Garay, J., Givens, C., Ostrovsky, R.: Secure message transmission by public discussion: a brief survey. In: Chee, Y.M., Guo, Z., Ling, S., Shao, F., Tang, Y., Wang, H., Xing, C. (eds.) IWCC 2011. LNCS, vol. 6639, pp. 126–141. Springer, Heidelberg (2011)

[GGOR13]   Garay, J.A., Givens, C., Ostrovsky, R., Raykov, P.: Broadcast (and round) efficient verifiable secret sharing. In: Cryptology ePrint Archive. Report 2012/130, September 2013

[GIKR02]   Gennaro, R., Ishai, Y., Kushilevitz, E., Rabin, T.: On 2-round secure multiparty computation. In: Yung, M. (ed.) CRYPTO 2002. LNCS, vol. 2442, pp. 178–193. Springer, Heidelberg (2002)

[GL05]   Goldwasser, S., Lindell, Y.: Secure multi-party computation without agreement. J. Cryptol. **18**(3), 247–287 (2005)

[GMW87]   Goldreich, O., Micali, S., Wigderson, A.: How to play any mental game or a completeness theorem for protocols with honest majority. In: Proceedings of the 19th Annual ACM Symposium on Theory of Computation, pp. 218–229, May 1987

[GO08]   Garay, J.A., Ostrovsky, R.: Almost-everywhere secure computation. In: Smart, N.P. (ed.) EUROCRYPT 2008. LNCS, vol. 4965, pp. 307–323. Springer, Heidelberg (2008)

[HR13]   Hirt, M., Raykov, P.: On the complexity of broadcast setup. In: Fomin, F.V., Freivalds, R., Kwiatkowska, M., Peleg, D. (eds.) ICALP 2013, Part I. LNCS, vol. 7965, pp. 552–563. Springer, Heidelberg (2013)

[KK06]   Katz, J., Koo, C.-Y.: On expected constant-round protocols for Byzantine agreement. In: Dwork, C. (ed.) CRYPTO 2006. LNCS, vol. 4117, pp. 445–462. Springer, Heidelberg (2006)

[KK07]   Katz, J., Koo, C.-Y.: Round-efficient secure computation in point-to-point networks. In: Naor, M. (ed.) EUROCRYPT 2007. LNCS, vol. 4515, pp. 311–328. Springer, Heidelberg (2007)

[KKK08]   Katz, J., Koo, C.-Y., Kumaresan, R.: Improving the round complexity of VSS in point-to-point networks. In: Aceto, L., Damgård, I., Goldberg, L.A., Halldórsson, M., Ingólfsdóttir, A., Walukiewicz, I. (eds.) ICALP 2008, Part II. LNCS, vol. 5126, pp. 499–510. Springer, Heidelberg (2008)

[Koo07]   Koo, C.-Y.: Studies on fault-tolerant broadcast and secure computation. Ph.D. thesis (2007)

[KPC10]   Kumaresan, R., Patra, A., Pandu Rangan, C.: The round complexity of verifiable secret sharing: the statistical case. In: Abe, M. (ed.) ASIACRYPT 2010. LNCS, vol. 6477, pp. 431–447. Springer, Heidelberg (2010)

[LSP82]   Lamport, L., Shostak, R., Pease, M.: The Byzantine generals problem. ACM Trans. Program. Lang. Syst. 4, 382–401 (1982)

[PCRR09] Patra, A., Choudhary, A., Rabin, T., Pandu Rangan, C.: The round complexity of verifiable secret sharing revisited. In: Halevi, S. (ed.) CRYPTO 2009. LNCS, vol. 5677, pp. 487–504. Springer, Heidelberg (2009)

[PW96]   Pfitzmann, B., Waidner, M.: Information-theoretic pseudosignatures and byzantine agreement for $t \geq n/3$. Technical report RZ 2882 (#90830), IBM Research (1996)

[Rab94]   Rabin, T.: Robust sharing of secrets when the dealer is honest or cheating. J. ACM 41(6), 1089–1109 (1994)

[RB89]   Rabin, T., Ben-Or, M.: Verifiable secret sharing and multiparty protocols with honest majority. In: Proceedings of the 21st ACM Symposium on the Theory of Computing, pp. 73–85 (1989)

[Upf92]   Upfal, E.: Tolerating linear number of faults in networks of bounded degree. In: PODC, pp. 83–89 (1992)

Leakage Resilience of the Blom's Key Distribution Scheme

Michał Jastrzębski[1,2] and Stefan Dziembowski[2](✉)

[1] Institute of Informatics, University of Warsaw, Warsaw, Poland
[2] Google Inc., Zurich, Switzerland
std@mimuw.edu.pl

Abstract. We initiate the study of the leakage-resilience of the information-theoretic key distribution schemes. Such schemes, originally proposed in the 1980s, have recently attracted a lot of interest in the systems community. This is because, due to their extreme efficiency, they can be executed on low-cost devices such as sensors, where the use of the public-key cryptography is infeasible. We argue that the study of leakage resilience of such schemes is particularly well-motivated, since, unlike more expensive devices, the sensors (or other similar devices) are unlikely to be physically resilient to leakage.

We concentrate on the classical scheme of Blom (CRYPTO 1982), since it is known to be optimal in a large class of such schemes. We model the leakage as an input-shrinking function. In this settings we show that Blom's scheme is leakage-resilient in a very strong model, where the adversary can (1) compromise completely some nodes in a "standard" way, and (2) leak information *jointly* from the remaining nodes. The amount leakage that we can tolerate can be up to $(0.5 - \epsilon)$ of the total amount of information on the leaking nodes. We also show that this bound is optimal, by providing an attack that breaks the scheme if more leakage is available to the adversary. This attack works even in a weaker model, where the nodes leak information independently.

In the proof we make use of the theory of the randomness extractors. In particular we use the fact that inner product over a finite field is a good 2-source extractor. This is possible since the Blom's scheme is based on the matrix multiplication.

1 Introduction

A recent trend in theoretical cryptography, initiated by [29,30,36], is to design schemes that are provably-secure even if implemented on devices that are not

---

This work was partly supported by the WELCOME/2010-4/2 grant founded within the framework of the EU Innovative Economy Operational Programme. The European Research Council has provided financial support for this work under the European Community's Seventh Framework Programme (FP7/2007-2040213)/ERC grant agreement no CNTM-207908.
Stefan Dziembowski leave from *Sapienza* University of Rome.

C. Padró (Ed.): ICITS 2013, LNCS 8317, pp. 220–237, 2014.
DOI: 10.1007/978-3-319-04268-8_13, © Springer International Publishing Switzerland 2014

fully trusted. The motivation for this research comes from the fact that, instead of breaking the mathematical foundations of a cryptosystem, in real life it is often much easier to attack its physical implementation. Such "physical attacks" are usually based on the *side-channel information* about the internals of the cryptographic device that the adversary can obtain by measuring its running-time, electromagnetic radiation, power consumption (see e.g. [38]), or even by actively tampering with it (see e.g. [4]) in order to force it to reveal information about its secrets. Practitioners have developed several remedies to these attacks, however, they are usually ad-hoc and lack a formal security argument.

Contrary to the approach taken by the practitioners, security of the constructions developed by the theoreticians is always analyzed formally in a well-defined mathematical model, and hence covers a broad class of attacks, including those that are not yet known, but may potentially be invented in the future. Over the last few years several models for passive and active physical attacks have been proposed and schemes secure in these models have been constructed (see e.g. [1,2,7,8,11,14,15,19–21,23–25,27,29,30,32,33,37,40]). Some of these papers [19,23,27,29,30,32] present the so-called *general compilers* i.e. algorithms that transform any cryptographic functionality into a "physically-secure" one. These generic constructions, although very inspiring theoretically, are of a limited practical relevance mostly because of the huge blow-up in the complexity of the computed functionality. In another class of papers the authors develop new schemes for concrete cryptographic task such as stream-ciphers [20,40], public-key primitives [8,11,14,33,34,37], multiparty computation protocols [7] or zero-knowledge schemes [24]. While some of these schemes can be quite efficient, it is unclear if they will ever be used in practice, one of the reasons being that their deployment would require a change in the existing industrial standards.

Therefore an alternative natural approach is to analyze the leakage-resilience of *existing* cryptosystems in order to find among them those that exhibit good leakage-resilience properties. One example of such work is the influential paper of Akavia et al. [2] where the authors show leakage-resilience of the public-key encryption scheme of Regev [42] and the identity-based encryption scheme of Gentry et al. [26]. Another example can be found in [3] where the leakage-resilience of the Okamoto identification scheme [39] is shown and used in a construction of a signature scheme secure in the bounded-retrieval model. The schemes in these examples are computationally secure and we are not aware of any non-trivial example of a practical information-theoretically secure scheme whose leakage-resilience has been shown in the literature.

Usually the information-theoretically secure schemes are considered not very practical since, for various reasons, they are cumbersome to use in real-life, the classical example being the one time pad encryption scheme that requires the users to store very large keys. Nevertheless, some of the information-theoretically secure schemes have found practical applications, due to their simplicity and efficiency. One of such examples is the Shamir's secret sharing scheme [44], which is used as a building block for several cryptographic protocols. Another prominent example are the information-theoretically secure *key distribution schemes*

(KDS). The leakage resilience of one of such schemes, namely the classical Blom's scheme [5] is the main topic of this paper. Below we first give a brief introduction to the KDS's and then informally describe our leakage model.

Key Distribution Schemes (KDS). Since currently the main application of the KDS's are the sensor networks we will use the sensor network terminology. We note, however, that the mathematical idea appeared much before the emergence of such networks (Blom's paper was published in 1982), and such schemes have also other applications, one example being the HDCP (High-Bandwidth Digital Content Protection) system created by Intel.

A sensor network consists of a large number m of autonomous devices denoted by natural numbers $1, \ldots, m$. In many cases, sensors are being deployed in hostile environment and are exposed to diverse malicious adversaries. In this case security of communication between nodes becomes essential. Sensors need to be able to communicate directly with each other over encrypted and authenticated channels. Such communication requires that each pair of nodes share a common secret key (which is used by this pair for encryption). After they are deployed, the nodes should communicate without relying on any trusted third party. Therefore, before the deployment, a trusted setup phase, called the *key predistribution*, is executed. Since the sensors have a limited computing power the use of the public-key cryptography is not an option, and the solutions based on the symmetric-key primitives are preferred.

One obvious solution is for each sensor to store the secret key to pair with any other node. In this case the common key of a pair would be secret and known only to the nodes in this pair. This approach is not practical because of the nature of sensors - the devices have limited memory, whereas the total number of stored keys grows quadratically in the size of the network. Another extreme is to give the same fixed key to every sensor in the network. While this scheme would be very memory efficient its security is quite low, since the adversary who *compromises* just one node, and extracts the key from it, would be able to decrypt the communication between each pair of the not compromised nodes sharing the same key.

Rolf Blom in [5] proposed a key distribution scheme which provides a nice tradeoff between security and memory efficiency. Description of the Blom key distribution scheme as well as its security can be found in Sect. 2. Informally speaking, the idea of [5] is to fix a number n of nodes that the adversary needs to compromise in order to break the security of the system. More precisely: as long as the number of compromised nodes is smaller than n then the keys shared by any pair of not compromised nodes is unknown to the adversary. The size of the stored information on each sensor is $n \cdot |K|$ bits (where $|K|$ is the length of the key that the sensors establish). Note that Blom's scheme can be viewed as a generalization of the schemes described above: by setting $n = m$ we obtain the scheme with high resilience against compromising of the nodes, but high memory requirements, and by setting $n = 1$ we obtain the other extreme case (low resilience and low memory requirements). For a formal analysis of Blom scheme see e.g. [6], where it is also shown that the Blom's scheme is optimal in terms of the amount of data that the sensors need to store (as a function of n, m and $|K|$). Practical key predistribution schemes were also proposed by Eschenauer and Gligor [22] who construct a scheme where two nodes can establish the common key only with some probability. Other *key predistribution* schemes providing different tradeoffs can be found for instance in [9,17].

Leakage Resilience of the KDS's. The sensors that execute the key distribution schemes are supposed to be low-cost, and therefore they cannot be assumed to be leakage-proof, as physical protections against leakages is expensive. Therefore analyzing the side-channel leakage-resilience of the key distribution schemes is particularly well-motivated, and it is natural to pick the Blom's scheme as the first target for this analysis (for its optimality and simplicity). Let us start with the description of our leakage model. As we already mentioned, several models have been proposed for reasoning about the side-channel leakages, for example the early approaches considered the leakages of the individual bits only [13,30]. In this work we follow a very popular paradigm in which the leakage is modeled as an *input shrinking function*, i.e. a function f whose output is much shorter than its input (the length of the output of f will be called the *amount of leakage*). Such functions were first proposed in cryptography in the so-called bounded-storage model of Maurer [35]. Later, they were used to define the memory leakage occurring during the virus attacks in the bounded-retrieval model [3,12,18]. In the context of the side-channel leakages they were first used in [20] with an additional restriction that the memory is divided into two separate parts that do not leak information simultaneously, and in the full generality in the paper of Akavia et al. [2].

Our Contribution. In this paper we use the model of Akavia et al. i.e. we do not impose any restrictions on the input of the leakage function, except that we require only that the size of its output is bounded. Several other papers in this model, already mentioned in the introduction, have been published in recent years. A popular tool that is used in these works are the randomness extractors (see e.g. [43]). Since some of these extractors are based on linear algebra (in particular the famous inner product extractor of Chor and Goldreich [10]) hence the Blom's scheme, which itself uses the matrix multiplication, seems to be a promising candidate for a leakage-resilient key distribution scheme. We confirm this intuition in this paper.

More precisely, but still informally, we show that the Blom's scheme is leakage-resilient in the following sense. In our model we allow the adversary to both perform the standard "non-leakage" attacks (i.e. to compromise the nodes) and to leak from the uncompromised nodes[1]. Recall that $n - 1$ is the maximal number of nodes that the adversary can compromise while attacking the scheme

---

[1] For simplicity of the notation in our formal model the leakage function is in fact also applied to the compromised nodes.

without leakage. In order to show the leakage-resilience we will now treat n as a security parameter and allow the adversary to compromise significantly less nodes than $n-1$. Let $j \leq n-1$ denote the number of nodes that the adversary actually compromised. It turns out (cf. Theorem 2) that if j is close to $n-1$ than the leakage-resilience of the Blom's scheme is very low. In particular if $j = n-1$ then the scheme can be broken with leaking just $|K|$ bits from the uncompromised nodes, and in general Blom's scheme can be broken in with leakage of size that is $\approx 0.5(n-j)^2 \cdot |K|$. Therefore we assume that $n-j$ is linear in n. Under this assumption we show (Theorem 1) that the key established between a pair of nodes, 1 and 2, say, remains secret even if the adversary (additionally to the information that he got by compromising the nodes) learns the value of the leakage function f on the concatenation of the internal data of all the other nodes. The maximal amount of leakage (i.e. the length of the output of f) that we can tolerate is at most $c(n-j)^2 \cdot |K|$, where c can be any constant such that $c < 0.5$. A small caveat is that the leakage function cannot depend on the identifiers[2] of the sensors 1 and 2, and hence in this sense it is non-adaptive.

Traditionally, the leakage resilience of the cryptographic schemes is measured in terms of the *relative leakage* λ that they can tolerate, which is defined as the ratio between the length of the output and the input of the leakage function. In order to talk in these terms let us assume that the parameter n is linear in m, i.e. there exists a constant α such that $n = \alpha m$. Our Theorem 1 implies (cf. Corollary 1) that the maximal achievable value of λ depends on the fraction γ of compromised nodes in the following way: $\lambda \leq c \cdot (\alpha - \gamma)^2 / \alpha$ (where c is any constant such that $c < 0.5$). Hence, e.g., if the adversary did not compromise any node then λ can be close to 0.5, if we choose α close to 1.

As highlighted above we also prove that the bound given in Theorem 1 is optimal by showing an attack that uses leakage of size $\approx 0.5(n-j)^2 \cdot |K|$. This attack actually works in a weaker model, where the sensors leak information independently, i.e. separate leakage function is applied to each sensor and the restriction on the leakage size concerns the sum of the lengths of the outputs of these functions (cf. Definition 2). The leakage functions in this attack can be chosen in advance, however they need to adaptively depend on the identifiers of the sensors, hence we call it an *adaptive model*. In Sect. 7 we show an even weaker attack (with slightly worse bounds) when the adversary does not even need to adaptive in the sense that the leakage functions do not depend on the identifiers of the sensors.

Before we present our contribution in detail we first describe formally (in Sect. 2) the Blom scheme and its security in the standard model without leakages. Then, in Sect. 3 we incorporate leakage into this model. Our main results are stated in Sect. 4 and their proofs are given in Sects. 5–6.

---

[2] In the Blom's scheme every node i has its *identifier* i that is chosen randomly and is used by the other nodes to compute the keys for communicating with i.

2 Blom's Key Distribution Scheme

In this section we give a formal definition of the Blom's scheme that was already informally introduced in Sect. 1. Let $\mathbb{F}$ denote some finite field (for instance $GF(p)$), $\mathbb{M}_n(\mathbb{F})$ and $\mathbb{S}_n(\mathbb{F})$ will denote respectively the set of all matrices and symmetric matrices of size $n \times n$ over field $\mathbb{F}$. If m is the size of the network (number of sensors participating in the protocol), then the scheme will be parameterized by n being a security parameter indicating the number of nodes which needs to get compromised before the adversary is able to break the scheme. The protocol setup requires that all secrets are being predistributed before the network is deployed. To formalize, the protocol setup for an $(\mathbb{F}, n, m)$ -*Blom scheme* (for the network size m and security parameter n) works as follows

- Central server selects publicly known identifiers $x_1, \ldots, x_m$, where each $x_i \in \mathbb{F}^n$. Nodes are labeled $1, 2, \ldots, m$ so that x_i is the identifier of the node i. Next, server chooses uniformly at random as symmetric matrix $R \in \mathbb{S}_n(\mathbb{F})$. The matrix is kept secret and will be destroyed after this step. The secret stored on device i consists of value $Rx_i \in \mathbb{F}^n$. After this step each node is associated with two values

$$(x_i, Rx_i)$$

where x_i is publicly known and Rx_i is kept secret. The network is deployed.
- If nodes i and j wish to establish a shared key, then i computes $x_j^T(Rx_i)$, whereas j computes $x_i^T(Rx_j)$.

The symmetry of R assures that

$$x_i^T R x_j = (x_i^T R x_j)^T = x_j^T R^T x_i = x_j^T R x_i$$

which guarantees that computed keys match on both sides of the channel.

It can be proven that if every n of the identifiers $x_1, \ldots, x_m$ are linearly independent, then the adversary compromising any $n-1$ of the nodes (apart from i and j of course), cannot determine the secret key which would be computed by nodes i and j. Moreover, such an adversary cannot gain any knowledge on this key. More formally, we can show [5] that

$$H(x_i^T R x_j | \text{secrets of } n-1 \text{ nodes}) = H(x_i^T R x_j)$$

where $H(\cdot)$ and $H(\cdot|\cdot)$ denote respectively the entropy and conditional entropy of a random variable. Formal proofs and extensions to conference keys can be found, for instance, in [6]. In practical applications, to ensure this notion of security, identifiers can be chosen as columns from a Vandermonde matrix (for definitions, consult for instance [28]). In this paper we will assume that the identifiers are simply uniformly and independently at random from $\mathbb{F}^n$. This, of course, can generate problems if, by accident, the selected identifiers are not linearly independent. Fortunately, the probability that this happens will be negligible and will disappear under the asymptotic notation.

3   Leakage Attacks on the Blom's Scheme

Consider a regular Blom scheme described in the previous chapter which is determined by $\mathbb{F}$, n and m being respectively the finite field, dimension of the random symmetric matrix and the number of participants. Matrix R is randomly chosen from $\mathbb{S}_n(\mathbb{F})$. Participants are receiving publicly known random identifiers $x_1, \ldots, x_m \in \mathbb{F}^n$ as well as secrets of the form Rx_i. The adversary wants to find the common key of two nodes. To simplify the exposition let us assume that these nodes are always 1 and 2, and therefore the key between them is $x_1^T R x_2 = x_2^T R x_1$.

In our work, we will consider the scheme in a general framework of the memory leakage. We allow the adversary to chose any function f and apply it to the secrets $Rx_3, \ldots, Rx_m$ giving $f(Rx_3, \ldots, Rx_m)$. The function f models an arbitrary memory leakage or an eavesdropping device which can be used on stored secrets. It is worth noticing that compromising several nodes is just a simple sub-case of the leakage function. Our results show that if the size of the image of f is *small enough*, the distribution of $x_1^T R x_2$ conditioned on the value of f is *close* to the uniform.

We wish to make our adversary adaptive, which means that it would choose the leakage function f based on the publicly known identifiers. Note that it is impossible to consider the leakage model when an adversary would be able to choose f based on all the identifiers, namely $x_1, \ldots, x_m$. Indeed, in this case, if $m > n + 2$, f could just compute R based on $Rx_3, \ldots, Rx_m$ and output $x_1^T R x_2$. Size of the image of f equals $|\mathbb{F}|$ and completely compromises the protocol, which is unacceptable. Instead, we will allow an adversary to chose f based on $x_3, \ldots, x_m$.

A part from the model in which the function f operates simultaneously on $Rx_3, \ldots, Rx_m$ we would consider the leakage model in which the adversary is choosing functions $f_3, \ldots, f_m$ operating respectively on $Rx_3, \ldots, Rx_m$. It seems that such an adversary would be significantly weaker then the one using the joint function. Our results show that it is not the case. We will also consider the non-adaptive adversary which needs to choose f before identifiers are being set up.

Our security models are incorporating both the notion of regular sensor compromising (as considered in the usual security analysis of the Blom scheme) as well as leakage functions. Next sections provide detailed descriptions of our security definitions in terms of games between an *adversary* $\mathcal{A}$ and an *oracle* Ω.

Notation.   For a random variable X we would define its support as $\mathrm{supp}(X) := \{x : \mathbb{P}(X = x) > 0\}$. We will also need a notion of *min-entropy* $H_\infty(X) := \min_{x \in \mathrm{supp}(X)} -\log(\mathbb{P}(X = x))$. Statistical distance is defined as $\Delta(X; Y) := \frac{1}{2} \sum_x |\mathbb{P}(X = x) - \mathbb{P}(Y = x)|$. By a distance to uniform distribution, conditioned on a random variable we will understand $d(X|Y) := \sum_x \mathbb{P}(Y = x) \cdot d(X|Y = x)$ where $d(X) := \Delta(X; U)$ for U uniform independent on X.

Strong Adaptive Adversary (Joint Leakage). Fix some parameters n, m, j, k and the finite field $\mathbb{F}$. There are m participants in the protocol. Consider the following game between the oracle Ω and the adversary $\mathcal{A}$.

1. $\mathcal{A}$: The adversary chooses j nodes among $3, 4, \ldots, m$ which we will call compromised. We may assume that the nodes chosen by an adversary are numbered $3, 4, \ldots, j + 2$.
2. Ω: The oracle chooses $R \in \mathbb{S}_n(\mathbb{F})$ uniformly at random. Oracle chooses $x_1, \ldots, x_m$ from $\mathbb{F}^n$ independently uniformly at random. Values of $x_3, \ldots, x_m$ are sent to $\mathcal{A}$.
3. $\mathcal{A}$: The adversary chooses a function $f : \mathbb{F}^{n(m-2)} \to \{1, \ldots, |\mathbb{F}|^k\}$.
4. Ω : The oracle sends to the adversary x_1, x_2 as well as $Rx_3, \ldots, Rx_{j+2}$ (secrets from compromised nodes) and $f(Rx_3, \ldots, Rx_m)$.

Observe that, in order to simplify the notation, we measure the size of the leakage not in terms of bits but in terms of the field elements and the function f can also be viewed as having a type $f : \mathbb{F}^{n(m-2)} \to \{0, 1\}^{k \log_2 |F|}$. For an adversary $\mathcal{A}$, by $View^{\mathcal{A}}$ we will denote the vector of values of all random variables which were observed by the adversary during its game with the oracle.

Definition 1. *We say that the $(\mathbb{F}, n, m)$-Blom scheme is strongly (j, k, ϵ) - secure if for any Adversary $\mathcal{A}$ in the game above we have that*

$$d(x_1^T R x_2 | View^{\mathcal{A}}) \leq \epsilon.$$

Weak Adaptive Adversary (Separate Leakages). The setting is the same as in the strong adversary model. The difference between this model and the strong one is in Steps 3 and 4:

3. $\mathcal{A}$: Adversary chooses a functions $f_3, \ldots, f_m$ such that $f_i : \mathbb{F}^n \to \{1, 2, \ldots, |\mathbb{F}|^{k_i}\}$ where $k_3 + \cdots + k_m \leq k$.
4. Ω : Oracle sends to the adversary x_1, x_2 as well as $Rx_3, \ldots, Rx_{j+2}$ (secrets from compromised nodes) and $f_3(Rx_3), \ldots, f_m(Rx_m)$.

Definition 2. *We say that $(\mathbb{F}, n, m)$-Blom scheme described above is weakly (j, k, ϵ)-secure if for any Adversary $\mathcal{A}$ in the game above we have that*

$$d(x_1^T R x_2 | View^{\mathcal{A}}) \leq \epsilon.$$

4   Our Results

In this section we state our main security results.

Theorem 1. *For every n consider a $(\mathbb{F}, n, m)$-Blom scheme and $j(n)$ and $k(n)$ such that $n - j(n) = \Omega(n)$. Let $c < 0.5$ be an arbitrary constant. If $k(n) \leq c(n - j(n))^2$ then the scheme is strongly $(j(n), k(n), |\mathbb{F}|^{-\Omega(n)})$-secure. Moreover the constant hidden in $\Omega(n)$ does not depend on $|\mathbb{F}|$.*

The proof of this theorem is presented in Sect. 6 and the main technical machinery is developed in Sect. 5. Observe that the leakage resilience (measured by the parameters $j(n), k(n)$ and $|\mathbb{F}|^{-\Omega(n)}$) does not depend on the number of the parties, but only on the difference between the parameters n and $j(n)$. Traditionally, the leakage resilience of a scheme is measured in terms of the relative size λ of the leakage with respect to the total size of data that can leak, which in our case is $n(m - 2)$. The following corollary of Theorem 1 serves for interpreting our result in this way. We will assume that there exists a constant α such that $n = \alpha m$, in other words: the security parameter (and hence the size of the data stored by each node) is linear in the number of sensors.

Corollary 1. *Let* $\lambda, \gamma, \alpha \in [0, 1]$ *and* $c < 0.5$ *be constants such that*

$$\lambda \leq \frac{c \cdot (\alpha - \gamma)^2}{\alpha}, \tag{1}$$

and let $\mathbb{F}$ *be an arbitrary finite field. Then for every m the* $(\mathbb{F}, n, m)$-*Blom scheme (with $n = \alpha m$) is* $(\gamma \cdot m, \lambda \cdot n(m - 2), |\mathbb{F}|^{-\Omega(n)})$-*secure.*

Proof. Let $j := \gamma \cdot m$ and $k = \lambda \cdot n(m - 2)$. It is a straightforward calculation that $k \leq c(n - j(n))^2$. Hence, by Theorem 1, the corollary is true. □

The corollary implies that, as long as the number j of compromised nodes is a constant fraction of the total number of nodes, we can tolerate a constant relative leakage λ with respect to the total size of the data. Observe that in the extreme case when no parties are compromised we have $\gamma = 0$, and hence λ is at most $c\alpha \approx \alpha/2$, which, for α close to 1, means that the relative leakage can be close to 0.5.

As mentioned in the introduction, the parameters obtained in Theorem 1 are optimal. Indeed, even if we pass to the *weak model*, the adversary can fully compromise the protocol for $k(n) \approx |\mathbb{F}|^{0.5(n-j(n))^2}$. To formalize, we can prove the following.

Theorem 2. *For every n consider a* $(\mathbb{F}, n, m)$-*Blom scheme and n and $k(n)$ such that* $k(n) = 0.5(n - j(n))(n - j(n) + 1)$. *Such scheme is not weakly* $(j(n), k(n), \epsilon)$-secure *for any* $\epsilon < 0.1$.

The proof appears in the full version of this paper [31]. Theorems 1 and 2 show together, that two considered *adaptive* models, namely models with *joint* and *separate* leakages can be considered as equivalent in terms of asymptotic security. This means that allowing the adversary to compute leakage function "mixing" the secrets stored at different nodes, gives him no significant advantage over the model in which we allow only to leakages from separate nodes. This may be viewed as counterintuitive, as one may expect that *joint leakage* model would allow to significantly reduce the leakage size necessary to compromise the protocol. The main technical tool that we use to prove Theorem 1 is the lemma that appears in the next section.

5   The Main Technical Lemma

Lemma 1. *Let X, Y be independent random vectors uniformly distributed over $\mathbb{F}^n$. If R is a random matrix uniformly distributed among $\text{supp}(R) \subset M_n(\mathbb{F})$ and independent of (X, Y), then for an arbitrary function $f : M_n(\mathbb{F}) \to \{1, \ldots, |\mathbb{F}|^k\}$ we have that*

$$d(X^T R Y | X, Y, f(R)) \leq |\mathbb{F}|^{u-n+1} + \frac{|\mathbb{F}|^{k/8n}}{|\text{supp}(R)|^{1/8n}} |\mathbb{F}|^{(n-u+7)/2}$$

for any $u < n$.

One may be tempted to think about this fact as a simple corollary from leftover hash lemma (LHL), because we can treat the variable $X^T R Y$ as coming from a family of hash functions $H_{(x,y)}(R) = x^T R y$ indexed by random choice of (x, y). It turns out that this is not the case since this hash family is only about $2/|\mathbb{F}|$ - almost universal which does not allow us to use the LHL. Trying modifications of the LHL proof using, for instance, conditioning on the rank of the random matrix R also does not seem to provide sufficiently good estimates.

Before we present our proof we need some technical tools. We start with the useful notion of an inner product extractor, then develop linear algebra lemmas and finally move towards the core of the proof.

5.1   Strong Two Source Extractors

Definition 3. *We will call a function $\text{Ext} : \mathbb{F}^n \times \mathbb{F}^n \to \mathbb{F}$ a strong (k_1, k_2, ϵ) -two-source extractor if and only if for any independent random variables X, Y in $\mathbb{F}^n$ such that $H_\infty(X) \geq k_1$ and $H_\infty(Y) \geq k_2$ we have*

$$d(\text{Ext}(X, Y) | X) \leq \epsilon.$$

If X and Y are random vectors in $\mathbb{F}^n$, then recall that by $X^T Y$ we will denote the regular dot product of vectors X and Y [10]. For $\text{Ext}(X, Y) = X^T Y$, [16] provides a simple proof of the bound on ϵ for $|\mathbb{F}| = 2$. This result can be extended to an arbitrary finite field $\mathbb{F}$ and follows easily from the work of [41].

Theorem 3 ([41]). *(Inner product extractor) The function $\text{Ext} : \mathbb{F}^n \times \mathbb{F}^n \to \mathbb{F}$ defined as $\text{Ext}(X, Y) = X^T Y$ is a strong $(k_X, k_Y, |\mathbb{F}|(2^{u-k_X} + |\mathbb{F}|^{(n+1)/2} 2^{-(u+k_Y)/2}))$-two source extractor for any $u \leq k_X$.*

5.2   Linear Algebra Tools

This section develops linear algebra tools ending with a following combinatorial lemma which is crucial for the proof of our results.

Lemma 2. *Let* $\{\mathcal{M}_v\}_{v \in \mathbb{F}^n}$ *be any family of subsets of* $\mathbb{M}_n(\mathbb{F})$ *satisfying*

$$\forall_{v \in \mathbb{F}^n} \forall_{M_1, M_2 \in \mathcal{M}_v} M_1 v = M_2 v.$$

Then

$$\sum_{v \in \mathbb{F}^n} |\mathcal{M}_v| \leq |\mathbb{F}|^4 \cdot |\mathbb{F}|^n \cdot \left| \bigcup_{v \in \mathbb{F}^n} \mathcal{M}_v \right|^{1 - 1/4n}.$$

Lemma 2 shows that sets $\mathcal{M}_v$, $v \in \mathbb{F}^n$ must be overlapping *considerably* compared to $|\bigcup \mathcal{M}_v|$. Technical proof of this lemma appears in the full version of this paper [31].

5.3   Proof of Lemma 1

Let us recall that we have set an integer n and an arbitrary function $f : \mathbb{M}_n(\mathbb{F}) \to \{1, 2, \ldots, |\mathbb{F}|^k\}$ for some k. We are given independent random variables X, Y, R such that X, Y are uniformly random vectors from $\mathbb{F}^n$ and R is random matrix chosen uniformly at random from $\mathrm{supp}(R) \subset \mathbb{M}_n(\mathbb{F})$. Let us define

$$\mathcal{M}_i = \{M \in \mathrm{supp}(R) : f(M) = i\}.$$

and note that $\sum_i |\mathcal{M}_i| = |\mathrm{supp}(R)|$. Also, let $|R| := |\mathrm{supp}(R)|$. We wish to estimate

$$d(X^T R Y | X, Y, f(R))$$

$$= \underbrace{\sum_i \left(\mathbb{P}(R \in \mathcal{M}_i) \sum_{y \in \mathbb{F}^n} \mathbb{P}(Y = y) d\left(X^T R y \middle| X, Y = y, R \in \mathcal{M}_i \right) \right)}_{(*)}$$

For a fixed y and $\mathcal{M}_i$ we may look at

$$d\left(X^T R y \middle| X, Y = y, R \in \mathcal{M}_i \right)$$

as an inner product extraction from independent random variables X and Ry, conditioned on event that $\{R \in \mathcal{M}_i, Y = y\}$. By $H_\infty^i(y)$ we will denote

$$H_\infty^i(y) := H_\infty(Ry | R \in \mathcal{M}_i).$$

Of course $H_\infty(X) = n \log(|\mathbb{F}|)$. Let us fix some $u < n \log(|\mathbb{F}|)$. Using independency of X, Y, R, Theorem 3 concerning inner product extraction gives us

$$d\left(X^T R y \middle| X, Y = y, R \in \mathcal{M}_i \right) \leq |\mathbb{F}| \left(\frac{2^u}{|\mathbb{F}|^n} + |\mathbb{F}|^{(n+1)/2} 2^{-(u + H_\infty^i(y))/2} \right)$$

Plugging this estimation into $(*)$ gives us

$$(*) \leq |\mathbb{F}| \cdot \frac{2^u}{|\mathbb{F}|^n} + \sum_i \left(\mathbb{P}(R \in \mathcal{M}_i) \sum_{y \in \mathbb{F}^n} \mathbb{P}(Y = y)|\mathbb{F}|^{(n+3)/2} 2^{-(u+H_\infty^i(y))/2} \right)$$

$$\leq |\mathbb{F}| \cdot \frac{2^u}{|\mathbb{F}|^n} + \frac{|\mathbb{F}|^{-n}}{|R|} \sum_i \left(|\mathcal{M}_i| \sum_{y \in \mathbb{F}^n} |\mathbb{F}|^{(n+3)/2} 2^{-(u+H_\infty^i(y))/2} \right)$$

$$= |\mathbb{F}| \cdot \frac{2^u}{|\mathbb{F}|^n} + \frac{|\mathbb{F}|^{-n}}{|R|} |\mathbb{F}|^{(n+3)/2} 2^{-u/2} \sum_i \left(|\mathcal{M}_i| \sum_{y \in \mathbb{F}^n} 2^{-H_\infty^i(y)/2} \right) \qquad (2)$$

Let us focus on estimating the term $\sum_i \left(|\mathcal{M}_i| \sum_{y \in \mathbb{F}^n} 2^{-H_\infty^i(y)/2} \right)$. We will use the following Holder inequality

$$\sum_i^r x_i^\alpha \leq r^{1-\alpha} \left(\sum_i^r x_i \right)^\alpha \qquad (3)$$

valid for any $0 < \alpha < 1$ and $x_i > 0$. Definition of $H_\infty^i(y)$ and Lemma 2 yield

$$\sum_i \left(|\mathcal{M}_i| \sum_{y \in \mathbb{F}^n} 2^{-H_\infty^i(y)/2} \right)$$

$$= \sum_i \left(|\mathcal{M}_i| \sum_{y \in \mathbb{F}^n} \sqrt{\max_{z \in \mathbb{F}^n} \mathbb{P}(Ry = z | R \in \mathcal{M}_i)} \right)$$

$$= \sum_i \left(\sqrt{|\mathcal{M}_i|} \sum_{y \in \mathbb{F}^n} \sqrt{\max_{z \in \mathbb{F}^n} |\{R : Ry = z\} \cap \mathcal{M}_i|} \right)$$

$$\leq |\mathbb{F}|^{n/2} \sum_i \left(\sqrt{|\mathcal{M}_i|} \cdot \sqrt{\sum_{y \in \mathbb{F}^n} \max_{z \in \mathbb{F}^n} |\{R : Ry = z\} \cap \mathcal{M}_i|} \right) \qquad (4)$$

$$\leq |\mathbb{F}|^n |\mathbb{F}|^2 \sum_i \left(|\mathcal{M}_i|^{1-1/8n} \right) \qquad (5)$$

$$\leq |\mathbb{F}|^n |\mathbb{F}|^2 |\mathbb{F}|^{k/8n} |R|^{1-1/8n} \qquad (6)$$

Inequalities (4) and (6) come from applying (3) for $\alpha = 1/2$ and $\alpha = 1 - 1/8n$ respectively. Estimation in (5) can be deduced by applying Lemma 2 to receive that

$$\sum_{y \in \mathbb{F}^n} \max_{z \in \mathbb{F}^n} |\{R : Ry = z\} \cap \mathcal{M}_i| \leq |\mathbb{F}|^4 |\mathbb{F}|^n |\mathcal{M}_i|^{1-1/4n}$$

Plugging obtained inequality (6) into (2) we receive

$$d(X^T RY | X, Y, f(R)) \leq |\mathbb{F}| \frac{2^u}{|\mathbb{F}|^n} + \frac{|\mathbb{F}|^{-n}}{|R|} \mathbb{F}^{(3n+7)/2} 2^{-u/2} |\mathbb{F}|^{k/8n} |R|^{1-1/8n}$$

$$= 2^u |\mathbb{F}|^{-n+1} + \frac{|\mathbb{F}|^{k/8n}}{|\mathrm{supp}(R)|^{1/8n}} 2^{-u/2} |\mathbb{F}|^{(n+7)/2}$$

for any $u \leq n \log |\mathbb{F}|$, which completes the proof with substitution $u := u/\log |\mathbb{F}|$.

$\square$

6   Proof of Theorem 1

Theorem 1 can be seen as a corollary from Lemma 1. We will need a following lemma, counting the number of symmetric matrices given its values on a chosen set of vectors.

Lemma 3. Let $c_1, c_2, \ldots, c_j$ and $v_1, v_2, \ldots, v_j$ be vectors such that $c_i \in \mathbb{F}^n$, $v_i \in \mathbb{F}^n$ and $j \leq n$. In this setting, either

$$\{M \in \mathbb{S}_n(\mathbb{F}) : \forall_i Mv_i = c_i\} = \emptyset$$

or

$$|\{M \in \mathbb{S}_n(\mathbb{F}) : \forall_i Mv_i = c_i\}| \geq |\mathbb{F}|^{(n-j)(n-j+1)/2}$$

Proof. The size of such set is minimal for $v_1, \ldots, v_j$ being linearly independent which we will assume from this point. We are able to choose vectors $v_{j+1}, \ldots, v_n$ so that $v_1, \ldots, v_n$ form a basis of $\mathbb{F}^n$. To uniquely determine M it is enough to set $Mv_{j+1}, \ldots, Mv_n$. Note, that

$$M \in \mathbb{S}_n(\mathbb{F}) \iff \forall_{a,b} : v_a^T Mv_b = v_b^T Mv_a.$$

This means, that if there exist $a, b \leq j$ such that $v_a^T c_b \neq v_b^T c_a$ then we fall into the first case of our lemma. Otherwise, Mv_{j+1} can be set into one of $|\mathbb{F}|^{n-j}$ ways. Indeed, $c_{j+1} := Mv_{j+1}$ must fulfill $v_a^T c_{j+1} = v_{j+1}^T c_a$ for all $a < j + 1$, which gives us a linear space of dimension $n - j$. Similarly, having set c_{j+1}, the value $c_{j+2} := Mv_{j+2}$ can be set into one of $|\mathbb{F}|^{n-j-1}$ possibilities, etc. In total we receive $|\mathbb{F}|^{(n-j)+(n-j-1)+\cdots+1}$ possibilities of choosing M which completes the proof. $\square$

Proof (of Theorem 1). Proving the Theorem 1 is equivalent to estimating

$$d\left(X_1^T RX_2 \middle| X_1, \ldots, X_m, RX_3, \ldots, RX_{j+2}, f(X_3, \ldots, X_m, RX_3, \ldots, RX_m) \right) \tag{7}$$

where $X_1, \ldots, X_m$ are m independent random vectors from $\mathbb{F}^n$, R is a random matrix from $\mathbb{S}_n(\mathbb{F})$ independent on $(X_1, \ldots, X_m)$ and f has a type $\mathbb{F}^{n(m-2)+n(m-2)} \to \mathbb{F}^k$. Denote (7) with D.

$X_1, \ldots, X_m$ are random variables denoting identifiers attached to participants. Values of $RX_3, \ldots, RX_{j+2}$ come from fully compromised nodes. One may
easily observe that the statistical distance described above indeed corresponds
to our model, as allowing the adversary to adapt to $X_3, \ldots, X_m$ is equivalent to
increasing the number of arguments of function f.

Assume that we have set $m - 2$ vectors $x_3, x_4, \ldots, x_m$, $x_i \in \mathbb{F}^n$. To shorten
notation, $R(c_3, \ldots, c_{j+2})$ will denote the event $\{Rx_3 = c_3, \ldots, Rx_{j+2} = c_{j+2}\}$.
Define $D(x_3, \ldots, x_m)$ to be equal to

$$d\left(X_1^T R X_2 \middle| X_1, X_2, Rx_3, \ldots, Rx_{j+2}, f(x_3, \ldots, x_m, Rx_3, \ldots, Rx_m) \right).$$

Obviously, this is equal to

$$\sum_{(c_3,\ldots,c_{j+2}) \in \mathbb{F}^{jn}} \mathbb{P}(R(c_3, \ldots, c_{j+2}))$$

$$\cdot d\left(X_1^T R X_2 \middle| X_1, X_2, f(x_3, \ldots, x_m, Rx_3, \ldots, Rx_m), R(c_3, \ldots, c_{j+2}) \right)$$

Lemma 3 implies, that for any $c_3, \ldots, c_{j+2}$, we receive

$$|\{a : \mathbb{P}(R = a|R(c_3, \ldots, c_{j+2})) > 0\}| = 0$$

or

$$|\{a : \mathbb{P}(R = a|R(c_3, \ldots, c_{j+2})) > 0\}| \geq |\mathbb{F}|^{(n-j)(n-j+1)/2}.$$

Also, computing $f(x_3, \ldots, x_m, Rx_3, \ldots, Rx_m)$ is equivalent to computing $g(R)$
for some $g : \mathbb{M}_n(\mathbb{F}) \to \mathbb{F}^k$. Using Lemma 1 we obtain

$$D(x_3, \ldots, x_m) \leq |\mathbb{F}|^{u-n+1} + |\mathbb{F}|^{k/8n - (n-j)(n-j+1)/16n} |\mathbb{F}|^{(n-u+7)/2}.$$

Averaging over $x_3, \ldots, x_m$ results in the same estimation for D :

$$D \leq |\mathbb{F}|^{u-n+1} + |\mathbb{F}|^{k/8n - (n-j)(n-j+1)/16n} |\mathbb{F}|^{(n-u+7)/2}.$$

Plugging $k = c(n - j)^2$ leads us to

$$D \leq |\mathbb{F}|^{u-n+1} + |\mathbb{F}|^{7/2} \exp\left\{ \log(|\mathbb{F}|) \left(\frac{n - u}{2} + \frac{(2c - 1)(n - j)^2}{16n} \right) \right\}$$

As $n - j(n) = \Omega(n)$, there is a constant j_0 such that $n - j(n) \geq j_0 n$, which gives

$$D \leq |\mathbb{F}|^{u-n+1} + |\mathbb{F}|^{7/2} \exp\left\{ \log(|\mathbb{F}|) \left(\frac{n - u}{2} - \frac{(1 - 2c)j_0^2 n}{16} \right) \right\}$$

By an arbitrary choice of $u < n$ we obtain $D = |\mathbb{F}|^{-\Omega(n)}$. $\square$

7   An Even Weaker Adversary

As described in Sect. 1 we can weaken our adversary even more (with respect to the one in the proof on Theorem 2), and the negative result will still hold (with slightly worse parameters). The definition of this new weaker model follows.

Weak Non-adaptive Adversary (Separate Leakages). The setting and the security definition is the same as in the weak adaptive model (cf. Definition 2). This only difference is that in this case the adversary will not adapt to $x_3, \ldots, x_m$. More precisely, the security game is as follows:

1. $\mathcal{A}$: Adversary chooses j nodes among $3, 4, \ldots, m$ which we will call compromised. We may assume that the nodes chosen by an adversary are numbered $3, 4, \ldots, j + 2$. Adversary chooses functions $f_3, \ldots, f_m$ such that $f_i : \mathbb{F}^n \to \{1, 2, \ldots, |\mathbb{F}|^{k_i}\}$ where $k_3 + \cdots + k_m \leq k$
2. Ω: Oracle chooses $R \in \mathbb{S}_n(\mathbb{F})$ uniformly at random. Oracle chooses $x_1, \ldots, x_m$ from $\mathbb{F}^n$ independently uniformly at random. Oracle sends to the adversary $x_1, x_2, x_3, \ldots, x_m$ as well as $Rx_3, \ldots, Rx_{j+2}$ (secrets from compromised nodes) and $f_3(Rx_3), \ldots, f_m(Rx_m)$

Definition 4. *We say that* $(\mathbb{F}, n, m)$ *scheme described above is* weakly non-adaptively (j, k, ϵ)-secure *if for any Adversary* $\mathcal{A}$ *in the game above we have*

$$d(x_1^T Rx_2 | View^{\mathcal{A}}) \leq \epsilon.$$

Theorem 4. *For every n consider a $(\mathbb{F}, n, m)$-Blom and $j(n)$ and $k(n)$ such that $k(n) = 0.5(n - j(n))(n - j(n) + 1)$. Such scheme is not weakly non-adaptively $(j(n), k(n), \epsilon)$-secure for any $\epsilon < 0.5(1 - 1/|\mathbb{F}|)^{n-1}$*

Proof of this theorem can be found in a full version of this paper [31].

In fact, in proofs of Theorem 2 as well as Theorem 4 we are *explicitly* constructing adversaries breaking the scheme with probabilities as indicated in statements. Obtained result would suggest that the scheme in the non-adaptive model cannot be yet considered as *compromised*, as $(1 - 1/|\mathbb{F}|)^{n-1}$ for growing n tends exponentially to 0. Note, however, that this term is strongly dependent on $|\mathbb{F}|$ (as we already mentioned, this is not the case in Theorem 1). In fact, for practical consideration, if we would take $|F| \approx 2 \cdot 10^9$, (32-bit integers) then even for very large $n \approx 2 \cdot 10^9$ we have

$$(1 - 1/|\mathbb{F}|)^{n-1} \approx 1/e$$

which allows us to treat this error as constant for practical applications. Thus, we may say that the leakage of size $k(n) \approx 0.5(n - j(n))^2$ compromises the protocol in practical setting and demonstrates that in practice *non-adaptive* and *adaptive* models are also equivalent in terms of security.

References

1. Akavia, A., Goldwasser, S., Hazay, C.: Distributed public key schemes secure against continual leakage. In: PODC 2012 (2012)
2. Akavia, A., Goldwasser, S., Vaikuntanathan, V.: Simultaneous hardcore bits and cryptography against memory attacks. In: Reingold, O. (ed.) TCC 2009. LNCS, vol. 5444, pp. 474–495. Springer, Heidelberg (2009)
3. Alwen, J., Dodis, Y., Wichs, D.: Leakage-resilient public-key cryptography in the bounded-retrieval model. In: Halevi, S. (ed.) CRYPTO 2009. LNCS, vol. 5677, pp. 36–54. Springer, Heidelberg (2009)
4. Anderson, R., Kuhn, M.: Tamper resistance - a cautionary note. In: The Second USENIX Workshop on Electronic Commerce Proceedings, November 1996
5. Blom, R.: Non-public key distribution. In: CRYPTO '82 (1982)
6. Blundo, C., De Santis, A., Herzberg, A., Kutten, S., Vaccaro, U., Yung, M.: Perfectly secure key distribution for dynamic conferences. Inf. Comput. **146**(1), 1–23 (1998)
7. Boyle, E., Goldwasser, S., Kalai, Y.T.: Leakage-resilient coin tossing. In: Peleg, D. (ed.) DISC 2011. LNCS, vol. 6950, pp. 181–196. Springer, Heidelberg (2011)
8. Brakerski, Z., Tauman Kalai, Y., Katz, J., Vaikuntanathan, V.: Overcoming the hole in the bucket: public-key cryptography resilient to continual memory leakage. In: FOCS 2010 (2010)
9. Chan, H., Perrig, A., Xiaodong Song, D.: Random key predistribution schemes for sensor networks. In: S&P 2003 (2003)
10. Chor, B., Goldreich, O.: Unbiased bits from sources of weak randomness and probabilistic communication complexity. SIAM J. Comput. **17**(2), 230–261 (1988)
11. Chow, S.S.M., Dodis, Y., Rouselakis, Y., Waters, B.: Practical leakage-resilient identity-based encryption from simple assumptions. In: CCS 2010 (2010)
12. Di Crescenzo, G., Lipton, R.J., Walfish, S.: Perfectly secure password protocols in the bounded retrieval model. In: Halevi, S., Rabin, T. (eds.) TCC 2006. LNCS, vol. 3876, pp. 225–244. Springer, Heidelberg (2006)
13. Dodis, Y.: Exposure-resilient cryptography. Ph.D. thesis, Massachussetts Institute of Technology, August 2000
14. Dodis, Y., Haralambiev, K., López-Alt, A., Wichs, D.: Cryptography against continuous memory attacks. In: FOCS 2010 (2010)
15. Dodis, Y., Tauman Kalai, Y., Lovett, S.: On cryptography with auxiliary input. In: STOC 2009 (2009)
16. Dodis, Y., Oliveira, R., Pietrzak, K.: On the generic insecurity of the full domain hash. In: Shoup, V. (ed.) CRYPTO 2005. LNCS, vol. 3621, pp. 449–466. Springer, Heidelberg (2005)
17. Du, W., Deng, J., Han, Y.S., Varshney, P.K., Katz, J., Khalili, A.: A pairwise key predistribution scheme for wireless sensor networks. ACM Trans. Inf. Syst. Secur. **8**(2), 228–258 (2005)
18. Dziembowski, S.: Intrusion-resilience via the bounded-storage model. In: Halevi, S., Rabin, T. (eds.) TCC 2006. LNCS, vol. 3876, pp. 207–224. Springer, Heidelberg (2006)
19. Dziembowski, S., Faust, S.: Leakage-resilient circuits without computational assumptions. In: Cramer, R. (ed.) TCC 2012. LNCS, vol. 7194, pp. 230–247. Springer, Heidelberg (2012)
20. Dziembowski, S., Pietrzak, K.: Leakage-resilient cryptography. In: FOCS 2008 (2008)

21. Dziembowski, S., Pietrzak, K., Wichs, D.: Non-malleable codes. In: ICS 2010 (2010)
22. Eschenauer, L., Gligor, V.D.: A key-management scheme for distributed sensor networks. In: CCS 2002 (2002)
23. Faust, S., Rabin, T., Reyzin, L., Tromer, E., Vaikuntanathan, V.: Protecting circuits from leakage: the computationally-bounded and noisy cases. In: Gilbert, H. (ed.) EUROCRYPT 2010. LNCS, vol. 6110, pp. 135–156. Springer, Heidelberg (2010)
24. Garg, S., Jain, A., Sahai, A.: Leakage-resilient zero knowledge. In: Rogaway, P. (ed.) CRYPTO 2011. LNCS, vol. 6841, pp. 297–315. Springer, Heidelberg (2011)
25. Gennaro, R., Lysyanskaya, A., Malkin, T., Micali, S., Rabin, T.: Algorithmic tamper-proof (atp) security: theoretical foundations for security against hardware tampering. In: Naor, M. (ed.) TCC 2004. LNCS, vol. 2951, pp. 258–277. Springer, Heidelberg (2004)
26. Gentry, C., Peikert, C., Vaikuntanathan, V.. In: STOC 2008 (2008)
27. Goldwasser, S., Rothblum, G.N.: How to compute in the presence of leakage. Electronic Colloquium on Computational Complexity (ECCC), 19:10 (2012)
28. Horn, R.A., Johnson, C.R.: Topics in Matrix Analysis. Cambridge University Press, Cambridge (1991)
29. Ishai, Y., Prabhakaran, M., Sahai, A., Wagner, D.: Private circuits II: keeping secrets in tamperable circuits. In: Vaudenay, S. (ed.) EUROCRYPT 2006. LNCS, vol. 4004, pp. 308–327. Springer, Heidelberg (2006)
30. Ishai, Y., Sahai, A., Wagner, D.: Private circuits: securing hardware against probing attacks. In: Boneh, D. (ed.) CRYPTO 2003. LNCS, vol. 2729, pp. 463–481. Springer, Heidelberg (2003)
31. Jastrzębski, M., Dziembowski, S.: Leakage resilience of the blom's key distribution scheme. Cryptology ePrint Archive (full version of this paper)
32. Juma, A., Vahlis, Y.: Protecting cryptographic keys against continual leakage. In: Rabin, T. (ed.) CRYPTO 2010. LNCS, vol. 6223, pp. 41–58. Springer, Heidelberg (2010)
33. Katz, J., Vaikuntanathan, V.: Signature schemes with bounded leakage resilience. In: Matsui, M. (ed.) ASIACRYPT 2009. LNCS, vol. 5912, pp. 703–720. Springer, Heidelberg (2009)
34. Lewko, A., Lewko, M., Waters, B.: How to leak on key updates. In: STOC 2011, New York (2011)
35. Maurer, U.M.: Conditionally-perfect secrecy and a provably-secure randomized cipher. J. Cryptol. 5(1), 53–66 (1992)
36. Micali, S., Reyzin, L.: Physically observable cryptography (extended abstract). In: Naor, M. (ed.) TCC 2004. LNCS, vol. 2951, pp. 278–296. Springer, Heidelberg (2004)
37. Naor, M., Segev, G.: Public-key cryptosystems resilient to key leakage. In: Halevi, S. (ed.) CRYPTO 2009. LNCS, vol. 5677, pp. 18–35. Springer, Heidelberg (2009)
38. European Network of Excellence (ECRYPT). Side channel cryptanalysis lounge. http://www.emsec.rub.de/research/projects/sclounge
39. Okamoto, T.: Provably secure and practical identification schemes and corresponding signature schemes. In: Brickell, E.F. (ed.) CRYPTO 1992. LNCS, vol. 740, pp. 31–53. Springer, Heidelberg (1993)
40. Pietrzak, K.: A leakage-resilient mode of operation. In: Joux, A. (ed.) EUROCRYPT 2009. LNCS, vol. 5479, pp. 462–482. Springer, Heidelberg (2009)
41. Rao, A.: An exposition of bourgain's 2-source extractor. Electronic Colloquium on Computational Complexity (ECCC) 14(034) (2007)

42. Regev, O.: On lattices, learning with errors, random linear codes, and cryptography. In: STOC 2005 (2005)
43. Shaltiel, R.: Recent developments in explicit constructions of extractors. Bull. EATCS **77**, 67–95 (2002)
44. Shamir, A.: How to share a secret. Commun. ACM **22**(11), 612–613 (1979)

Detection of Algebraic Manipulation in the Presence of Leakage

Hadi Ahmadi$^{(\boxtimes)}$ and Reihaneh Safavi-Naini

Department of Computer Science, University of Calgary, Calgary, Canada
{hahmadi,rei}@ucalgary.ca

Abstract. We investigate the problem of algebraic manipulation detection (AMD) over a communication channel that partially leaks information to an adversary. We assume the adversary is computationally unbounded and there is no shared key or correlated randomness between the sender and the receiver. We introduce leakage-resilient (LR)-AMD codes to detect algebraic manipulation in this model.

We consider two leakage models. The first model, called *linear leakage*, requires the adversary's uncertainty (entropy) about the message (or encoding randomness) to be a constant fraction of its length. This model can be seen as an extension of the original AMD study by Cramer et al. [3] to when some leakage to the adversary is allowed. We study *randomized strong* and *deterministic weak* constructions of linear (L)LR-AMD codes. We derive lower and upper bounds on the redundancy of these codes and show that known optimal (in rate) AMD code constructions can serve as optimal LLR-AMD codes. In the second model, called *block leakage*, the message consists of a sequence of blocks and at least one block remains with uncertainty that is a constant fraction of the block length. We focus on deterministic block (B)LR-AMD codes. We observe that designing optimal such codes is more challenging: LLR-AMD constructions cannot function optimally under block leakage. We thus introduce a new optimal BLR-AMD code construction and prove its security in the model.

We show an application of LR-AMD codes to tampering detection over wiretap channels. We next show how to compose our BLR-AMD construction, with a few other keyless primitives, to provide both integrity and confidentiality in transmission of messages/keys over such channels. We discuss our results and suggest directions for future research.

1 Introduction

In a basic message authentication scenario, Alice wants to deliver a message to Bob in the presence of Eve, who can arbitrarily manipulate the communication. The goal is to enable Bob to detect adversarial manipulation with high probability. This objective is achieved by appending to the message a relatively short authentication tag, calculated based on the message and a shared secret key between the legitimate parties. In the computational setting, message authentication is also attained via public key cryptography using digital signatures.

C. Padró (Ed.): ICITS 2013, LNCS 8317, pp. 238–258, 2014.
DOI: 10.1007/978-3-319-04268-8_14, © Springer International Publishing Switzerland 2014

The classical message authentication problem adopts the strong Dolev-Yao attacker model [5], which possesses complete read and write access to the communication and modifies messages arbitrarily in real-time. Keyless detection of such a powerful adversarial manipulation is impossible. When a less powerful adversary is present however, alternative solutions to keyless manipulation detection may exist. In this work, we consider a theoretical model of communication where Alice is connected to Bob through a channel whose content can be manipulated by an additive (algebraic) noise chosen by Eve. There is no shared key between Alice and Bob and the adversary is computationally unbounded.

Detection of algebraic manipulation has already been studied by Cramer et al. [3]. There, the authors assumed that the communication system keeps its content "private" and designed *algebraic manipulation detection* (AMD) codes to provide message integrity, only when the adversary cannot view the codeword. This restrictive assumption, however, makes the adversary of an oblivious nature since manipulation will be solely based on the public codebook knowledge. We relax this assumption and study leakage-resilient (LR)-AMD codes for situations where the adversary obtains partial information about the codeword.

1.1   Problem Definition and Results

An *LR-AMD* code is defined by a pair of encoding and decoding functions. When a message is encoded, the codeword is "partially" leaked to Eve. She then uses this to determine an arbitrary noise variable and adds it to the codeword. We say that decoding fails if the manipulated codeword is decoded to a message other than the original one. The LR-AMD code must satisfy *correctness* and *security*. Correctness means in the absence of noise, decoder returns the original message. Security means small decoding failure probability for a non-zero adversarial noise. The *optimality* of a code construction on the other hand is measured via *effective tag length* or *asymptotic rate*: The former is the code redundancy and the latter is the asymptotic message length divided by the code length.

We define two classes of LR-AMD codes, namely *linear* (L)LR-AMD and *block* (B)LR-AMD codes. LLR-AMD coding is an extension of AMD coding [3] to when Eve's uncertainty about the message (or code randomness) stays proportional to the length. We consider *deterministic weak LLR-AMD codes* which provide security guarantee for a randomly chosen message as well as *randomized strong LLR-AMD codes* that provide security for any message. BLR-AMD codes are for detecting algebraic manipulation in the block leakage scenario, where the message is a sequence of blocks and Eve's uncertainty for (at least) one block stays proportional to its length. We only focus on *deterministic weak* BLR-AMD codes. The leakage in LR-AMD codes is specified by *leakage rate* $0 \leq \alpha \leq 1$, i.e., the fraction of message/randomness that can be leaked in terms of min-entropy.

AMD Codes vs. LLR-AMD Codes. We show that optimal AMD code constructions work optimally as well under linear leakage. We first prove general bounds on the failure probability of AMD codes when used in the linear leakage model. Applying these results to optimal AMD constructions suggests strong

LLR-AMD constructions with the asymptotic rate of 1 and weak LR-AMD codes with the asymptotic rate of $1/(1+\alpha)$. This implies upper bounds on the effective tag lengths of weak and strong LLR-AMD code families. The more challenging question is whether the bounds can be improved, especially for weak codes. The answer is negative: We derive lower bound expressions on the effective tag lengths of LLR-AMD code constructions, which are (almost) equal to the upper bounds, thus implying the optimality of the code constructions.

BLR-AMD Codes. It is impossible to accomplish deterministic LLR-AMD with rate over $1/(1+\alpha)$, revealing that when α tends to 1 the maximum achievable rate is bounded by $1/2$. This leads us to a question whether there are reasonably interesting leakage scenarios for which deterministic AMD with higher rates (less redundancy) is possible. We consider the *block-leakage* model, described above, and introduce an efficient systematic BLR-AMD code construction that hat achieves the asymptotic rate of 1. We note that this construction can be used as a weak LLR-AMD code and also a strong LLR-AMD code by choosing part of the message string to be used for encoding randomness.

Manipulation Detection Over Wiretap Channels. In the wiretap channel [13], the sender sends a message to the receiver over the main channel, while the eavesdropper receives a noisy version via a probabilistic wiretapping channel. Wyner showed that transmission with perfect security is possible using randomized wiretap codes [13]. To protect against tampering however, one needs keyless manipulation detection which is impossible if the adversary's manipulation power is unrestricted. We thus restrict the adversary to "algebraic manipulation" over the wiretap channel. We consider a wiretap channel with noise-free main channel and u-ary erasure/symmetric wiretapping component with symbol erasure/corruption probability p. We show that the LLR-AMD codes detect algebraic manipulation when $p > 0.5$, whereas the BLR-AMD code construction protects against a wider range of p. Finally we consider the case that symbols are binary and manipulation is *"unrestricted"*, i.e., *the adversary is not limited to additive tampering and can apply all bitwise tampering functions*. We will use the following construction. Alice encodes her message using a BLR-AMD code, passes it to a Manchester encoder, and transmits the resulting codeword over the channel bit-by-bit via on-off keying. We will argue that the combination of Manchester coding and on-off keying restrict the manipulation of the adversary to algebraic ones, which can be detected with high probability by our BLR-AMD code construction. The above construction can be composed with wiretap codes to provide both privacy and manipulation detection in secret key/message transport.

1.2   Discussion and Related Work

Error Correcting Codes. Shannon's seminal work [12] provides the first formal treatment of *reliable message transmission* when the communication channel is corrupted by *probabilistic noise*. The adversarial channel model was later proposed by Hamming [10] as an alternative to Shannon's model. Existence and construction of error correcting codes over oblivious adversarial channels (corrupting up to a p-fraction of bits) has been studied in [9,11]. Our goal in this paper is *detection of errors* in adversarial channels.

Deterministic vs. Randomized Coding. We study both randomized and deterministic LR-AMD codes. Randomized coding is interesting as it allows us to detect algebraic manipulation of any messages, as opposed to a random message. But nevertheless, the study of deterministic code constructions is crucial because generating "true" randomness can be hard, e.g., for low-cost devices. When true randomness is not available but the input message itself is a (random) secret key deterministic LR-AMD coding becomes interesting.

Communication Channel Model. The application of LR-AMD codes to tampering detection over wiretap channels suites for instance a scenario where a covert adversary tries not to use high-energy jamming/overshadowing attacks to avoid the risk of being detected. This adversary rathers annihilate, amplify, and/or flip communication symbols using same energy signals. When binary modulation is used, this is translated as the four bitwise tampering functions: keep, flip, set-to-0, and set-to-1. Binary modulation is popular in many communication systems such as fiber optics.

Integrity Codes. We show an interesting application the BLR-AMD codes for message integrity over tamperable wiretap channels. Similar problem has been addressed by integrity codes [2]. We mention the main advantages of our approach over the solution in [2]. The construction of an integrity code consists of on-off keying and unidirectional coding. The authors realize that on-off keying does not prevent all 1-to-0 errors if the adversary knows the modulator carrier. They resolve this by encoding bit "1" to a long random (e.g., 48-bit [2, Sect. 4]) string. This solution however requires a lot of local secret randomness (per transmitted bit) and causes a huge bandwidth waste by drastically decreasing the transmission rate. Our approach alternatively benefits from the BLR-AMD code construction that detects 1-to-0 conversions made by bit-flipping: It does not need randomness and more importantly is much more efficient in rate.

Non-malleable Codes. Dziembowski et al. [7] introduced non-malleable (NM) codes which relax the definition of error correction and detection: non-malleability requires manipulation to result either in the original message or in an unrelated variable. NM codes have found application in algorithmic tamper-proof security [8]. Authors of [7] built an NM code construction for bitwise manipulation which takes advantage of AMD codes. This sparks the idea of using LR-AMD codes to build NM codes for leakage scenarios.

2 Notations and Preliminaries

We use calligraphic $\mathcal{X}$ and bold $\mathbf{X}$ letters to denote sets and their sizes, and use uppercase X and lowercase x letters to denote random variables and their realizations over sets. X^n indicates a sequence of length n and X_i represents its ith element. We use $\Pr_X(\mathcal{E})$ to show the probability of $\mathcal{E}$ over distribution X, and use $E_x(Y)$ to indicate the expectation of Y over choices of x. Logarithms are by default to base 2. The following definitions are used throughout the paper.

Definition 1. (Min-entropy) *For a random variable $X \in \mathcal{X}$ with distribution P_X, its min-entropy is obtained as $H_\infty(X) = -\log \max_x P_X(x)$.*

Definition 2. (Conditional min-entropy) *Given random variables $X \in \mathcal{X}$ and $Y \in \mathcal{Y}$ with joint distribution P_{XY}, the (average) conditional min-entropy of X given Y is obtained as $\tilde{H}_\infty(X|Y) = -\log(E_y(\max_x P_{X|Y}(x|y)))$.*

Definition 3. (Weak source) *A random variable X over the set $\mathcal{X}$ of size $\mathbf{X}$ is called a β -weak source if it holds $H_\infty(X) \geq \beta \log \mathbf{X}$. The source is called β-weak conditioned on the random variable Z if it holds $\tilde{H}_\infty(X|Z) \geq \beta \log \mathbf{X}$.*

3   LR-AMD Codes: Definitions

A leakage-resilient algebraic manipulation detection (LR-AMD) code is specified by a pair of encoding/decoding functions $Enc : \mathcal{M} \to \mathcal{X}$ and $Dec : \mathcal{X} \to \mathcal{M} \cup \{\bot\}$, where $\mathcal{M}$ is the message space, $\mathcal{X}$ is the additive group of the codeword space, and $\bot$ is the manipulation detection symbol. Figure 1 illustrates Alice using this code to send Bob a message M over an algebraically manipulable channel with leakage. Alice encodes $X = Enc(M)$ and sends it. The channel leaks information Z to Eve. Eve uses Z to choose $\Delta \in \mathcal{X}$ and replaces X with $Y = X + \Delta$. Bob receives Y and decodes it to $\hat{M} = Dec(Y)$. We say *decoding fails* if $\hat{M} \notin \{M, \bot\}$.

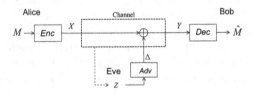

Fig. 1. Algebraic manipulation with leakage.

An LR-AMD code must satisfy *correctness* and *security*: The former means decoding of encoding of a message should return the message itself, and the latter requires negligible failure probability (when $\Delta \neq 0$). Depending on whether security is for a random message or for all messages, we define weak and strong LR-AMD codes, respectively. The random-message security for a weak LR-AMD code lets the encoding function be deterministic. In this work, we only consider "deterministic" weak LR-AMD codes. A strong LR-AMD code, however, must be randomized to work for all messages. We define two classes of LR-AMD, namely LLR-AMD and BLR-AMD, codes. Throughout, we let $0 \leq \alpha, \epsilon \leq 1$ be real values and $\mathcal{M}$, $\mathcal{R}$, and $\mathcal{X}$ be the message, randomness (if applicable), and codeword spaces of sizes $\mathbf{M} = |\mathcal{M}|$, $\mathbf{R} = |\mathcal{R}|$, and $\mathbf{X} = |\mathcal{X}|$, respectively.

3.1 LLR-AMD Codes

A linear (L)LR-AMD code guarantees security if the message/randomness min-entropy is above a certain fraction of its length given the leakage information.

Definition 4. (Weak LLR-AMD code) *The deterministic block code with encoding function $Enc : \mathcal{M} \rightarrow \mathcal{X}$ and decoding function $Dec : \mathcal{X} \rightarrow \mathcal{M} \cup \{\bot\}$ is a $(\mathbf{M}, \mathbf{X}, \alpha, \epsilon)$-weak LLR-AMD code if $\forall m : Dec(Enc(m)) = m$, and for any adversary $\mathcal{A}dv$ and variables $M \in \mathcal{M}$ and Z such that M is $(1 - \alpha)$-weak conditioned on Z, it holds:*

$$\Pr_{M, \mathcal{A}dv} \Big(Dec(Enc(M) + \mathcal{A}dv(Z)) \notin \{M, \bot\} \Big) \leq \epsilon. \tag{1}$$

The code is systematic if $Enc(M) = (M, \mathbf{Tag}(M))$ for $\mathbf{Tag} : \mathcal{M} \rightarrow \mathcal{T}$, where $\mathcal{M}$ and $\mathcal{T}$ are additive groups.

Definition 5. (Strong LLR-AMD Code) *The randomized block code with encoding function $Enc : \mathcal{R} \times \mathcal{M} \rightarrow \mathcal{X}$ and decoding function $Dec : \mathcal{X} \rightarrow \mathcal{M} \cup \{\bot\}$ is a $(\mathbf{M}, \mathbf{X}, \mathbf{R}, \alpha, \epsilon)$-strong LLR-AMD code if $\forall m : Dec(Enc(m)) = m$, and for any adversary $\mathcal{A}dv$ and variables $R \in \mathcal{R}$ and Z such that R is $(1 - \alpha)$-weak conditioned on Z,*

$$\forall m : \quad \Pr_{R, \mathcal{A}dv} \Big(Dec(Enc(R; m) + \mathcal{A}dv(Z)) \notin \{m, \bot\} \Big) \leq \epsilon. \tag{2}$$

The code is systematic if $Enc(R; M) = (M, \mathbf{Tag}(R; M))$ for some function $\mathbf{Tag} : \mathcal{R} \times \mathcal{M} \rightarrow \mathcal{R} \times \mathcal{G}$, where $\mathcal{M}$, $\mathcal{R}$, and $\mathcal{G}$ are additive groups.

Remark 1. Definitions 4 and 5 restrict leakage in terms of leftover min-entropy. This is a general form of that used by the leakage-resilient cryptography literature [6] which assumes leakage of a uniform source via a limited-length function.

For consistency with [3] when there is no leakage ($\alpha = 0$), we drop α from the notation and use $(\mathbf{M}, \mathbf{X}, \epsilon)$-weak AMD and $(\mathbf{M}, \mathbf{X}, \mathbf{R}, \epsilon)$-strong AMD codes.

3.2 BLR-AMD Codes

The block leakage model captures a scenario where the message is a sequence of (equal-sized) blocks and the leakage information leaves (at least) one message block with some leftover min-entropy proportional to its length. A BLR-AMD code is a scheme that detects algebraic manipulation with the codeword in the block leakage model. Here, we focus on deterministic weak BLR-AMD codes.

Definition 6. (BLR-AMD code) *Let $Enc : \mathcal{U}^d \rightarrow \mathcal{X}$ and $Dec : \mathcal{X} \rightarrow \mathcal{U}^d \cup \{\bot\}$ denote a deterministic block code. For $\mathbf{U} = |\mathcal{U}|$, $\mathbf{X} = |\mathcal{X}|$, $0 \leq \alpha < 1$ and $0 < \epsilon \leq 1$, the code is a $(\mathbf{U}^d, \mathbf{X}, \alpha, \epsilon)$-(weak)BLR-AMD code if for any adversary $\mathcal{A}dv$, message $M \in \mathcal{U}^d$ and leakage Z such that $\exists o \in \{1, \ldots, d\} : \tilde{H}_\infty(M_o | Z, (M_j)_{j \neq o}) \geq (1 - \alpha) \log \mathbf{U}$, the security property (1) holds.*

An instance of block leakage is when the message is a uniform secret and the adversary can observe $Z = (f_1(M_1), \ldots, f_d(M_d))$, for d arbitrary functions f_1 to f_d, provided that the sum of function lengths stays $\leq \alpha d \log \mathbf{U}$. This follows that at least one of the functions f_o should be of length $\leq \alpha \log \mathbf{U}$, satisfying the block leakage model. Another scenario where BLR-AMD codes can be used is the tamperable wiretap channel, discussed in Sect. 5.

3.3   LR-AMD Code Optimality

It is of theoretical and practical significance to design LR-AMD code constructions with flexible parameters, rather than a single code.

Definition 7. (LR-AMD code family) *A class $\mathcal{F}$ of LR-AMD codes is called an LR-AMD code family if for any integers $\kappa, \nu \in \mathbb{N}$ and real $0 \leq \alpha \leq 1$, it contains an LR-AMD code with message size $\mathbf{M} \geq 2^\nu$ and failure probability $\epsilon \leq 2^{-\kappa}$ for leakage rate α.*

We use *effective tag length* [2] and *asymptotic code rate* to measure the optimality of an LR-AMD code family in concrete and asymptotic ways, respectively.

Definition 8. (Effective tag length) *For $\kappa, \nu \in \mathbb{N}$, $0 \leq \alpha \leq 1$, the effective tag length of an LR-AMD code family $\mathcal{F}$ is $\varpi_{\mathcal{F}}^*(\kappa, \nu, \alpha) = \min_{\mathcal{F}^*} \log \mathbf{X} - \nu$ where $\mathcal{F}^* \subseteq \mathcal{F}$ has all codes with $\mathbf{M} \geq 2^\nu$ and $\epsilon \leq 2^{-\kappa}$ for leakage rate α.*

Definition 9. (Asymptotic rate) *For $0 \leq \alpha \leq 1$, the asymptotic rate of an LR-AMD code family $\mathcal{F}$ equals $Rate_{\mathcal{F}}(\alpha) = \lim_{\kappa \to \infty} \max_\nu \max_{\mathcal{F}^*} \frac{\nu}{\log \mathbf{X}}$ where $\mathcal{F}^* \subseteq \mathcal{F}$ has all codes with $\mathbf{M} \geq 2^\nu$ and $\epsilon \leq 2^{-\kappa}$ for leakage rate α.*

4   Optimal LR-AMD Constructions

4.1   LLR-AMD Code Constructions

This section aims to give optimal and efficient constructions of weak and strong LLR-AMD code families. We show that there is no need for designing new codes since an optimal AMD code construction (for no leakage) works almost optimally when there is linear leakage. We show this by (1) proving general upper-bounds on the failure probability of weak and strong AMD codes when used under linear leakage, and (2) proving lower-bounds on the effective tag length (and failure probability) of LLR-AMD code families. The former is shown below.

Theorem 1. (Appendix A) *Any $(\mathbf{M}, \mathbf{X}, \mathbf{R}, \epsilon)$-strong AMD code is a $(\mathbf{M}, \mathbf{X}, \mathbf{R}, \alpha, \mathbf{R}^\alpha \epsilon)$-strong LLR-AMD code, and any $(\mathbf{M}, \mathbf{X}, \epsilon)$-weak AMD code is a $(\mathbf{M}, \mathbf{X}, \alpha, \mathbf{M}^\alpha \epsilon)$-weak LLR-AMD code.*

We apply the above result to examples of optimal AMD code constructions. Lemma 1 shows a strong AMD construction suggested by Cramer et al. [3].

Lemma 1. [3] *Let* $\mathbb{F}$ *be a field of size* q *and characteristic* p, *and* d *be any integer such that* $d + 2$ *is not divisible by* p. *The tag generation function* $f_s :$ $\mathbb{F} \times \mathbb{F}^d \to \mathbb{F} \times \mathbb{F}$, *such that*

$$f_s(r; m) = (r \ , \ r^{d+2} + \sum_{i=1}^{d} m_i r^i)$$

gives a family of systematic $(q^d, q^{d+2}, q, \frac{d+1}{q})$-*strong AMD codes with effective tag length* $\varpi_s^*(\kappa, \nu) \leq 2\kappa + 2\log(\nu/\kappa + 3) + 2$ *when* $p = 2$.[1]

Combining Theorem 1 and Lemma 1 gives us a family of $(q^d, q^{d+2}, q, \alpha, \frac{d+1}{q^{1-\alpha}})$-strong LLR-AMD codes whose failure probability becomes arbitrarily small by choosing q sufficiently large. The effective tag length of this family, when $p = 2$, is upper bounded as

$$\varpi_s^*(\kappa, \nu, \alpha) \leq \frac{2}{1 - \alpha} (\kappa + \log(\nu/k + 3)) + 2.$$

Below, we provide an optimal weak AMD code construction, whose security is proven in Appendix B.

Theorem 2. (Appendix B) *Let* $\mathbb{F}$ *be a field of size* q *and characteristic* p, $d \in$ $\mathbb{N}$, *and* $t \in \{2, 3\}$ *be such that* $t \neq p$. *The tag generation function* $f_w : \mathbb{F}^d \to \mathbb{F}$, *such that*

$$f_w(m) = \sum_{i=1}^{d} (m_i)^t$$

gives a family of systematic $(q^d, q^{d+1}, \frac{2}{q})$-*weak AMD codes with the effective tag length* $\varpi_w^*(\kappa, \nu) \leq \kappa + 1$ *when* $p = 2$.

Applying Theorem 1 to this construction results in a family of $(q^d, q^{d+1}, \alpha,$ $\frac{2}{q^{1-\alpha d}})$-weak LLR-AMD codes. The effective tag length of this code family is generally upper bounded by $\varpi_w^*(\kappa, \nu, \alpha) \leq \frac{\kappa + \alpha\nu + 1}{1 - \alpha}$, but becomes as low as $\frac{\kappa}{1-\alpha} +$ $\alpha\nu + 3$ when $1/\alpha$ tends from below to a natural number.

Compare the effective tag lengths of the two LLR-AMD constructions. For the strong code, the tag length remains always logarithmic to ν (hence the message length) regardless of leakage rate α. For the weak code however, the tag length increases linearly with ν when $\alpha \neq 0$, and thus it cannot be negligible to the message length for arbitrarily small decoding failure. This can also be seen comparing the decoding failure probabilities $\frac{1}{q^{1-\alpha}}$ and $\frac{1}{q^{1-\alpha d}}$ for the strong and weak LLR-AMD codes: Letting these terms tend to zero, the two constructions achieve the asymptotic rates of 1 and (at most) $1/\alpha$, respectively. It is crucial to know whether the above rates are the highest achievable. We obtain a positive answer to this question by proving non-trivial (almost) tight lower bounds on the effective tag lengths of weak and strong LLR-AMD code families.

---

[1] We slightly modified the original code description [3] for consistency reasons. We used r and ν in place of x and u, respectively, and let randomness r be part of the $f_s(., .)$ function's output.

Theorem 3. (Appendix C) *Any weak, resp. strong, LLR-AMD code family $\mathcal{F}$ has an effective tag length lower bounded as*

$$\varpi_{\mathcal{F}}^*(\kappa,\nu,\alpha) \geq \max\{\frac{\kappa}{1-\alpha}-2\,,\kappa+\alpha\nu-2\}, \quad resp. \quad \varpi_{\mathcal{F}}^*(\kappa,\nu,\alpha) \geq \frac{2\kappa}{1-\alpha}-2. \quad (3)$$

The effective tag lengths of the AMD constructions (Theorem 2 and Lemma 1) closely match the lower-bound expressions. This indicates the optimality of those constructions under leakage. Again observe that unlike strong ones, weak LLR-AMD codes cannot achieve more than $1/(1+\alpha)$ asymptotic rate under linear leakage rate of α. We ask whether deterministic LR-AMD coding with higher rate (less redundancy) is possible for other leakage scenarios. This is addressed for the block leakage model in the following section.

4.2   BLR-AMD Code Construction

Theorem 4 introduces a novel deterministic BLR-AMD construction that is optimal as it achieves the asymptotic rate of 1. The construction can be also used as weak and strong LLR-AMD codes. The reason the code stays secure under block leakage is that its tag generation function is nonlinear to all message blocks, and leftover min-entropy even in one message block suffices to protect against algebraic manipulation. This is in contrast with strong LLR-AMD codes (e.g., Lemma 1) which relies only on the min-entropy of the encoding randomness.

Theorem 4. (Appendix D) *For positive integers q and (odd) d, $\mathbb{F}_{q+1}$ be a field of size $q+1$ with primitive element τ, and G be a $d \times d$ non-singular matrix over $\mathbb{Z}_q$ such that*
- each column of G consists of distinct entries, i.e., $\forall j, i, i' \neq i: g_{i,j} \neq g_{i',j}$;
- entries of G (as integers) are at most ψd for constant ψ, i.e., $\forall i, j: g_{i,j} \leq \psi d$.
The tag generation function $f_{blr} : \mathbb{Z}_q^d \to \mathbb{F}_{q+1}$, such that

$$f_{blr}(m) = \sum_{i=1}^{d} \tau^{\sum_{j=1}^{d} g_{i,j} m_j} \mod q \in \mathbb{F}_{q+1},$$

gives a systematic $(q^d, (q+1)q^d, \alpha, \frac{\psi d}{q^{1-\alpha}})$-BLR-AMD code.

Remark 2. There are possible ways to construct the matrix G in Theorem 4, e.g., using non-singular circulant matrices [4]. In Appendix H, we give one example of constructing G with $\psi = 3$ when q is prime.

The effective tag length of the above construction for $\mathbb{F}_{q+1}$ of characteristic 2 is

$$\varpi_{blr}^*(\kappa,\nu,\alpha) \leq \frac{\kappa + \log(\psi\nu/\kappa + 3)}{1-\alpha} + 3.$$

4.3   Comparing the Three Constructions

Figure 2 graphs the effective tag lengths of the three LR-AMD constructions defined by $f_s(.;.)$, $f_w(.)$, and $f_{blr}(.)$ with respect to message length parameter $2^7 \leq \nu \leq 2^{20}$, letting leakage rate $\alpha = 0.49 < 0.5$ and security parameter $\kappa = 128$. For the strong LLR-AMD and the weak BLR-AMD constructions, the tag length stays almost constant (around 520 and 260 bits, respectively). This promises the asymptotic rate of 1 when ν tends to infinity. Of course $f_s(.;.)$ bears around two times redundancy of $f_{blr(.)}$ since it carries the encoding randomness. The minimum possible tag length of the weak LLR-AMD construction, however, grows linearly with ν, leading to an asymptotic rate of 0.66.

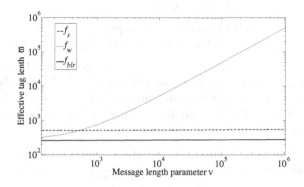

Fig. 2. Comparing the redundancies in the LR-AMD constructions ($\alpha = 0.49$).

5   Wiretap Channels: Manipulation Detection

Consider a special case of Fig. 1 when leakage is through a probabilistic wire-tapping channel. For a passive wiretapper, Wyner [13] proved that keyless private communication is possible with a slight noise over the wiretapping channel. Keyless manipulation detection however is trivially impossible if the adversary's manipulation power is not restricted. We first study "algebraic" manipulation detection over wiretap channel and next show how coding and modulation can be combined to detect "unrestricted" manipulation over this channel.

5.1   Algebraic Manipulation

We consider symmetric and erasure u-ary wiretap channels, defined as follows.

Definition 10. (SWC/EWC) *A (u,p)-symmetric wiretap channel (SWC) transmits codeword as a sequence of elements of set $\mathcal{F}_u$ of size u, such that its wiretapping component, $SC_{u,p}$, either transmits a symbol correctly with probability $1 - p$ or corrupts it, i.e., converts to it any other symbol with probability $p/(u-1)$.*

A (u,p)-erasure wiretap channel (EWC) is defined similarly, expect the wire-tapping component, $EC_{u,p}$, erases (converts to Λ) symbols instead of corrupting.

When $u = 2$, the definitions lead to the common binary wiretap channels, denoted by p-BEWC and p-BSWC. Observe that the wiretap channel is a special case of linear leakage when leakage is probabilistic, so one may use LLR-AMD codes for them. Applying the construction of Lemma 1 gives the following result.

Corollary 1. *The construction of Lemma 1 detects algebraic manipulation of any message over the (u,p)-EWC with $p > 0.5$, with failure probability*

$$\leq \min_{0.5 < \beta < p} \left(\frac{d}{q^{2\beta-1}} + q^{-\frac{(p-\beta)^2}{p \ln(u)}} \right).$$

Here d and q are defined in Lemma 1. The proof of this result is given as part of the proof for Theorem 5 below. Informally, the upper-bound is calculated as follows: Except with probability $\leq q^{-\frac{(p-\beta)^2}{p \ln(u)}}$, the erasure channel erases β fraction of symbols from the randomness R and the tag $T = f_s(R; m)$, where m is the message. This implies the leftover min-entropy of $1 - \alpha \geq (2\beta - 1) \log q$ for R, and decoding failure of $\leq \frac{d}{q^{2\beta-1}}$. Similarly, the following can be obtained for the weak LLR-AMD construction of Theorem 2.

Corollary 2. *The construction Theorem 2 detects algebraic manipulation of a uniform message over the (u,p)-EWC with $p > \frac{d}{d+1}$, with failure probability*

$$\leq \min_{\frac{d}{d+1} < \beta < p} \left(\frac{2}{q^{(d+1)\beta-d}} + q^{-\frac{(d+1)(p-\beta)^2}{2p \ln(u)}} \right).$$

Observe that when $p \leq 0.5$, the LLR-AMD code constructions provide no security guarantees regardless of the value of u. This raises the question of the possibility of tempering detection for $p \leq 0.5$. We show a positive answer through modeling the wiretap channel by block leakage, where only one message block needs to have leftover uncertainty. Theorem 5 proves that the BLR-AMD code construction of Theorem 4 detects algebraic manipulation over a wider range of EWCs, i.e., when $p > 0.5$ or $p^{p^{-1}} > u^{-1}$, which covers e.g., $p > 0.25$ for $u = 2^8$.

Theorem 5. (Appendix E) *The BLR-AMD code construction of Theorem 4, with q such that $\log_u(q + 1) \in \mathbb{N}$, detects algebraic manipulation of uniform message over the (u,p)-EWC with failure probability of at most*

$$\epsilon_{blr1} = \min_{0.5 < \beta < p} \left(\frac{\psi d}{q^{2\beta-1}} + (q + 1)^{-\frac{(p-\beta)^2}{p \ln(u)}} \right) \quad \text{for } p > 0.5, \quad \text{and} \tag{4}$$

$$\epsilon_{blr2} = \min_{\zeta < \beta < p} \left(\frac{\psi d}{q^\beta} + (q + 1)^{-\frac{(p-\beta)^2}{2p \ln(u)}} + e^{\frac{d}{(q+1)^\zeta}} \right) \quad \text{for } p^{p^{-1}} > u^{-1}, \tag{5}$$

where $\zeta = -\log_u(p) < p$.[2]

---

[2] ϵ_{blr2} can be made arbitrarily small, e.g., by choosing $d \approx q^{(\beta+\zeta)/2}$ and q sufficiently large.

Proposition 1. *Theorem 5 also holds for* (u, p')-*SWC with* $p' = (1 - u^{-1})p$ *and p given in the theorem.*

Proposition 1 holds since for the codeword X, the adversary's view $Z' = SC_{u,p'}(X)$ can be simulated from the erasure channel output $Z = EC_{u,p}(X)$ by letting $Z_i' = r$ for uniformly random $r \in \mathbb{F}_u$ when $Z_i = \Lambda$, or $Z_i' = Z_i$ otherwise.

The construction of "optimal" AMD codes remains open for wiretap channels that violate the condition on p and u in Theorem 5 and Proposition 1. This includes p-BEWC with $p < 0.5$ and p-BSWC with $p < 0.25$.

5.2   Unrestricted Manipulation

We show how the code can be used in practice to detect unrestricted manipulation over tamperable erasure/symmetric wiretap channels. To send a message to Bob, Alice (i) encodes it by the BLR-AMD construction, (ii) applies *Manchester coding*, and (iii) transmits the resulting codeword bit by bit separately using *on-off keying*. The construction does not require any sort of extra randomness (except message/key) in the system. Manchester code is a simple binary error-detecting code that appends to each bit its complement. On-off keying is a common transmission method in digital data communication (esp. fiber optics), in which bits "1" and "0" are represented by carrier wave signal's presence and absence, respectively. Because of binary communication, the adversary can only tamper with each bit using one of the four bitwise functions, i.e., keep, flip, set-to-0, and set-to-1. Proposition 2 proves that assuming certain property for on-off keying, BLR-AMD code can detect unrestricted manipulation.

Proposition 2. (Appendix F) *Let* Enc_{mn}/Dec_{mn} *be the Manchester encoding/decoding functions, and* f_{blr} *be the BLR-AMD code of Theorem 4, where* $q = 2^v - 1$ *and* $\mathbb{F}_{q+1} = GF(2^v)$. *The code* $Enc_b(m) = Enc_{mn}(m, f_{blr}(m))^3$ *and*

$$Dec_b(c) = \begin{cases} \hat{m}, & \text{if } Dec_{mn}(c) = (\hat{m}, \hat{t}) \neq \bot, \text{and } \hat{t} = f_{blr}(\hat{m}) \\ \bot, & \text{else} \end{cases}, \qquad (6)$$

has code rate almost $\frac{d}{2(d+1)}$ *and detects manipulation of uniform message over a p-BEWC (or p/2-BSWC) with* $p > 0.5$ *with failure probability at most* ϵ_{blr1} *(as in Theorem 5), if the codeword is sent via on-off keying.*[4]

It can be argued that the assumption that the on-off keying prevents the adversary from using the set-to-0 function is plausible. More details can be found in the e-print version of the paper [1, Appendix I].

---

[3] For binary transmission, assume each message block $m_i \in \mathbb{Z}_q$ is mapped to its v-bit string representation before being given to Manchester code (there would be no mapping to 1^v string).

[4] The result assumes that on-off keying prevents the adversary from using the set-to-0 function.

5.3   Wiretap Codes for Active Adversaries

We compose the construction of Proposition 2 with wiretap codes [13] for both privacy and integrity of message/key transmission over wiretap channels.

Definition 11. *The code with functions $Enc_w : \{0,1\}^t \rightarrow \{0,1\}^k$ and $Dec_w : \{0,1\}^k \rightarrow \{0,1\}^t$ is a (t, k, ϵ)-wiretap code over the p-BEWC (resp. p-BSWC) if $\forall m \in \{0,1\}^t : Dec_w(Enc_w(m)) = m$ and for uniform $M \in \{0,1\}^t$ it holds $I(M; Z)/t \leq \epsilon$, where $Z = BEC_p(Enc_w(M))$ (resp. $Z = BSC_p(Enc_w(M))$).*

Proposition 3. (Appendix G) *Let Enc_w/Dec_w denote a (t, k, ϵ)-wiretap code over the p-BEWC (resp. p/2-BSWC), for $p > 0.5$, such that $Enc_w(M)$ is uniform for uniform M. Let Enc_b/Dec_b be the code construction of Proposition 2 with $v \leq t\epsilon$. The code $Enc_{wb}(m) = Enc_b(Enc_w(m))$ and*

$$Dec_{wb}(c) = \begin{cases} Dec_w(Dec_b(c)), & Dec_b(c) \neq \perp \\ \perp, & else \end{cases}. \qquad (7)$$

is a $(t, n, 2\epsilon)$ wiretap code, with $n = \frac{2k(d+1)}{d}$, which detects manipulation of M over the p-BEWC (or p/2-BSWC) with failure probability at most ϵ_{blr1} (as in Theorem 5), if the codeword is sent via on-off keying.

Known results give (t, k, ϵ)-wiretap code constructions over p-BEWC (resp. p-BSWC) with arbitrarily small $\epsilon > 0$ and of rate arbitrarily close to p (resp. $h(p) = -p\log(p) - (1-p)\log(1-p))$ [13]. The above code construction achieves rates arbitrarily close to $(p)/2$ (resp. $h(p)/2$) and provides both privacy and integrity of transmission with arbitrarily small failure probability.

6   Conclusion

The AMD study in linear and block leakage models captures interesting scenarios of reliable communication in the presence of an adversary who receives arbitrary but bounded leakage about the communication. We proved optimal LLR-AMD and BLR-AMD constructions and showed an application of these codes to manipulation detection over wiretap channels. This work raises a number of directions to future work. These include manipulation detection over more general wiretap channels and finding applications of LR-AMD codes to other areas of cryptography. An example of the latter is adding robustness to non-perfect secret sharing schemes, which is a subject of our ongoing work.

A   Proof of Theorem 1: LLR-AMD

We prove the theorem for strong AMD codes (similar proof can be given for weak AMD codes). Let Enc/Dec denote a $(\mathbf{M}, \mathbf{X}, \mathbf{R}, \epsilon)$-strong AMD code. The security property implies (when there is no leakage)

$$\forall m: \quad \max_{\delta} \Pr_{R}(Dec(Enc(R; m) + \delta) \notin \{m, \perp\}) \leq \epsilon, \qquad (8)$$

where R is the uniform randomness of the encoder. For any m and δ, define $\mathcal{R}_{fail}(m, \delta) \subseteq \mathcal{R}$ as the set of r values that lead to the verification failure, by satisfying $Dec(Enc(R; m) + \delta) \notin \{m, \perp\}$. Since R is uniform, the probability that $R \in \mathcal{R}_{fail}(m, \delta)$ equals to $|\mathcal{R}_{fail}(m, \delta)|/\mathbf{R}$; thus, to write (8) as $\forall m : \max_\delta |\mathcal{R}_{fail}(m, \delta)| \leq \epsilon \mathbf{R}$. Let Z be any random variable such that the randomness R is $(1 - \alpha)$-weak conditioned on Z for $0 \leq \alpha \leq 1$, i.e., $E_z \left(\max_r \Pr(R = r | Z = z) \leq \mathbf{R}^{\alpha-1} \right)$. For any message m, the probability of failure when Z is leaked to the adversary $\mathcal{A}dv$ is upper bounded as

$$\Pr(Dec(Enc(R; m) + \mathcal{A}dv(Z)) \notin \{m, \perp\}) = E_z \left(\Pr(Dec(Enc(R; m) + \mathcal{A}dv(z)) \notin \{m, \perp\} | Z = z) \right)$$

$$\leq E_z \left(\max_\delta \Pr(R \in \mathcal{R}_{fail}(m, \delta) \mid Z = z) \right) \leq E_z \left(\max_\delta |\mathcal{R}_{fail}(m, \delta)| \max_r \Pr(R = r | Z = z) \right)$$

$$= \max_\delta |\mathcal{R}_{fail}(m, \delta)| \; E_z \left(\max_r \Pr(R = r | Z = z) \right) \leq \epsilon \mathbf{R}^\alpha.$$

B   Proof of Theorem 2: Weak AMD

We shall show that for the uniform message $M \in \mathbb{F}^d$ and any $(\delta_m, \delta_t) \in \mathbb{F}^d \times \mathbb{F}$ such that $\delta_m \neq 0$, it holds $\Pr_M (f_w(M + \delta_m) = f_w(M) + \delta_t) \leq \frac{2}{q}$. Since $\delta_m = (\delta_{m,1}, \ldots, \delta_{m,d}) \neq 0$, there exists at least non-zero one element $\delta_{m,o} \neq 0$ for $1 \leq o \leq d$. This lets us write the term $f_w(M + \delta_m) - f_w(M) - \delta_t$ as a polynomial of degree $t - 1$ with respect to the variable M_o, i.e., $Poly(M_o) \triangleq$

$$f_w(M + \delta_m) - f_w(M) - \delta_t = \left[\sum_{i=1}^d (M_i + \delta_{m,i})^t - M_i^t \right] - \delta_t = \sum_{j=1}^t \binom{t}{j} \delta_{m,o}^j M_o^{t-j} + a_0,$$

where $a_0 = \left[\sum_{i=1, i \neq o}^d (M_i + \delta_{m,i})^t - M_i^t \right] - \delta_t$ is the constant term. For any values of $(M_i)_{i \neq o}$, hence fixed a_0, the polynomial $Poly(M_o)$ evaluates to zero for at most $t - 1 \leq 2$ (out of q) values of M_o. The polynomial thus becomes zero with probability at most $(t-1)/q \leq 2/q$, implying the failure probability bound.

The effective tag length of this code family when $p = 2$ is obtained as follows. For integers $\kappa, \nu \in \mathbb{N}$, let $q = 2^{\kappa+1}$ and $d = \lceil \nu / \log q \rceil$ so that both $\epsilon = 2/q \leq 2^{-\kappa}$ and $|\mathcal{F}^d| = q^d \geq 2^\nu$ are satisfied. By restricting the source space $\mathcal{F}^d$ to only $M = 2^\nu$ elements the code range will also reduce to $\mathbf{X} = q2^\nu$ elements in $\mathcal{F}^{d+1}$. This leads to $\log \mathbf{X} - \nu = \nu + \log q - \nu = \kappa + 1$.

C   Proof of Theorem 3: Tag Length

The proof relies on the results of the following lemma.

Lemma 2. *For any weak, resp. strong, LLR-AMD code the failure probability is lower bounded as*

$$\epsilon \geq \max\left\{\left((1-e^{-1})\frac{\mathbf{M}-1}{\mathbf{X}-1}\right)^{1-\alpha}, \ (1-e^{-1})\mathbf{M}^{\alpha}\frac{\mathbf{M}-1}{\mathbf{X}-1}\right\}, \tag{9}$$

$$resp. \quad \epsilon \geq \left((1-e^{-1})\frac{\mathbf{M}-1}{\mathbf{X}-1}\right)^{(1-\alpha)/2}. \tag{10}$$

Proof. We start by the $(\mathbf{M}, \mathbf{X}, \alpha, \epsilon)$-weak LLR-AMD code. We shall show that for any such code there exists a message distribution $M \in \mathcal{M}$, a leakage variable Z with $\tilde{H}_\infty(M|Z) \geq (1-\alpha)\log\mathbf{M}$, and an adversary whose success chance in changing M is lower bounded by (9). We choose M to be uniform and Z to be an $\alpha\log\mathbf{M}$-bit string that represents answers to the adversary's $\alpha\log\mathbf{M}$ questions about the codeword. The variable Z is such that each bit Z_i is defined by $Z_i = Query_i(Z_1^{i-1}, M)$, where $Query_i$ shows the ith question. Let $X = Enc(M)$ be the codeword for M. The adversary can choose any non-zero adversarial noise $\delta \in \mathcal{X}/\{0\}$ to be added to the X. There are $n = \mathbf{X}-1$ values for δ, at least $t = M-1$ of which lead to valid codewords $X+\delta$. Let $\mathcal{X}^+$ be the set of such valid δ values. If the adversary picks δ randomly, her success chance will be $\geq t/n$. We now describe the adversary's strategy as follows. She first chooses a random subset $\mathcal{H}_0 \subseteq \mathcal{X}/\{0\}$ of size $k = n/t$ and runs the following algorithm.

$\mathcal{H} \leftarrow \mathcal{H}_0$.
for $(i = 1$ to $\alpha\log\mathbf{M})$
    Partition $\mathcal{H}$ arbitrarily to $\mathcal{H}_1$ and $\mathcal{H}_2$ of (almost) equal sizes.
    Set $Z_i \leftarrow$ whether $|\mathcal{H}_1 \cap \mathcal{X}^+| > 0$.
if $Z_i = 1$ (Yes) **then** $\mathcal{H} \leftarrow \mathcal{H}_1$.
else $\mathcal{H} \leftarrow \mathcal{H}_2$.
return δ that is randomly chosen from $\mathcal{H}$.

The size of $\mathcal{H}$ at the end of the algorithm decreases to $k/\mathbf{M}^\alpha$. The adversary succeeds with probability $\mathbf{M}^\alpha/k$ if and only if $\mathcal{H}_0 \cap \mathcal{X}^+$ is not empty, whose probability is obtained as

$$\Pr(|\mathcal{H}_0 \cap \mathcal{X}^+| > 0) = 1 - \Pr(|\mathcal{H}_0 \cap \mathcal{X}^+| = 0) = 1 - \frac{\binom{n-t}{k}}{\binom{n}{k}}$$

$$= 1 - \frac{(n-k) \times \cdots \times (n-k-t)}{n \times \cdots \times (n-t)} \geq 1 - (1-k/n)^t = 1 - (1-1/t)^t \geq 1 - e^{-1}.$$

This concludes the adversary's success probability is at least $\epsilon \geq (1-e^{-1})\mathbf{M}^\alpha/k = (1-e^{-1})\mathbf{M}^\alpha\frac{\mathbf{M}-1}{\mathbf{X}-1}$, which is the second term of (9). For the first term, we use the fact that the message size $\mathbf{M}$ is such that after $\alpha\log\mathbf{M}$ questions the adversary cannot guess the correct message with probability more than ϵ, and this implies $\mathbf{M}^{1-\alpha} \geq 1/\epsilon$. We use this to write (noting that $0 \leq \alpha \leq 1$)

$$\epsilon^{1/(1-\alpha)} \geq (1-e^{-1})\frac{\mathbf{M}-1}{\mathbf{MT}-1} \implies \epsilon \geq \left((1-e^{-1})\frac{\mathbf{M}-1}{\mathbf{X}-1}\right)^{1-\alpha}.$$

A similar argument can be used for the $(\mathbf{M}, \mathbf{X}, \mathbf{R}, \alpha, \epsilon)$-strong LLR-AMD code: For uniform randomness R and the variable Z such that $\tilde{H}_\infty(R|Z) \geq (1-\alpha)\log\mathbf{R}$, the adversary can use a similar strategy to Algorithm 1 with $\alpha\log\mathbf{R}$

questions to achieve the success chance of $\epsilon \geq (1 - e^{-1})\mathbf{R}^\alpha \frac{\mathbf{R}(\mathbf{M}-1)}{\mathbf{X}-1}$, noting that there are at least $\mathbf{R}(\mathbf{M} - 1)$ valid δ values in $\mathcal{H}_0$. In a strong LLR-AMD code, the adversary is assumed to know the message. So the randomness size $\mathbf{R}$ should be large enough to satisfy $\mathbf{R}^{1-\alpha} \geq 1/\epsilon$. Combining this with the above shows the following for $0 \leq \alpha \leq 1$ which proves (10).

$$\epsilon^{2/(1-\alpha)} \geq (1 - e^{-1})\frac{\mathbf{M}-1}{\mathbf{X}-1} \implies \epsilon \geq \left((1 - e^{-1})\frac{\mathbf{M}-1}{\mathbf{X}-1}\right)^{(1-\alpha)/2}. \qquad \square$$

We use (9) to bound the effective tag length of weak AMD code families as

$$\log \mathbf{X} - \nu \geq \log \frac{\mathbf{X}}{\mathbf{M}} = \log\left(\frac{\mathbf{X}}{\mathbf{M}-1} \times \frac{\mathbf{M}-1}{\mathbf{M}}\right) \geq \log \frac{\mathbf{X}-1}{\mathbf{M}-1} + \log(1 - \mathbf{M}^{-1})$$

$$\geq \max\{\frac{1}{1-\alpha}\log\frac{1}{\epsilon}, \ \log\frac{1}{\epsilon} + \alpha\log\mathbf{M}\} + \log(1 - e^{-1}) + \log(1 - \mathbf{M}^{-1})$$

$$\geq \max\{\frac{\kappa}{1-\alpha}, \ \kappa + \alpha\nu\} - 2.$$

Similarly, (10) is used to bound the effective tag length of strong code families

$$\log \mathbf{X} - \nu \geq \frac{2}{1-\alpha}\log\frac{1}{\epsilon} + \log(1 - e^{-1}) + \log(1 - \mathbf{M}^{-1}) \geq \frac{2\kappa}{1-\alpha} - 2.$$

D   Proof of Theorem 4: BLR-AMD

The code construction Enc_{blr}/Dec_{blr} is systematic, so we only need to show the security property. Let the message $M \in \mathbb{Z}_q^d$ and Z follow the block leakage model such that for some $o \in \{1, \ldots, d\}$ it holds that $\tilde{H}_\infty(M_o|Z, (M_j)_{j\neq o}) \geq (1-\alpha)\log q$. The decoding failure probability when Z is leaked to the adversary Adv is upper bounded as

$$\Pr_M(Dec_{blr}(Enc_{blr}(M) + Adv(Z)) \notin \{M, \bot\})$$

$$= E_z\left(\Pr_M(Dec_{blr}(Enc_{blr}(M) + Adv(z)) \notin \{M, \bot\}|Z = z)\right)$$

$$\leq E_z\left(\max_\delta \Pr_M(Dec_{blr}(Enc_{blr}(M) + \delta) \notin \{M, \bot\}|Z = z)\right)$$

$$\overset{(b)}{=} E_z\left(\max_{\delta_m \neq 0, \delta_t} E_{(m_j)_{j\neq o}|Z=z}\left(\Pr_{M_o}(f_{blr}(M + \delta_m) = f_{blr}(M) + \delta_t|Z = z, (M_j = m_j)_{j\neq o})\right)\right)$$

$$(11)$$

Equality (a) follows from the law of total probability and the systematic construction of the BLR-AMD code. For fixed $(M_j = m_j)_{j\neq o} \in \mathbb{Z}_q^{d-1}$, $\delta_m \in \mathbb{Z}_q^d$, and $\delta_t \in \mathbb{F}_{q+1}$, we write the term $f_{blr}(M + \delta_m) - f_{blr}(M) - \delta_t$ as

$$\sum_{i=1}^d \left[\tau^{\sum_j g_{i,j}(M_j + \delta_{m,j})} - \tau^{\sum_j g_{i,j}M_j}\right] - \delta_t = \sum_{i=1}^d \left[\left(\tau^{\sum_j g_{i,j}\delta_{m,j}} - 1\right)\tau^{\sum_{j\neq o} g_{i,j}m_j}\tau^{g_{i,o}M_o}\right]$$

$$- \delta_t = \sum_{i=1}^d \left[a_i Y^{g_{i,o}}\right] + a_0 \overset{\triangle}{=} P_{\delta,(m_j)_{j\neq o}}(Y), \qquad (12)$$

letting $a_0 = -\delta_t$, $Y = \tau^{M_o}$, and a_i be the coefficient of $Y^{g_{i,o}}$ in the summation, i.e., $a_i = \left(\tau^{\sum_j g_{i,j}\delta_{m,j}} - 1\right)\tau^{\sum_{j\neq o} g_{i,j}m_j}$. Applying this to (11), we need to find an upper-bound on

$$E_z\left(\max_{\delta_m\neq 0,\delta_t} E_{(m_j)_{j\neq o}|Z=z}\left(\Pr_{M_o}(P_{\delta,(m_j)_{j\neq o}}(Y) = 0|Z = z, (M_j = m_j)_{j\neq o})\right)\right). \quad (13)$$

The polynomial $P_{\delta,(m_j)_{j\neq o}}(Y)$ is of degree at most $\max_i(g_{i,o}) \leq \psi d$ over $\mathbb{F}_{q+1}$. Lemma 3 shows that the polynomial is non-constant since it has at least one non-zero coefficient.

Lemma 3. *For any choice of message blocks* $(M_j = m_j)_{j\neq o}$, $\delta_m \neq 0$, *and* δ_t, *the polynomial* $P_{\delta,(m_j)_{j\neq o}}(Y)$ *has at least one non-zero coefficient.*

Proof. We prove the claim by contradiction. Assume that all a_i's are zero, implying (τ is a primitive element in $\mathbb{F}_{q+1}$)

$$\forall 1 \leq i \leq d: \quad \left(\tau^{\sum_j g_{i,j}\delta_{m,j}} - 1\right)\tau^{\sum_{j\neq o} g_{i,j}m_j} = 0 \in \mathbb{F}_{q+1} \Rightarrow \sum_{j=1}^{d} g_{i,j}\delta_{m,j} = 0 \in \mathbb{Z}_q.$$

The above can be written as $\delta_m.G = 0$ over $\mathbb{Z}_q$, which holds only if $\delta_m = 0$ as G is non-singular. This contradicts the adversarial assumption $\delta_m \neq 0$. $\square$

For any δ (such that $\delta_m \neq 0$) and $(M_j = m_j)_{j\neq o}$, at most ψd values of Y (hence M_o) make the polynomial evaluate to zero. Let $\mathcal{M}_{o,fail}(\delta,(m_j)_{j\neq o})$ of size at most ψd be the set of such M_o values that lead to decoding failure, implying

$$P_{\delta,(m_j)_{j\neq o}}(Y) = 0 \iff M_o \in \mathcal{M}_{o,fail}(\delta,(m_j)_{j\neq o}).$$

We prove security by upper-bounding the failure probability (13) as follows.

$$E_z\left(\max_{\delta_m\neq 0,\delta_t} E_{(m_j)_{j\neq o}|Z=z}\left(\Pr_{M_o}(P_{\delta,(m_j)_{j\neq o}}(Y) = 0|Z = z, (M_j = m_j)_{j\neq o})\right)\right)$$

$$= E_z\left(\max_{\delta_m\neq 0,\delta_t} E_{(m_j)_{j\neq o}|Z=z}\left(\Pr_{M_o}(M_o \in \mathcal{M}_{o,fail}(\delta,(m_j)_{j\neq o})|Z = z, (M_j = m_j)_{j\neq o})\right)\right)$$

$$\leq E_z\left(\max_{\delta_m\neq 0,\delta_t} E_{(m_j)_{j\neq o}|Z=z}\left(|\mathcal{M}_{o,fail}(\delta,(m_j)_{j\neq o})|\max_{m_o}\Pr_{M_o}(M_o = m_o|Z = z, (M_j = m_j)_{j\neq o})\right)\right)$$

$$\overset{(a)}{\leq} \psi d E_z\left(\max_{\delta_m\neq 0,\delta_t} E_{(m_j)_{j\neq o}|Z=z}\left(\max_{m_o}\Pr_{M_o}(M_o = m_o|Z = z, (M_j = m_j)_{j\neq o})\right)\right)$$

$$\overset{(b)}{=} \psi d E_z\left(E_{(m_j)_{j\neq o}|Z=z}\left(\max_{m_o}\Pr_{M_o}(M_o = m_o|Z = z, (M_j = m_j)_{j\neq o})\right)\right)$$

$$\overset{(c)}{=} \psi d E_{z,(m_j)_{j\neq o}}\left(\max_{m_o}\Pr_{M_o}(M_o = m_o|Z = z, (M_j = m_j)_{j\neq o})\right)$$

$$\overset{(d)}{\leq} \frac{\psi d}{q^{1-\alpha}}.$$

Inequality (a) holds since we have $|\mathcal{M}_{o,fail}(\delta,(m_j)_{j\neq o})| \leq \psi d$, equality (b) is attained by removing $\max_\delta$ as the expression has become independent of this parameter, equality (c) uses the law of total probability, and inequality (d) follows the assumption that $\tilde{H}_\infty(M_o|Z,(M_j)_{j\neq o}) \geq (1-\alpha)\log q$.

E   Proof of Theorem 5

For uniform message $M \in \mathbb{Z}_q^d$, let $T = f_{blr}(M) \in \mathbb{F}_{q+1}$ denote the tag calculated by the BLR-AMD code and $X = (M, T) = (X_1, \ldots, X_{d+1})$ denote the codeword. Let $\eta = \log_u(q+1) \in \mathbb{N}$. For the purpose of u-ary transmission over (u, p)-EWC, we replace each message block in the codeword by a sequence of η symbols over $\mathcal{F}_u$; hence, each codeword element X_i consists of η channel symbols. The theorem provides two bounds, namely ϵ_{blr1} (4) and ϵ_{blr2} (5), on the BLR-AMD detection failure probability under two different conditions of $p > 0.5$ and $p^{p^{-1}} > u^{-1}$, respectively. To prove the two bounds, we provide different approaches to bounding the failure probability of the code.

Approach 1: Proving ϵ_{blr1} in (4) for $p > 0.5$. Considering $0.5 < \beta < p$, any message block M_o for $o \in \{1, \ldots, d\}$, and the tag T, we shall study two events: $\mathcal{E}_1$ that the channel leakage leaves $(2\beta - 1) \log(q)$ bits of leftover min-entropy in M_o and $\mathcal{E}_2$ that the BLR-AMD decoder detects adversarial tampering (assuming $\mathcal{E}_1$ holds). The failure probability will be then bounded as $\epsilon_{blr1} \leq \Pr(\overline{\mathcal{E}_1}) + \Pr(\overline{\mathcal{E}_2})$.

Let η_o and η_t be the numbers of symbols erased from M_o and T, respectively. We have from the chain rule of min-entropy

$$\tilde{H}_\infty(M_o | Z, (M_i)_{i \neq o}) \geq \tilde{H}_\infty(M_o | (M_i)_{i \neq o}) - (\eta - \eta_t)\log(u) = (\frac{\eta_o + \eta_t}{\eta} - 1)\log(q).$$

Noting that $\Pr(\overline{\mathcal{E}_1}) = \Pr(\eta_o + \eta_t < 2\beta\eta)$, we obtain this probability as

$$\Pr(\overline{\mathcal{E}_1}) = \sum_{i=0}^{\lfloor 2\beta\eta \rfloor} \binom{2\eta}{i} p^i (1-p)^{2\eta - i} \leq e^{-\frac{(p-\beta)^2}{2p}2\eta} = e^{-\frac{(p-\beta)^2}{p}\log_u(q+1)} = (q+1)^{-\frac{(p-\beta)^2}{p\ln(u)}},$$

where the inequality follows the Chernoff bound. When $\mathcal{E}_1$ holds, the leftover min-entropy of M_o shows the uncertainty rate of $1 - \alpha \geq 2\beta - 1$. From Theorem 4, the BLR-AMD decoder fails with probability $\Pr(\overline{\mathcal{E}_2}) \leq \frac{\psi d}{q^{2\beta - 1}}$. Proof is completed.

Approach 2: Proving ϵ_{blr2} in (5) for $p^{p^{-1}} > u^{-1}$. The condition on p implies $p > \zeta$ for $\zeta = \log_u(1/p)$. Choosing $\zeta < \beta < p$, we consider three events: $\mathcal{E}_1$ that there is (at least) one message block M_o, $o \in \{1, \ldots, d\}$ that is completely erased, $\mathcal{E}_2$ that at least $\beta\eta$ symbols are erased from the tag T, and $\mathcal{E}_3$ that the BLR-AMD decoder detects adversarial tampering (assuming that $\mathcal{E}_1$ and $\mathcal{E}_2$ hold). The overall failure probability is bounded as $\epsilon_{blr2} \leq \Pr(\overline{\mathcal{E}_1}) + \Pr(\overline{\mathcal{E}_2}) + \Pr(\overline{\mathcal{E}_3})$.

A message block M_i is completely erased with probability $p' \geq p^\eta = p^{\log_u(q+1)} = (q+1)^{\log_u(p)} = (q+1)^{-\zeta}$. This implies $\Pr(\overline{\mathcal{E}_1}) = (1 - p')^d \leq e^{-p'd} = e^{-\frac{d}{(q+1)^\zeta}}$. On the other hand, $\mathcal{E}_2$ holds except with probability

$$\Pr(\overline{\mathcal{E}_2}) = \sum_{i=0}^{\lfloor \beta\eta \rfloor} \binom{\eta}{i} p^i (1-p)^{2\eta - i} \leq e^{-\frac{(p-\beta)^2}{2p}\eta} = (q+1)^{-\frac{(p-\beta)^2}{2p\ln(u)}}.$$

Provided that $\mathcal{E}_1$ and $\mathcal{E}_2$ holdd, the leftover min-entropy of M_o is bounded as

$$\tilde{H}_\infty(M_o | Z, (M_i)_{i \neq o}) \geq \tilde{H}_\infty(M_o | (M_i)_{i \neq o}) - (1 - \beta)\eta\log(u) = \beta\log(q),$$

which implies the uncertainty rate of $1 - \alpha \geq \beta$ and BLR-AMD decoding failure probability of $\Pr(\bar{\mathcal{E}}_3) \leq \frac{\psi d}{q^\beta}$ (from Theorem 4). This completes the proof.

F   Proof of Proposition 2

The code rate $\frac{d}{2(d+1)}$ comes from the product of rates of the Manchester and the BLR-AMD codes. We show that the failure probability is precisely that of the BLR-AMD code over p-BEWC (or $p/2$-BSWC), which equals ϵ_{blr1} for $p > 0.5$. We show this by discussing that using on-off keying and Manchester coding causes a bitwise manipulation adversary to be either detected or behave like an additive (keep and flip) adversary, whose manipulation is detected by the BLR-AMD code from Theorem 5. For message M, we denote the n-bit codeword $X = Enc_b(M)$, where $n = 2(d+1)v$, by $X = (X_1, X_2, \ldots, X_n)$.

On-off keying prevents the adversary from set-to-0 tampering [1, Appendix I]. She thus remains with keep, flip, and set-to-1 functions. Considering such an adversary, let $Tamp_A = (t_1, t_2, \ldots, t_n)$ be the sequence of bit-manipulation functions over the set of keep, flip, and set-to-1. We claim that $Dec_{mn}(Tamp_A(X)) \in \{\perp, Dec_{mn}(Tamp_S(X))\}$, where $Tamp_S = (t'_1, t'_2, \ldots, t'_n)$ is an "additive" manipulation sequence such that $\forall 1 \leq i \leq n/2 : (t'_{2i-1}, t'_{2i}) =$

$$\begin{cases} (\text{keep, keep}), & (t_{2i-1}, t_{2i}) \in \{(\text{keep, set-to-1}), (\text{set-to-1, keep}), (\text{set-to-1, set-to-1})\} \\ (\text{flip, flip}), & (t_{2i-1}, t_{2i}) \in \{(\text{flip, set-to-1}), (\text{set-to-1, flip})\} \qquad (14) \\ (t_{2i-1}, t_{2i}), & \text{else} \end{cases}$$

We consider the case where $Dec_{mn}(Tamp_A(X)) \neq \perp$ since otherwise we are done with the proof. For every $1 \leq i \leq n/2$, the pair of codeword bits (X_{2i-1}, X_{2i}) are either 01 or 10. We prove the claim by showing in both of these cases $(t'_{2i-1}(X_{2i-1}), t'_{2i}(X_{2i})) = (t_{2i-1}(X_{2i-1}), t_{2i}(X_{2i}))$. We show the equality for $(X_{2i-1}, X_{2i}) = 01$ and the other case can be argued similarly: The equality holds trivially from (14) if the pair (t_{2i-1}, t_{2i}) does not include any set-to-1 function; if not, the only valid options are $(t_{2i-1}, t_{2i}) \in \{(\text{keep, set-to-1}), (\text{set-to-1, flip})\}$ for which the equality again holds.

G   Proof of Proposition 3

For parameters d and v of the BLR-AMD code, let $n = 2(d+1)v$ and $k = dv$. The codeword $C = Enc_{wb}(M)$ is obtained by applying three encoding functions sequentially. The first (wiretap) encoding gives $X = Enc_w(M) \in \{0,1\}^k$ which is uniform for the uniform message $M \in \{0,1\}^t$. The second (BLR-AMD) encoding gives $Y = (X, f_{blr}(X)) \in \{0,1\}^{n/2}$, and the third (Manchester) encoding results in $C = Enc_{mn}(Y)$. The code rate is $t/n = (td)/(2k(d+1))$. The detection failure probability equals that of the code Enc_b/Dec_b and uniformity of X (see Proposition 2). It remains to prove the privacy property of the code.

We prove privacy for p-BEWC (noting that it also works for $p/2$-BSWC). Manchester encoder Enc_{mn} appends to each bit of Y its negation. If both a bit and its negation are erased by p-BEWC (which occurs with probability $p' = p^2$), Eve cannot discover the bit. This implies that Eve's view $Z = BEC_p(C)$ can be built from $Z' = BEC_{p'}(Y)$, i.e., the view over the p'-BEC without Manchester coding. We thus remove Manchester coding and assume that Eve's view is $Z' = (Z'_1, Z'_2)$, where $Z'_1 = BEC_{p'}(X)$ and $Z'_2 = BSC_{p'}(f_{blr}(X))$. We conclude

$$I(M; Z) = I(M; Z'_1, Z'_2) = I(M; Z'_1) + I(M; Z'_2 | Z'_1) \le I(M; Z'_1) + H(Z'_2)$$
$$\le I(M; Z'_1) + (n/2 - k) \le I(M; Z'_1) + v \quad \Rightarrow \quad I(M; Z)/t \le \epsilon + v/t \le 2\epsilon.$$

H   Non-singular Matrix Construction

Let H be a $d \times d$ diagonal matrix over (field) $\mathbb{Z}_q$, where q is prime and $d < 3q$, with entries $H_{i,i} = i$ for $1 \le i \le d$. The following algorithm converts H into a non-singular matrix that has non-identical entries in each and every column. It is easy to show that the value of s is always upper bounded by $2i$ and thus at the end, all entries in resulting matrix are less or equal to $2d + d = 3d$.

> $G \leftarrow H$
> **for** $(j = 1$ to $d - 1)$
> > Add column j of G to its column $j + 1$.
> $s \leftarrow 2$
> **for** $(i = 2$ to $d)$
> > **while** $(s$ equals any entry of G up to row $i - 1)$
> > > $s \leftarrow s + 1$
> > Add s times the first row of G to row i.
> **return** G

References

1. Ahmadi, H., Safavi-Naini, R.: Detection of Algebraic Manipulation in the Presence of Leakage. Cryptology ePrint Archive, Report 2013/637 (2013)
2. Capkun, S., Cagalj, M., Rengaswamy, R.K., Tsigkogiannis, I., Hubaux, J.P., Srivastava, M.: Integrity codes: message integrity protection and authentication over insecure channels. IEEE Trans. Dependable Secure Comput. 5(4), 208–223 (2008)
3. Cramer, R., Dodis, Y., Fehr, S., Padró, C., Wichs, D.: Detection of algebraic manipulation with applications to robust secret sharing and fuzzy extractors. In: Smart, N.P. (ed.) EUROCRYPT 2008. LNCS, vol. 4965, pp. 471–488. Springer, Heidelberg (2008)
4. Davis, P.J.: Circulant Matrices. Chelsea Publishing Company, New York (1994)
5. Dolev, D., Yao, A.: On the security of public key protocols. IEEE Trans. Inf. Theory 29(2), 198–208 (1983)
6. Dziembowski, S., Pietrzak, K.: Leakage-resilient cryptography. In: 49th Annual IEEE Symposium on Foundations of Computer Science (FOCS), pp. 293–302 (2008)
7. Dziembowski, S., Pietrzak, K., Wichs, D.: Non-malleable codes. In: ICS, pp. 434–452 (2010)

8. Gennaro, R., Lysyanskaya, A., Malkin, T., Micali, S., Rabin, T.: Algorithmic tamper-proof (atp) security: theoretical foundations for security against hardware tampering. In: Naor, M. (ed.) TCC 2004. LNCS, vol. 2951, pp. 258–277. Springer, Heidelberg (2004)
9. Guruswami, V., Smith, A.: Codes for computationally simple channels: explicit constructions with optimal rate. In: IEEE Symposium on Foundations of Computer Science (FOCS), pp. 723–732 (2010)
10. Hamming, R.W.: Error detecting and error correcting codes. Bell Syst. Tech. J. **29**(2), 147–160 (1950)
11. Langberg, M.: Oblivious communication channels and their capacity. IEEE Trans. Inf. Theory **54**(1), 424–429 (2008)
12. Shannon, C.E.: A mathematical theory of communication. Bell Syst. Tech. J. **27**(3), 379–423 (1948)
13. Wyner, A.D.: The wire-tap channel. Bell Syst. Tech. J. **54**, 1355–1367 (1975)

Author Index